British industrial relations

2nd edition

Howard F. Gospel and Gill Palmer

London and New York

First published 1983 by George Allen & Unwin (Publishers) Ltd
© Gill Palmer 1983

Second edition published 1993
by Routledge
11 New Fetter Lane, London EC4P 4EE

Simultaneously published in the USA and Canada
by Routledge
29 West 35th Street, New York, NY 10001

© 1993 Howard F. Gospel and Gill Palmer

Typeset in Times by LaserScript, Mitcham, Surrey
Printed and bound in Great Britain by
Mackays of Chatham PLC, Chatham, Kent

British Library Cataloguing in Publication Data
A catalogue record for this book is available from the British Library

ISBN 0–415–08453–9

Library of Congress Cataloging in Publication Data
Gospel, Howard F.
   British industrial relations/Howard F. Gospel and Gill Palmer. –
   2nd rev. ed.
   p.   cm.
   Rev. ed. of: British industrial relations/Gill Palmer. 1983.
   Includes bibliographical references and index.
   1.Industrial relations – Great Britain. I.Palmer, Gill.
   II. Palmer, Gill. British industrial relations. III. Title.
   HD8391.G65   1993
   331'.0941 – dc20   92-28827
                                                                    CIP

Contents

Figures and tables

FIGURES

TABLES

Preface

In recent years there has been much talk about the transformation of industrial relations and the development of a new approach to the management of human resources in Britain. Some would even say that, since the advent of the Thatcher administration, industrial relations problems have been resolved to the extent that the subject no longer exists. We hope that the broad conceptual and historical perspective of this book will show that industrial relations problems ebb and flow and change in nature. We also hope that the book will enable the subject to be seen in a long-term historical perspective and will demonstrate the continuing importance of a broad industrial relations approach.

The book is a second and greatly revised edition of Gill Palmer's *British Industrial Relations*, first published in 1983. We would like to thank again those who commented on the first edition of the book. We also acknowledge a debt to those who commented on the whole manuscript or on various chapters of the second edition. In particular we would like to thank various colleagues at the University of Kent, F. Whitemore, M. Gilbert, R. Brown, A. Carruth, A. Dickerson and R. Crompton. We would also like to thank J. Kelly, S. Wood, T. Keenoy, F. Bayliss, R. Bean, A Pendelton, G. Poynter, R. Edwards, A. Starkman, R. Carr and J. Whitlow. Finally, we would like to thank the British Council for support with the coordination of the writing of the book.

1 Introduction

Industrial relations is a frequently discussed, but often little understood subject. Stories of wage demands and industrial disputes get into the news and, from time to time, the subject looms large in political debate, throwing up major differences between the political parties, employers, employees and other interest groups. In Britain over the last quarter century, industrial relations has been an issue of widespread public interest and concern, but this attention has not always been matched by growing understanding. Instead of analysis there is often confusion, wishful thinking and prejudice. In the absence of any systematic analysis and understanding, crude assumptions and assertions are made. Industrial relations suffers the fate of any subject that becomes an ideological issue in the absence of analytical debate. Simplistic assumptions lead to ill-conceived prescriptions and policies. The problem with such policies is that they tend not to have the expected results, and misconceived policies generate further confusion. This book concentrates on the need to understand and analyse a subject which continues to generate considerable concern.

WHAT IS THE SUBJECT ABOUT?

Studies of industrial relations coverage by the press and television show that, as far as the media are concerned, the subject is about trade unions and, in particular, about strikes and their consequences. Surveys show that 'industrial disputes' account for much of the television news time devoted to the subject and about the same amount of national press stories on the topic.[1] The media treat the subject as being about trade union 'demands' over wages or 'resistance' to redundancies, often involving the threat of 'strikes', and this perspective is probably followed by the public at large and by many politicians. The crucial roles of management and the government tend to be neglected as does the day-to-day smooth running of industrial relations in most organisations.

However, we clearly need a wider definition of the subject matter if we are to analyse and understand not just what appears in the media, but also what really happens in industrial relations. No subject can be understood if it is too narrowly conceived. Just as the complexities of family relationships could not be grasped by looking at the formal terms of marriage contracts or divorce settlements, so no analysis of industrial relations will get far if it looks only at collective agreements and industrial disputes. We need to go behind the dramatic events that from time to time attract media attention and look at the more basic social processes that underlie them. In addition we need to look at the actions of ordinary employees at work, at management within employing organisations, and at the actions of the state within the broader economic, political and legal context.

For many years academics in the UK also saw the subject as being about the study of trade unions and only later did they come to focus much on management. As a result, much early work took the form of detailed descriptions of unions and management–union arrangements, often boring the student with facts but giving little insight into what was going on. British studies started to move to overcome this tradition in the 1960s when Flanders argued that industrial relations should be seen as the study of the 'institutions of job regulation'.[2] By this he meant the way rules governing employment are created, administered and changed, and this widened the focus from trade unions to include broader aspects of management, the government and other institutions concerned with regulating terms and conditions of employment. Flanders also tried to define more precisely what these institutions are concerned to do. He picked up ideas developed in the US by Dunlop[3] and argued that work is governed by a mass of rules and regulations covering criteria for recruitment, effort, performance, pay, hours, holidays and a myriad of other details of employment. These rules may range from the very formal, such as legislation and written collective agreements, through to very informal customs and understandings which exist in all workplaces. Flanders argued that these rules and regulations are what industrial relations actors and institutions try to determine.

This approach opened the way for a more conscious attempt to understand what management and trade unions are about, but it has itself been criticised for concentrating too much on the workplace and for focusing on overt rules and regulations at the expense of less visible methods of control and motivation. If the subject is only about more formal structures of management, trade unions and the government, it will miss the importance of informal groupings – like interactions between groups of workers at the workplace or between managers within a firm. If the subject is only about rules and regulations, it will ignore the importance of personal attitudes and beliefs – for example, the personal friendship between workmates which may lead them to act collectively or the antagonism between a manager and union official which can sour relations in a workplace. Finally, a focus on rules and regulations may lead us to expect order, where there may be considerable disorder and where there may exist a wide gap between formal rules and actual practice.

The more people have tried to analyse what is happening in industrial relations, the wider they have had to cast their net to comprehend significant institutions, interactions and events. For this reason this book will define the subject as concerned with the processes of control over the employment relationship, the organisation of work, and relations between employers and their employees. This broad definition, we hope, will help us move beyond the simple description of institutions and events to the more important task of analysis.

The employment relationship is an economic, social and political relationship in which employees provide manual and mental labour in exchange for rewards allotted by employers. The details of this exchange take many forms. 'Rewards' from employment can be economic, social and psychological. They may give the employee a high income, power and social prestige, or a degraded, dead-end job with poor pay and benefits. On the side of the provision of labour and the organisation of work, employee contributions range from unskilled and semi-skilled labour to scarce, highly flexible and creative skills. Employees may find the effort they are expected to provide is rigidly specified and controlled or left free to individual interpretation and initiative. We can contrast factory assembly-line workers with journalists or research scientists, or bus drivers with airline pilots, or supermarket check-out cashiers with highly skilled computer staff, to find considerable variations in the type and autonomy of labour exchanged for rewards. Industrial relations is certainly not restricted just to the study of blue-collar manual workers, and 'industrial' does not just mean manufacturing industry. The subject covers all areas of paid employment and all forms of work organisation.

The employment relationship can be short-term and temporary, as for a casual labourer on a British building site, or it can envelop much of an employee's life, as in the case of the Japanese large-firm employee whose house, leisure and career will sometimes all be on one company's premises. The relationship may be set in a private firm or in a public enterprise, in a unionised or a non-unionised workplace, since we do not define industrial relations as being only about relations between employers and unionised workforces. It may cover the relationship between an employer and the most junior employee, or the relationship between an employer and well-paid professional employees. Potential variations are enormous, but of one thing we can be sure: the employment relationship, the way work is organised, and relations between employers and employees are important. They are important for employees in determining their life-style and future prospects; for the employer concerned to control and develop an organisation; and for society at large in terms of the climate and productiveness of the economy. The forms of employment relationship that develop, the criteria for recruitment to the most desired jobs and the mobility between types of job, will all have an impact on society's political and social culture and on the relationship between different social groups that emerges. Given this importance, it is hardly surprising that there will be many people and groups interested in influencing the employment relationship and the way work is organised, or that the processes that shape these phenomena should form a complex area for study.

ISSUES IN INDUSTRIAL RELATIONS

In any society there are a number of economic, social and political issues to be resolved in structuring employment relationships and the way work is organised. In industrial relations it is customary to distinguish between substantive and procedural issues. Substantive issues cover the details of the reward–effort exchange such as wages and benefits and levels of performance. Procedural issues surround the question of how the substantive issues are decided, for example, who has the power to set substantive terms and through what administrative or bargaining arrangements.

Substantive issues include pay, holidays, overtime arrangements and any less direct 'fringe benefits' like pensions, company health-care subscriptions and company cars. They also cover training and the prospect of promotion to better-paid jobs. There may be many questions surrounding pay determination, not only how basic levels of pay are set, but also whether there is a regular fixed rate of pay or whether earnings vary according to effort or performance. Most industrial disputes appear to arise from issues concerned with pay, but the 'effort', as opposed to the 'reward', issues in employment relationships can be equally, or often more difficult to resolve. In any society decisions are needed on what work is done and on the way the labour process, required to complete this work, is divided up between jobs. This division of labour affects the type of skill, the skill level, degree of specialisation and type of effort required of employees. The level and intensity of effort also need to be determined. Surrounding these details of the reward–effort exchange will be personnel issues, for example, the criteria of recruitment and promotion to jobs, whether recruits are trained and offered careers or given only short-term contracts, the criteria for dismissal and any compensation for dismissal or redundancy.

If the substantive issues that surround the employment relationship are complex, the procedural issues are equally so. They cover relations between employers and employees and deal with the following kinds of questions. What people or groups control the substantive decisions? Are decisions to be taken unilaterally by the employer, or bilaterally by the employer and the employees? What influence should employee institutions, such as trade unions and professional associations, have? What rules should the state lay down in legislation? If more than one party has some influence on these issues, what procedures and mechanisms are, or should be, used to reach jointly agreed decisions? How are disputes about the application of the substantive rules to be resolved? In Chapter 2 we take an initial look at the debate surrounding these procedural questions, a debate to which we will be returning throughout the book.

WHO IS INVOLVED?

There are nearly 22 million employees in employment in the UK, employed by private companies ranging from British and foreign-owned giants to small local firms and corner shops, by central and local government, and by state-owned corporations and industries such as the Post Office and British Rail. All these people are directly involved in the employment relationship and are concerned to influence the shape it takes and the way work is organised. However, in this book we shall be concerned not so much with individuals as with groups. This is not to say that individuals and their views are unimportant. Personal or unstructured relations have their importance for managers and workers. But groups can mobilise more resources than individuals and can exert more pressure to achieve their ends. The way groups form is important, for groups help articulate values and interests and identify issues which a number of people are prepared to support. Group formation and the relative power of different groups have a fundamental impact on the way employment relationships develop and the work process is organised.

The groups most frequently associated with industrial relations in the UK are, in the first place, groupings of managers both within the employing organisation and between organisations in employers' associations. Employers and managers are too often taken for granted in discussions of industrial relations. In Chapter 3 we discuss the strategies that have been used by employers to control the organisation of work, to shape the employment relationship, and to deal with trade unions. That chapter also looks at the different ideological perspectives and styles of employers in Britain. Chapter 4 analyses the structures which employers have developed within their organisations to pursue and implement their strategies. It also discusses employer groups more directly parallel to trade unions – the employers' associations formed to coordinate employers' labour policies.

In Chapter 5 we look at employees as individuals and in groups, considering both formal and informal groupings, and how their actions shape the organisation of work and the employment relationship. This leads on in Chapter 6 to a consideration of trade union objectives, structure, government and power. We also look at other institutions formed to represent occupational interests, such as professional associations, and at forms of representation in non-union workplaces.

There are many other groups which may be concerned to influence the employment relationship, including political, economic and religious groups; institutions such as the media, which try to endorse or encourage what they see as 'reasonable behaviour'; and pressure groups such as the Institute of Directors or the Low Pay Unit, which advocate particular points of view. However, the most important body apart from the groups formed by employers and employees is the state. The state acts as employer for a substantial proportion of employees, but even when not in this role, government economic policy, law and the activity of government departments or agencies fundamentally affect employment issues. Chapter 7 provides a discussion of the state's involvement in industrial relations and touches on the likely future impact of membership of the European Community and the growth of an emergent European superstate. Chapters 8, 9 and 10 deal with the interaction between employers and their organisations, workers and their organisations, and the state and its agencies. They focus on the British system of collective bargaining and attempts to restructure and reform it over the last quarter-century. Finally, Chapter 11 looks at outcomes and draws some general conclusions. All these chapters give prominence to the changing nature of control over the employment relationship, the organisation of work and relations between employers and their employees.

CONFLICT OR COOPERATION?

Given the range of issues to be decided, and the people and groups concerned with those decisions, what assumption should be made about the extent to which cooperation or conflict is inherent in industrial relations? The basic premises here may seem obvious, but as this is an area that causes much confusion and lies at the heart of much ideological debate, basic premises need to be emphasised. The employment relationship, like any other social relationship, involves *both* cooperation and conflict between those involved. Cooperation is needed for any social interaction to persist – for example, studies of the relationship between prisoners and their guards show that some form of cooperation invariably develops. Of course, employers and their employees have a more positive relationship than this. On the other hand, even the closest relationships, such as within the family, generate conflict over ends, means to ends, values and priorities. Employment relationships provide plenty of scope for conflict on substantive and procedural issues.

Can we be more specific about the degrees of conflict and cooperation to expect? The many assumptions and assertions that exist in this area are introduced in Chapter 2. For the purpose of introducing the subject matter, we need only emphasise that it would be absurd to start with the assumption that employment issues will be non-problematic and easy to resolve to everyone's satisfaction. There is no industrial society in the world that does not have conflict and disputes at work – even though in some countries strikes are illegal and in other countries cultural and other arrangements place a great emphasis on cooperation. There is no organisation, whether it is run on principles of managerial prerogative or extensive joint consultation, that does not experience conflicts in this area. Even small, self-managing worker cooperatives generate conflicts over the allocation of people to jobs, over supervision, over differences in interests between groups and between individual versus collective goals. Conflicts like these arise from the basic need to organise people at work and over differences of interest, they arise in some form whatever the particular organisational structure.

Industrial relations is a subject, like politics and economics, where, because of the different interest groups and the different individual perspectives which exist, there are likely to be conflicting expectations and demands on limited resources and there are no perfect answers capable of satisfying everyone involved for all of the time. Conflict will never be eliminated, but the *form* it takes and its *severity* will vary. Policies adopted by different groups will affect the extent to which conflict is overt or muted, exacerbated or contained. But no policies will achieve the impossible aim of resolving all the issues to the satisfaction of all the goals of all the people involved.

We have, from the start, emphasised the inevitability of conflict in industrial relations because there is a widespread bias against accepting this idea. This bias contributes to the distortions and confusions to be found in much public discussion of the subject in the press and in some management declarations. Anyone who expects relations in employment to be always harmonious and problem-free is likely to react with bewilderment and anxiety when difficulties arise. If one feels that everything in a relationship *should* be based entirely on cooperation, then one is likely to believe there has been a serious breakdown or transgression when confrontations occur. If, on the other hand, one believes that conflict in a relationship is normal and could even be beneficial, then one is prepared and better equipped to deal with it. In order to live at peace together, it is necessary to understand the nature of conflict and to devise agreed methods for resolving it.

It is common, in industrial relations literature, to identify two broad perspectives on industrial relations, a 'unitarist' and a 'pluralist' perspective.[4] (We will examine other perspectives in the next Chapter.) People who look at employment and work relations with a *unitarist perspective* tend to believe that there is only one source of authority within the organisation. They see conflict as abnormal, only arising when employment organisations are not working correctly because of, for example, personality disorders, inappropriate recruitment or promotion, the deviance of dissidents or poor communications. They believe, or purport to believe, that in a 'normal' organisation everything will be peacefully ordered and co-operative. A rational and benign management will arrange things in everyone's interest. From this perspective any sign of conflict will be a cause of great concern and it will be assumed that someone is acting irrationally and illegitimately. Conflict will often be dealt with by attempts to ignore or suppress it.

The alternative, and we will argue more realistic, perspective on work life accepts the inevitability of conflict at work. This *pluralist perspective* recognises the existence within organisations of several legitimate sources of authority; it therefore sees organisations as complex social structures formed of a plurality of potentially conflicting interest groups. Conflict is bound to arise as people enter the employment relationship with expectations that cannot be matched with scarce resources and as groups form with differing interests and values. There will always be something of a gap between what management wants and what employees expect and vice versa. From the pluralist perspective conflict is not only inevitable but may be necessary. 'Conflict, however distasteful it may be in practice, has a consequence that is useful for society, namely to determine the next steps it will take'.[5] The pluralist's response to conflict will not be to try to suppress it, but to try to find a method of handling disputes that will produce the most desired results. (However, as we will see in the next chapter, there are other perspectives of a more radical nature which see this gap as more fundamental and irreconcilable.)

There are many managers in Britain who would appear to operate with a unitarist perspective. They may express the view that conflict at work is morally wrong and that all the issues surrounding employment should be resolved in harmonious agreement. However, it is probably true to say that in practice most managers are more aware of the complexities of the social situations in which they find themselves. The unitarist perspective is probably not, in reality, subscribed to by most managers. Nevertheless, many profess to believe it and try to persuade others to do so also, and the perspective underlies much public debate, with industrial relations often being discussed on the basis of a set of assumptions which, if challenged, would be acknowledged to be misconceived.

There are many reasons why widespread and dominant ideas about a subject may fail to reflect the realities of how people actually behave. First, the idea that conflict is an inevitable part of social life is disquieting; many people find the notion of conflict as inherent in the employment relationship to be threatening. Second, the view that particular conflicts of interest are unjustified or immoral is very convenient for anyone trying to maintain a particular authority or cast doubt on the legitimacy of dissenting views. Later in the book we will examine the value of ideological appeals in support of group strategies. Here we need only note that the common bias against the idea that conflict is inevitable in work situations can easily distort the analysis of industrial relations.

At the same time, however, we come back to the complementary point that cooperation also exists in all work organisations. As Rose has pointed out, 'Conflict is always paired with cooperation.'[6] It is what predominates in most organisations on a day-to-day basis and it is essential to ensure the production of goods and services. According to one management writer, Ouchi, cooperation, both between workers and between workers and managers, is what is essential to create more efficient and competitive firms. For him, 'Organisations exist only to enable individuals to cooperate in some integrated activity.'[7] This may be to overstate the point and to ignore the fact that cooperation also differs in degree and quality. In some organisations and circumstances, cooperation may be only limited, instrumental and conditional; in others it may be fuller and based on greater commitment and trust. The extent to which real cooperation can be developed is one factor affecting the social and economic well-being of the organisation, and many managers have increasingly become aware of the need to move from simply controlling workers to developing relations based more on cooperation and commitment.[8]

Conflict and cooperation therefore coexist within organisations. From an industrial relations point of view, the recognition and resolution of conflicts of interest opens the door to agreed compromises and cooperation. The institutions which handle conflict in relations between employers and employees can therefore at the same time promote cooperation. It is important to study and understand these institutions.

In summary, the issues in the employment relationship are varied and complex. It would be remarkable if everyone acted in agreement and harmony over the organisation of people at work. If even the smallest organisation generates problems, then the employment problems thrown up by ICI or British Aerospace or the Civil Service are likely to test the social skills of managers and employees alike. Cooperation and conflict must both be expected: it is the form that cooperation and conflict takes and the way that they are dealt with that should be the subject of discussion and analysis. The form that industrial relations cooperation and conflict take will depend on how work is organised, the way group interests form, the strategies and relative power of the various interested groups, and the institutional arrangements for handling their conflicts. These are the subject areas of this book.

2 Perspectives on industrial relations

How should we approach the analysis of industrial relations? What types of theory should we use? What are the major academic perspectives on the subject? These questions are not easily answered, for most writing in the area has been prescriptive or descriptive rather than explicitly based on theory. Prescription lies at the centre of government, management and trade union debates on the subject. Over the last quarter-century there has been a succession of prescriptions for changes in industrial relations, for new ways of managing human resources and for the introduction of industrial relations legislation of various kinds. Such proposals are often highly contentious, the theoretical assumptions on which they are based are rarely spelt out and the debates on public policy contain biases and misunderstandings. Academic studies of industrial relations have traditionally emphasised description of historical events and institutions rather than theoretical analysis. There are some widely discussed middle-range theories – for example on trade union growth or workers' propensities to strike – but at the level of macro-theory there is little agreement on how the subject should be interpreted. Prescriptions and descriptions often purport to be based on pragmatic, non-theoretical common sense. In fact there is no such thing as non-theoretical common sense, for any discussion of social behaviour requires that some assumptions and generalisations be made. In industrial relations, the existence of contentious and conflicting proposals from the different participants suggests that, whatever the assumptions are, they are certainly not 'common' to all. For example, while some people assume that employers always have the real power in industrial relations, others assume that employees when organised into trade unions can be as powerful or more so. While some assume the government adopts a neutral stance on industrial matters, others assume the government is always active, but disagree over whether governments usually act primarily in the interests of employers or employees. If we try to sort out the theoretical generalisations and assumptions behind different public policy proposals, we find ourselves faced with a great range of different approaches. As they are usually not presented as clearly delineated theories, we can best speak of the existence of a number of broad theoretical perspectives on the processes of control over the employment relationship, the organisation of work, and relations between employers and their employees.

This chapter examines a number of such broad theoretical perspectives on industrial relations and considers a number of different prescriptions. It assesses the assumptions that lie behind them and notes the different value judgements often associated with certain perspectives. In part, the perspectives correspond with some of the main stages of public policy as developed over the course of the twentieth century; in part, they represent more genuinely academic theories of industrial relations. In practice, academic theories and policy prescriptions have often overlapped and influenced one another. However, this has not always been the case and it is necessary to distinguish the two. It is hoped that the chapter will provide an initial insight into the broad range of perspectives on industrial relations and will show how the subject matter can be analysed.

UNITARIST PERSPECTIVES AND PRESCRIPTIONS

As was noted in Chapter 1, the unitarist perspective assumes that organisations have a single source of authority, a common set of goals and objectives agreed to by everyone. Cooperation at work is seen as the natural order of things and conflict is both unnatural and unnecessary. This perspective has a simple ideological appeal – employers use it to reassure themselves about the correctness of their actions and to try to persuade others, especially employees, of the legitimacy of managerial action. Various types of assumptions and prescriptions are associated with this perspective.

If one assumes that there are no genuine, significant differences in the interests, objectives and values of people at work, then any sign of conflict between employer and employee must derive from deviance. Individuals who are 'difficult' or who have some personal or political 'axe to grind' must have generated the problems, aided by the preparedness of their fellow employees to be led astray. If the deviants were removed by dismissal, or if their behaviour was suppressed by discipline or the law, all would be well. This perspective on industrial relations is subscribed to by many managers. It also surfaces in media comment, as journalists or broadcasters search for quick, easy explanations to involved and opaque problems. It has also been promoted by governments, in particular under Conservative administrations.

A practical example of the unitarist perspective may be given from a large construction site which was plagued with industrial relations problems, culminating in an unofficial strike by the electricians. The local press and television were ready with quick explanations of what had gone wrong. Their interpretation was that the trouble was caused by militants and troublemakers. One of the employer's spokesmen pointed out that the leaders of the strike were leftwingers and other malcontents. A closer investigation of the site quickly undermined this theory. Indeed, no one on site who had detailed knowledge of the situation presented troublemakers as the major problem. Instead they pointed to complex and deep-seated factors common on large building sites, exacerbated in this case by fixed-cost contracts given to many separate firms. Uncoordinated policies between different firms operating on the site had given rise to bizarre pay structures, so that men working next to each other on identical jobs earned very different pay, and the skilled electricians found themselves earning less per hour than the unskilled men in several other companies.[1] Problems associated with coordinating personnel policies on large sites are well known within the construction industry. However, such problems were complex and took time to understand and to communicate to an uninitiated audience. In contrast, an explanation in terms of deviant behaviour and militancy was simple and neatly fitted a popular stereotype of the industrial relations world.

Individual beliefs and personalities may, of course, have an impact on the course of events, but individuals operate in social and economic contexts that need to be understood. The removal of significant individuals or leaders may alter the behaviour of other employees, but it will not turn complex social situations into a unitary utopia where everyone is of one mind.

More sophisticated unitarist prescriptions argue the need for the good management of human relations and the careful handling of employment relations by managers, to remove the sources of potential conflicts. There are many managerial prescriptions on human relations at work and they are not all premised on unitarist perspectives. However, some major managerial theories have been based on unitary assumptions about relations at work, or at least the theorists have held up the prospect of harmonious, conflict-free employment relations as an incentive for the adoption of the managerial techniques they favour. The Human Relations theories, which emerged from the USA in the 1930s and were associated with the social psychologist Elton Mayo, emphasised the need that workers have to belong to a work community.[2] They also stressed the need for consultation and participative supervision as a way of creating harmony at work. Later neo-Human Relations theorists called for job enrichment, employee involvement and other forms of consensual decision making. These schools of thought have had protagonists who implied that they had identified the source of conflict at work and that their proffered solutions could cure the problems of industrial relations. In recent years, with the growing economic importance of Japan, a new generation of business gurus prescribes so-called Japanese managerial techniques and makes similar claims that the adoption of supposedly consensual Japanese management techniques will eliminate all the problematic conflicts of employment relationships.[3]

In recent years there has also been a growth of so-called Human Resource Management, with origins in part in the USA, but also drawing some inspiration from Japan and from indigenous developments in Britain in the 1980s.[4] Some of this is unitary in nature, and reminiscent of the earlier Human Relations approach, in that it talks about creating common participatory cultures, stresses shared values and objectives, emphasises individual relations at work, and denies the legitimacy of employee organisation in trade unions. This particular approach to personnel management has been very much a result of political and economic developments in the 1980s and will be discussed in more detail in subsequent chapters. What we would say here is that the management of human resources is not necessarily unitarist nor anti-union in nature. However, in some of the recent literature and practice, the term Human Resource Management has been associated with an approach that is individualist and unitarist in orientation.

All the remaining perspectives on industrial relations reviewed below are of a pluralist nature in that they recognise several sources of authority and a complex plurality of interests in employment, they accept that conflicts of interest between people at work are inevitable, and they acknowledge that power will be used in the resolution of those conflicts. However, that does not imply a single theoretical perspective, for the plurality of interests and the inevitability of conflict can be interpreted in different ways. There are conflicting notions about what are the significant conflicts and which the significant interest groups. There are different views about the balance of power between groups – whether some have a dominant position or whether there can be a balanced, mutual alliance that satisfies everyone. There are disagreements over which group, if any, has wider, more legitimate interests than the others and which groups make the key decisions. Underlying these differences are contrasting evaluations of co-operation and conflict. Some pluralists only accept conflict if it is expressed in certain ways and is designed to promote cooperation. Others value it only when it is the result of some group successfully pursuing desired policies, for example, policies leading to 'higher productivity' or to 'democracy' or 'equality'. We review these differences in terms of a number of variants of the pluralist perspective.

LIBERAL COLLECTIVISM AND COLLECTIVE BARGAINING

One school of thought in British industrial relations has always accepted the inevitability of conflict between employers and employees on economic issues and believes that employees need to act collectively in order to protect their economic interests. It prescribes collective bargaining as the fairest and most efficient method of institutionalising and resolving conflict at work and generating employment rules. These ideas are sometimes simply labelled 'pluralist' in industrial relations literature, but as there are other analyses that assume a plurality of interests, we shall label this school the 'liberal collectivists'. It is liberal because it traditionally advocated a limited role for government and the use of law and because it sees agreements, freely negotiated between conflicting parties, as the best method for resolving disputes. It is collective because, unlike the liberal individualists we mention later, it accepts the legitimate right of employees to form collective organisations to increase their bargaining power when negotiating contracts. This is seen as legitimate, and indeed desirable, given that the individual employee is believed to be in a weaker bargaining position than the individual employer.

The liberal collectivist perspective lies behind much academic writing in the UK. It is often associated with the so-called 'Institutionalist' tradition, with origins going back to Sydney and Beatrice Webb in the late nineteenth century;[5] it is an approach that stresses the need for a knowledge of the institutional arrangements of the labour market. In the post-Second World War period in Britain this perspective has also been associated with the so-called 'Oxford School', named after a number of academics at Oxford University.[6] In practice this perspective, with its emphasis on the benefits of freedom of association, collective bargaining and negotiated agreements, has also had the support of British trade unions and many managers and it has traditionally been the stance of many politicians not only on the left but in the centre and centre-right of British politics.

The ideas behind liberal collectivist support for collective bargaining are not difficult to unravel. Collective bargaining is the process by which trade unions and similar associations, representing groups of employees, negotiate with employers or their representatives with the object of reaching collective agreements. Through collective bargaining conflict can be brought out into the open, channelled into various institutional arrangements, and thereby defused. Collective agreements specify jointly agreed terms on a range of employment issues such as pay, hours and basic conditions of employment. The process requires a political system that allows employees freedom of association and action so that they can organise into economic pressure groups which are independent of employers or the state. It also requires the mutual recognition of divergent interests by employers and employees and their willingness to accept the compromise of jointly agreed terms. In addition it requires a market system which allows the price of labour and of goods and services to fluctuate according to supply and demand. It is to be noted, however, that collective bargaining seeks to regulate the labour market and prevent a competitive 'free-for-all' – in this respect it differs from liberal individualism, to which we refer below.

Collective bargaining is a power bargaining method in which the negotiating positions of the two sides are backed by economic sanctions. On the employees' side, this requires the legal right and practical ability to take industrial action if necessary. On the employers' side, it requires the right to act in the last resort according to managerial prerogatives and to dismiss employees in dispute. It is felt that the state's role in this bargaining process should be essentially limited and the government should not attempt to regulate terms and conditions of employment in any detail. The role of government is to provide a framework of legislation within which bargaining takes place and the parties pursue their organisational and collective interests.

Liberal collectivists argue the case for collective bargaining in terms of industrial and political advantages. They argue that, industrially, collective bargaining creates a form of industrial democracy by allowing employees a voice in the determination of their pay and conditions of employment, while at the same time largely conceding the employers' freedom to take unilateral decisions on commercial, investment and other managerial issues. Politically, it is argued, collective bargaining helps enhance the stability of a society by providing a safety valve, by excluding potentially disruptive industrial conflicts from the political arena, and by providing a set of institutions for the relatively peaceful resolution of employment-based conflicts. As the American writer Robert Dubin once put it:

> Collective bargaining is the great social invention that has institutionalised industrial conflict. In much the same way that the electoral process and majority rule have institutionalised political conflict in a democracy, collective bargaining has created a stable means for resolving industrial conflict.[7]

In summary, collective bargaining is seen to be a flexible and democratic method for the satisfactory resolution of inevitable conflicts at work. These arguments had wide support in the western world after the Second World War.[8] At that time political theorists in the Anglo-Saxon world emphasised the need for strong voluntary groups to represent different economic interests in society if democratic, rather than totalitarian, government were to survive. Such functional interest groups were seen to create a balance of power and prevent too great a concentration of power in the hands of employers or the state. For this reason trade unions, of a liberal and pluralistic persuasion, were encouraged in postwar Germany and Japan and collective bargaining advocated as a safeguard against the return of totalitarian regimes. Such institutions, it was argued, provided a more secure base for long-term economic and political stability than the arrangements in countries such as the USSR and China.

Some form of collective bargaining has developed in all the market economies of the world and the arguments for it have a strong ideological appeal for many. Nevertheless from the 1980s onwards collective bargaining in the UK has come under attack from a variety of directions, and there have been many prescriptions for change. The criticisms which have been mounted against British collective bargaining take a number of forms and will be considered in detail in later chapters. One set of arguments, especially from the right wing of politics, asserts that collective bargaining is too disruptive, either because the level of industrial action is too high and costly for a nation competing in global markets, or because employers and employees collude to push up wages and prices without due regard to consumers, or because collective bargaining gets in the way of individual rights and so complicates the relationship between the employer and the employees. Rather different criticisms come from those, on the left wing of politics, who assert that unions are usually too weak and that employee involvement in decision making is too limited under collective bargaining. These argue that employees should not be limited in their influence to basic pay and conditions of employment but should have a voice on a much wider range of decisions related to work. Employee representatives should be accepted in collective bargaining and other processes, in order to ensure genuine social dialogue and the adequate representation of the labour force's interests.

From such criticisms have come a variety of actions and proposals for action on the part of government. Some have called simply for government action to reduce the power of trade unions by adopting tight economic policies and restrictive industrial relations laws. Others have advocated management action to give individual employees more say. Again, from the left wing of politics, others have advocated a strengthening of collective bargaining and other forms of collective representation at various levels of society. An assessment of these different proposals is one of the themes of this book. At this stage we need only note that the proposals which call for new types of decision-making machinery can imply perspectives on the subject matter which deviate from traditional liberal collectivism.

The systems model of industrial relations

Before turning to other perspectives it is appropriate to refer here to the systems model of industrial relations, an attempt within the liberal-collectivist perspective to develop a more formal, academic theory of industrial relations. This is usually associated with the American economist and industrial relations academic, John Dunlop, who argued that industrial relations should be seen as a social sub-system, parallel to but distinct from the economic and political systems.[9] The industrial relations system consists of four elements – actors, contexts, a binding ideology and a body of employment rules which are the outcome of the interaction process between the actors. The actors are employers and their organisations, employees and any groups they have formed to represent them, and the state and government agencies. Thus a plurality of interest groups are recognised. The main external contexts influencing their behaviour are threefold – technology, market or budgetary constraints, and the distribution of power in the wider society. Within these constraints, the actors establish substantive and procedural rules to govern the employment relationship, by unilateral action, by bilateral collective bargaining or by tripartite action involving the state. The whole system, it is contended, is held together by certain shared understandings and beliefs. The outcome of the system and the centre of attention in industrial relations should be seen as 'a network or web of rules'.

In constructing this model, Dunlop was heavily influenced by the ideas about social systems developed by sociologist and fellow American, Talcott Parsons.[10] Dunlop argued that it was necessary to see industrial relations as a system because a change in one part would have repercussions on other parts and because relations in the system were largely self-adjusting. A major upset in one area would lead to adjustments in relations until new rules, and a new equilibrium, were reached. Thus, central to this stabilising process is a binding ideology, which all parties share on the basic need for mutual survival and for procedures for conflict resolution.

This model has been widely used in industrial relations literature because it has proved a useful framework for description and as such there are elements of it in our own approach. However, despite over thirty years' use, most comment on the model still takes the form of criticism or attempts at refinement, rather than attempts to use it to explain industrial behaviour. It has generated limited analytical insights and has been most useful as a way of organising facts.

Parsons's 'structural-functionalist' approach has often been criticised for an inability to explain social conflicts. Systems models rarely give adequate attention to fundamental sources of conflict and instability in society and they overemphasise the stabilising force of common ideas or ideologies. The analytical device of separating out self-contained, self-adjusting 'systems' from the complex totality of social behaviour obscures the fact that broad-based social divisions can cut across political, economic and industrial relations systems, destabilising them all. By specifying three types of actor and assuming a mutual interest in survival, Dunlop's model discounts the possibility that interest groups may seek to eliminate rivals and in certain circumstances may succeed in doing so and thus entirely change the system.

Most countries' industrial relations are relatively stable from year to year, but, at times, the conflicts generated within society can be sufficiently severe to rupture the 'normal' or pre-existing rules and procedures. In some instances, for example, employers have successfully destroyed trade unionism within their companies. In some countries governments have outlawed free trade unions and have expropriated employer capital. Recently in the former Soviet Union and Eastern Europe upheavals have fundamentally transformed long-established industrial relations arrangements. In such circumstances it makes little sense to talk of self-adjusting social systems. Certainly ideology does not prevent change. If conflicts are severe, then, rather than acting as a unifying force, the ideas that people hold can entrench opposed positions. Ideology can reinforce conflict as well as cooperation.

In summary, then, in what ways does this discussion of theory help us sort out liberal collectivist perspectives? Academics advocating collective bargaining have been closely associated with Dunlop's model. Their analyses have often been attacked for theoretical weaknesses that can be blamed, in part, on an over-reliance on Dunlop's framework. Free collective bargaining is advocated on the grounds that it satisfactorily resolves conflicts at work and usually serves to remove economic conflicts from the political arena. For the first twenty-five years after the Second World War these assumptions seemed valid, and it was argued by its supporters that collective bargaining provided a stable, self-adjusting system of conflict resolution buttressed by the ideological support of different groups. In the 1980s, however, collective bargaining came under attack in Britain, and the systems-based assumptions that industrial relations can be largely separated from politics, or that there is consensus support for collective bargaining, became much more suspect.

Other perspectives are based on theoretical assumptions which give more attention to the questions of the relative power of different interest groups and the role of the state. These we review below.

CORPORATIST PERSPECTIVES

Up to now we have been concerned with perspectives which have not been very concerned with the interaction between the industrial relations and the political systems. Perspectives which call for more active state intervention and for some measure of tripartite decision making involving government with employer and employee representatives are often labelled 'corporatist'. Yet, clear definitions of corporatism are hard to pin down. The label is sometimes used very broadly to refer to any policies which depart from the clear-cut separation of the state and governmental agencies from the economy and economic interest groups such as prevailed under traditional liberalism.[11] In more stringent definitions, corporatism is characterised as a system of interest representation in which the state plays a more active part in directing the activities of predominantly privately owned industries in partnership with the representatives of capital and labour. Both employer and employee representatives are able to help the state administer agreed policies because their organisations have controls or influence over their respective constituents, namely union members and individual firms.[12] Corporatist policies have in practice ranged from the voluntary tripartite participation of trade unions and employers' associations in government decision making such as was much favoured in Britain in the 1970s; to more elaborate systems of interest representation and concerted action by government, employers and unions such as have existed in some continental European countries such as Sweden and Germany; to the highly coercive, regimented, administrative structures associated with the Fascist regimes of the interwar years and of some present-day Latin American states. Because of this range the concept is usually subdivided to contrast looser, more voluntary and liberal tripartism from more rigidly organised, hierarchically structured, compulsory corporatism.[13]

It is also useful to distinguish the level at which interest groups are incorporated into administrative structures. Macro-, mesa- and micro-levels of corporatism may be identified.[14] Macrocorporatism (which we tend to stress in this book) involves an active role for the state and the development of tripartite relations at national level, such as we have outlined above. Mesacorporatism involves the incorporation of interest groups within structures which regulate industries – elements of this are to be found in the industry-wide system of collective bargaining in Germany and the Australian system of compulsory arbitration.[15] In microcorporatism, at the level of the firm, the role of the state is less important, and the concept refers to the incorporation of employee interest groups into the administrative structure of the firm. A good example of this level of corporatism is to be found in the enterprise unionism and workplace consensus which is said to exist in Japan or in some tendencies in British firms which we will discuss in Chapter 3.[16]

The arguments backing corporatist prescriptions are in part that liberal competition, pure market forces and unbridled bargaining between groups in society produce results that are socially divisive and unjust and that more coordinated, centrally administered, tripartite decision making can produce more efficient and fairer results. The case has moral and pragmatic components.

A moral case for corporatism was put by Emile Durkheim, the French social theorist.[17] He argued that the division of labour in modern society had created numerous conflicting interest groups. Competition between these groups was the essence of social life, but a key problem in modern society was keeping this competition within reasonable bounds. With the rapid development of modern industry there was a danger of 'anomie' – a state of unbridled competition in which groups were totally unrestrained in their pursuit of naked sectional interests. Anomie was socially unhealthy. To be socially valuable, pluralist competition must be regulated and restrained by 'social norms' – i.e., agreed rules about fair play, fair rewards and just means to group ends.

In discussing how the anomic tendencies of modern industry should be cured and how acceptable regulating norms could be established, Durkheim emphasised the need to involve people in the decisions that governed their lives. The citizen should be integrated into society by means of self-government at work and the development of functionally distinct corporations which would each be governed democratically by a miniature industrial parliament, nominated by election. The state would be responsible for coordinating and planning the activities of the economic corporations and would administer its policies through them. In this way economic life would be organised and regulated without losing any of its diversity. Durkheim envisaged the gradual development of this system until the functional corporations became the main way in which people participated in national government and corporatism would develop into a new political and economic system which was neither strictly capitalist nor socialist.

This type of moral argument for corporatism has been more acceptable on the continent of Europe than in the UK or USA, where liberal notions and suspicion of government intervention have had a more dominant impact on political attitudes. In Europe there has traditionally been and there is today more talk about 'social partnership' and 'social dialogue'. Nevertheless, moral arguments for corporatism have been heard in the UK. In the interwar years, for example, Harold Macmillan advocated corporatist policies to overcome class conflict and create 'One Nation' in Britain. At the same time, there were some employers and trade union spokesmen who put a moral case for giving workers a say in national-level forums.[18]

In the 1970s Britain adopted corporatist prescriptions which emphasised more pragmatic arguments. The main argument was that the functional interest groups had grown to such a size that power bargaining between them was too disruptive in terms of strikes and cost-push inflationary pressures. The state had to take the responsibility for intervening to regulate the activities of these powerful groups and to harness their potential for the national economic good. In this way it might be possible to control inflationary wage and price movements and to encourage economic efficiency. In addition it was argued that state policies of non-intervention were premised on fiction. In complex modern economies, state activity inevitably has a major impact on the economy. The state directly employs a large proportion of the labour force and the public sector provides the infrastructure on which private industry depends. Government economic and fiscal policies crucially affect the distribution of economic resources. The state therefore has very considerable economic responsibilities and once these are openly accepted then it should become apparent that the best way to develop and administer national economic policy is with the cooperation of the two main producer interest groups in society – organised business and labour.

The arguments backing corporatist prescriptions tended to rest on important assumptions about the distribution of power in society. Moral advocates of corporatism tended to assume that society is subdivided between numerous competing groups, that there is a sufficiently complex balance of power to ensure that no group dominates and that the state will adopt a neutral 'umpire' role between competing interests. In the UK, the corporatist policies which were advocated have been at the voluntary or bargained end of the range of corporatism. Advocates of this type of corporatism assume two dominant interests in society – capital and labour. They then assume that there is a sufficient equivalence of power between capital and labour to prevent state intervention degenerating into the oppression of one group by the other. Critics of the corporatist perspective believe that capital and labour interests are not matched in power and that therefore state intervention is likely to be uneven.

Corporatism was an important aspect of, and perspective on, industrial relations in the UK in the 1970s. Commentators at the time discussed the inevitable development of corporatist policies. Within politics, the programmes of the Labour Party, the centre parties and the left wing of the Conservative party contained many corporatist prescriptions, and the Trades Union Congress (TUC) and Confederation of British Industry (CBI) advocated forms of corporatist state intervention.[19] Today such perspectives still find some support, especially with elements within the Labour Party and the trade unions. Though any hint of corporatism was rejected by Mrs Thatcher and though Mr Major can hardly be said to be much more favourably inclined, there are those within the Conservative Party who have shown more sympathy for state intervention and mediation. In the European Community there are also strong tendencies which stress social dialogue and tripartism and which keep the corporatist perspective alive. However, in Britain, the election in 1979 of an anti-corporatist Conservative government brought to prominence a very different perspective on industrial relations.

LIBERAL INDIVIDUALISM AND NEO-*LAISSEZ-FAIRE*

Liberal individualism shares certain similarities with the unitarist perspective in that it tends to believe that organisations are best led by those who have property rights of ownership or their representatives who have superior technical knowledge and expertise. However, it recognises conflicts of economic interest between employers and employees, but deplores both collective bargaining and corporatist arrangements for handling that conflict. Instead, the prescribed mechanism is the individual contract of employment as determined by market forces and common law notions of the rule of law.

The classical *laissez-faire* economists of the nineteenth century focused on exchange in the market and argued that economic conflicts of interest should be resolved by contracts, freely entered into by people operating in competitive markets. Any combination by the buyers or sellers of any commodity would reduce market competition and this would upset the invisible hand of the free-market mechanism which, left to itself, ensured the greatest possible benefit for all. In the employment field this meant that individual workers should bargain with individual employers to agree contracts of employment for themselves. There would inevitably be conflicts as employees sought the highest price, the best conditions and the least onerous work, and employers wanted the lowest price, the least costly conditions and the most effective and flexible service. However, these conflicts should be resolved in the agreed terms of the employment contract. Thereafter the relationship should be conflict-free. If employees were not prepared to seek other work, renegotiate their contract or challenge their employers' interpretation of the contract in court, they should give the service they were contracted to provide without dispute or grievance and accept the unitary authority of the firm as in the best interests of all. Any combination by trade unions or associations of employers to influence the terms of employment contracts was to be deplored, because it would upset the allocative working of labour supply and demand. Following on from this, any corporatist state intervention and tripartism would inevitably work against individual choice and efficient outcomes.

These arguments are liberal because they assume a society composed of an aggregation of relatively equal individuals capable, if free from state or other interference, of pursuing their own best interests by freely entering into contracts with others. The arguments are individualist because they follow *laissez-faire* doctrine in deploring pressure groups, monopolies and 'combinations'. Market and moral reasons are given for this. Market reasons we have already mentioned – that, in a competitive market, forces exist to determine a just and fair price for labour that also ensures the greatest efficiency in terms of the production and the allocation of resources. Combinations, on the employer or employee side, would upset this mechanism by creating too great a concentration of power and enabling some workers and employers to profit at the expense of others. Moral liberalism provides an attack on combinations on ethical and political grounds. It argues that the equal right to vote in a parliamentary democracy grants everyone equal power in society. Pressure groups of any kind seek to coerce their own members or the rest of society and they upset the mechanism of popularly elected governments. It also provides an attack on collectivism on individual grounds. It is best for individuals, in a free society, to take responsibility for their own actions and not to rely on others, such as trade unions or the state.[20]

To some, the nineteenth-century assumptions and arguments of liberal individualism fit uneasily into a world where large corporations and combinations of employees have gained considerable size and influence and where perfectly competitive markets are a rare feature of the world economy. Accordingly, the liberal individualist perspective was once presented in industrial relations literature as an outdated hangover from the nineteenth century confined to a few employers and the right wing of politics. It was seen as barely worthy of consideration in an age which has seen the emergence of giant multinational enterprises with oligopolistic control of many product and labour markets, the development of trade unions in every industrial society of the world, and the activities of increasingly interventionist welfare states.

Nevertheless, the liberal individualist perspective has significant historical origins and traditions which have long supported an anti-collectivist stance among certain employers, politicians and other significant individuals and groups in the UK. Some have pointed out that an important custodian of moral liberalism has always been the judiciary and that the Conservative Party had always contained a right wing of market liberals.

The economic and ideological shifts which led to the election of President Reagan in the US and of Mrs Thatcher in the UK, both relying on neo-*laissez-faire* economic policies, brought new life to this perspective. It is true that in the US liberal individualism had always continued to exist and anti-collectivism was always strong among employers. But in Britain the change in direction was more striking – though it would be more accurate to say that the change represented a reversion to nineteenth- and early twentieth-century traditions. The industrial relations policy of the Conservative governments after 1979 displayed a suspicion and distrust of trade unionism often expressed in liberal individualist terms by questioning the process of collective bargaining. It purported to believe that the state should not intervene in collective bargaining in the private sector where market forces should reign. Nor should it intervene unnecessarily in the labour market with so-called protective legislation which in practice brought about only inflexibilities and inefficiencies. This swing of the ideological pendulum led to a revival or more open espousal of unitarist ideas among employers and an increased emphasis on individual relations within industry. The implications and outcomes of this will be dealt with in later chapters and questions will be asked about the continuity of this perspective in the 1990s under the Major government which some argue represents a shift away from the harsher aspects of liberal individualism.

RADICAL PERSPECTIVES

Some of the perspectives to which we have already referred might be described as radical: for example, some of the more far-reaching aspects of corporatism and some of the more vigorous elements of liberal individualism have radical connotations and involve active policies of radical reform. However, under this title we refer here to a number of different traditions on the left of the political spectrum which have involved a critical perspective on relations between employers and employees in industrial society and which have sought fundamental change.

Under this heading we would include in the first place, in the British context, a radical democratic tradition going back at least as far as Robert Owen and the Chartists in the early part of the nineteenth century and including William Morris and the Christian Socialists in the second half of the nineteenth century. Proponents of this tradition tended to take a critical view of many aspects of industrialism, pointing to the degradation of much industrial labour, the absence of democracy in the workplace and the need for more fulfilling work and fairer rewards. They were distrustful both of employers and of the state, which they believed supported the employing class. Though sometimes Utopian and lacking in a well-formulated analysis, this dissenting perspective provided a critique of capitalism which always had an appeal and which has never been quite lost on the left of British politics and industrial relations.

In another tradition we would place the Guild Socialists who, at the beginning of this century, stressed conflicting employer and employee class interests as working to the detriment of industrial democracy and economic efficiency. They sought, via encroaching control from workers, to put the government of each industry in the hands of industrial unions or 'guilds': they believed that the abolition of traditional property ownership, the negotiation of 'collective contracts' between the state and workers' guilds, and a full provision of opportunities for all employees to concern themselves with the conduct and policies of the organisation, would result in a greater moral commitment and involvement on the part of workers.[21] A more militant tradition, which developed in France and the USA at the turn of the century and which had some influence among British thinkers and British trade unionists, was the Syndicalist tradition. Syndicalists criticised the distribution of power at work and argued for the development of spontaneous worker action within industry capable of a fundamental challenge to employers and government. Georges Sorel, in France, advocated the use of mass strikes, as a real or mythical political weapon, to win control of industry and the state.[22] This would bring about a freer society founded on industrial associations and workers' control. Syndicalist ideas were never widespread within the UK, but in 1910 Tom Mann started a syndicalist journal and an articulate expression of syndicalist thought was published in 1912 by the Unofficial Reform Committee of the South Wales Miners' Federation. *The Miners' Next Step* called for the end of private ownership and the administration of the economy by industrial unions. Ideas of the type favoured by the Guild Socialists and Syndicalists have appealed to a minority in the union movement in Britain and other countries right up to the present day.

A further strand in the radical approach to the study of relations between employers and employees has been various Marxist and neo-Marxist perspectives on industrial relations. Marxism traditionally had a weaker influence on British intellectual thought than in continental European countries. It also had less influence on British trade union ideology than on some other European trade union movements such as those in France and Italy. In recent years the prediction that a workers' revolution and the elimination of private property would ultimately remove alienation and conflicts at work has been discredited by the existence of industrial conflict and lack of workers' rights in the former Soviet Union and the Communist societies of Eastern Europe, where, in some cases, workers' organisations helped bring down the old regimes. Nevertheless, although Marxist prescriptions for a future conflict-free society are generally rejected, a Marxist-type analysis of existing employment relations has had a wider following and provides a radical critique of the different liberal perspectives.[23] As such it can still offer some insights and a critical way of viewing the employment relationship and the labour process in capitalist society.[24]

Marxists see the process of control over employment relations as inescapably bound up with the economic base of society and class relations. The economic structure of society and broad inequalities shape the consciousness and action of classes. Under capitalism they see a hierarchy of social relations and a constant struggle between the buyers and sellers of labour which extends past economic issues to a political struggle for control. In this process, there can be no stable balance of power and any accommodation made by worker representatives with the forces of capital must be unstable.

Yet Marxists have varied on how they view the actions taken by employee institutions under capitalism. Two broad schools of thought are relevant to our discussion. One view traditionally rejected the value of institutional change as long as the political economy was capitalist. The other, less dogmatic, has argued that institutional reform may be used gradually to transform the hegemony of capitalist interests in society.

The more doctrinaire Marxists, such as were to be found in the former Soviet Union and Eastern Europe and who continue to exist in China, argued that, under capitalism, both collective bargaining and corporatism merely integrated working-class leaders into the existing political structures to the long-term enhancement of employer control and to the detriment of the working class. Trade union activities promote narrow, sectional interests and do not serve the interest of the working class as a whole; the growth of collective bargaining leads unions to accommodate employer interests and to support capitalist employment relations. 'As institutions trade unions do not *challenge* the existence of a society based on a division of classes, they merely express it. . . . They can bargain within the society, but not transform it.'[25] This attitude in part helps explain why collective bargaining has been less developed in France, where the main union, the Confédération Générale du Travail (CGT), for many years opposed what they termed collaboration with employers through collective bargaining. Corporatist institutions involving collaboration with government were equally suspect. No government, constrained by the economic power of big business, could implement progressive policies unless they were being used to weaken workers' aspirations. Only under socialism or communism could industrial relations be transformed. In that state, they argued, fundamental conflicts of interest would no longer exist at work. Trade unions could still exist, but their role would be only to take up minor grievances and to act as a transmission mechanism between the state and workers in industry. This hardline position has now been discredited.

Those Marxists who rejected this approach and who have been less dismissive of independent employee action within capitalism have been able to quote Marx's support for trade unions as the organisations through which workers would gain the experience and consciousness which would lead them on to effective demands for social change and they also cite his support for factory legislation in the UK. With the Italian theorist, Gramsci, they argue that political change can occur through slow, institutional reforms that gradually increase working-class power.[26] This less doctrinaire stance has had the support of most recent British radical theorists who argue that collective bargaining has benefited British workers. This is a form of Marxism which still has some credible adherents and which has some influence in Social Democratic and Socialist parties throughout the world.

In their analysis of the prescriptions arising from other perspectives, radicals have insisted that economic and political issues cannot be separated; they place great emphasis on the antagonistic interests between the buyers and sellers of labour power; and they focus, in a way that many other perspectives do not, on the importance of assessing the power held by opposing interest groups. Their approach therefore focuses much more on power relations. Radicals have differed among themselves in that there are those who emphasise more the degradation of work in modern society and the absence of democracy at the workplace and those who stress the purported total incompatibility of employer and employee interests. In their prescriptions, the latter have called for the total abolition of capitalism; the former groups have sought an ideal of greater economic and political equality in the labour market and the wider society, of more fulfilling work, and of greater equality in decision making in the workplace.

THE PERSPECTIVE OF THIS BOOK

This chapter has reviewed a number of different types of analysis and prescription for British industrial relations. Tangled up with prescription and analysis are different value judgements on cooperation and conflict and on the role of management, trade unions and the state. Table 2.1 summarises the different perspectives and their implications. As we have seen, there is much controversy about the analysis and interpretation of industrial relations behaviour, and industrial relations debate has often been less concerned with the careful, systematic analysis of evidence than with the search for propaganda to support entrenched value judgements and to persuade others. This is not surprising; few people are indifferent to the social arrangements that regulate employment and, as in politics, it would

Table 2.1 Value judgements associated with different perspectives

Likely judgement on	Unitarist	Liberal-collectivist	Corporatist	Liberal-individualist	Radical
Conflict and cooperation	Conflict unnecessary and harmful; cooperation the natural order.	Group conflicts on economic issues inevitable, beneficial if institutionalised through collective bargaining.	Group conflicts on economic and political issues inevitable, beneficial if institutionalised by incorporating the different interests into decision-making bodies.	Individual conflicts on the economic terms of employment inevitable. Can be resolved in the individual contract of employment.	Class conflict inevitable within capitalism. Cannot be successfully institutionalised unless radical change leads to greater workers' control.
Management role	Leadership. Enhances general interests through economic development.	Coordinator: Represents employer interest and can help institutionalise conflict through collective bargaining.	Coordinator. Can organise to represent owner interests and help build corporate arrangements.	Leadership. Enhances general interests through economic development.	Control. Servants of power, helping to exploit the workforce.
Trade union role	Harmful and unnecessary.	Interest groups which can help institutionalise conflict through collective bargaining.	Interest groups which can help incorporate workers onto governing bodies.	Harmful and unnecessary.	Potentially valuable organs of working-class struggle. Harmful if they dissipate the energy of the working class and prevent change.
The state's role	Guardian of the national interest.	First among equals. Role in the economy should be minimised.	Tha active guardian of the national interest.	First among equals. Role in the economy should be minimised.	Under capitalism, the state is the agent of capital.

be a very strange person who had no views to express on the issues involved. Nevertheless, we need to recognise that prejudice is rife in discussions on industrial relations and we need to be aware of how our own value biases may distort our view of reality. With this in mind, we can briefly set out our own perspective which draws from different approaches and which guides the analysis of this book.

In the first place we follow the social theorist Max Weber in seeing both conflict and cooperation as inherent in social relations: cooperation because humans are social animals unable to survive, let alone achieve higher objectives, without the collaboration of others; conflict because both within and between social groups there will be competition over resources, values, and power. All societies develop social institutions, i.e. regular patterns of behaviour for dealing with family relations, moral values, work and so on. However, the fact that these institutions invariably exist in one form or another does not automatically give any particular institution social value. Weber rejected the common bias – ingrained in the structural-functionalist school of sociology and systems theory – which assumes that existing social institutions have developed to serve some social purpose and therefore must have social value. He argued instead that social institutions develop out of the inevitable power battles between interest groups and he placed an emphasis on the analysis of power, ideology and techniques of control that we shall be referring to again.

We also draw on the institutionalist and systems schools. The institutionalist approach is useful in that it is based on the belief that, since industrial relations processes take place primarily through and between institutions, one should have a good knowledge of these institutions. In particular one should have some understanding of the historical origins and development of key institutional arrangements. This book seeks to provide that historical understanding of institutions. Similarly we draw on the systems perspective, with its emphasis on the contexts of industrial relations and its identification of three main actors – employers and their organisations, employees and their organisations, and the state and governmental agencies. This in part we use for arranging our own presentation of material and for focusing on the study of the formal and informal rules which govern employment. From what we have already said, however, it should be clear that we do not accept the approach's emphasis on shared ideology nor do we think that institutions can be examined outside their broader power contexts.

One criticism of the systems approach has always been that it is over-deterministic and mechanistic, placing too much emphasis on the context and insufficient on the perceptions, motivations and actions of the parties. In recent years academic analysts have sought to emphasise more the choices which the parties make and in particular the major *strategic choices* which shape the system of industrial relations within an organisation, industry or country.[27] The notion of choice is a relatively simple idea, but we think it is important since it stresses that the actions of the parties themselves are important. The notion does not mean that there are no constraints on the parties; nor does it mean that major choices are being made all the time. It means rather that, at certain key junctures in the history of nations, firms and trade unions, major choices are made (including decisions not to make changes) which have a profound impact on future developments. We will develop this further in subsequent chapters where different choices will be examined in more detail.

This book also attempts to be comparative in the sense of drawing examples from a number of different countries, especially from the USA, Germany and Japan. The advantages of this, we hope, are that a comparative perspective enables us better to understand the distinctive features of the past development of British industrial relations, and we believe also that it may give some clues to future developments. In addition in an increasingly competitive, but interdependent, world it is more and more necessary to view British industrial relations in a comparative context. This is especially the case given two continuing developments, the increasing impact of subsidiaries of multinational companies on British employment practices and the growing effect of European Community membership on British industrial relations.

Finally, throughout the book we draw on a number of different academic disciplines depending on the area of analysis. For example, an understanding of industrial relations requires some knowledge of history. It requires a knowledge of Political and Economic History to understand the context within which industrial relations has developed; it also requires some knowledge of Business and Labour History in order to understand the origins and development of the main institutions of employers and employees. In this book we seek to give such a historical perspective. The study of industrial relations also requires some understanding of Politics and Labour Law so as to be able to understand how government action and legislation affects the actions of the parties and determines employment rules. At the level of the individual and the small group, a Social Psychological perspective is useful to understand the motivations and the dynamics of individual and group behaviour. Similarly, we also adopt a Sociological perspective to analyse the wider organisational and social structures which affect work and the employment relationship. Sociological and psychological approaches to employment and work in organisations are often combined in a study of Organisational Behaviour, and this can also offer insights into industrial relations. Last, but not least, we seek to put industrial relations into its economic context and to consider economic consequences. Labour and Industrial Economics have much to offer to an understanding of industrial relations institutions and outcomes. It is obviously not possible to master all these different academic disciplines, but we hope to be able to draw on them as required and to show the value of an approach which is interdisciplinary.

CONCLUSION

This chapter has reviewed a complex range of different approaches to industrial relations. Any reader who started without any familiarity with these debates may well be baffled by the array of 'isms' and 'ists'. However this categorisation of different perspectives on the subject matter should have demonstrated that the analysis of industrial relations is contentious and should help explain why there have over the years been so many contrasting proposals for reform. Far from being a descriptive subject, based on common sense, industrial relations is subject to considerable political and theoretical controversy. There is a multitude of ways of interpreting what *is* going on and a multitude of views about what *should* be happening in the area.

This means that here are no generally accepted global theories in industrial relations. Neither unitarist perspectives, liberal collectivism, corporatism, liberal individualism nor radical perspectives provide explanations that can account for the main industrial relations trends in the modern world. However, these perspectives provide a rich source of ideas that can be used to understand behaviour in particular circumstances at particular times. For example the liberal collectivist analysis of collective bargaining goes a long way to explaining the stability of collective bargaining systems, given certain contexts. The industrial relations policies of Germany and some Scandinavian countries and some periods in the UK are best illuminated by an understanding of the debate about corporatism. The Marxist argument that class interests and conflicts underlie ideological differences may still offer some insights into industrial relations. Of course, these perspectives cannot always be mutually consistent, but they can offer insights into different aspects of industrial relations, at different times, and at different levels.

In the rest of this book we shall look at the raw material around which these perspectives have been drawn. We study employers, employees, the representative institutions that they form, and the activities and role of the state. In this study we will be concerned to assess the types of cooperation and conflict that seem to predominate, the power available to back up different interests, and the social and political consequences of unilateral management regulation, collective bargaining or state intervention in employment relations. These are the issues which need to be clarified if we are to judge between the different assumptions and analyses currently made about British industrial relations.

3 Employers and their strategies

The first of the groups we choose for analysis are employers and their organisations. This choice of starting point needs explanation. A commonly held view is that industrial relations is primarily about trade unions and that they are the most important group involved. Unions are certainly the focus of most public debate in the area and they receive most attention in broadcast and newspaper coverage. Certainly in situations where there is a 'problem', such as a strike or a threatened plant closure, trade unions are likely to be quoted. Employers, on the other hand, are more likely to be absent from television news coverage of industrial relations.[1]

The low profile of employers in the media obscures the importance of employer behaviour for shaping industrial relations. Employers are certainly not powerless or ineffective compared to trade unions, but their power has a different base and its exercise attracts less attention. Employer influence can pass unobserved. Union strength rests largely on the power to strike. This is a very visible weapon and can be powerful if the strikers represent indispensable labour, or if the production lost during the strike is of crucial importance to the employer's interests, or if the strikers have considerable public support. However, there are many situations where the strike is a double-edged and dubious weapon. It is doubled-edged because strikers risk loss of income which may take years to recover.[2] It is dubious because success depends not only on correct tactics against opponents, but also on the strikers' ability to maintain a united stand. If the union membership is divided or loses confidence, then the credibility of the strike as a powerful weapon can vanish overnight.

In contrast to union power, employer power is less visual and newsworthy and can often be used more flexibly. Capital, unlike strike power, can be converted into other profit-generating activities, or even moved out of the country, without the constant need to win the active support of a mass of people. Employer power is not unconstrained but it is considerable.

Union power may be considerable, but, even where this is the case, it is usually so constrained by the problems of mobilising strikes that its use is limited to defensive issues where numbers of people clearly see they have a common interest. British union power has traditionally been reactive, directed at the defence of living standards and the improvement of a narrow range of related issues like hours or holidays. Employers are in a better position to take initiatives and introduce broader change. They can usually exert a greater influence on the control of employment relations. We will try to show that historically employers have played the major part in shaping the British system of industrial relations.

Governments have often seemed to pay more attention to trade unions, but some have also concluded that the main power and therefore the main responsibility for reform lies with employers.[3] Increasingly, academic work has come to emphasise the importance of employer initiatives in shaping personnel policies and the framework of industrial relations institutions.

WHO ARE THE EMPLOYERS?

A stereotyped view of the employer is of a besuited businessman, clearly visible at the top of the firm, directly controlling the workforce by issuing personal instructions. This model is too simple, even for the nineteenth century, when 'the boss' often related to his workforce only through sub-contractors or foremen. It is even more misleading for modern industry, where 'the employer' is likely to be the board of directors of a public company, often in a different location, sometimes in a different country, and where the management of the workforce is delegated to a hierarchy of managerial employees.

Most of Britain's employed population of over 22 million work for large employers. The government is, of course, the largest employer, with about one quarter of the labour force working in the public sector. It is, for example, the direct employer of 1.1 million people in central government and the indirect employer of 1.2 million in the National Health Service, 1.5 million in local authorities and 1.4 million in education.[4] In the private sector 50 per cent of all employees work for firms which employ more than 100 workers, though such firms constitute less than 1 per cent of the total number of businesses in the UK; 20 per cent of employees work for firms which employ more than 1,000 workers, though such firms constitute a tiny proportion of the total number of businesses. At the other end of the spectrum 25 per cent of the labour force work for firms which employ 10 workers or fewer and such firms make up 90 per cent of the total number of businesses.[5]

One of the most significant trends in the twentieth century has been the concentration of modern industry into fewer, giant companies. This long-term concentration has occurred both in terms of turnover and the employment size of firms and of individual plants or establishments. It has had important industrial relations implications which we will discuss below. It is to be noted, however, that from the 1980s onwards, there has been a growth in the relative size of the small firm sector. As a result of restructuring and downsizing, there has also been a reduction in the employment size of many big firm. This has been accompanied by a reduction in the number of big plants and in the average size of plant.[6]

The concentration of business over the course of the twentieth century has not just been a UK phenomenon. It has also occurred in all other major industrial countries.[7] The global concentration of business has been accentuated since the Second World War by the rapid development of multinational enterprises. Such firms spread their boundaries across nation states and employ people in different countries. In most major industries there are today a small number of multinational firms which tend to dominate world markets.[8] Within Europe the UK has the largest number of firms with over 1,000 employees and the largest number of non European multinational enterprises employing more than 1,000 workers within a European country.[9]

The concentration of business and the growth of multinational enterprises introduces into the industrial relations scene employers who have the financial resources of small nation states and enough employees to populate large towns. British Telecom, for example, has about 200,000 employees, most of whom are employed in the UK. Other large British employers, with staffs of about 100,000 and with most of these employed within the UK, include the big high street banks, such as Barclays, National Westminster and Lloyds, and the major supermarket and retailing chains, such as Sainsbury, Tesco and Marks & Spencer. The prominence of such firms as major employers reflects the growth in the postwar period of the services sector of the economy. Other large British companies such as ICI, British American Tobacco and BP, with substantial labour forces, employ a significant proportion of their employees outside the UK. Other large firms, such as Unilever and Shell, have joint British and foreign ownership and management. In this book we are mainly concerned with the UK activities of such firms. We are also concerned with the activities of foreign multinationals in Britain – most of the large foreign multinationals such as Ford, General Motors, IBM and a growing number of Continental and Japanese multinationals have operations in the UK.

As we have said, the development of large organisations has not eliminated the medium and small employer, but it has often changed the smaller employers' position in product and labour markets. Some economists and business historians speak of the development of a dual economy. Large monopolistic or oligopolistic corporations operate in the primary economy,

surrounded by a secondary economy of smaller, often more fiercely competitive organisations. The employers in the secondary economy often
service the core organisations of the primary sector and are likely to be
more vulnerable to market forces and to be pressurised by the primary
sector in economic recession. As we will see, from an employment point of
view, these smaller firms are likely to offer less good terms and conditions
of employment and are less likely to have bureaucratised employment and
industrial relations systems.

Employer objectives

Asked about their objectives in industrial relations, employers and their
spokesmen rarely say that they wish to achieve maximum effort and production and maximum subordination to managerial objectives from their
employees, in return for minimum costs. Yet both classical economic and
radical theories of capitalist production posit employer objectives in these
terms. These economic theories state that if an employer is to succeed, or
even survive in the face of competition, he must treat his labour force as a
factor of production, a cost to his business, like his non-human raw
materials. Some theorists add the argument that the struggle to control the
labour power that has been purchased must be the employers' *main* priority
in the search for profit or capital accumulation.[10]

Any employers who see their function as simply to minimise labour
costs and maximise the effort of their labour resources are unlikely to say
so in public. The questioning of the legitimacy of such objectives has been
sufficient over the years to make discussion of employer objectives a
value-laden, smoke-screened topic. Employers have developed a defence
against attacks on their objectives towards labour. This defence emphasises
the long-term interest of both employer and employee in a profitable
enterprise. At the present time, often under the banner of new-style Human
Resource Management, there is increasing talk about the need to treat the
workforce as a resource and an asset to be retained and developed for the
longer term, though how far this has been implemented in practice is not
clear. (See Chapters 9 and 11.)

The pressures on employers to treat their labour force as a resource and
the problem of legitimising the policies which flow from this are both
neatly illustrated by a historical study of Quaker employers such as Cadburys and Rowntrees, which suggests that market pressures will constrain
policy towards employees, even for entrepreneurs whose values and beliefs
might favour very different policies. Child identified four Quaker business
beliefs:[11] a dislike of exploitation and profit at the expense of others; the
importance of service, stressing hard work and personal renunciation in the

service of others; egalitarianism and the need for democratic relations between people; and an abhorrence of social conflict. In the early twentieth century, Quaker employers came under pressure from fellow Quakers to renounce the profit motive and establish democratically run businesses based on moral rather than material objectives. Child charts the response to this pressure and shows that Quaker employers choose to reject the values of egalitarian relations and the arguments that employers renounce privileged rewards. Instead they emphasised a general notion of service and the abhorrence of conflict, i.e. those values that conflicted least with conventional business objectives.

Quaker employers were spurred to produce an articulate defence of management in social terms, which has been widely adopted by other employers. They argued that employers had the moral and social responsibility to lead their organisations effectively and use the most efficient managerial techniques. This would enable them to serve the community – without personal renunciation – by improving the pay and conditions of their employees. It was more socially responsible to be efficient than to be democratic. The Quaker employers led the way in introducing welfare measures for employees like paid holidays, sick pay, pensions and in providing a better quality of working life. These benefits would traditionally have seemed harmful to employer interests because they raised labour costs, but there were real economic returns in terms of reduced labour turnover and increased productivity. Enlightened policies did not alter the basic authority relationships at work or represent any radical rejection of the employer objectives posited by classical economic theory.[12]

In competitive markets, owner-managers have usually been forced to minimise labour costs in order to keep the price of their products competitive and make the profits necessary to attract support from financial markets and suppliers. However, there is still a debate about the extent to which changes in ownership, or changes in business concentration, have lessened market-based constraints on employer policy towards employees.

Ownership, control and objectives

Most large firms are no longer run by proprietors. We therefore need to ask whether the separation of ownership from management, and along with this various forms of public ownership, has fundamentally altered the constraints that shape employers' objectives in the employment relationship.

The diffusion of ownership in scattered shareholdings and the growth of salaried, professional management have been the subject of a long debate in the social sciences about the effects of the divorce of ownership from control. Many writers have adopted a 'managerialist' stance. They argue that managers rather than owners now direct business affairs and that managers pursue objectives that differ from those of the owner-entrepreneur. The managerialists can be divided into those who believe managerial interests will be sectional and those who do not.

Sectional managerialists take a pessimistic view of managers' wider social responsibilities. They argue that managers are less constrained by shareholders and have more autonomy in running businesses, but they believe this freedom is used in the pursuit of the managers' own sectional interests. They argue that managers seek to maximise sales revenue or growth, rather than profits, and that they are concerned with a 'quiet life' or with increasing promotion prospects, as well as financial returns. They are not necessarily more concerned than owner-managers or shareholders about their employees' welfare, although they will have a greater common interest with employees in the organisation's survival. Non-sectional managerialists take a more optimistic view and argue that managers, freed from the controls exercised by a previous owning elite, are likely to pursue objectives that benefit the community as a whole. Managers form a powerful new group acting as a neutral buffer between the warring interests of capital and labour. They are more concerned with employee and community welfare, or with public opinion, than are shareholders.[13]

Counter-arguments against the managerialist views are put by radical economists and sociologists.[14] They accept that many large companies are no longer controlled by majority shareholders, but they argue that this does not result in managers pursuing fundamentally different economic or social objectives. Senior managers often still have a considerable stake in companies. In a competitive market economy they have to act as long-term profit maximisers and cost minimisers. Moreover, despite claims about more widely dispersed share ownership, it is large financial institutions, such as banks, insurance companies and pension funds, that influence key decisions and perforce take a short-term market perspective.

There is much evidence to support the radical rather than the managerialist view of top management objectives. Owner interests can have a direct impact on managerial decisions even when no majority shareholder exists. Diversified shareholding may simply mean that a minority shareholder, with a significant block of voting shares, can exercise the traditional owners' role on the board. Indeed, owner control may be increasing as the growth of institutional shareholding produces 'professional' shareholders more skilled in judging company affairs. Senior managers tend to adopt values and objectives very like the traditional shareholder.[15] Top managers adopt the same ideology and objectives as shareholders because they tended to come from the same background, share the same social relations and have a high proportion of their own personal wealth in shares. Studies suggest managerial decisions are constrained by capital markets, even when the direct intervention of shareholders or the shareholder orientation of managers are absent. The threat of takeover, and the need for capital support to finance investment, place considerable constraints on the extent to which any manager can diverge from conventional business objectives.[16]

Yet, one can criticise the radical view of employer objectives on the grounds that there may be differences between shareholders (for example, differences between national and international or large group and individual interests) which can blur the edges of the division of interest between capital and labour. Moreover, the traditional owner-entrepreneur may never have pursued profit maximisation as single-mindedly nor as successfully as either radical or classical economists assume, often because of weak accounting techniques and a lack of detailed knowledge.

The experience of state ownership in the UK lends some support to the view that, in modern capitalist societies, there are wider economic and technological constraints operating on the business enterprise. These constraints tend to minimise the differences between owner-managers and non-propertied managers. Calls for nationalisation in the early twentieth century were based on the belief that public ownership would radically change relations at work and herald a new era where the good of the community would prevail. There were different suggestions on how publicly owned enterprises should be run. Guild Socialists advocated the self-management of industry by democratically run guilds, which would contract with the employers to produce a certain output, at a given price. The miners' and railwaymen's unions suggested schemes for their industries involving government by councils composed of union officials and technical experts.[17] A more moderate view was that publicly owned enterprises should be managed entirely by expert managers free to take decisions on the normal criteria of business efficiency, though managers would be subject to the supervision of a board, appointed by government. It was this last model that was adopted after the Second World War. However, experience suggested that the objectives which lay behind nationalised managements' approach to employment relations did not differ very radically from those in private industry. There was the same concern with labour as a cost, the same need to maximise the effort and flexibility of labour, and the desire to control labour in order to pursue more dominant objectives of efficiency and return on investment. During the 1970s and 1980s, government guidelines placed these managers under increasingly tight economic constraints in relation to their employees. There *are* differences in managerial behaviour between the public and private sectors, but these can often be explained in terms of the type of industry and political contingency rather than as evidence of fundamentally different objectives.[18] For example, in the public sector employment relations are likely be more heavily bureaucratised and, in the past, jobs have tended to be more secure. Recent privatisations of publicly owned enterprises have led to reductions in the labour force and some decentralisation of collective bargaining, but have left most other aspects of industrial and employment relations intact.[19]

There is then considerable uniformity in the objectives pursued by employers in the employment field, but the strategies, defined as the major techniques and long-term policies, adopted in pursuit of those objectives and used to convert purchased labour power into valuable work for the employer take many forms.

MANAGERIAL STRATEGIES OF MOTIVATION AND CONTROL

At this point some might question whether employers have had policies and techniques which added up to anything so grand as strategies. Many might feel that employers merely reacted opportunistically to events and at best muddled through. In the case of British employers, there is indeed historically much to this contention. In considering strategies, a useful distinction may be drawn between intended and enacted strategies: intended strategies are those which are consciously and purposively developed *ex ante*; enacted strategies are those practices which grow incrementally over time and which, with the benefit of hindsight, reveal a certain pattern of actions *ex post*.[20] Historically, most British employers did not intentionally develop and implement long term strategies.[21] Instead they reacted in an *ad hoc* and often opportunistic manner, responding to market conditions. Despite this general pattern, however, there were always some firms which did consciously develop strategies of a more consistent nature, and their number has increased over time.

The benefit of an historical perspective is that it enables one to discern long-term patterns of action. The vast majority of British employers did not have strategies in the sense of long-term, consciously devised, coherent policies. However they did act in the long-term with a certain degree of regularity and they did make decisions which, when viewed cumulatively, reveal patterns of behaviour over time.

The employer's interest in the employment relationship is a by-product of the pursuit of more primary objectives. If these objectives can only be achieved through the efforts of employees, then the employer needs to recruit staff and build an organisation through which employee behaviour can be coordinated, monitored and controlled in a way that will ensure that the employer's plans are executed. Simply buying labour power on the labour market will not be enough, since in the market the employer buys hours of work or labour potential. In order to turn this potential into something of value to the employer, labour needs to be directed and organised, it needs to be motivated and controlled.

What techniques can be used by an employer wanting to organise and coordinate employees? A very simple typology showing the broad range of managerial techniques was set out by Etzioni.[22] He identified three main types of strategies: coercive, remunerative and normative.

Coercive

The employer uses compulsion or the 'stick' to control the labour force. Historically, this was common in the early factories of the Industrial Revolution and exists in situations of forced labour. The question then is, can it be talked about as a strategy in modern-day Britain? Coercive sanctions are still used in that firms have disciplinary rules and procedures, and breach of these rules can lead to discipline of various kinds, from suspension without pay to the ultimate sanction of dismissal. However, as Etzioni pointed out, an organisation which relies exclusively or mainly on coercive sanctions is likely to elicit an alienated response, with lack of commitment and cooperation.

Remunerative

All employers use financial rewards or the 'carrot' as a basic means of motivation and control. In Britain, employers traditionally placed very great reliance on incentives such as payment-by-results and today there is still considerable emphasis on performance pay as a way of motivating workers. In practice, the use of remunerative control and motivation techniques can have all sorts of industrial relations problems. Too great a reliance on the 'cash nexus' leads to a form of attachment which is instrumental, or in other words workers' attachment is limited, strictly conditional, and is focused on the level of reward.

Normative   — Soft HRM (some of it)

The employer may try to get more thorough commitment in various ways which Etzioni referred to as normative. By this he meant control or motivation by giving employees a sense of belonging, a voice in the organisation, and more satisfying work and by trying to develop reciprocity and trust. Such an approach is more likely to develop moral commitment where the worker more thoroughly identifies with the organisation. This is discussed further below where we look at paternalism of various kinds in Japan and Britain.

This typology is of some use in that it might give an insight into historical stages of development, with movement over time from coercive to remunerative and to normative emphases. It is also of some use for analysing how different groups of workers are managed, for example, more emphasis might be placed on coercive and remunerative techniques with unskilled workers, and more on normative techniques with professional and managerial staff. It might also be of some use to analyse differences between countries, for example, it could be argued that more emphasis has been placed on remunerative controls in countries like Britain and the US and on normative controls in Japan. On the other hand, the typology suffers from the disadvantage that it is very broad and it tells us little about the situations in which different approaches are adopted.

A different typology developed by Woodward places managerial strategies more firmly in their situational contexts.[23] She identified three basic types of managerial control: personal supervision, mechanical controls and administrative controls.

Personal supervision

The employer personally allocates work, issues instructions, checks on the methods being used, and monitors the standard of performance. In organisations of increasing size this function of personal supervision is delegated to managers and a pyramidal hierarchy of 'line management' can ensure that many people are receiving instructions from the top. Hierarchies of supervision are familiar in all organisations of any size. However, most employers no longer rely on direct personal supervision to express and enforce their demands on organisation behaviour. More impersonal mechanical and administrative controls have replaced personal supervision as the most significant managerial techniques.

Mechanical controls

Mechanical controls are a further step towards 'impersonal' control, for the required rules on the speed of work and standards of performance are planned and built in at the design stage of automated machines or process plant. Decisions about the planning and design of work may be taken at a different time and place from where the work is eventually executed. For example, crucial decisions about the pattern of jobs and the organisation of work in a chemical process plant will have been taken by the firm of consultant engineers employed before the plant was built. This is discussed further below when we look at the concept and practice of Taylorism.

Administrative controls

Administrative controls are based on rules. Impersonal rules specify desired behaviour, and rules may regulate recruitment, hours, wages, effort, promotion or discipline and may be elaborated to provide complex programmes for production planning, measurement mechanisms or cost control systems. Since this is an increasingly important aspect of control, we discuss this type further under the heading 'bureaucracy' below.

A similar typology was developed quite independently by the radical economist, Richard Edwards, who identified three similar managerial strategies: simple or direct, technical and bureaucratic.[24]

Simple or direct

This refers to close supervision by the employer or his representative who directly allocates work, issues instructions, and monitors results. Simple sanctions such as the threat of dismissal and simple incentives such as payment-by-results are used. This was the predominant pattern historically, and it still exists today in many smaller firms. However, as firms grew in size and as new more sophisticated production technologies became available, so firms developed new strategies.

Technical

Again this is an attempt at impersonal control through the use of technology or machines. Employers, Edwards contends, have consciously built performance and effort standards into machines and production systems. It is through these that they control the speed of work and reduce the autonomy of the worker. The classic example of this is the motor-car assembly line as developed by Henry Ford; another example might be the large office where employees process information at computer terminals. Both of these involve close control through machine-pacing. A crucial stage in the development of employer control, according to Edwards, was the advent of Scientific Management and Taylorism in the US at the beginning of the twentieth century and elsewhere from the interwar years onwards. We will deal with Taylorism in more detail below, but here we would say that it offered a set of techniques for studying worker effort, for reorganising work in a way that maximised employer control, and then relating work to financial incentive schemes. At the same time, this approach also had its disadvantages and contradictions: it tended to lead to worker alienation and discontent, and large factories managed on these lines were a breeding place for militant trade unionism.

Bureaucratic

This is seen by Edwards as the final stage of a movement towards less obtrusive, more impersonal controls. In large organisations management tries to build control into the social relations of the organisation and to develop complex rules and procedures which simultaneously bind and motivate employees. Thus firms develop rules and procedures, either unilaterally or bilaterally in negotiation with trade unions, which govern authority relations, promotion hierarchies, pay and benefit systems. Such arrangements were developed in the first place for managerial and white-collar workers, but have spread in recent years to manual staff also.

This typology may be of more use than that of Etzioni or Woodward because it is more grounded historically and seeks to relate control strategies to particular market conditions. The hypothesis is that competitive product markets, loose labour markets and small firms are likely to be associated with personal or simple control; less competitive product markets tighter labour markets, and larger firms, employing more capital-intensive technologies, are likely to lead to mechanical or technical control; and oligopolistic or monopolistic product markets, with shortages of labour and large firms, are likely to lead to administrative or bureaucratic controls.

Thus, various writers have noted a general historical trend away from personal supervision and towards other methods of control. Now we look in more detail at how aspects of mechanical or technical control and administrative or bureaucratic control intersect.

Taylorism – technical and bureaucratic control

The revival of one particular perspective on employer strategies started with a vivid and controversial analysis of Taylorism by Braverman.[25] Braverman argued that work has been progressively degraded over the course of industrialisation. The dominant strategy employed by American business in relation to its workforce has been to deskill jobs. This had enabled them to hire cheaper, semi-skilled or unskilled labour and to exercise tighter control over how work is done.

Central to Braverman's case is the argument that the theories and methods of F.W. Taylor, who worked in the late nineteenth and early twentieth centuries, were widely adopted by employers and still provide the criteria used by industrial engineers and work study departments to divide the labour process into jobs. Taylor initiated the 'Scientific Management' movement in the US and his ideas on work study, job design and individual incentives had a major impact on both sides of the Atlantic and, through Lenin's interest, in the Soviet Union. Taylorist schemes have been introduced into many companies over the years, and Braverman's argument is that, despite some resistance and the rise of new fashions like 'Human Relations' or 'Job Redesign', Taylor's basic principles have not been superseded where it matters most – in the organisation of work.

Taylor advocated certain techniques for analysing, measuring, allocating and rewarding work on the grounds that they would greatly increase the efficiency and productivity of labour. Braverman sees these techniques not in terms of improvements, designed to benefit everyone, but in terms of a strategy designed to improve the employer's position in conflicts over the control and price of labour. Braverman suggests that before Taylor's work study techniques were introduced, workmen themselves could plan and pace their own methods of work; they, rather than the employer, knew the best way of doing a job. Men with skills learnt from years of experience had a valuable asset which they could sell to the employer in the labour market. Taylorism enabled employers to break down this employee-held asset. It taught employers to analyse the work process so that the design and planning stages could be moved from the shop floor to new production engineering and work study departments. These departments could specify the remaining tasks and divide them between simple, repetitive jobs. Such jobs required low-grade labour, which was available cheaply and easily from the labour market. The jobs required little training and so labour could be seen as a disposable resource, with the employer needing to employ workers only when they could be immediately used. Through work study techniques, the effort required from workers could be precisely calculated and this could be carefully matched to the amount paid by the employer, by Taylor's payment-by-results incentive schemes. In addition, simplified, prescribed tasks made it easier to check worker performance and adherence to rules and this facilitated management control.

Braverman therefore argues that Taylorism is not a science of work, but a science of the management of others' work. It is not a strategy for scientific workmanship, but a strategy of deskilling, for employers to gain closer control over employee behaviour and cost. He concludes that, having deskilled manual labour, employers also have moved on and deskilled clerical, administrative and managerial work.[26]

Braverman's argument can be criticised on the grounds that he exaggerates the universality of this employer strategy and that he oversimplifies and romanticises the system of work organisation before Taylor.[27] However, his book usefully sets a spotlight on managerial strategies in the area of work organisation.

Recent studies have traced the significance of Taylor in different societies.[28] Taylor's ideas were significant in the development of modern work organisations, though they spread unevenly and in competition with other rationalisation movements. Scientific management was adopted but interpreted in different ways in the contrasting economic and social contexts of the US and UK. In the US it was more successfully introduced in the first half of the twentieth century; in Britain, because of weak managerial structures and more opposition from the workforce, it was less effectively implemented. In Japan Taylorism had a different impact again: it was introduced, but was modified by managerial attempts to gain greater flexibility and cooperation from the labour force. The Japanese development of modern work organisation, based more on flexibility, demonstrates that Taylorism is not the only strategy available to capitalist employers.[29]

Taylorism had important implications for bureaucracy. Scientific management gave employers the techniques to tighten the hierarchy of supervision, to create a systematic division of labour, and to elaborate written rules about task performance. However, Taylorism did not involve the bureaucratisation of personnel policy. Although Taylor accepted the need for improved recruitment criteria, he did not advocate giving workers greater job security or paying them according to career progression or extending fringe benefits. Instead, he sought the complete substitutability of labour. Workers would have a casual relationship with any particular employer and employers should not attempt to induce organisational loyalty. Rather than bureaucratic personnel policies Taylor advocated a minimum interaction policy between employer and employee based on a rudimentary wage–effort exchange.[30]

Bureaucracy and bureaucratic managerial controls

In conventional stereotypes, bureaucracy is often seen as a cumbersome, inefficient form of organisation hampered by red tape and rigidity. Nevertheless, much organisation theory revolves around the concept of bureaucracy, and many studies of employer strategies towards employees have used the concept of bureaucracy as a guide.[31] In modern organisation theory the concept is used in different ways. It is therefore useful to return to the classic analysis of bureaucratic organisation developed at the start of the century by Weber.

Weber saw the widespread development of bureaucratic administration as one of the most significant, far-reaching social changes in the modern world.[32] Bureaucratic techniques gave organisational controllers the potential for unprecedented control over social resources in pursuit of their objectives and enabled them to build organisations that were larger and more complex than ever before. Because these control techniques were so superior to other methods of organisation, they were likely to dominate modern business and political organisations, regardless of the particular political economy in operation.

What are the features of bureaucracy in the context of modern employer strategies? We may separate Weber's bureaucratic control techniques into two sets. One set consists of the provisions that surround the appointment, promotion, rewarding, and disciplining of employees. We can call this the bureaucratic personnel policy. The other set concerns the structure of hierarchical control, the design of jobs and the direction and monitoring of work. We can call this bureaucratic control over task performance.

Why would such techniques be effective in achieving employer objectives? Weber argued that the impersonal, hierarchical, rule-bound characteristics of bureaucratic organisation gave organisational rulers an unprecedented ability to direct the behaviour of large numbers of people towards organisational ends. They enabled the people at the top of an organisation to incorporate expertise, plan work, and then allocate tasks throughout the organisation, while specifying the criteria on which any decision should be based. They also guarded against the danger of senior managers becoming dependent on any particular employee. On the personnel policy side, the much maligned position of bureaucrats with their formal recruitment, job security, careers and incremental pay scales, Weber saw as designed to build loyalty and motivation into the organisation's workforce.

Bureaucratic administrative techniques have become widespread and, as Perrow argued, 'the vast majority of large organisations are fairly bureaucratic. . . . Without this form of social organisation, the industrialised countries of the west could not have reached the heights of wealth that they currently enjoy', but 'by its very nature, and particularly because of its superiority as a social tool over other forms of organisation, bureaucracy generates an enormous degree of unregulated and often unperceived social power in the hands of a very few leaders'.[33]

Virtually all modern organisations use some of the managerial, bureaucratic techniques charted above. However, there are different forms of bureaucracy. Employers pursue different strategies and different policies towards their employees using different versions of bureaucratic techniques. Employee reactions may themselves force bureaucratic adjustments to managerial controls. We need to look at the different types of bureaucratic strategy that are adopted.

Technical and bureaucratic control have therefore been strategies used by modern employers to manage employees. In Britain both kinds of motivation and control techniques have been important, though, on the whole, they have probably been less well developed and elaborate than in countries such as the US and Germany. Another form of control, which we will call bureaucratic paternalism, incorporating aspects of normative control, now needs to be considered.

Bureaucratic paternalism in Japan

A classic comparison of employment policies in Britain and Japan is that by Dore.[34] He contrasted large companies in the engineering industries of each country in a study in which two factories from English Electric (now GEC) were matched by product and technology with two from Hitachi. Although there have been changes in employment practices in both countries since the case studies were completed, the basic distinctions highlighted by the research remain and have been underlined by more recent analysis and studies of Japanese plants in Britain.[35]

Dore characterises the broad difference between British and Japanese management by saying that the British are market-orientated, whereas the Japanese are organisation-orientated. British employers and employees relate to a general labour market; there is no permanent commitment between employer and employee. Employees are expected to return to the labour market if their skills are no longer required or if other employers offer higher pay. In contrast, Japanese large-scale companies do not relate to an external labour market for the provision of the core of their workforce. They expect regular employees to be permanently committed to one employer. These employees' future careers, and much of their non-work activities, depend on their employing organisation.

Dore's study showed that manual employees working on similar production processes and similar machinery can have radically different employment relations. Three differences arising from the British/Japanese contrast are worth emphasising.

Lifetime commitment versus minimum interaction

Many employees in large Japanese companies have a permanent status; they are recruited straight from the education system and expect, and are expected, to remain with the company until retirement. It is only in the most extraordinary circumstances that these regular employees are dismissed or made redundant, and the strength of the tie between employer and employee is caught by the term 'lifetime commitment'.

The difference between British and Japanese practice on job tenure in Dore's study is most marked for manual workers, because it is for unskilled and semi-skilled operatives that the British 'minimum interaction' principle operates. For British manual workers the more temporary relationship with the firm is compounded by the lower provision of pensions, sickness pay and other fringe benefits. Japanese firms provide more fringe benefits of this sort, and make them equally available to all regular employees, whether of manual or managerial status. As Dore writes:

> In English Electric there is a considerable difference between managers, skilled men and operatives in the degree to which they are given cause to consider themselves 'members of the firm' rather than mere employees. This difference is much less marked at Hitachi; the official ideology, in fact, holds there to be no difference.[36]

In Japan, status distinctions exist but are attached to seniority. Status graduations are numerous and all regular workers can increase their seniority and status. In the UK there are much sharper divisions into two or three 'classes'. The move in recent years by British firms to give, and by unions to negotiate, 'staff status' for manual workers has only gone some way to soften the differences in status long symbolised by the distinction between 'staff' and 'works'.[37]

Group versus individual responsibility for tasks

In British factories responsibilities and tasks tend to be allocated to individuals rather than groups. Again, this is most pronounced for manual workers who have the most closely prescribed, work-studied jobs. In Japan the division of labour is less minutely prescribed and responsibilities are allocated to groups rather than individuals. Associated with the less detailed regulation of task by specialised work study or industrial engineering departments, there is far more consultation within the department or workgroup before decisions are taken on how to execute a job. Although the head of the group has formal responsibility for seeing that work is done, there is no suggestion that the results depend on his efforts; the leader can play a figurehead role while more junior and possibly more competent people openly carry the load. The performance of work tasks is therefore subject only in part to neo-Taylorist controls. Employers rely more on group working and ideological appeals for group loyalty. Once again, the introduction in recent years by some British firms of team working and quality control circles has only gone a short way towards introducing such practices in Britain.[38]

Reward systems; salary scales and career progression versus payments-by-results

Traditionally, many British manual workers had two basic components to their pay: a 'basic rate for the job' which depended on going rates for unskilled, semi-skilled or skilled workers, and weekly bonuses from payment-by-results schemes. If the individual completed work-studied tasks faster than the time allowed, he received a bonus. British managers and administrative staff were less likely to receive these direct monetary incentives and were paid salaries with annual increments depending on their superiors' discretion.

In Japan all regular workers in large companies are placed on incremental salary scales. There is less attempt to pay 'the market rate' for skills; indeed, the market is largely irrelevant except at the start of the scales, for the school or graduate intake. Thereafter, employees move along their incremental scale and all regular employees, even the most unpromising, are guaranteed gradual upgrading, with the high-flyers progressing more quickly. Bonuses are paid but these are group-based and usually allocated on the same criteria used to place employees to their salary grade – i.e. seniority and merit.

With such stable pay and with employment security, how do Japanese employers motivate their employees? They provide the bureaucratic motivator that Weber believed would be so effective in encouraging obedience to organisational rules, the organisation-based career. Conformity to organisational requirements is rewarded, not just by seniority-based salary increments, but by promotion to higher status and more highly paid jobs. Recruitment to the better-paid posts in the managerial hierarchy comes from within the organisation and all regular employees can progress up one of the company's promotion lines.

It might be asked, how do Japanese employers, operating with a fixed and increasingly costly labour force, respond to market fluctuations and the potential need to cut labour costs? Japan has a dual economy and the regular employee in the primary economy is protected from the vagaries of labour demand by the secondary economy. Large companies subcontract much work to a myriad of small- to medium-scale subcontractors whose workers do not enjoy the privileges of the permanent employee, even though they may be employed to work on the premises of the large concern. A secondary labour market also exists in the large companies, operating alongside the internal labour market of the regular employee. Temporary workers are taken on who do not get the tenure or benefits of the regular workforce and female employees are expected to leave the company on marriage or childbirth. As we will see in Chapter 6, trade unions in Japan are enterprise-based, tend to have in membership only full-time workers, and do not press for changes in the system. With these arrangements for support, Japanese 'lifetime commitment' has proved remarkably resilient in the face of economic recessions.

In conclusion, there is more than one way to organise tasks into jobs and to relate to a labour market. It is too easy to take familiar practices for granted or assume they have an inviolate logic. British practices were historically influenced by attempts to introduce Taylorism and have tended not to be particularly bureaucratised; Japan provides a contrast – the emphasis has been on the construction of bureaucratic personnel policies and less on bureaucratic controls over task performance. Yet, though Japan provides the most highly developed example of bureaucratic paternalism, policies designed to bureaucratise personnel policies are by no means unique to Japan.

Bureaucratic paternalism elsewhere

In Britain bureaucratic personnel policies with job security, internal promotion and seniority-based benefits are most evident in areas of the public sector such as the Civil Service and in the private sector in areas such as banking. Workers in a number of large private-sector companies, such as ICI or BP, are also managed in this way. Bureaucratic personnel policies have rarely been adopted for British manual workers, although some large nineteenth-century organisations did attempt to create career ladders for key manual workers, and aspects of these are still found in the railway, post office and steel industries. Quaker employers like Rowntree, Cadbury and J & J Clarke had developed paternalistic practices from the 1890s. They emphasised welfare, for example building model factory villages, but tended not to provide extensive employment tenure or career progression and their welfare model did not spread beyond a minority of employers.[39]

Bureaucratic paternalism was also evident in Germany and the US. In Germany large companies like Siemens and Krupp were highly paternalistic in 1900.[40] In the US even Ford, though adopting Taylorist job design and work study in 1914, sought to reduce the costs of a very high labour turnover by instituting a fixed, high day-wage and creating a 'Sociology Department' to cater for the moral welfare of employees.[41] Later in the middle of the twentieth century, large American companies created elaborate career ladders and put great effort into the generation of organisational loyalty, combined with policies of anti-unionism and 'human relations' techniques for careful communication to, and supervision of, employees.[42]

A summary of some of the ideas about employer strategies is provided in Figure 3.1.

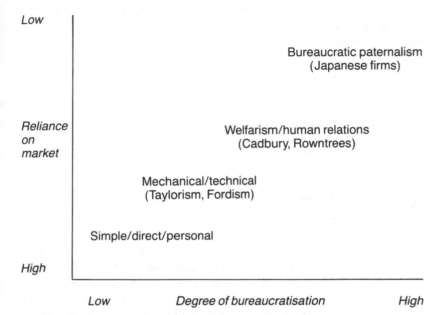

Low

Bureaucratic paternalism
(Japanese firms)

Reliance
on
market

Welfarism/human relations
(Cadbury, Rowntrees)

Mechanical/technical
(Taylorism, Fordism)

Simple/direct/personal

High

Low   *Degree of bureaucratisation*   High

Figure 3.1 Typology of managerial strategy

An economic interpretation of employer strategies

So far we have dealt with typologies of employer strategies which are primarily sociologically based. Some of these same phenomena have been analysed in slightly different ways by economists.

In analysing economic processes, economists use the notions of markets and firms. A market exists when there is an exchange of goods or services between sellers and buyers, shaped by the forces of supply and demand and coordinated by the price mechanism. Such an exchange is usually a short-term and relatively impersonal transaction. Firms, on the other hand, are economic institutions which operate in markets, but which are distinct from them. Activities within firms are coordinated and controlled by a hierarchy of managers, and relations within the firm are more likely to be longer term. One way to see the firm is as an administrative mechanism which comes into being and supersedes the market mechanism when it becomes more efficient or more effective to coordinate activities and allocate resources internally within the firm rather than externally in the market.[43] Where the costs of using the external market mechanism (costs such as those of obtaining information, preventing opportunistic behaviour and reducing uncertainty) are relatively low, the firm will choose to transact through the market; where the costs of market transactions are too high, the firm will prefer to internalise activities within its boundaries; the limits to the growth of the firm will be fixed by the volume of transactions which can be efficiently internalised.

These ideas can be developed and used to understand employers' labour strategies. In making labour decisions, there are a number of choices open to the employer. But these choices are not limitless. One way to conceive the choices is as follows: the employer can either externalise activities in the market, internalise them within the boundaries of the firm, or coordinate them by various combinations of the two. Gospel has applied this concept to decisions in the three areas of work organisation, employment relations and management–union relations.[44]

In terms of work organisation (taken to cover the way workers are organised around technology and processes), the concepts of internalising and externalising can be used to analyse a number of important labour decisions. For example, the firm can externalise by relying on different forms of subcontracting to organise production, or it can internalise by more directly organising its own workforce. Thus, one significant historical change was the movement from putting-out systems of production, to various forms of subcontracting, and to direct production within the firm. Over time, there has been some backward and forward movement between these different ways of organising work. The notion of internalising and externalising can also be used to analyse skill formation and transformation, in other words, training arrangements. Thus the firm can externalise by doing little or no training and poaching or recruiting labour in the market which others have trained. Also, it could be said to externalise by relying on apprenticeship arrangements which are occupationally orientated or by making extensive use of state training facilities which train in externally marketable skills. On the other hand, the firm can internalise by doing its own training and making training more firm-specific.[45] Where and how workers acquire skills is of extreme importance: it affects their attitude towards those skills, their control over them, and their attitude to technical change.

In terms of employment relations (taken to cover the way people are recruited and employed, job tenure and promotion, and wage and benefit arrangements), the firm can externalise by relying on the external market for labour; by recruiting and laying off as demand changes; by filling higher positions with external as well as internal candidates; and by fixing wages according to external market signals. Alternatively, the firm can internalise the employment relationship by more systematically screening and recruiting workers; by making every effort to make them permanent employees; by developing internal job ladders and using internal promotion wherever possible; by fixing wages more according to internal administrative principles than to market forces; and by developing more extensive fringe benefits, often based on seniority within the firm. In the former situation, where strategies of externalisation are pursued, the employment contract is likely to be of a minimal kind; in the latter it will be more complex and there will be a more highly developed internal labour market.[46] The term 'internal labour market' is often used to describe an elaborate internal employment system relatively insulated from external market forces. In this sense the term is now widely accepted; however, it is something of a misnomer, since what is being described is less of a market and more of an internal administrative system.

In management–employee relations (taken to cover systems of representation, relations with employees and trade unions, and the process of collective bargaining), managements can internalise by seeking to promote their own employee representation system, such as a works council, or by sponsoring a company union. Where management does recognise an outside union, it will seek to bargain domestically within the firm and will handle grievances and disputes internally through its own in-house procedures. By contrast, a firm can be said to externalise its industrial relations when it hands dealings with a trade union over to an association of employers outside the firm. This type of employers' organisation sets wages according to external market criteria and processes grievances through an external disputes procedure. This use of employers' associations is a form of externalisation, though it might perhaps be better termed 'coordination by cooperation'.[47] Certainly it represents a form of delegation to an outside body.

In reality, firms will often use a combination of these strategies. For example, they may use different strategies for different types of labour, showing more of a tendency to internalise in the case of higher level employees who are in short supply or who possess firm-specific skills. They may also move between different types of strategy over time as market conditions change. But such moves occur infrequently and come about slowly.

In general, in the nineteenth and early twentieth centuries, British employers tended to prefer market mechanisms and to externalise their labour activities and they only slowly and hesitantly built strong internal structures. This contrasts with tendencies in other countries, especially among large firms in the USA, Germany and Japan, where there was a stronger tendency to rely more on internal systems of coordination. Yet the British system showed some diversity, and it is significant that there were always exceptions to the general pattern. These exceptions tended to be large, well-organised firms which had relatively stable and growing product markets and which often needed to attract and retain a particular type of labour which was not readily available in the external labour market. Among these were a significant number of private-sector organisations.

These therefore tended to be organisations which had the incentive (in terms of attracting and retaining skills), the resources (in terms of product market success) and the organisational capability (in terms of corporate structure and managerial hierarchy) to institute and develop such systems.

The notion of internalising and externalising can be used to analyse managerial strategies in the labour area. It can be used to understand the slow growth of internal labour markets in Britain where employers had long relied on external markets for labour supply and wage fixing. It can also be used to examine various aspects of work relations. For example, it can be employed to describe the historical move from various forms of sub-contracting to more direct forms of work organisation. More contemporaneously, in different economic circumstances, it can be used to understand the re-emergence of various forms of subcontracting, temporary and part-time working. It can be used to focus on one important aspect of training, namely whether training is organised under company control and is firm-specific, or whether it is more market-orientated. The concept is also helpful in understanding the significance of industry-wide, multi-employer bargaining which may be seen as a form of externalisation and the growth of single-employer bargaining which was seen as a form of internalisation.

There is obviously much overlap between the different approaches we have reviewed and developed. Thus, for example, sociologists might talk about strategies of minimum interaction as opposed to bureaucracy; in a very similar way economists might conceptualise the same activities in terms of market externalisation and firm internalisation.

WHY ARE DIFFERENT STRATEGIES ADOPTED?

We have seen that employer strategies can vary considerably. The question then becomes why are different policies and techniques adopted and why do some employers choose one set of strategies rather than another? Indeed, how much choice is there and how constrained are employers? There are no definitive theories in this area, but plenty of ideas which shed varying degrees of light.

Some have offered broad cultural explanations and, for example, have sought to explain the employment differences between Japan and Britain on cultural lines. After the Second World War it was common for western observers to assume that Japanese policies were irrational; they represented the unconscious hangover of feudal and paternalistic customs, and in time more 'modern', rational, market-orientated, western policies would be adopted. In the context of British industrial history, there were certain attitudes which had considerable tenacity: in employment relations a strong tradition of *laissez-faire* individualism and rather looser notions of paternalism; in work relations a 'gentlemanly' lack of interest on the part of many senior managers and a belief in the 'practical' approach on the part of many lower-level managers;[48] in dealing with unions a belief in maintaining managerial prerogatives at the cost of developing closer consultative and better bargaining arrangements. Such traditional attitudes were deeply entrenched and affected the choice of labour strategies.

However, there are a number of major problems with cultural arguments. Their origins have to be explained and located in historical and institutional contexts. Broad cultural arguments fail to explain the substantial differences between different firms *within* Britain and *within* Japan. The success in introducing Japanese-style practices in modified form into Britain and other western countries have also cast doubts on cultural arguments.[49]

More sophisticated explanations recognise the possibility that employers may choose to adopt different policies to suit different historical circumstances and that the employers' freedom of choice may be subject to various types and degrees of situational constraint. Dore explained the difference between Britain and Japan in terms of the technological and social environment facing those who first established business organisations in each country. Britain was an early developer and her entrepreneurs presided over the gradual development of industrial organisation from the top of businesses that were small and insecure in the face of market pressures. The agricultural sector and the craft trades provided an existing labour force of relatively mobile workers whose labour could be bought as need arose. Japanese business operated in a very different situation. Japan developed late and the early entrepreneurs ran large, secure bureaucracies owned by the state or merchant-family groups. The advanced modern technology which they imported required labour skills unlike any in the existing adult labour force. However, comprehensive primary schooling had already developed and employers could use school results to cream off the best school-leavers for company training. Contingent historical factors of this type could mix with cultural preferences to provide rational explanations for the choice of different policies by different employers. Once the framework of employment relations was established, this itself set constraints on the options of those who followed.

Organisation theory provides many studies of constraints or 'contingencies' that influence employers' adoption of business strategies.[50] Relevant here are the studies that suggest top management may attempt to centralise planning and decision making within the organisation in order to achieve maximum control over business operations, but that this desire to gather all control into central hands can meet various obstacles. Centralised decision making is difficult if there is a need for constant and varying adjustments to behaviour. For example, if there is great unpredictability in the product market or in the production process, then it may be impracticable for the employer to centralise all decisions about how work should be carried out and it may be too costly to design systems that would specify in advance how to cope with all potential variations. The employer will need to accept decentralised decision making.

One study contrasted the management of a rayon mill with the management of a research and development facility in the electronics industry.[51] The highly predictable market, materials and production process of the rayon mill permitted the development of highly centralised, bureaucratic control over the labour process, with work tasks closely prescribed and all possible contingencies planned for in the reference 'book of rules'. However, the successful R & D organisations in electronics were managed in a way that permitted more fluid adjustment to constantly changing tasks by relying, not on centrally defined and controlled work roles, but on 'professional' workers, highly trained to take their own decisions in the light of the circumstances.

Similar arguments have been produced to explain the different management organisations in construction and manufacturing industries.[52] Manufacturing, with its stable production locations and relatively stable workflows, enables management to use modern administrative and mechanical techniques to centralise decision making and closely prescribe the jobs of those lower in the organisation's hierarchy. In construction, these managerial techniques are used much less, and constantly changing work sites and seasonal shifts in demand make it more rational for management to continue to rely on personal supervision and a more decentralised work structure. Many decisions are left to be taken by the workers on site on the basis, not of head office instructions, but of experience and craft training. In the unpredictable circumstances of the construction industry 'craft administration' rather than 'bureaucratic administration' can still be the most rational managerial technique.

Another example of organisation theory's contribution to the analysis of managerial control comes from a government-owned industrial manufacturing monopoly in France. Crozier noted that a high degree of organisational security and market stability had made possible the development of a highly centralised, tightly controlled, bureaucratic management structure. In only one area did unpredictability cause the failure of centralised managerial controls: machine breakdown could not be predicted in advance and the maintenance department retained considerable autonomy and freedom from administrative regulations.[53] Here management control and motivation strategies had to be more indirect and flexible.

There is, therefore, an extensive body of work within organisation theory which suggests that the tightness of bureaucratic controls used by employers will depend on the predictability of the work to be controlled. These theories tend to focus on the contingencies which affect employer control over task performance. They say less about bureaucratic personnel policies.

As has already been suggested, economists studying internal labour markets can throw some light on bureaucratic personnel policies. Many of them have noted an association between large-scale, monopolistic or oligopolistic firms, and the development of internal labour markets.[54] Why should employers in monopolistic positions adopt bureaucratic personnel policies? Piore suggests that employers in control of giant monopolies are able to respond more flexibly to employee demands for job security and career progression. Employers operating under competitive market conditions will be constrained to adopt the direct controls and labour-cheapening methods of Taylor. By contrast, if an employer can exploit a monopolistic position to raise profits, then the containment of labour costs may be less important. In these circumstances employees may be able to win the greater security and better conditions provided by bureaucratic personnel policies. Edwards and Lazonick stress advantages to employers rather than employees as the reasons why bureaucratic personnel policies will be adopted.[55] Internal labour markets increase an employee's dependence on his employer. For employers who have the resources to provide these conditions, internal labour markets may represent the most effective strategy of managerial control.

The state of the economy will also affect employer strategies. Friedman argued that there are two main employer control and motivation strategies. *Direct control* involves the use of simple and tough techniques such as close supervision, piecework, and the threat of discipline and dismissal. By contrast, *responsible autonomy* involves controlling and motivating workers by giving them more discretion and say, though within fixed limits, and gaining more normative commitment to the enterprise. These strategies, according to Friedman, are very much determined by the state of the business cycle: in periods of depression, when trade unions are weak and management may be in a stronger position, they are more likely to use direct control strategies; in periods of economic upswing and prosperity, by contrast, they are more likely to resort to the more sophisticated techniques of responsible autonomy.[56]

Gospel has suggested that strategies of externalisation existed where product markets were small, fragmented and competitive, and where labour markets provided an ample supply of workers.[57] They also existed where firms had simple divisions of labour and lacked the organisational capability (or bureaucratic structures) to develop and administer strong internal systems. In these circumstances, it made more sense for employers to rely on market rather than administrative coordination. Strategies of internalisation occurred when administrative coordination permitted a more effective and efficient labour management than coordination by market mechanisms. Internalisation therefore depended on markets, was related to more sophisticated divisions of labour, and required more advanced managerial hierarchies.

The labour market for particular classes of labour also affected strategies. Where classes of labour were in short supply or where they acquired firm-specific skills (such as has often been the case with many white-collar and managerial workers), employers were more likely to pursue strategies of internalisation. Where, by contrast, employees were in plentiful supply or possessed general skills which were easily acquired in the market (such as was the case with many less skilled manual workers), employers were more likely to pursue strategies of externalisation. Large employers may therefore use internal labour markets for some workers and external labour markets for other workers depending on the type of job and the availability of market skills.

The state of demand in the labour market also directly affected industrial relations in that it shaped the opportunism which was often the hallmark of employer policies, inducing cooperative attitudes in times of prosperity and more adversarial attitudes in times of recession.[58]

Thus organisational, technological and market forms have been important in shaping labour management strategies. However, this is not to deny that there were other forces operating. The influence of the state, both negative and positive, also had an important effect, especially at certain key points in time. As we will see in Chapter 7, at the most fundamental level, from the nineteenth century onwards, the support of the British state for *laissez-faire* employment principles and non-intervention in the employment relationship was of great importance. Similarly, the provision from the nineteenth century onwards of legal immunities for unions and later the support for collective bargaining, especially during the period of the two world wars and in the post-Second World War years, had an important effect on British industrial relations. In the 1980s the Thatcher administration, with its commitment to market principles and individualism and its introduction of legal restraints on unions, has also had a significant effect on the conduct of industrial relations, by reshaping the agenda and making possible what had previously seemed difficult for employers to attain.

Some independent effect on employer strategies has to be assigned to the actions of trade unions. In Britain, the strength of craft unionism, the persistence of workplace organisation, and the complexities of multi-unionism had an effect on the division of labour, employment practices, and collective bargaining arrangements. However, on the whole, union impact has tended to be exaggerated in both popular and academic commentary. Employers had initiatory power, while union power was largely reactive and defensive. Ultimately employers made the decisions, or failed to make the decisions, which counted most. Indeed, corporate structure and management choice of bargaining arrangements had a substantial effect on the organisation and power structure of trade unions in Britain. Thus, traditional structures provided the basis for craft unionism in the nineteenth century; the resort to employers' organisations led to increasing centralisation of union organisation and decision making in the early twentieth century; the persistence of loose forms of corporate oganisation and the weakness of employers' associations in Britain ensured the strength of fragmented shopfloor unionism through the first three postwar decades; more recently the development of stronger corporate structures have encouraged a more enterprise-orientated trade unionism.

In answer to the question, 'Why are different policies adopted?' it would seem that employers choose those policies which gave them the greatest control over the work of their employees for the minimum economic cost, but this 'rationality' is bounded by constraints arising from the employers' situation. The practicability of different policies, and their cost, will be subject to contingent factors over which the employers have no control. From the available literature it is evident that history, the nature of labour and product markets, the structure of the business organisation and the nature of managerial hierarchies, the role of the state, and countervailing pressures from employees all need to be considered.

For some employers the pressure of contingent factors may seem so great that to talk of choice or deliberate policy may seem absurd. Historically, in Britain many firms felt so buffeted by their environment or workforce that they coped from day to day without any attempt to plan rationally a policy for handling their employees.[59] In this case it is difficult to talk about *intended* strategies. For some employers options are more restricted than for others, but this does not prevent them from taking decisions on employment matters, and their decisions may add up to patterns of action which are *enacted* strategies.[60] Employers are certainly important actors in industrial relations, although at different times they may have greater or lesser power to make innovative changes.

Obviously the strategies adopted for the organisation of labour have an impact on other aspects of industrial relations. For example, employees who have job security and career prospects develop different interests and priorities than those without and employees with a minimal relationship with their employer, attached by short-term economic rewards to tightly controlled jobs, are likely to respond by seeming to maximise short-term rewards. Taylorist policies for controlling work create a vicious spiral of distrust between employer and employee which has served to embitter British industrial relations.[61] The scientific management of worker effort and reward can degenerate into a continuous battle over prices for jobs as each new job becomes the focus for bargaining and every hitch in production or shortage of supplies generates conflicts over compensatory payments for time lost. Conflicts over rewards for effort are, of course, present in all employment relationships but not all management systems stimulate the constant opening of hostilities throughout the day. Workers who see themselves as members of an organisation rather than as a commodity on the labour market are likely to form organisation-based rather than market-based, unions.

Comparative studies suggest that Britain has a relatively low development of bureaucratic managerial policies and techniques.[62] The bureaucratic techniques used for the management of manual workers have traditionally been those that focus on task performance, rather than on the motivators of bureaucratic personnel policy. The latter have, however, been growing slowly but surely.

A summary framework for analysing managerial strategies in their context is presented in Figure 3.2.

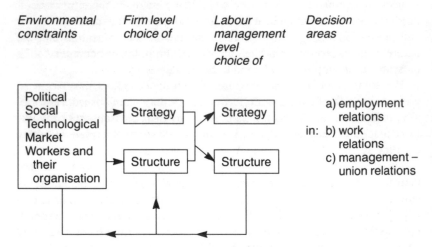

Figure 3.2 A framework for the analysis of managerial strategies

EMPLOYER IDEOLOGY AND STYLES

So far we have talked about employer strategies, policies and techniques. However, it is not only employers' strategies and techniques that shape events, but also managerial beliefs and ways of thinking. Though less concrete and substantial, these are often the origins of policies and the filter through which they are implemented. It is important therefore to consider the ideological perspectives of employers, the operational styles of managers and the kinds of cultures they seek to create within their organisations.

An ideological perspective we define as a set of beliefs, held by a specific interest group. These beliefs are not necessarily well articulated or internally consistent, but they serve two important functions: first, they are a method of reassurance and self-legitimation for the holder of the beliefs; second, they are an instrument of persuasion and a means whereby the employer seeks to persuade employees to act in a certain way. Managerial style we define as something rather more practical and operational: it is the way an individual manager or group of managers act on a day-to-day basis and how they manage their employees. This in turn relates to the cultural climate which managers seek to create. At the organisational level, we define culture as the set of norms, values and assumptions which exist within an organisation and which underpin the operation of the organisation. Managers seek to create cultures in line with their ideologies and styles and which will reinforce their strategies and techniques.

There have been various attempts to develop typologies of managerial ideologies, styles and corporate cultures. Many hinge on how autocratic or participative management is *vis-à-vis* its employees, or how goal-centred or people-centred managers are, or how mechanistic or flexible management is in running the organisation.[63] However, these typologies often tend to be more prescriptive than analytical. Another typology which is useful in industrial relations is that developed by Fox.[64] He identified two main ideological perspectives or 'frames of reference' in British industrial relations which have affected managerial styles, corporate cultures, and managerial practice. This typology overlaps with the perspectives set out in Chapter 2.

One main perspective is the *unitarist* ideology: managers with this view see the organisation as hierarchically structured with themselves at the top as leaders, albeit benign leaders; a single source of authority, a common set of objectives, and a shared set of values are stressed; the only rational form of employee behaviour is seen as being congruent with that of management and conflict is seen as being undesirable and illegitimate. In such a firm trade unions and collective bargaining are seen as unnatural and unnecessary and the employer tries to emphasise the relations between management and the individual employee. This is the ideological perspective which one finds in many small family-owned firms; it is also to be found in larger entrepreneurial companies which have grown rapidly, but where the owner still remains in control, such as perhaps Alan Sugar's Amstrad, Richard Branson's Virgin or Anita Roddick's Body Shop.[65] Among large British firms, examples might range from Marks & Spencer through to the more macho and aggressive unitarism of News International or P&O. It is also to be found in some large foreign multinationals operating in Britain, such as IBM, Texas Instruments, Hewlett-Packard, Mars and some of the Japanese companies which have located in Britain.

By contrast the *pluralist* ideological perspective sees the firm as being made up of a plurality of interest groups each with different and legitimate aspirations and objectives; within such an organisation conflict is not seen as being something which can always be avoided and trade unions may play a role; the role of management within the pluralist organisation is less one of leadership and more of coordination. The pluralist enterprise therefore recognises trade unions and is prepared to share rule-making within the firm with them. It therefore takes a less individualist and more collectivist view of the enterprise. Traditionally in Britain management in the public sector was usually pluralist and in most medium-sized and large firms also pluralistic perspectives tended to predominate.

This broad typology of unitarist and pluralist can be applied in different ways. It can be applied to managers in different firms and sectors of the economy, with, for example, managers in large firms in manufacturing being in general more pluralistic than managers in smaller firms in the service sector. It may illuminate differences between different groupings of managers within a firm, with, for example, personnel managers being rather more pluralistic than finance or marketing managers. It can also be used to analyse differences in emphasis over time. For example, managers have adopted rather more pluralistic stances during periods when unions were strong such as during the two world wars and in the 1960s and 1970s; in periods when unions were relatively weak, such as the interwar years or the 1980s, there has been a trend towards more unitarist styles.[66]

The typology is obviously rather crude and there have been various attempts to make it more elaborate and to use it to classify differences in policies and practices.[67] These centre primarily on further subdividing unitarist and pluralist approaches into traditional and sophisticated, thus giving us four ideal types of management style as in Figure 3.3. Here traditional means 'old-style', favouring customary notions and practices, and largely *ad hoc* and reactive; sophisticated means more 'modern', innovative and proactive, and more systematic and strategic in the sense of integrating together various policies and practices. Thus traditional unitarist managers would be found in small firms, often owner-controlled and managed, or in the newer entrepreneurial firms of the 1980s which have taken a tough stand on trade unionism – an example might be Eddy Shah of the Stockport *Messenger* and *Today* newspapers; the sophisticated unitarists are firms like Marks & Spencer or IBM with their emphasis on individualism and their more elaborate human resource management policies. The traditional pluralists, in some respects the standard modern firm, would include many medium-sized to large British firms, especially in the engineering industry, where a firm like the old British Leyland had to deal with trade unions, but did so often in a reactive and opportunistic manner. More sophisticated pluralists, it has been suggested, are of two types: there are those such as Ford which take a very constitutionalist approach to the management of industrial relations stressing contract bargaining and more bureaucratic written agreements; and those such as ICI or Unilever which have engaged in collective bargaining but which have also usually adopted a rather more consultative or participative approach to the management of industrial relations.

	Unitarist	Pluralist	
			Low
Traditional	Many small firms	Standard moderns	
			Consultative Cooperative
Sophisticated	Marks & Spencer IBM	Adversarial/ constitutionalist; Ford	
	Japanese firms	Consultative/ cooperative; ICI, BP	
			High
	Low	Collectivism	High

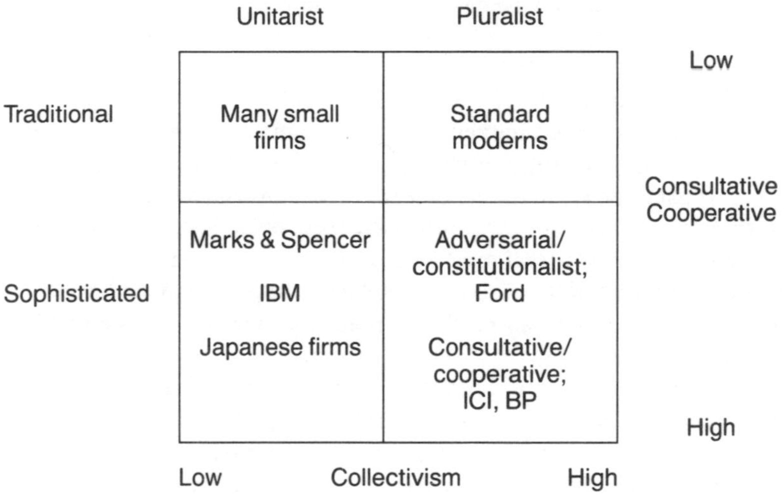

Figure 3.3 Typology of management styles
Source: Adapted from A. Fox, *Industrial Sociology and Industrial Relations* (1966); J. Purcell and K. Sisson, 'Strategies and Practices in the Management of Industrial Relations', in G. S. Bain (ed.), *Industrial Relations* (Oxford, 1983); J. Purcell, 'Mapping Management Styles in Employee Relations', *Journal of Management Studies* (1987).

A slightly different but overlapping approach is to be found in the work of Purcell, who has identified two dimensions.[68] The individualist ideology represents an attempt to communicate and deal with employees as individuals and to use their creative potential for the corporate good. Here there is a spectrum which runs from the 'hire and fire', 'pounds, shillings and pence' approach of the cost-cutter to the newer more Human Resource

Management approach of a number of high-wage, high-benefit companies. The collectivist ideology, by contrast, represents the extent to which the organisation recognises the right and usefulness of employees to have a say in managerial decision making. Again there is a spectrum from representational systems based on consultation and works councils through to collective bargaining of varying degrees of coverage and depth.

Figure 3.3 combines and adapts these different typologies and shows how the intersection of different dimensions provides a multiplicity of ways of understanding managerial styles.

Of course, these are ideal types and in practice firms are more complex. Managers may believe and say one thing and yet do another. Moreover, none of this is to say that managerial ideologies and corporate cultures will be accepted by the workforce. Acceptance depends on how these ideologies and cultures are 'sold', how consistent management is in their implementation, and the strength of occupational subcultures and counter-cultures. These topics will be dealt with in Chapter 5.

CONCLUSION

Employers are the prime movers and the dominant influence in shaping industrial relations. In spite of changes in the ownership and structure of business organisations, employer objectives in industrial relations must still be seen as dependent on their primary business objectives. Employers are likely to try to maximise their control over employee behaviour at work and to minimise the cost of their labour resources in the pursuit of the business's major objectives of making profits or remaining viable in a competitive, market environment.

Most modern organisations are bureaucratic, but the degree of bureaucracy and the particular set of bureaucratic techniques which are adopted can vary. There is no simple or inevitable way to organise and structure the employment relationship or to control work. We have contrasted strategies of Taylorism and bureaucratic paternalism and of externalisation and internalisation. In the UK bureaucratic paternalism or strategies of internalisation have developed only slowly and unevenly. Managers also have different styles and organisations have different cultures. Typologies here distinguish between managers and organisations in terms of levels and varieties of unitarism and pluralism.

This chapter has focused on employer strategies, especially at the level of the firm. However, employers' organisation and structures are also important because organisation and structures shape strategies and are the manifestation of strategies. In the next chapter we turn to the structure of employers at firm, industry, and national levels.

4   Employers and their organisation

The organisational forms or structures which firms and other employing institutions assume have important implications for the management of industrial relations. We have put structure after the consideration of employer strategies in the previous chapter because in many respects structure follows strategy. In other words, the strategies which firms pursue largely shape the structures which they adopt. However, structure can also precede strategy in the sense that organisational arrangements can facilitate or constrain the pursuit of certain types of strategies. For example, the absence of a well-developed structure can impede the development of sophisticated, internal bureaucratic strategies or make it more likely that the firm will rely on strategies of externalisation, as described in the previous chapter.

This chapter will examine the overall structure of firms and other organisations, managerial hierarchies, methods of industrial relations management, the development of personnel management and the role of employers' associations. The aim is to show how these structures have been shaped by employer strategies and how, in turn, structural forms and arrangements have shaped strategies.

THE ORGANISATION OF THE FIRM

In looking at structure it is useful to start with the overall structure of the firm or employing organisation because how it is organised for general business purposes will have profound effects on where and how decisions about industrial relations are taken. Here one useful typology, as found in the works of the historian Alfred Chandler and the economist Oliver Williamson, may be outlined.[1]

In the nineteenth century the majority of firms were *S-form* companies in that they were small, had a single plant, and usually produced a single product or product range. Such firms, being small, tended to be owner-controlled and managed and did not have extensive managerial hierarchies;

rather they relied on various forms of subcontracting and on the foreman to perform many functions, including those of labour management. Of course, today the majority of firms are still small and produce only a limited range of products. In such firms the employment relationship is likely to be more personal; control and motivation strategies are likely to be relatively simple and direct and based on personal and often close supervision.

Over time small firms grew in size and in many cases, especially in Britain, they grew through acquiring and merging with other firms. In this way they grew into large, multi-plant enterprises. Often such firms were organised on *H-form* lines as holding-companies. In other words, the holding-company had a small head office which only loosely controlled and coordinated the constituent plants of the company. The firm was often no more than a federation with weak controls and largely autonomous plants. In such firms also managerial hierarchies tended to be limited and weak. Historically the H-form company was very common in Britain especially in the engineering industry, where a firm such as British Leyland (now Austin Rover and a part of British Aerospace) grew out of a whole series of mergers from the 1950s onwards. In terms of industrial relations, such firms had at best a small headquarter's personnel function, industrial relations were left to plant level, and as a result there was considerable diversity and often inconsistency within the firm. In other words this reflected loose, *ad hoc* strategies towards labour management. Such firms did not have the capability to develop sophisticated internal bureaucratic strategies and often pursued strategies of externalisation and relied on employers' organisations for many aspects of industrial relations.

Some firms, as they grew in size by internal expansion and by merger, adopted a *U-form* structure, in other words a more unified and centralised form of organisation. Such firms tended to have larger head offices, with more extensive managerial hierarchies divided into a series of specialised functions such as production, marketing, finance and personnel. These functions were then duplicated at the level of each individual plant and were the means by which central management controlled its operating units. Historically, examples were firms such as ICI, Ford and Pilkingtons in the private sector and the Post Office and British Rail in the public sector. From an industrial relations point of view such firms tended to have large central personnel departments and more centralised and bureaucratic systems and styles. This made it more possible for them to develop strategies of internalisation and made it less necessary to rely on employers' organisations. In the case of ICI, for example, it has had a central personnel department since 1927 which has largely controlled industrial relations throughout the company and developed a uniform set of policies and practices.

In the post-Second World War period, as firms have increasingly diversified by moving into new product and geographical areas, so they have come to adopt an *M-form*, or multidivisional structure. In other words the firm has been consciously divided up into semi-autonomous divisions, usually based on product lines. Headquarters management has responsibility for making strategic decisions and for monitoring lower-level activities, but operational decisions are left to management within each division. These days many large British firms are organised on these lines. From an industrial relations point of view this tends to mean that they have a planned decentralisation, with a number of different systems within the firm for the different divisions of the company. Thus, in the case of Unilever, for example, there are significant differences between industrial relations in its soap and detergent plants, its food plants and its chemical plants, but all are monitored by the headquarter's personnel department. Such firms have also been more likely to pursue strategies of internalisation, but with differences between divisions.

In recent years there have been four further sets of developments in overall organisational structures which have important implications for industrial relations.

First, there has been the growth of a number of large conglomerate firms which are even more diversified than the M-form firms. Some of the largest British firms fall into this category, including British American Tobacco, Hanson, BET and Lonrho. These firms have, within their portfolios, operations as diverse as mining and minerals processing, heavy manufacturing of various kinds, food, drink and tobacco manufacturing, publishing, insurance and financial services, and distribution and retailing. They are prepared to consider acquiring firms in almost any industry if those firms are likely to provide a good return. These firms have some similarities with the older H-form companies in that they tend to be organised on holding-company lines and to have only a small headquarters senior management who are mainly concerned with financial performance. However, they differ in that they are much more diversified, much more consciously decentralised, and their constituent parts are more closely monitored from a financial point of view. In such companies, top management tends to take little interest in industrial relations and personnel matters (except for the management of senior managerial staff), and industrial relations and personnel systems vary greatly between the different parts of the conglomerate company.

Second, in many private-sector firms, there has been a growing tendency towards greater decentralisation within previously U- and M-form structures. This has often meant the creation of so-called profit- and cost-centres or operational business units at the level of the plant or even lower. Again, this decentralisation is more planned and monitored than in the older H-form companies, but nevertheless the degree of decentralisation may have come to constrain the development of overall, corporate industrial relations strategies in some firms.[2] In the 1980s economic pressures led in some cases to what is probably an excessive devolution of responsibility with only financial control remaining at the centre.[3] These developments have put pressure on labour management systems and have led to greater industrial relations diversity and differences in the treatment of employees within firms.

Third, a wave of mergers and acquisitions in the 1980s, the increased importance of institutional investors, and the growth of what has been termed a 'market for corporate control' have begun to have important implications for industrial relations.[4] Senior managers have increasingly to worry about the threat of a hostile take-over; more importance has to be placed on short-term profits and share prices rather than long-term growth and market share; and takeovers have led to British firms, often still searching for improved corporate structures, being bought, dismembered or reconstituted as subsidiaries of bigger, often foreign, companies. These phenomena have often diverted the attention of top management away from long-term planning and from developing industrial relations and personnel strategies.

Finally, in the public sector, where historically centralised U-form structures were predominant, there has also been a growing decentralisation. This has occurred in central government with the creation of semi-autonomous agencies, in local government with devolution of budgets and competitive tendering, and in the NHS and school teaching with the advent of opting-out and local financial management. A consequence of this redrawing of organisational boundaries is the creation of greater autonomy and diversity in personnel and industrial relations arrangements within the sector.

Thus the overall structure of the firm, its organisation, the degree of centralisation and the tightness of control, has important implications for industrial relations and is an essential starting point for examining the organisation of industrial relations management.

MANAGERIAL HIERARCHIES

As organisations grow in size, they develop more elaborate and complex hierarchies, and we also need to consider these in order to understand the management of industrial relations. These can be viewed in various ways. They can be seen *vertically* as ranging from top management responsible for strategy, to middle management responsible for policy and operational matters, and to lower management responsible for the day-to-day implementation of policy. Thus we need to be aware of management from the top level down to the level of the foreman. How managers act and think, how well or badly they are trained, and the extent to which they are coordinated or segmented have profound implications for industrial relations.

We also need to be aware of the *functional* organisation of management. Here the most common distinction is between line and staff managers. The former constitute the hierarchy of control over the production of the product or the service and will have titles such as general manager, works manager or foreman; by contrast staff managers are in advisory and support positions within the managerial hierarchy. The main staff areas are usually finance or accounting, sales or marketing, distribution, and personnel.

The degree of integration or segmentation between levels and functions within a firm can have important effects on industrial relations. Thus where senior management might be cut off from lower-level management and unaware of what is going on, or where production management seldom talk to personnel, a firm is likely not to have very good industrial relations. Historically, in Britain, managerial hierarchies were often not very well organised. For example, senior management often tended to be cut off from lower levels by background and status distinctions. Traditionally they were not particularly interested in industrial relations matters. Management was strictly divided into specialisms, among which the personnel function was frequently of low status and was not well integrated into the senior management team.

British management has often tended to be less well educated and trained, especially in technical and production areas, than management in the USA, Germany and Japan. In Britain the finance function often dominates and accountants are more likely to get to the top of firms than engineers or production managers.[5] Studies in the 1980s have shown that British management on the whole still remains less well educated and trained than its American, European and Japanese counterparts.[6]

In Britain, weaknesses have often been particularly acute at lower levels in the management hierarchy. Middle managers in Britain have been likely to work their way up through the company's ranks and, in the production area, in industries like engineering and printing, many have been ex-craft apprentices. These tend to be less well educated and formally trained than their overseas counterparts and probably on the whole less open to new management techniques.[7] At the base of the management hierarchy, the position and status of the foreman has long been eroded and encroached upon by line managers and specialist departments. In Britain this continued through the Second World War and postwar period, despite some attempts at the training and upgrading of supervisory staff. Overall, the vast majority of foremen in British industry have been recruited mainly from manual jobs, are usually selected in an *ad hoc* manner, and receive little further technical or managerial training which would enable them to ascend the managerial hierarchy.[8] Moreover, higher-level management seems to have been less concerned to integrate them into the management team. One recent study suggested that, 'The major break in the vertical structure of British companies comes between shopfloor supervision and management proper, rather than between supervision and shopfloor.'[9] The weakness of supervisory staff in Britain posed problems for the management of production and industrial relations. For example, it has often been observed that foremen have acquiesced in, or colluded with, various shopfloor customs and practices. Though this phenomenon is to be found in many countries, it may have been more pronounced in Britain, given the weakness of managerial control systems above and the strength of shopfloor trade unionism below.[10] Only in recent years have a growing number of British firms begun to realise that there is an increasing need to train and develop their supervisory staff and to integrate them more into the management hierarchy. Along with this is growing a belief that supervisory staff should be given more responsibilities for motivating and managing lower-level employees.[11]

METHODS OF INDUSTRIAL RELATIONS MANAGEMENT

Schematically we can say that senior management within the firm or employing organisation can manage industrial relations in various ways.

In the first place, they can rely on *line management*. In other words they can rely on middle and junior managers to deal with various personnel matters – to recruit, to direct the work process and to deal with worker representatives. In many firms this was the traditional way that things were done and this approach persists in many small firms today. It has the advantages that line managers know the processes and work involved and can integrate the management of the product with the management of people. However, reliance on line management can also have certain disadvantages. Dealing with industrial relations takes line managers away from their main task which is the management of production; different line managers can take different decisions and this can lead to inconsistencies which cause industrial relations problems; line managers are prone to take a short-term view of personnel matters. Because of these problems, as the management of people has become more complex, as a result of the growing size and diversity within organisations, of more extensive employment legislation and of rising worker aspirations, so in larger organisations, employers came to use staff specialists in the personnel area.

Thus, the use of *staff specialists* is the second way that labour can be managed. We will deal with the development of personnel management in more detail in the following section. Here we would just say that the allocation of responsibility between staff and line has always been a shifting one. Through the 1960s and 1970s the personnel function grew in power and influence, in part reflecting growing trade union power, increasing legislative intervention, and the institutionalisation of industrial relations. In the 1980s, however, there has been a shift back from managing through the personnel function towards giving line managers more responsibility for personnel matters, especially in areas such as selection, appraisal, and training. In more complex areas such as the design of pay and benefit systems, many firms are also using specialist external consultants. This sometimes leaves personnel departments with a mixture of more strategic planning functions and lower-level administrative functions.

A third way that senior management has managed industrial relations is through the medium of an *employers' association*. Again we will deal with these in more detail later in this chapter. Here we would simply note that employers' organisations can be defined as outside associations of firms in a particular industry which provide various services for member firms. In particular they have handled dealings with trade unions and collective bargaining. As we will see, this offers member firms certain advantages. Employers' organisations reduce the time and costs the firm incurs in handling industrial relations; they are a way that employers can pool their strength; and they can create rules and procedures for a whole industry, which provides some degree of standardisation and predictability.

A fourth means whereby firms have managed their labour has been via various forms of *subcontracting*. This was important historically, but has increased also in recent years. Subcontracting means not employing the labour force directly, but indirectly through a subcontractor or agent. Under subcontracting systems, the functions of recruiting a labour force, monitoring production and paying workers were handed over to a subcontractor. Such arrangements were widespread in nineteenth-century industries such as coal mining and iron making. So also were systems where skilled men hired, supervised and paid their own helpers or underhands, as was the custom in cotton spinning, shipbuilding and pottery.[12] Such practices seem to have persisted longer in Britain than in other countries. By the late nineteenth century, however, internal subcontracting had been considerably reduced as competitive and technological changes pressured employers to cut out these middle-men and replace them with their own foremen. Today subcontracting is to be found in industries like building and agriculture. It has also grown in recent years in clerical and secretarial work, in catering and maintenance areas within firms, in some of the services provided by local authorities, and in franchises such as fast food. As we pointed out in Chapter 3, large Japanese firms make extensive use of subcontracting arrangements. Subcontracting has the advantage that labour matters are handed over to someone else, the firm does not need to take on a large staff directly, and it is easier to lay workers off if necessary. It has the disadvantages, however, that organisations using subcontracted labour have less direct control over labour costs and over the effort and compliance of workers.

The use of different structures depends on many factors, especially changes in the overall structure and growth of the firm and pressure from the labour force. Thus, historically, small S-form firms in the nineteenth and early twentieth centuries did not have the organisational resources to develop complex hierarchies. They relied instead on subcontracting and on the foreman for the management of labour within the firm. For dealing with trade unions they relied on employers' organisations. This often persisted with loosely coordinated H-form firms. As companies grew in size in the twentieth century, so they were able to develop staff specialisms. In the post-Second World War period, because of tight labour markets and more competitive product markets, they came to rely less on employers' organisations and further developed their internal managerial structures.

The growth of personnel management

Personnel management had its origins in a few large firms in the late nineteenth century. At that time, however, many firms still relied on forms of subcontracting and on line managers, foremen and employers' organisations for the management of labour and industrial relations. The First World War gave personnel management a considerable boost when, with the advent of large numbers of workers into the munitions factories, especially large numbers of female workers, both government and employers thought it necessary to employ personnel or welfare managers, as they were often called at that time, to recruit labour, to keep records, to administer recreational and other facilities, and to deal with other aspects of employment relations. Many of the early personnel managers were women, usually middle-class, with social work or religious background. The number of full-time welfare specialists grew from under 100 before the war to over 1,000 in 1918.[13]

After the war many firms got rid of their personnel departments, seeing them as an unnecessary luxury. However, others kept them, and it was during the interwar period that in a few large firms these came to be called Labour, Employment or Personnel Departments. In such firms, usually of the U-form type, the personnel departments increasingly came to be staffed by men and became responsible for industrial relations as more broadly defined, including increasingly dealings with trade unions. By 1939 there were around 2,000 managers engaged full time on labour matters.

The Second World War also gave a positive stimulus to personnel management again, with the need to further the war effort and raise productivity. The number of personnel managers increased to around 5,000 by the end of the war. This time the impact was more lasting and in most cases personnel departments survived after the war. Thereafter, through the next two decades, there was a slow increase in their number. However, not all firms employed formally qualified specialists and few gave the personnel function board-level representation.[14] Overall, the majority of personnel managers in Britain lacked formal qualifications and personnel management remained relatively low status in the management hierarchy. Their role was usually administrative and reactive rather than strategic or proactive and, in dealings with trade unions, much was still left to employers' organisations. It was only later in the 1960s and 1970s, as firms grew in size, as labour problems accumulated, and as more complex employment legislation had to be applied, that the number of personnel managers again rose, increasing from about 15,000 in the mid-1960s to around 50,000 by the late 1970s.[15]

The number of personnel managers continued to increase through the 1980s and the membership of the main professional body, the Institute of Personnel Management, has grown by about 10 per cent a year over the last few years. Today most large and medium-sized firms employ specialist staff and many have main board directors with responsibility for personnel management.[16] However, smaller firms often still do not have personnel managers, there are fewer in the public sector per employee than in the private sector, and foreign-owned firms are more likely to have specialists both at plant and board level than their British-owned counterparts.[17] As has already been noted, in the 1980s, there has been a growing trend towards giving line managers more responsibility for personnel matters; this is in line with new thinking about Human Resource Management and with the view that every manager should be a human resource manager. However, in more specialist and strategic areas, including dealings with trade unions, the Personnel Department (sometimes re-named the Human Resource Department) still plays a dominant role.[18]

In conclusion, weaknesses in corporate structures and managerial hierarchies constrained managerial strategies and exacerbated many of the industrial relations problems of the 1960s and 1970s. Improvements in structure and hierarchy in those decades provided a basis for changes in labour strategies in the 1970s and 1980s. From the mid-1960s, as British firms reformed their overall organisational structures, they also began to sort out their industrial relations problems. Indeed there was a significant connection between overall organisational change and industrial relations. The restructuring of firms, often on multidivisional lines, and the development of managerial hierarchies provided firms with a better organisational capability to act. Such reorganisation simultaneously facilitated the setting of strategic goals and imposed more effective control over lower management.[19] The development of managerial hierarchies, especially the growth in the number and professionalism of personnel specialists, has facilitated the planning and coordination of industrial relations strategies.[20] However, continuing weaknesses, combined in some instances with an excessive decentralisation and an emphasis on short-term financial considerations, have remained a constraint on the development of labour strategies.

EMPLOYERS' ASSOCIATIONS

Employers' associations have had a significant influence on the development of British industrial relations. They were formed by employers who chose to pursue strategies external to the individual firm and they have affected employers' relations with trade unions, the structure of collective bargaining, and the nature of relations with government in the UK.

Although employers' associations seem similar in structure to trade unions – 'bosses unions' as they are sometimes labelled – they are not functionally equivalent as institutions. Employee interests, as we see in Chapters 5 and 6, are primarily represented in groups. Individual employees rarely have the power to influence major issues alone. However, individual companies are often in a position to represent their own interests in dealings with government or unions. Indeed multinational companies or firms in a dominant position in their industries may exert more influence than an employers' association. Employers' associations can also be distinguished from unions on the grounds that their members are likely to see them as more limited representative bodies. Trade unions are arguably the main institutions for representing the interests of labour in our society and they adopt broad industrial and political objectives. Employers' associations are not equivalent as representatives of capital. Britain's employers' associations primarily represent the labour market interests of the manufacturing and service sectors of industry. There are other channels for the representation of different types of interest. For example, many trade associations concern themselves with product rather than labour markets issues and there are specialised associations for the finance industry and commerce.

Employers form associations to provide mutual support when they feel a common vulnerability and to defend themselves against industrial or political threats from other power-holders. Organisations concerned with the employment relationship have been formed to pursue strategies in four broad areas: to regulate the labour market through the fixing of wages and conditions; to oppose trade unions; to deal with trade unions through multi-employer collective bargaining; to influence government policy and legislation.[21]

The history of British employers' associations is as old or older than that of trade unions. In the eighteenth century Adam Smith noted that 'combinations of masters' were widespread and powerful although they attracted less attention and condemnation than combinations of workers. These early employers' organisations were specialised and locally based. Because of the prevailing *laissez-faire* ideology any collusion to reduce market competition was unlikely to be broadcast, and the early associations operated quietly and informally. Adam Smith wrote that employer agreements to cut wages or agree maximum rates were always conducted 'with the utmost silence and secrecy' and could pass unnoticed unless the workforce caused an outcry.[22]

Some associations of employers were agreeing standard rates for wages or piece work prices before trade unions appeared in their industries. In the early nineteenth century, the coal and iron owners established local agreements on the selling price for their product and on the wages of their labour, before their workers were unionised. However, there were other employers who determined their own pay policies and collaborated with fellow employers only on trade or product-market issues, limiting joint activity towards the labour market to the exchange of information, petitioning justices to suppress combinations of workers or petitioning Parliament to strengthen the master and servant laws.[23]

The main boost to the growth of employers' associations was the growth of trade unions in the late nineteenth century. New associations were formed, specifically concerned to coordinate responses to the threat of an organised workforce, and existing local organisations were formalised and centralised into stronger, nationally based federations.

A number of policies were chosen by associations adopting the strategy of outright opposition to trade unionism. One such policy used by employers associations on the docks and in shipping was the use of blackleg or replacement labour.[24] Another method was the use of 'the Document'. This was a signed undertaking in which a worker accepted, as a condition of employment, that he would leave, or not join, a trade union. Its use by employers in the mid-nineteenth century helped defeat various attempts at unionisation.[25] A less publicised but longer-lasting policy to prevent the spread of union membership was the use of blacklists of union activists, compiled and circulated by the employers' associations.

Strategies of outright opposition to trade unionism did not succeed in eliminating unions nor stem the gradual growth of union membership from the end of the nineteenth century. Employers therefore moved towards accommodation with trade unions and used employers' associations to develop strategies of externalisation and a system of collective bargaining that limited trade union influence to external labour market issues and sought to preserve managerial prerogatives within the workplace by formally excluding matters such as the organisation of production from collective bargaining. There was a marked expansion of new or more visible associations, especially in the late nineteenth and early twentieth centuries and during the First World War.[26] Within the general strategy of accommodation with trade unions were four distinct policies, pursued through employers' associations, which had a major impact on the development of British collective bargaining. There were:

(a) insistence on multi-employer bargaining;
(b) limits on the content of agreements;
(c) the insistence that disputes be dealt with through official procedures, and
(d) industry-wide or 'national' bargaining.

We return to these policies again in Chapter 9, but a brief explanation here will show why employers chose to act through associations and how they profoundly influenced the development of collective bargaining in Great Britain.[27]

Multi-employer bargaining

Employers who decided to respond to union demands for improved conditions often chose to do so collectively, rather than individually, even when the union strength and union attack had been directed at one employer. Multi-employer bargaining had several advantages for late nineteenth-century and early twentieth-century employers. By combining in negotiations they could pit their united strength against union tactics of picking off the most vulnerable employer and then using improvements there as the base of leapfrogging wage claims elsewhere. Multi-employer agreements also reduced labour market competition and gave employers the assurance, especially important in labour-intensive industries. that they all had to pay the same wage rate and that no employer could compete 'unfairly' on wage costs because he was more efficient or more ruthless than his rivals. Companies, it should be remembered, were usually small S-form firms. For them there were economies of scale in dealing with unions collectively. They did not possess managerial staff with specialist knowledge or skills in handling trade unions and they were unable to adopt sophisticated internal bureaucratic policies for managing their employment relations. By delegating responsibility to their employers' association, employers could handle their new and more complex employee relations without fundamental change in the structure of their companies. Collective agreements with employers' associations also had advantages for trade union officials. Although any improvement in terms might not be as favourable as they could expect from the most profitable or most unionised employers, the multi-employer agreements had a much wider coverage than they might otherwise have hoped to achieve.

In some trades the development of multi-employer bargaining with unions occurred as a relatively smooth transition because agreements merely replaced, or made additions to, pre-existing district wage or piece rates. In some industries, such as the printing and some building trades, district rates had a long history in earlier craft-methods of regulating the labour market, whereas in iron and coal, district rates were already set, unilaterally, by the employers. Elsewhere, in industries such as chemicals and food processing, the transition to multi-employer collective bargaining represented a more radical change in the employers' approach to the labour market.

Agreements to exclude control of the labour process

When employers moved to recognise trade unions, they were concerned to place firm boundaries around what they were prepared to negotiate about. Employers came to accept negotiation on external, labour-market-related issues, covering basic wages, hours of work and overtime rates. However, in an effort to help neutralise the workplace from trade union activity, they resisted any negotiation on internal or 'managerial' issues – on how labour, once bought, should be used.[28] The history of employer–union relations in Britain has been coloured by periodic large-scale, confrontations between unions and employers' associations, some on the initial principle of recognising unions at all, but many on the equally intensely felt issue of managerial prerogative and the preservation of non-negotiable subjects. Managerial rights which employers sought to exclude from collective bargaining included hiring and firing, the use and manning of machines, promotion, supervision and discipline, and the methods and techniques of production.

In the engineering industry, the protection of managerial prerogatives came to dominate employer association policy and lay behind major confrontations with the unions in 1851–2, 1897–8 and 1922. The skilled engineering workers formed the first central, national union in the UK.[29] In the latter half of the nineteenth century they felt that their traditional craft status and job control was threatened by new technology which enabled once-skilled metal-working jobs to be accomplished by unskilled machine-minders. They used their union to demand that the new machine-tools be manned by craftsmen at skilled rates and they resisted the introduction of piecework. On their side, the employers were eager to take advantage of the new technology to increase their control over work and reduce the power of craft groups, as was discussed in the previous chapter. They sought to cheapen the labour process by employing less skilled labour and to manage the deskilled work by introducing piecework systems. The battles over managerial prerogative did not occur simply because unions were challenging employers' controls of the labour process, but because employers themselves were tightening and centralising their control of workplace activity. The engineering union lost the confrontations referred to above and was forced to sign agreements accepting management's right to operate machines and manage labour as management chose.

However, this strategy was not totally successful in eliminating employee control at the place of work. In some crafts such as printing workers kept very considerable controls and many strongly placed work groups within engineering were able to retain an influence on the day-to-day management of their own work. Employee involvement on issues of workplace management often took place in the twilight zone of unofficial shopfloor activity and it grew after the Second World War. Productivity bargaining in the 1960s brought these issues within the scope of more formal collective bargaining, but even then this was initially resisted by some employers' associations on the old grounds of not negotiating areas of managerial prerogative (see Chapter 9). From that time onwards, as we will see, firms have sought to deal internally within the firm with questions of managerial prerogatives.

Disputes procedures to resolve disputes away from the workplace

Industry-wide dispute procedures were adopted by many employers' associations in the late nineteenth and early twentieth centuries as a way of helping members handle pressures from trade unions. A typical procedure required that any dispute which threatened a stoppage of work be referred to a series of meetings of union and employer association officials. Work would continue while the officials heard the case by the conflicting parties and attempted to conciliate or resolve the dispute. If they failed, the issue was referred to higher regional or industry-side meetings. Only when this procedure had been followed could a constitutional strike or lockout be called.

The advantage of industry disputes procedures for employers was that they brought the full weight of the employers' association into negotiations and they delayed constitutional strike action until the most senior officials had been involved. Such procedures were not always resisted by unions, for although they acted as a block to the union tactic of concentrating their strength against the most vulnerable employer, they had some advantages for union officials. They provided a channel for resolving disputes, and backward employers might be pressured to provide average terms by their co-employers. They also helped to increase the authority and role of the trade union officials and executives over local rank and file groups. 'Procedures' provided a major institution through which unions and employers could relate and helped establish the emphasis on joint discussion, rather than on formalised legal agreements, that is still a major feature of the British system of collective bargaining.

National or industry-wide agreements

Once employers' associations and unions had national-level meetings to discuss disputes, it was a small step to the establishment of industry-wide agreements on wage rates, basic hours and overtime premiums. During the First World War the government encouraged employers to take this step by endorsing and approving the spread of industry-wide collective bargaining. The number of employers' associations rose until there was one major association or federation for each of the main industries and national agreements on hours and basic pay rates covered most manual workers in most industries. Industry-wide bargaining developed further, again with government encouragement, in the Second World War. For employers, national agreements had the advantages of maximising employer strength in wage bargaining, fixing basic rates and conditions for a certain period for a whole industry, providing some predictability and taking wages out of competition between employers. However, it should be stressed that usually such agreements fixed only minimum wages and conditions and this constituted a problem for the regulatory effectiveness of agreements.

In conclusion, employers' associations were used by employers to shape the level and content of negotiations with employees and thereby accommodate the growth of trade unionism in a way that enabled employers to protect managerial prerogative at the place of work and to externalise many aspects of industrial relations.

The use of employers' associations to influence government policy and legislation has been less evident than the collective bargaining role in the history of British employers' associations. Indeed government influence on employers' associations has been as, or more, apparent than influence the other way round. The government encouraged the development of employers' associations by advocating industry-wide agreements in the

period around the First and Second World Wars. The growth of interventionist government economic policies in the 1960s and 1970s also
stimulated employers' organisations and the creation of the Confederation of
British Industry (CBI) in 1965. As we will see in Chapters 7 and 10, British
governments in the 1960s and 1970s chose to administer economic and
social policies through tripartite semi-official institutions, which expanded
the representative role of both employers associations and trade unions.
Tripartite institutions also surround the international governmental agencies,
such as the EC and the UN, and have encouraged the development of
international employers organisations. Corporatist industrial policies
required employers' representatives for their implementation and acted as a
stimulus to the development of British employers' associations.[30]

The current functions of employers' associations

Unilateral regulation of labour markets by employers organisations does
not really exist today. However, informal wage clubs for the exchange of
information on the timing and amount of major changes in pay still exist in
many areas and industries including those where trade unions do not
negotiate. In the North Sea Oil industry, for example, there are a number of
such employer clubs; in computer manufacturing there is a twenty-four-
member club which shares information on wages and salaries.[31] Strategies
of using employer associations to oppose trade unions have also declined in
the UK. Employers who refuse to accept particular unions within their
companies may receive advice from their associations on how to maintain
this position. However, most British employers' associations are not these
days opposed to union recognition as a matter of principle.

The main strategy pursued through British employers' associations has
been to accommodate trade union pressure by structuring collective bargaining to determine pay and conditions at multi-employer or industry-
wide levels. As we will see in Chapter 9, the relevance of this strategy for
employers has also declined. Industry-wide agreements can set standard
terms which are actually applied by all employers or minima below which
employers will not drop. The initial industry agreements generally set
standards for pay and conditions which were then applied across the industry concerned. The Electrical Contracting Association is one association
which still sets and enforces standard rates in its national agreements.
However, in most other industries, the control of the national agreements
has declined, and on pay, if not conditions, association agreements are
treated as a minima, or are totally ignored.

Various types of employer policy have weakened association control of
collective bargaining. The main policy might be termed strategic

independence and is associated with the adoption of internalised or bureaucratic policies by large companies who have their own specialist personnel
departments for managing employment policy.[32] Such companies prefer to
negotiate independently and internally with trade unions, relying on their own
strength and expert staff. They treat employers' association agreements as
minima and in many cases have chosen to leave their associations entirely.

Some have argued that employer association control of collective bargaining declined from as early as the late 1930s as employers responded to
tighter labour markets.[33] Small firms undercut industry rates and large firms
began to develop self-sufficient, bureaucratic management hierarchies. ICI,
for example, having developed its own central personnel department, withdrew from its employers' association in the mid-1930s.[34] However,
although some weakening of association control can be traced back this far,
most employers continued well into the post-Second World War period to
make use of employers' associations in their dealings with trade unions. In
1968 the Donovan Royal Commission argued that employers' associations
acted as a significant bar to the development of modern personnel policies
in the UK and it recommended that employers rely less on associations and
more on the development of their own internal policies.

Many firms undergoing reorganisation in the 1960s and 1970s felt less
need for employer organisation membership, since they were increasingly
able to provide their own services internally.[35] For them employers' organisations no longer performed any real protective function. In fact, as
Donovan suggested, for many, membership could even be prejudicial. It
exposed firms to national claims while at the same time restricting the
development of their own internal policies. Diversified firms, which might
be members of two or more separate associations, found it difficult or
meaningless to reconcile the different national agreements to which they
were parties. A number of large firms therefore left their employers'
associations. Some, such as Ford and ICI, had never been members or had
left many years previously. Others, for example, Esso, Shell, BP and Alcan
left their associations or loosened their ties in the mid-1960s. By the time
of Donovan others were expressing doubts. In evidence to the Royal
Commission, the International Publishing Corporation stated that the value
of its membership of the British Federation of Master Printers was 'very
slight indeed';[36] the electrical company, Philips, stated, 'It is our view that
the Engineering Employers' Federation is far too large and ponderous to
continue filling what was once a constructive role';[37] and Cadburys
resigned from its employers' bargaining body 'primarily because of the
rigidity of the national wage system under which flat wage awards are
given without recognition of local needs'.[38] There was a similar trend in the
engineering industry, where, after a national strike in 1979, in which many

companies felt unnecessarily involved, the two largest firms in the industry, GEC and British Leyland, withdrew from membership.[39] Many foreign firms, such as the Japanese companies which located in Britain in the 1980s, did not feel tied by traditional British industrial relations practices and never joined employers' associations.

Thus national bargaining became less important and national wage agreements became more like safety nets, with decreasing relevance to companies. Some agreements, as in rubber and parts of the food-processing industry, collapsed altogether. In the case of national procedural agreements, a significant event occurred in 1971 when the engineering unions terminated the historic engineering industry procedure. The unions had objected to various aspects, especially the managerial prerogatives clause. When agreement could not be reached on a new procedure, they therefore gave notice to terminate the procedure and the large firms in the industry did nothing to save it.[40] In 1988 the employers withdrew from industry-wide wage negotiations (though they have continued to exist for the foundry and engineering construction industries).[41]

However, it should be stressed that not all employers' organisations declined in membership or importance. Some large firms remained in membership, though usually in order to obtain advisory and lobbying services rather than for collective bargaining purposes. Many medium-sized and small firms continued to rely on their associations and on national agreements and, for them, there was some justification in terms of administrative economies and protection against trade unions.[42] In some industries, such as parts of building, printing, textiles, footwear, clothing and motor repair, employers' organisations remained relatively more important. These tended to be industries dominated by smaller firms which failed to develop internal organisational capabilities and for which national collective bargaining still provided some real benefits in terms of controlling competition based on wage-cutting.

Thus, company-based, bureaucratic personnel policy have gone a considerable way in replacing the traditional British employers' reliance on employers' associations. Employer association bargaining now provides only a floor of terms and conditions.[43] However, national agreements still determine the length of the working week and holiday provisions, subjects which have an important impact on labour costs and where employers still prefer to establish terms together rather than alone.

Many associations have adjusted to their lost role as the employers' main negotiating agent by developing general services and providing assistance to company negotiations. The CBI runs a computerised databank of information on pay claims and settlements. Individual associations organise the exchange of information on wage movements and provide advice and guidelines to help in local negotiations. Even companies who are confident about handling their own relations with unions or with government may decide it is worth their affiliation fee to have access to information collected in confidence by the association from all employers in their industry.

The strategy of using associations to influence government has not been as significant in the history of British associations as in many other countries. In Germany and Sweden a major stimulus to the creation of strong, centralised employers' associations was the threat and possibility of government intervention. In the UK both employers and trade unions were traditionally reluctant to pursue industrial relations policies through legislation. However, British employers' organisations do lobby British governments and the EC on employment legislation. We return to the complex relationship between employers and the state in more detail in Chapter 7.

Today British employers' associations range from large organisations employing several hundred staff, to tiny specialist associations, and to organisations which are informal and more like loose employer clubs. The largest employers association in Britain, in terms of income from members, is the National Farmers' Union. It does have a role to play in representing large farmers and agribusinesses in terms of industrial relations and employment matters. However, like many employers' associations, it also doubles as a trade association and lobbying group for its industry, and this is its main function. In the case of bodies which are much more prominently and exclusively employers' associations, there is a considerable spread according to size and importance. At one end of the scale is the Engineering Employers' Federation (EEF) and its local associations, with 5,000-member establishments throughout the country covering more than 800,000 employees and itself employing a large staff of officials; or the equally well-staffed Building Employers Confederation (BEC), with 9,000 UK company members covering about 75 per cent of private-sector building activity in Britain. In the public sector, the Local Government Management Board is an employers' organisation which represents most local authorities in their dealings with trade unions.[44] At the other end of the scale are many small organisations in industries such as textiles, footwear and clothing, with tens or at most hundreds of member firms, covering relatively small workforces.

THE CONFEDERATION OF BRITISH INDUSTRY

The CBI was formed in 1965 to act as a central voice for all employers. Initially created by the merger of three previous federations that acted in the manufacturing industry, the CBI now recruits in all sectors of business

Table 4.1 Some major employers' associations ranked according to membership income, 1989

Association	Income (£ million)
National Farmers' Union	11.9
Engineering Employers' Federation	7.2
Building Employers' Confederation	6.3
Chemical Industries Association	3.2
Motor Agents Association	2.8
British Printing Industries Federation	2.7
National Federation of Retail Newsagents	2.7
Newspaper Society	2.5
Federation of Master Builders	1.8
Electrical Contractors' Association	1.6
Federation of Civil Engineering Contractors	1.6
Freight Transport Association	1.6
National Association of British & Irish Millers	1.4
Road Haulage Association	1.4
Heating & Ventilating Contractors' Association	1.3
Publishers Association	1.2

Source: Annual Report of Certification Officer (1989), p. 50.

including the nationalised industries. It has over 180 employers and trade organisations and over 12,000 individual firms in membership. About 10 million of Britain's 22 million employees work for employers affiliated to the CBI.

The CBI is organised into regions and members elect representatives to regional councils. CBI policy is formulated by elected policy makers and its membership generally. The governing body of the CBI is a central council of some 330 people; it meets monthly. The council covers a cross-section of members to reflect the highly diverse interests within the CBI. There are numerous committees and sub-committees of the national and regional councils actively involving many hundreds of directors and managers. For industrial relations there is an Employment Policy Committee which formulates broad policy and coordinates policy work carried out by the Industrial Relations and Wages and Conditions Committee, the Health and Safety Policy Committee, the Social Security Panel, the Pensions Panel and a number of other specialist groups. Confidential discussions between companies and employers' organisations engaged in collective bargaining take place in the Wages and Conditions Committee.

An International Employment Affairs Panel coordinates CBI work at the EC in Brussels and the International Labour Organisation in Geneva.

The CBI's activities are restricted by the unwillingness of its large and disparate membership to agree common policy or to fund an extended role for the CBI. The conflicts of interest can be great, spanning as it does large and small firms in different industries and in the public and private sector. Only occasionally since its formation in 1965 has the CBI been able to coordinate employers to present united policies towards trade unions. The opposition in the mid-1970s to the recommendations of the Bullock Commission of Inquiry on Industrial Democracy was one such example, and its threats to mount a major campaign of non-cooperation if the government passed the recommendations into law were taken seriously. Despite tendencies towards corporatism at various times, it has never developed central negotiations with the trade unions, though this has been attempted both formally and informally. Since the advent of the Thatcher government in 1979 and the decline in trade union power, it has been particularly reluctant to develop central negotiations with the trade unions. In this respect it is not as strong as the more centralised organisations abroad like the BDA in Germany or the SAF in Sweden, both of which have played a more powerful role in coordinating wage bargaining or in actively negotiating with trade union counterparts.

THE POWER OF BRITISH EMPLOYERS' ASSOCIATIONS IN COMPARATIVE PERSPECTIVE

The main determinant of the power of an employers' association is the extent to which its members choose to act together rather than handle their employment policies alone. If employers do choose to collaborate on policy, then their power will depend on the unity they can maintain and the sanctions they can use against other power groups.

Problems in establishing common policy

There are various centrifugal forces which may operate against united action such as: employers' quest for competitive advantage over labour or product market rivals; managerial attempts to keep marginal enterprises afloat; principled differences over policy; and trade union pressure to break ranks. Employers are more likely to form strong and united associations in some situations than in others. Homogeneous labour or product markets are more likely to be associated with a high degree of employer solidarity, but this relationship does not always hold, as organisation among national newspaper publishers has traditionally shown.[45]

Parts of printing, textiles, clothing, footwear and building (especially electrical contracting) are industries where employers' associations have had the most prominent and permanent influence over employer policy and where association agreements still regulate employer policy on pay and conditions. Three factors appear to increase the need for united employer policies: small company size, a low level of bureaucratic management control and, in some instances, the use of casual labour. Casual labour moves between employers and the use of standard, industry-wide rates of pay is convenient for employers because it prevents the need to negotiate terms at the start of each new job or contract. Effective industry agreements create stability in a situation in which employers would otherwise be vulnerable to the constant poaching of labour, to haggling and disputes at the start of each job, and to 'leapfrog' tactics by unions resulting in an inability to control labour costs. Small firms lack specialist managerial resources, are less able to internalise their industrial relations, and may feel more vulnerable to competition and trade union pressure than larger companies. Strong associations which establish standard employment conditions and act for the employer in negotiations are therefore likely to be attractive. Both small size and the use of casual or subcontract labour suggest a low level of bureaucratic managerial control. If an employer does not possess the administrative control techniques of modern bureaucratic organisation then one way of handling labour problems is to 'contract out' the labour relations policy. An organisation which has bureaucratised its personnel policy by offering internal careers and more extensive employment benefits is less likely to need to collaborate with other employers, because it does not share a labour market with them. Firms with internal labour markets are less concerned about the regulation of external labour markets.[46]

Factors affecting employer unity are thrown into relief by international comparisons. In Sweden the central employers' association, the SAF exhibits strong solidarity and has considerable power, funds, and influence. It has been argued that a country's industrial infrastructure determines the degree of employer unity.[47] Sweden industrialised late, industry is concentrated into a few, specialised industries, and within these industries a few firms dominate production. There are only a handful of major firms in the economy and, because of the small size of the home market, they see their main competition as coming from outside Sweden's boundaries, not from within. In contrast, the UK industrialised early and has a highly diverse, fragmented industrial base with a higher degree of internal competition. This argument is illuminating but has been found wanting in application to other societies.[48] A crucial further factor is the influence of other power groups on employer action. Employers are usually stimulated to submerge their differences and act together in response to some threat, especially a threat by employees acting through trade unions or through socialist political parties. In Sweden, such threats demonstrated the employers' need for strong, central coordination of policy and pushed employers towards the advocacy of central, nationwide collective bargaining. Such threats were not seen to exist to the same extent in the UK. In Germany, also, the central employers' association, the BDA, and its constituent member associations, are powerful. They play a central part in fixing terms and conditions of employment and also organise other important services such as training. In both Sweden and Germany employers' organisations have historically been effective and there is more of an incentive to preserve what works.[49]

In the UK employer solidarity on employment policy towards trade unions was at its peak in the late nineteenth and early twentieth centuries when predominantly S- and H-form firms, with weak hierarchies, faced the threat of growing unionisation and greater assertiveness among manual workers. Employer unity has declined as companies have become larger, more diverse and more bureaucratic and have adopted strategies of internalisation.

Power in relation to other groups

If employers *do* choose to act together through their associations, there are various ways they can mobilise their power.

Power vis-à-vis employees and trade unions

In industrial disputes with trade unions, employers' associations have the usual sanctions available to individual employers of lockouts, legal action, suspensions and dismissals. Associations can coordinate employers' use of such sanctions. They can provide moral or financial support, formally or informally, for members engaged in industrial action with unions. More secretly they may organise blacklists against individuals who have caused trouble for employers. British employers' reluctance to give their associations the authority or power to ensure united employer action is illustrated by their lack of interest in formal strike insurance schemes. Strike insurance is used by associations in Sweden and Germany. In the UK, schemes have existed in the electrical contracting, footwear and road haulage industries. However, when the CBI investigated the possibility of establishing a central strike insurance fund in the late 1970s, they found members unwilling to contemplate a formal, centralised fund on the grounds that it would give the CBI control over members' policies.

Power vis-à-vis government

Employers' main power in relation to government derives from the close interaction between government and business in the implementation of economic and industrial policy. Governments need information from, and the support of, industry for the implementation of policies and there is likely to be constant consultation between government departments and relevant interested employers. This close contact may take place between ministers and the directors or chief executives of powerful companies, but it also forms the staple work of many employers' associations. Constant access to, and influence on, government may appear to be strongest under Conservative governments, when personal friendships and careers which span industry and politics help strengthen the pressure that can be brought to bear. As we will see in Chapter 7, it is true that, under the Labour government of 1974–9, organised employer non-cooperation worked against parts of the government's industrial policy and its proposals for industrial democracy. However, under the Thatcher government from 1979 onwards, the CBI and major employers' associations did not have much influence on government policy and were largely excluded from decision making. The influence on that government was of a more indirect kind by individual companies and businessmen. Again, there is a contrast here with Germany, where the BDA and its constituent employers' associations have had considerable influence on the development of government macro-economic policy.

CONCLUSION

The overall structure of the firm, its size and organisational form, can have a profound effect on the management of industrial relations. So also can the sophistication or otherwise of the managerial hierarchy within the firm. It was the weakness of managerial structures in Britain and the lack of sophistication of managerial hierarchies which caused many of the traditional problems of British industrial relations and which limited the development of certain strategies. Improvements in these areas from the late 1960s onwards laid the basis for some of the reforms we will discuss in later chapters.

The British economy was long dominated by small, single-unit, family-owned and managed enterprises. Even where large, multi-unit firms emerged, these initially took the form of loosely coordinated holding companies in which subsidiaries were allowed considerable autonomy and traditional methods of administration persisted. Historically, there were a few large, more unified firms with more elaborate managerial hierarchies organised on functional lines. In most firms managerial and supervisory systems remained weak: managers were often poorly educated and trained; and levels and functions were inadequately integrated. Labour management was left to line managers and foremen within the firm and was delegated to employers' organisations outside the firm. It was only in the early post-Second World War years, after the mergers and diversifications of the 1960s, that an increasing number of large firms developed multidivisional forms of organisation, with centralised control over strategic matters and devolution of operational decisions to product divisions. At the same time firms began to pay more attention to developing their managerial hierarchies, not least in the personnel field. However, despite such changes, there is still abundant evidence that corporate structures in Britain remain weak and management is still less well educated and trained than its foreign counterparts, with particular weaknesses at production and operational level. In recent years further moves towards decentralisation and the pressure of short-term financial considerations may have constrained long-term strategic thinking in the industrial relations area.

Employers' associations have historically been important institutions in Britain. They are not functionally equivalent to trade unions because their individual members may be as powerful as, or more powerful than, their representatives and because the interests they represent are narrowly defined. In the UK, employers combined together on an industry by industry basis in the nineteenth and early twentieth centuries primarily in response to the growth of trade unions. Some of the arrangements the associations developed for handling trade unions by industry-wide collective bargaining arrangements on basic pay and hours of work remain important today. But, since the Second World War, an increasing number of employers have placed less reliance on their associations in negotiations with unions, preferring to decide on or negotiate employment policies internally within their own companies. Most large-scale companies have adopted strategic independence whereby industrial relations are internalised and controlled through the adoption of bureaucratic personnel policies. The growth of diversified firms and multinational companies who have powerful organisational resources and who do not fit neatly within industrial boundaries has spurred this type of development. Employer association power rests on the extent to which employers choose to unite to establish common policies and on the sanctions the associations can muster. Studies of employer solidarity suggest that coordinated policies are likely to develop where employers share a sense of vulnerability within a common labour market or see common interests in the face of threats from employees. British employers have formed less centralised, united employers' associations than exist in some continental countries.

5 Employees as individuals and in groups

The United Kingdom has a labour force of just over 28 million, of whom just over 10 per cent are self-employed. In recent years there have been significant changes in the structure of employment. Full-time, male manual workers, though traditionally the focus of much industrial relations study, now constitute only about one quarter of the employed labour force (although this leaves them still a large and significant category of workers). There has been an increase in the number of women workers, who now make up 41 per cent of those in employment; 24 per cent of the labour force, mainly female, are now in part-time jobs and this type of employment is likely to increase further. The proportion of the labour force in manual jobs and manufacturing employment has been declining for many years now and over two-thirds of workers are now employed in the service sector. In the 1980s there was also a decline in public-sector manual jobs as a result of cutbacks and privatisation, though public-sector workers still make up about one-quarter of the labour force.[1] Also in the early 1980s and again in the early 1990s, as unemployment has risen towards 3 million, the unemployed have constituted a larger proportion of the working population than in first three decades after the war.

What can we say about the expectations people have of work? How do they behave at work? What makes them act primarily as individuals or in groups? What influence do they have on their own terms and conditions of employment?

EMPLOYEE OBJECTIVES AND EXPECTATIONS

There have been many attempts to understand what employees want from work. Clearly, most people work to earn a living, but beyond the basic need for income lie more complex issues. Do employees limit their interest to the economic rewards of work or do they have a wider range of expectations and demands? Are they, for instance, concerned about job content, do they want to exercise skill or judgement at work? If they have an interest in the content and control of work, do they want to have a significant say or do they accept managerial authority but want some constraints on its use? Different answers to these questions lead on to very different predictions about how employees will behave and debates here centre on the concept of the 'work ethic' and on the prevalence of different value systems among employees.

Employees, the work ethic, and orientations to work

The work ethic can be defined as a set of assumptions and beliefs that give work a central meaning in our society. According to the work ethic, work is a major source of value. Good work is associated with social success and moral worth. Even a poor job, which offers few intrinsic satisfactions and is mainly a source of income, is invariably considered better than no job.[2] Thus, work integrates the worker into the community, giving the worker much of his or her wider social significance. Through work, many people define their identity and seek to achieve important life goals.

In *The Protestant Ethic and the Spirit of Capitalism*, Weber argued that the values of the work ethic combined with Protestant ideas about individual salvation to help motivate and sustain the merchants and entrepreneurs of the industrial revolution.[3] The question now is how far the values of the work ethic still permeate society and act as a motivator and source of expectations for employees.

The assumption that workers *do* operate in terms of the work ethic runs through theories as diverse as the managerial Human Relations School and radical approaches.[4] Human Relations theorists argue that workers demand and need interesting, stimulating work, where judgement can be exercised and where there are rewarding social contacts. Without such work, employees will be alienated and uncooperative and managerial objectives difficult to achieve. If, however, management can provide work with these features, then employees will be motivated and satisfied and will not press further demands. Radicals also assume that workers need self-fulfilling, interesting work but they distinguish between labour that is necessary and work that is dictated by the profit motive. They add the contention that much work in our society is boring and unfulfilling and there must be more worker involvement, better designed jobs and industrial democracy, if the ills of alienation are to be avoided. Radicals therefore assume extensive employee expectations including aspirations for substantial industrial changes. Corporatists also tend to make similar assumptions about employees' need of, and demand for, some form of industrial democracy, though with the emphasis more on better representational structures. These three sets of theories all assume that employee demands will stretch beyond an interest in economic rewards and will cover some managerial issues such as how work is organised and how business organisations are run. In contrast, many economists assume that employees undertake work primarily for pecuniary gain and in order to consume.[5] However, economists do acknowledge that there is a trade-off between income and leisure which may vary according to age, sex and marital status. Scientific management theorists like F. W. Taylor gave work a high priority (at least in instrumental terms), but argued that employee aspirations only relate to direct and immediate economic rewards. If employees are to achieve their life goals through work they should do so by maximising income, and the moral assumption is made that employees should not challenge managerial prerogatives by concerning themselves with managerial controls over work.

There is therefore no absence of theoretical and moral arguments about what people want or should want from work. Empirical evidence, however, suggests that work is valued in different ways by employees and that no simple set of assumptions can be seen to hold.

An early classic study by Goldthorpe *et al.* in the 1960s surveyed male, married manual workers in Luton and concluded that they had economic, instrumental orientations to work.[6] Their predominant interest was pay and they did not demand interesting or self-fulfilling work – indeed, several had given up more intrinsically satisfying work for the higher pay of their monotonous, dead-end jobs. Goldthorpe and his fellow researchers did not assume their sample represented the approach to work of all manual workers. Instead they suggested that different types of orientation to work might be associated with the community in which people lived. They argued that 'solidaristic orientations', placing high value on social relations with colleagues at work, would be found among groups such as miners, dockers or craftsmen. 'Bureaucratic orientations', valuing job security and prospects for promotion, would be held by salaried, middle-class workers. For both categories, work was of central importance and aspects of the work ethic might be held to apply. However, for the relatively affluent, semi-skilled workers, such as were in their sample, work was not given much value. It was merely seen as a means to achieve the money needed for more valued leisure or family activities. Workers with such 'instrumental orientations' were not likely to make demands for interesting work, for rewarding social contacts, or for participation in job control or management. Instead they would concentrate all efforts to achieve the maximum financial returns from work. As an aside, it should be noted, however, that they often had different and higher aspirations for their children.

Later studies have pointed to more varied orientations. One by Beynon and Blackburn found different orientations to work to be associated with particular family roles.[7] In one factory they found men working on the night-shift, who were older and had heavy family responsibilities, were primarily concerned about job security and pension rights. The day-shift men were younger, less concerned about these aspects of employment but had higher expectations for interesting work, good pay and promotion prospects. Full-time women valued social relations with colleagues and expected little discretion at work. Part-time women had low expectation in all areas and made low demands on pay, security, social relations or interesting work. This suggests that the demands made of work can vary according to gender and family commitments and can vary over a working lifetime.

In recent years more research has been devoted to women in employment.[8] This reflects the growing number of women in paid work, a proportion which is set to increase to 45 per cent of the labour force by the end of the century. It is well known that women tend to work in certain types of industries and jobs (clerical, educational and health care, semi-skilled factory, and semi-skilled domestic), that a large proportion of them (over two-fifths) work part-time, and that they tend to be less well paid and have poorer training and promotion prospects than men.[9] It is often assumed that paid employment is less important for women than for men and that work is therefore a less central life interest for them. However, most recent research shows that, in terms of their orientation to work and expectations, women see paid employment as a necessary and natural component of their lives and as a complement to family life and domestic responsibilities. It is difficult to make historical comparisons, and some women have always been in this position and have had this attitude to work; but it is probably true to say that this orientation to paid work as a central life activity has probably increased over the last few decades, reflecting economic necessity for women and their families. Another conventional stereotype is that women in work are different from men in that they stress social relations and convenience factors more than pay, or job prospects, or work content. Most recent research has shown how, in so far as this is true, women have tended to make pragmatic accommodations to the fact that they are less well paid, are less likely to get promotion and do in practice have to shoulder more domestic responsibilities.[10] By contrast, though, more skilled and qualified women who see themselves as following a career are more likely to have the same attitudes to work as their male counterparts, and this proportion is likely to increase in the future.[11] There is evidence also that working women, of all levels of skill and qualifications, are as, or more, demanding of their jobs and employers as are men. Though, as we will see, they are less likely to join trade unions and less likely to be active in them, they are no less likely to pursue work interests, indeed more so than men in areas such as equal opportunities and working time arrangements.[12]

There are other groups of workers with particular interests and demands at work. There are around a million people from ethnic minorities in the labour force. Their skill levels tend to be rather polarised, but the proportion with higher-level qualifications are above average and the proportion in good jobs below average. In the future, as the proportion of school- and college-leavers from the ethnic minorities increases, they will make stronger demands for fairer treatment at work. Also in the future, for demographic reasons, there will be fewer young people at work. The number aged under 25 in the labour market is projected to fall by 1.2 million between 1987 and 1995.[13] These young people, in a stronger position in the labour market than their older brothers and sisters were in the 1980s, may make new demands at work. There has been talk for some time of a growth in 'post-industrial' or 'post-materialist' values.[14] By this is often meant a rejection of traditional political ideologies based on class, a belief in personal development and autonomy at work, and in individualism rather than collectivism. However, others have added to such orientations a questioning of authority and a belief in commonly shared activities and have questioned whether younger workers are less materialistic than their elders.[15] In practice, it may well be that younger workers are not very different from older workers in their orientation to work and that differences in the type of work and the work context may be more important than factors such as age.

The experience of different types of work influences what people want from work. Professional workers with interesting jobs and rewarding relationships with colleagues usually value such advantages and expect to maintain them. The same is true of skilled manual workers with real skills and a sense of craft community with their workmates.[16] People learn from experience what can be asked of work. They use their own past experience and the experience of others in 'similar' jobs to define what they see as reasonable, legitimate demands. Past experience and the experience of others in comparable work also affects the demands made of work. Those who have never been used to much in terms of job content tend to adapt and to lower their expectations. Similarly, past experience and the experience of others in similar jobs can influence the straightforward economic demands made of work. Most employees can make an assessment of the state of supply and demand in their labour market and the effect this has on pay. However, they also make an assessment of how other workers in similar work are rewarded. These comparisons with reference groups have a powerful impact on the expectations people have of their rewards, and so do prevailing social ideas about 'fair wages' or a 'fair day's work'.[17] Simple economic models based on labour supply and demand cannot therefore be used to predict what employees will see as their legitimate expectations.

In addition, it must be recognised that employees make different demands in different contexts. Daniels studied worker attitudes during management–union negotiations which linked changes in pay with changing work methods and during more normal times.[18] He distinguishes between 'bargaining contexts' and 'work contexts'. When the workers were bargaining with their employer, they emphasised the economic rewards of work, apparently placing little value on job content, autonomy or other offered advantages. However, in the context of daily work, they expressed more interest in non-financial rewards and stressed more the intrinsic nature of the job. Instead of the oppositional stance towards management expressed during negotiations, they were more likely to emphasise teamwork and mutual cooperation with management to solve production problems.

People's expressed preferences alter with the constraints they see operating in different situations and with what they think they can achieve. The spread of more 'realistic' pay claims at times of high unemployment demonstrates this point. The sharp increase in unemployment in the early 1980s caused a reduction in employee expectations and demands compared with the 1970s, when unemployment was much lower and when there were growing demands for worker participation. However, when unemployment ceased to rise and then actually fell in the mid-1980s, old pay expectations reemerged and new demands started to stress such things as employee involvement. Again in the early 1990s, with further high levels of unemployment, pay claims have been moderated. Indeed, high unemployment highlights the fact that some kind of work ethic is held by many employees in society. The depression, the sense of worthlessness and the associated ill-health that often accompany long-term unemployment, derive in part from economic deprivation, but also from the ethic that sees work as the way of achieving adult status and full citizenship in society.[19]

Thus, workers' preferences and actions can vary over time with the constraints which they face. However, deeper orientations seem to remain more stable. For example, in the 1980s, the experience of high unemployment, the attempt to create an entrepreneurial culture and new approaches to the management of human resources seem to have had limited effect on the orientation of workers. They may have encouraged a greater individualism and an acquiescence among workers.[20] However, there is evidence that they have not changed basic 'us and them' attitudes nor led to an enhanced work ethic, nor undermined certain basic collectivist orientations.[21] Most employees' attachment to work remains primarily instrumental, though this must be subject to the important qualification that workers, as always, look to other things from work, including status, job satisfaction and some degree of control over what happens to them in their jobs.[22]

Employee ideologies and value systems

It is probably best to see various distinct types of value system within the British labour force. Parkin suggested a threefold typology:

(a) a *dominant* value system which asserts the value of work, insists that issues of a managerial nature are outside employees' legitimate sphere of interest, and that employees should be primarily concerned with pay;

(b) a minority *radical* value system which takes an oppositional stance and argues for substantially more workers' say and control at work; and

(c) a *subordinate* value system which does not reject the major tenets of the dominant ideology but which seeks to manipulate them and claim better treatment.[23]

Radical values have probably always been expressed by a minority. They had some influence at certain points in time such as during the shop stewards movement of the First World War period or among certain groups of workers such as the miners at various points in their history, but they are not a significant force in Britain, where the relevant values now are a mixture of (a) and (c). The dominant value system is widely disseminated, but its total acceptance presents problems for employees. The employment relationship does not involve a simple exchange of a certain quantity of labour for a certain price. As we have already suggested in Chapter 3, it is an exchange of labour potential and employers need to convert that potential into actual work performed. It is difficult, therefore, for employees to ignore managerial questions and all have some interest in how they are managed, if only in preserving any elements of discretion and self-determination that they may have. Subordinate values do not challenge managerial control of the hierarchical structure of authority at work, but assert the employees' right to fair treatment within that authority structure. The subordinate value system is probably widespread among British workers. Employees operating with such values do not make demands for radical or fundamental changes, but they claim fair treatment within existing structures and they exploit bureaucratic notions about the basis of rational administration by arguing that precedent, comparability or seniority be used as criteria in decision making.[24]

In summary, there are various theories about what people want or ought to want from their employment. The evidence presents a complex picture of a wide range of potential demands whose expression varies with the context and constraints that are seen to be operating. Most employees realise they have to, and are prepared to, work along with management. However, many employees do not totally accept dominant managerial values and their activities are probably best seen in terms of a subordinate value system where workers often acquiesce and seek to extract maximum advantage from the work provided within existing management systems. At times, when certain issues emerge, in certain economic and political contexts, more radical aspirations can come to the fore.

INDIVIDUAL EMPLOYEE ACTION

Can and do employees achieve what they want from their employment by their own actions? Theoretically the individual can choose the type of job he or she applies for, negotiate terms with the employer, and press his or her own interests once he is employed. Some employees with scarce skills or in strategic positions are able to do this very well. However, for most employees individual power in these areas is slight.

Blackburn and Mann studied the choice of jobs available to manual workers in the Peterborough labour market in the late 1970s.[25] They concluded that manual workers had little scope for choice even at a time of nearly full employment. The jobs available to external recruits were at the bottom of the heap in terms of job interest and financial and other rewards. Eighty-five per cent of manual jobs required less skill than would be involved in driving to work. Differences in pay or conditions were slight. No matter what individual preferences might be, the labour market gave the unskilled manual worker little choice. In the 1980s unemployment reduced the choice open to many other workers by cutting down on job opportunities, restricting workers to certain jobs and for long periods excluding some altogether from employment.

In the initial negotiations on terms of employment, most prospective employees are in a weak position compared to the employer. Competition for jobs is usually greater than competition for workers. In other words the employee usually requires a job more urgently than the employer requires one more employee, and so time works to the employer's advantage in negotiations. For the employer, vacancies can often be covered by rearranging the workforce or working time and lost production can be made up later. In contrast, the employee often needs an immediate sale of his or her labour because accumulated savings are small compared with outgoings and labour is a perishable product: it cannot be 'stored' and each day's unsold labour is a loss of part of the asset. Also, the management conducts more negotiations with employees than vice versa. This experience, coupled with higher social status and an accustomed position of authority, gives the employer an advantage in the 'art' of negotiating. The employer will also find it easier to get to know the other employers in the area, in order to exchange information or agree maximum rates. Employees, on the other hand, are less likely to know their competitors. For all these reasons, most individual employees are at a disadvantage in negotiating their contract of employment, for few are in that happy position of possessing essential, rare and desperately needed skills.[26]

Once in employment, can the individual act by himself or herself to improve his position at work? Of course, the individual can work hard, hope that his or her effort will be recognised, and hope to gain promotion to a better job. Equally, he or she may try to evade or manipulate managerially determined rules and regulation. Case studies have found employees evading rules they believed to be restrictive, manipulating payment systems to their own advantage, and generally attempting to expand their zone of discretion on the effort they put into work. This occurs in both blue- and white-collar situations.[27] However, individual manipulation of rules is essentially evasive and usually does little to change the basic, employer-determined features of the employment relationship.

Individual action can have more influence for the employee if the employer provides, or employees can create, an internal labour market so that existing employees have preferential access to the more interesting, better-paid jobs within the organisation. If clear promotion hierarchies are created by management as part of their internal personnel policy, then individual action to gain the favourable attention of superiors is expected and encouraged. Even where management does not consciously develop such career ladders, employees may be able to manoeuvre to get preferential access to better jobs, and it is usually the case that the better-rewarded and more interesting jobs are not available to external recruits but go to existing employees who used the 'discretion' inherent in their jobs to demonstrate reliability, compliance to supervisory demands, and a willingness to adopt managerial values and orientations.[28]

However, where the chances of promotion up the managerial hierarchy are slight or non-existent, then the scope for individual action to improve one's position at work is limited. Even with promotion opportunities, the individual can usually do little, alone, to alter the employer-determined rules of employment. For example, employees acting alone can rarely alter the criteria for recruitment or promotion, or prevent unfair dismissal or achieve major changes in the allocation of rewards or in methods of work. It should also be remembered that internal labour markets may segment workers and competition for promotion may divide them. We need to turn from individual to group action in order to see the most powerful methods used to achieve employee objectives at work.

GROUP ACTION BY EMPLOYEES

Employees form informal groups at work to provide support in terms of affiliation and identification and to protect and further their interests. These groups may be the same as formally constituted departments, sections, or teams as set up by management. But they may be different in membership and shape from managerially constituted groupings.

Workgroups may have boundaries which are wider than the boundaries as drawn by management; or they may be subgroups which have boundaries which are narrower than those constituted by management. An example of the former might be the secretarial staff of different departments within an organisation who feel they have wider group interests; an example of the latter might be the subgroups of electricians, engineers and joiners to be found in a maintenance department of a factory. They may also be more or less permanent than the groupings as set up by management. Some of them may be transient and shifting, formed for a particular reason and then ceasing to exist; others may have a longer-term existence based on friendship or self-interest, and managerial attempts to change formal groups may not prevent such informal groupings continuing to exist. A temporary work-group might be all the operating staff on the night shift in a particular workplace who are confronted by a particular set of difficulties; an example of a workgroup which continues to exist despite managerial attempts at reorganisation might be where management has set up mini-teams but where the whole former workforce feel they are a group. Workgroups are usually defined in interactive terms, as when workers have frequent face-to-face contact; however, they may also be defined cognitively as when workers believe they have interests in common even though they rarely meet. In the latter category might be long-distance lorry drivers working out of a parti-cular depot or railway signalmen working in separate signal boxes down a particular railway line. Whatever their configuration, such informal group-ings, as created independently by employees, are important for an under-standing of much of what happens in industrial relations. Such groups are extremely common among people at work.

Traditional studies of employee groups and action in the UK have focused on the more formal kind of organisations, namely trade unions and professional associations. However, the significance of less formal employee groups within the workplace has always been apparent.[29] If we can see when different types of workgroup form and note the factors which affect their strategies and power, then more formal employee associations can be understood as one particular form of the wider phenomenon of pressure group formation and action at work. In the rest of this chapter we review the various types of small informal groups that develop at the workplace. The next chapter surveys the larger and more formalised institutions created by employees.

Small groups of people identifying with one another, forming affiliations and friendships, and acting together to solve work problems or improve their working environment are widespread at work. Of course, there will always be some workers who act primarily as individuals and who do not collaborate with their colleagues, and some work situations appear to discourage group formation. For example, casual building workers traditionally tend to be individualistic, reluctant to make any commitments to either management or their mates, and they react to grievances by quitting rather than forming groups to pressure for change.[30] Workers in supermarkets and fast food restaurants also tend to think and act individualistically, in part because they work part-time and on shifts.[31] Travelling salesmen are another category of employees who tend to work and act in this way, especially when they are paid on a commission basis, and they do not form strong workgroups. However, such situations tend to be unusual, and, even within these categories, there are tendencies towards group formation and degrees of cohesion. Indeed, group formation at work is a common means whereby workers define their identity and establish a sense of belonging. In turn, this sense of identification and belonging can often be used, in a more functional or strategic sense, to further the employment interests of their members.

There are many studies of the small group activity of manual workers in various countries. Among the first and most famous were the Hawthorne studies in the USA. Set in the Human Relations tradition, these showed that, even at the height of the depression, and among groups of workers who might be unlikely to act collectively, workgroups emerged to provide social satisfaction and to control aspects of work.[32] In the UK in the 1960s and 1970s the activity of manual workgroups and the control they appeared to exercise over job tenure, work methods and pay arrangements caused considerable managerial and government concern. They also caused some concern to trade unions who often frowned on activities which they saw as unofficial. Many of the shifts in management and government policy which we discuss in Chapters 9 and 10 have been concerned to solve the 'problem' of manual workgroup power. Many managements in the 1970s tried to contain, some would say appease, workgroups. In the 1980s they came to take a tougher or more sophisticated approach and tried to neutralise or individualise workgroups and to reconstitute them more under management control. In this way they hoped to channel workgroup activity and potential to their advantage.[33] In the 1970s government action was aimed at the integration of such groups into more formal trade union hierarchies with the hope thereby of containing workgroup activity. Unions themselves were for the most part willing or keen to integrate workgroup and shop steward activities into formal union structures. In the 1980s government action was also aimed more at the individualisation of workers and at increasing their identification more with the companies for which they work by, for example, encouraging individual shareownership and merit pay. However, as we will see in subsequent chapters, such attempts have not always been successful.[34]

Although manual workgroups have attracted most attention, it is important to realise that small groups with an interest in improving employment conditions are *not* confined to manual workers. Workgroups active in their own self-interest can be found throughout most organisational structures. Strong white-collar and professional workgroups are to be found among process control staff in oil refineries and power stations, air traffic controllers and junior hospital doctors. Even among managerial staff, employees can be found pursuing their interests through informal, face-to-face 'cliques' and 'cabals'. In a classic study, Dalton investigated managers in a number of American firms.[35] He found managers creating informal groups to provide mutual aid in their pursuit of promotion, to develop their own departments and to protect their interests against attack. The operation of these subgroups was covert and difficult for a stranger to detect, but cliques and cabals had a major impact on organisational and individual behaviour.

In Japan, it has long been the management practice to encourage and shape formal and informal workgroups to overlap and to operate for the benefit of the firm. There group consultation, team working, and group social activities throughout the permanent workforce of large companies gives small groups an open and recognised channel through which to press their views and claims. Before we turn to the extensive literature on manual workgroups in the UK and US, it is worth asking why small group activity has been seen as less of a problem in Japan. This question highlights one of the themes of this book: that managerial control techniques and employee behaviour at work are interrelated. Employee behaviour cannot be isolated from the managerial strategies adopted by employers or the context and structure of the organisation.

Workgroups *vis-à-vis* management structures and strategies

The development of employee workgroups as a problem for management can be related to the strategies adopted by employers for the construction of their business organisations. Before modern, bureaucratic organisations developed, businessmen in Britain, the US and Japan were often reliant on the operation of largely autonomous, self-managing workgroups.[36] As we pointed out in Chapter 4, nineteenth-century entrepreneurs did not possess their own managerial capabilities. They controlled production by using work gangs as subcontractors within the early factories. From the late nineteenth century onwards, employers moved to gain more direct control over these workgroups and in Chapter 3 we noted the contrasting policies associated with Taylorism (influential in the US and to a lesser extent in the UK) and bureaucratic paternalism (more influential in Japan). Policies associated with Taylorism were designed to break up the pre-existing workgroup ties. Employees were seen as isolated individuals with temporary commitments to their employer and were subject to highly centralised, bureaucratic controls over work organisation and task performance. The managerial pressure to break or prevent workgroup ties is illustrated by comments about Ford's US plants in the 1920s and 1930s: 'There was to be no association with other men. Any association with other workers was frowned upon and chatting or fraternising with workmates during the lunch hour was taboo'.[37] Though extreme, this represented the attitude of many employers who preferred to ignore or who tried to suppress workgroup power.

In contrast, Japanese managerial policy was more often to incorporate workgroups as units into the new managerial structures. Many of the old subcontract group's functions in the allocation of work, work methods and quality control were retained, workgroup leaders were given more of a managerial status, and group members came to be guaranteed job security and prospects of seniority-based promotion. Under these policies workgroup activity continued to have a legitimate role to play within the managerial structure, and workgroups became less the focus of an alienated opposition to managerial controls. However, in those societies that relied on more Taylor-type policies, workgroup activity was either successfully crushed or continued to survive as the unofficial side of organisational life, often acting as a source of resistance to managerial control. Such resistance was more prevalent in the UK than in the US. The UK had weaker managerial structures and hierarchies and longer traditions of workgroup activity. In the US the transition to modern organisation and direct managerial control occurred in expansionary periods, which softened the impact of change on employees, and the later adoption of bureaucratic personnel policies by many large-scale American employers also helped lessen opposition to the new managerial structures by providing more long-term rewards for employee loyalty. With a more gradual, though often bitter, transition to direct, internal controls and the long absence of bureaucratic personnel policy, the UK was left with severe managerial problems for the control of large-scale production.[38] Workgroups continued a well-organised but unofficial existence on British shopfloors, often in opposition to managerial controls, and British managers have had to grapple for longer with the problems of managing such workgroups.[39]

In the UK workgroups have always been important in industries such as engineering, shipbuilding, steelmaking, printing and other craft-based trades. In the 1960s and 1970s, such activity became more visible and effective in other areas and came to be seen as a problem, especially at a time when tight labour markets enhanced workgroup power and when more competitive product markets put pressure on firms.[40] Employers sought to cut labour costs by mounting a new challenge to the workgroups' remaining areas of control and it was in this context that workgroup power came to be seen as a national problem. In the 1980s managements have tried more to individualise workgroups or to create their own managerially controlled teams with a view to improving quality or increasing productivity. This has meant redrawing the boundaries of workgroups on management terms and trying to create new flexibilities and team working.[41] The degree of success in this respect will be discussed more in Chapter 9.

Analysing workgroup activity and power

An early classic study by Sayles investigated 300 workgroups in US manufacturing industry and classified these according to the type of pressure they exerted on management, as shown in Figure 5.1.[42]

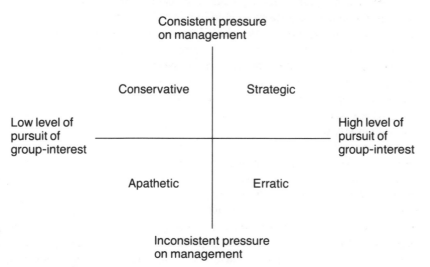

Figure 5.1 Typology of workgroup activity
Source: Adapted from L. Sayles, *Behavior of Industrial Work Groups* (New York, 1958).

Apathetic groups rarely mobilised themselves to act together in their own interests and did not consistently put pressure on management. Members acted more as individuals. Conservative groups were more united and had high morale, but they tended not to pursue group grievances and demands; in part this was because they were accepted as significant groups within the power structure of the organisation. By contrast, strategic groups were more active in the pursuit of their own self-interest and were more consistent in the pressure they put on management. Finally, erratic groups were unpredictable in that they could erupt in protest over minor issues and fail to react to major worsening of conditions, but overall they were often quick to pursue their own best interests.

Sayles argued that one could predict the classification of particular workgroups according to (a) whether the division of labour isolated workers or welded them into integrated teams and (b) whether they occupied a strategically powerful position in the production process. Apathetic groups were common in noisy, heavy work in the car industry or foundries, where working conditions militated against the formation of friendship networks and where the groups had only limited strategic power to stop production. Erratic groups were found on small assembly lines and among packers. Their cohesion and power was also weak, but they could occasionally be mobilised by strong or militant leadership. Strategic groups had less need for strong leadership; they tended to coalesce into strong social units with sufficient power to build confidence in their own negotiating abilities, and were to be found among welders in engineering, or internal truck drivers, or among the pressers in clothing manufacturing. The conservative groups were found among the skilled craftsmen in motor car plants or skilled cutters in clothing factories. They were highly skilled, played a crucial role in the production process and were accepted as a group with legitimate interests by management because of their strength; they did not need to use oppositional tactics and strike action to achieve their ends.

Sayles's analysis is useful but incomplete, for his technological factors do not entirely determine workgroup behaviour. As we have already suggested and will explore more below, workers' beliefs about group action and the market context within which these beliefs are formed are equally or more important.[43] Nevertheless his study shows how the division of labour within a factory can facilitate or hinder the development of strong group ties and can affect the extent to which workgroups adopt oppositional tactics. His work also demonstrates that group action by employees is not inevitable. In some situations even face-to-face groups may not see sufficient common interest or have sufficient confidence to overcome barriers or apathy or the pressures of individualism.

A major British set of studies by Batstone *et al.* in a plant of a multinational vehicle manufacturer in the late 1970s outlined a number of other factors influencing workgroup activity and power.[44] Their research found a marked contrast in the strength of workgroup organisation and activity between manual production workers and craftsmen on the shopfloor and white-collar staff in the office. On the shopfloor the strongest groups exercised an influence over many managerial issues. These workgroups had bargained to establish and maintain a set of arrangements that made decisions on job allocation, manning levels, methods of work, and piecework earnings accessible to workgroup pressure. Men were recruited with the help of the workers' trade union and obtained transfers to amenable jobs through the union. Each section had a shop steward who worked out the rotas for overtime working, night-shift working, and lay-offs. As part of a decentralised union structure the workgroup was responsible for ratifying agreements made between union officials and their management on basic rates of pay and conditions. Most of the sectional workgroups on the shopfloor had also developed their own rules to relieve the sick or those with domestic problems from night work and to relieve older workers from assembly-line work.

In contrast to the strong workgroups formed by workers on the shopfloor, workgroups among the white-collar workforce exerted much less influence on the day-to-day management of their own work. These white-collar groups were linked into white-collar trade union branches, but they did not have the protective and strategic functions of the shopfloor workgroups; their pay and conditions of work were determined at central, not workgroup level; and they were not active in pursuit of day-to-day improvements in employment conditions.

Batstone *et al.* offered a complex explanation of this contrast. The difference between shopfloor and white-collar workgroups could not be explained by any significant differences in the orientations of the workers themselves, for they all appeared to have similar objectives for employment. The researchers therefore analysed the contrast in terms of a range of factors, some arising from organisation structure, some from the centralisation of management's personnel policies and the distribution of power between managers, and some from the organisation and leadership of the workgroups themselves. They stressed in particular the felt need on the part of shopfloor workers for collective action and both the opportunity for, and pay-offs from, such action. They also stressed how, in large part for these reasons, workgroup leaders, shop stewards, were able to mobilise members more on the shopfloor than their counterparts in the office.

From a more social psychological perspective Brown *et al.* have studied various groups of workers, both blue- and white-collar.[45] They found what they called workgroup identification and intergroup differentiation was pervasive in all the workplaces they studied. However, they also found that group identification and intergroup differentiation varied considerably. Workgroup formation was more likely to occur and workgroups were more likely to be cohesive under certain conditions. This happened where workgroups perceived a conflict with other groups, especially with management. This the authors described as conflict between the ingroup and other outgroups. It was more likely to occur where workers made comparisons, for example, in terms of perceived contribution, with other groups which strengthened their differentiation from them. It also occurred where interpersonal relations were close and where there were friendships and other attachments within the group. Alongside such cognitive and interactive factors, Brown *et al.* also identified other more sociological and industrial relations variables. For example, in a study of a bakery, they drew attention to the broader orientation of workers: the cozy family-like atmosphere among the office staff and their more cooperative attitudes towards management; the more individualistic ethic among the bread roundsmen; and the more collectivist and oppositional orientation among the bakery worker subgroups. They also saw trade union membership and involvement in union action as significant contributory factors.

Thus differences in workgroup activity and power relate to the workgroup's position in the organisational structure and to the extent to which it occupies an important position in the production process (see Sayles's second factor above). Batstone *et al.* used strategic contingency theory (originally developed by organisation theorists to analyse the power of different *management* departments) to isolate four sources of power that may be available to any sub-group within an organisation. These power resources depended on:

1   The extent to which group members have skills which cannot be easily replaced or substituted.
2   The extent to which group members occupy a crucial position or bottleneck in the organisation's workflow.
3   The immediacy with which group action can affect or disrupt production.
4   The extent to which the group can create or exploit uncertainty in the production process.[46]

Therefore skilled men maintaining irreplaceable production machinery or technicians operating a central computer could be expected to exert more powerful pressure than storemen or canteen workers. In the case study, many of the shopfloor production workgroups had a higher rating on these variables than did the staff departments.

As an aside, it is interesting how these sources of power identified by sociologists overlap with the economist's approach to analysing the demand for labour. According to the so-called Marshall-Hicks conditions,[47] the demand for labour will be more inelastic (less responsive to wage changes) and therefore the power of labour will be greater:

1 Where it is more difficult to substitute other inputs such as capital or other classes of labour.
2 Where it is more expensive to make such a substitution.
3 Where the demand for the product is less responsive to the price.
4 Where the cost of labour is only a small proportion of total costs: and therefore it is less expensive to make concessions to workers and less likely to affect demand for the product.

Batstone *et al.* recognised that the power resources derived from organisational structure were not outside the scope of human influence but could be affected by the strategies pursued by managers or workgroups. The researchers did not consider the wider aspects of managerial strategy and workgroup control discussed above, but they did look at the impact of local management and workgroup strategy on the structural sources of power. They found unskilled men, who could easily be replaced by others, acting to increase management's dependence on their labour by preventing substitutes from 'blacklegging' when they were in dispute. At the time of the study, management rarely attempted to 'man-up' manual strikers' jobs because workgroup leaders could organise widespread manual worker opposition to such attacks on union principles. By applying the 'no blackleg' principle flexibly, shop stewards threatening to 'man up' jobs of certain strikers had effectively weakened groups whose claims they did not support. Workgroups also acted to increase their power in relation to the other power resources listed above. They attempted to increase the force of any industrial action by requests for sympathetic action in order to create a more crucial impact on production. The immediacy of a production group's actions depended upon stock levels; workgroups therefore attempted to reduce stocks by overtime bans or working to rule if a dispute seemed imminent. In these ways the manual shopfloor workgroups acted to increase their power resources. Management, of course, also manipulated power resources, for example, by building up certain stocks. Finally, the power derived from a crucial position in the production process could be turned against a group by other parties. Some assembly-line workers could have such an immediate impact on production that both management and other workers sought to curb their use of strike action. The researchers noted that if a group like this is very important in the production process, it is possible for management to stir them to strike action to avoid having to pay those laid off when markets slump, supplies run short or breakdowns occur.

In this case study the strongest and most active shopfloor workgroups had a strong sense that their interests were often opposed to those of management. Batstone *et al.* note the importance of employee values that represented a strong version of the subordinate value system, with traces of radical values (see above). Workgroup representatives acted to sustain this counter-ideology and develop workgroup strategies consistent with it. Focusing on workgroup leadership, the authors classified workgroup shop stewards into 'leaders' who saw themselves as representatives, responsible for guiding their members and upholding trade union principles in opposition to managerial objectives, and 'populists' who simply saw themselves as delegates responsible to their members alone and who were less committed to trade union principles. They noted how a higher proportion of 'leaders' on the shopfloor formed themselves into a tight network, headed by a 'quasi-elite' capable of mobilising considerable ideological and practical support and of developing and executing long-term strategies to increase workgroup power. Between the main types of 'leaders' and 'populists', there were 'nascent leaders' who over time might develop the prerequisites necessary to become 'leaders' and 'cowboys' who saw themselves as representatives but who were less consistently committed to acting in pursuit of collective interests. The study shows leadership and internal governance structures can play an important role in workgroup activity. (See Figure 5.2.)

Of course management action can do much to shape workgroup activity. A harsh management may stimulate workgroup counteraction; weak managerial controls may facilitate workgroup activity; while sophisticated managerial policies may defuse and channel workgroup activity. There have always been examples of the latter more sophisticated strategy. In the 1970s, a case study of Chemco, a pseudonym given to a modern plant of a large chemical company, describes a situation where the threat of oppositional workgroups was defused by careful managerial strategies on job design and trade union relations. The researchers suggested that Chemco's managers had adopted a number of policies to prevent the development of oppositional groups among their unskilled and semi-skilled workforce at the case study plant. The workforce was divided spatially and by means of a shift system, which meant that workers on one shift rarely met their colleagues on another. A trade union had been invited in by management and treated cooptively, so that no workgroup ties had formed around demands for union recognition. Managers aided the appointment of moderate shop stewards and the negotiation of company-wide collective agreements helped to ensure that strongly organised, oppositional workgroups did not emerge to create managerial problems on the shopfloor.[48]

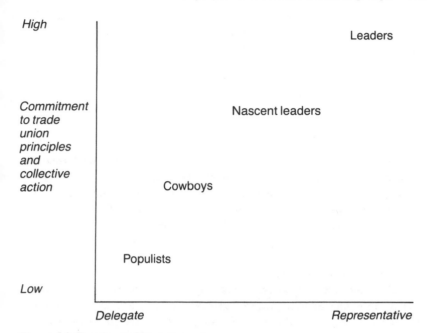

Figure 5.2 Typology of shop stewards
Source: Adapted from E. Batstone, I. Boraston and S. Frenkel, *Shop Stewards in Action* (Oxford, 1978).

In the 1980s and 1990s many more managements have shown greater sophistication in their approach to workgroups. They have developed a number of strategies and techniques aimed at neutralising the oppositional power of workgroups and redirecting their potential for management. In terms of work organisation, they have developed team working, small cell production and intergroup flexibilities which, among other things, have sought to break down old informal workgroups and to reconstitute these more under management control.[49] In terms of employment relations, some managements have consciously divided workers up into a core of more permanent staff, with advantageous pay and conditions, and a periphery of less well-placed staff, often part-time and temporary workers. Such differentiation has acted to redraw the boundaries of informal work-groups.[50] In terms of representational arrangements, managements have instituted new communications and consultative systems and so-called QC or Quality Control Circles which give employees a say and participation in decision making at the small group level, but in groups which management has established and largely controls.[51] Reforms in collective bargaining, which we will discuss in detail in Chapter 9, have also had a significant effect. Management insistence on more formal, often plant-wide bargaining, to the exclusion of lower-level workgroup bargaining, has often reduced the ability of workgroup leaders to pursue sectional interests and win benefits for their members. In some instances, the marginalisation of collective bargaining and the development of alternative management-controlled communication and representation systems has also constrained workgroup activity and power.[52]

The extent and persistence of workgroup activity

The studies discussed above follow a tradition of industrial relations research. They are concerned with workgroup activity which is perceived by workers and managers alike as being, in varying degrees, opposed to managerial controls, though not necessarily inhibiting of efficiency.[53] Other studies have shown that workgroup activity need not always be an industrial relations issue, for many workgroups are sufficiently incorporated into organisational structure to further their group's interests by using managerial rather than oppositional tactics.

Dalton showed this process operating within American management groups.[54] He referred to managerial groups as cliques and cabals, and noted that the strategies available to such groups were affected by the way the groups related to the organisation structure. *Vertical* cliques formed up and down the authority pyramid, while *horizontal* cliques formed across single grades in the hierarchy. Dalton argued that vertical cliques were most powerful. They were small groups formed by a senior officer and a few subordinates who were in constant contact and whose jobs required teamwork. With access to organisational resources and decision-making procedures, a cohesive vertical clique could initiate major policy changes which would help increase the group's power and aid members' chances of promotion. In contrast, horizontal cliques – for example, all foremen or all departmental heads – were more difficult to mobilise. They were not in constant contact and had disparate jobs. They could usually be organised to resist clearly perceived attacks on group interests, but once the immediate threat had passed, problems of communications and differences in immediate interests would cause the 'action group' to lapse. Horizontal management groups could be organised on defensive issues and could resist change by policies of non-cooperation, but they were not as powerful as the more integrated vertical groups because they could not initiate major changes in management structure.

Dalton's study reminds us that confrontational tactics are not necessarily an indication of the greatest workgroup power and that groups which can protect or enhance their interests without the need openly to oppose managerial controls may be in a more powerful position than those which cannot. Other studies within organisation theory also demonstrate that high levels of workgroup activity can exist in a managerial context and that such activity among professional or managerial groups may well be defined as part of the normal established process of managerial decision making. In this respect one thinks also of the considerable power of groups such as hospital doctors or airline pilots.

Accurate estimates of the extent of employee workgroup activity are not available. The fact that workgroup activity can be part of the normal administration of an organisation and that pressure on employment issues may be covert and transitory, all make it difficult to gauge the workgroup activity in the UK. The only attempts at measurement have been associated with studies of shop steward activity. Shop stewards may be used as a proxy for workgroup leaders. However, there are many problems with such an enterprise. Many workgroups are not unionised and therefore do not have the formal equivalent of a shop steward. Shop stewards may sometimes cover a number of different workgroups. Moreover, surveys of shop stewards have been noted for a tendency to underestimate their number. Despite these difficulties, in 1968 the Donovan Royal Commission estimated that there were 175,000 British shop stewards. A survey in the manufacturing industry a few years later revised the estimate from 250,000 to 300,000.[55] In the late 1970s, the TUC suggested that there were 300,000 shop stewards, 200,000 safety representatives and 100,000 union pension trustees, all with some representative functions at the workplace who might conceivably be in a position to mobilise workgroup pressures. In the early 1980s the number of shop stewards in manufacturing industry declined by about one-quarter, along with the reduction in employment and union membership which we will discuss in Chapter 6. However, the number of stewards rose by nearly 20 per cent in private services and 30 per cent in the public sector. Between 1980 and 1984 the total number of shop stewards increased from 317,000 to 335,000. The extent of reduction since then is unknown, but has probably been no more than the reduction in union membership.[56]

It is clear that the most visible, oppositional activity fluctuates with economic and other constraints. With a historical perspective, Goodrich saw the shopfloor as the 'frontier of control' between managerial and workgroup interests and noted that the frontier shifted as the strength of the parties was affected by the external economic and political context.[57] This became apparent in the 1980s when, with the advent of high unemployment and the reduction in formal trade union power, strong workgroup controls of the type described above came under concerted attack. The power of some workgroups, in industries like motor vehicles, printing and the docks, were greatly constrained; shop steward activity was limited; and management was able to reassert its prerogatives in many areas.[58] However, it should be stressed that such workgroups continued and were often able to turn changed circumstance to their advantage. Thus, more competitive product markets paradoxically made managements more vulnerable; new technologies and forms of work organisation which put a premium on flexibility and cooperation created new opportunities for the exercise of workgroup power; and new management techniques, such as performance-related pay, were often seen as a threat to workers and shop stewards were sometimes able to use them as a way of strengthening workgroup action. Managements who thought they could do without shop stewards often found that they could not dispense with them and, indeed, that there were advantages in continuing to deal with them.[59] Meanwhile in other areas, for example, among railway workers, skilled process workers in industries such as chemicals, and among some civil servants and Post Office staff, workgroup cohesion and activity remained strong or even grew. Among offshore oil workers, for example, where workers tend to be individualistic, work on shifts, and are often non-union, workgroup activity has developed and grown around issues such as health and safety. Many managers recognise the continued importance of workgroups and have seen advantages in continuing to deal with shop stewards.

CONCLUSION

There has been much debate about employee objectives at work. Some people argue that employees have limited, short-term and strictly economic objectives. Others contend that most employees hold some form of work ethic and are likely to demand interesting work and a say in decision making. Evidence suggests that employees have a wide range of objectives and that the demands made of work vary with individual circumstances and changing issues in the workplace. Studies of employee values conclude that a radical and fundamental rejection of employer authority is rare in the UK, but that there is widespread support for ideologies and actions which seek to protect employees by limiting and constraining the exercise of managerial authority.

Whatever their objectives, employees alone rarely have the opportunity to achieve major changes in the conditions of employment provided by their employer. If they have scarce skills or are in a strategic position in the work process, they can bargain individually with the employer for better conditions. If their organisation has a well-developed internal labour market so that employees can gain promotion to more interesting, better-paid jobs, then an employee may be able to achieve some of his objectives by individual effort and promotion. However, in most situations, individual efforts have only limited results, and it is common for employees to further their interests by acting with others in various types of group.

In this chapter we looked at the small, face-to-face, informal groups created by employees. Much managerial anxiety and industrial relations research has focused on workgroups formed by blue-collar workers. The power of manual workgroups has been blamed for low levels of productivity in the UK and for the British reputation for problematic industrial relations. However, various studies suggest that small groups of employees acting together to further their members' interests are not unique to manual shopfloors, but pervade organisations in most societies from management level downward. The way workgroups pursue their self-interest, how they relate to formal employee associations such as trade unions, and how they interact with managerial structures and strategies have great significance for industrial relations.

Some employee workgroups are incorporated into managerial structures of control and their activities are not regarded as much of an industrial relations issue. Strong and self-confident workgroups may operate to protect and enhance members' interests, but because they act by manipulating managerial resources, information flows, and arguments, they do not attract much attention. Sayles's 'conservative groups', Dalton's managerial cliques and cabals, groups of professionals such as doctors or academics, and the workgroups within the permanent workforce of Japan's large companies tend to be of this type. If these group members are involved in confrontational opposition to management, then this tends to take place in more formal forums. Other employee workgroups are active in opposition to management in their day-to-day activities at the place of work. They operate with values which emphasise differences of interest between employer and employee, and, for them. workplace activity is more of a 'frontier of control' between opposing interests. Studies of such groups show that the frontier shifts as the balance of power between employer and employee swings with economic and political changes.[60] It is also greatly influenced by the strategies and techniques which management uses to control and motivate employees.

Workgroup activity needs to be analysed in terms of different types of organisation structure and managerial control. Incorporated workgroups tend to be associated with internalised and bureaucratic personnel policies, while the most alienated, oppositional workgroups have emerged as the unintended consequence of strategies of externalisation and Taylorist policies designed to atomise the workforce and break traditional workgroup ties. More visible and oppositional forms of workgroup activity reached a peak in the 1970s in the UK. Recession and high unemployment in the early 1980s and again in the early 1990s have taken their toll of these kinds of workgroup activities. In recent years management has sought to create teams and other groupings more directly under their control. However, these attempts have not been universal nor always successful and they are subject to recurrent counterpressures from workers. Workgroups remain an important industrial relations phenomenon.

Face-to-face, informal workgroups are not the only groups formed by employees to further their interests at work. We turn in the next chapter to the larger, more formally constituted groups which seek to represent employees' interests at work, namely trade unions and professional associations of various kinds.

6 Employee institutions – trade unions

Informal employee workgroups can operate without complex institutional arrangements and supports. However, if local employee groups link up across workplaces and organise on a wider scale, then more formal organisations or institutions are needed. All industrialised societies develop formal institutions for the representation of employees at work, but the form that these take varies greatly. Most call themselves trade unions but, as we shall see below, there is often no clear distinction between employee institutions labelled unions and those labelled staff or professional associations.

In this chapter we look at the different types of formal employee institutions that exist. We review the historical development of large-scale employee organisation in the United Kingdom and note the impact that different bases of organisation have on the objectives, structure and internal government of employee institutions. As with management, so with employee institutions we can talk about the strategies, styles and structures of the organisations concerned.

TYPES OF EMPLOYEE INSTITUTION

Employee institutions can be independently created and shaped by their members or they can be established and structured by outside agencies. In the British case the latter type of employee institution has never been very important and we will deal with them more briefly at the outset.

Unions structured by external interests

In some countries employee institutions have been established and shaped by government action. Where this has been the case, as in former Communist and in some Third World countries, unions usually follow administrative or industrial structures as laid down by government. Such unions provide governments with channels of communication and consultation with employees and are often used in attempts to mobilise worker support for government policy. Lesser degrees of government influence may occur if, rather than forming or reshaping unions, legislation is passed to license or permit only those unions that conform to certain specifications in terms of their objectives or methods of operation. No government in the UK has ever attempted to form or reconstruct employee institutions in the way that occurred, for example, under Fascist, Communist and autocratic regimes elsewhere this century.

Employee institutions may also be established by employers. In the US and UK some large companies have formed staff associations or company unions to act as a channel of representation for their staff. In staff associations all company employees are usually members, they elect representatives who have rights to sit on various consultative committees with management, and they have a role in employee welfare. They are rarely intended to do more than inform management of staff views before decisions are taken, and the typical staff association does not have the right or the necessary sanctions seriously to challenge managerial decision. Institutions of this type are resented by independent trade unions, on the grounds that they were formed as part of a managerial strategy to prevent the spread of real trade unionism and thereby to protect managerial prerogatives. Such suspicions have been encouraged by the use in the past of company-sponsored 'sweetheart unions' which were used, for example, in the US in the interwar years to prevent the spread of independent unionism. In Japan trade unions are company-based, so that there is, for example, a Toyota Workers Union and a Nissan Workers Union which organise within the one company. Some of these are very much constrained in what they can do by the employer, while others have been able to assert more independence. In the UK there were also historically examples of company-based staff associations, but these are now mainly found in the finance sector. In the banks, insurance companies and building societies, staff associations exist. Some of these are sponsored by the employer; others, as in Barclays and Lloyds banks, are more genuinely independent. In some large manufacturing companies, staff associations are also still to be found representing white-collar and managerial staff.

With the exception of the finance industry, British employers have had little success in establishing staff associations and until recently British governments have not followed the strategy, common elsewhere, of attempting to shape or at least license approved trade unions. Employee institutions in the UK have essentially developed 'from the grass-roots' – created by employees themselves. Not only have they developed independently of governments and employers, but neither churches nor political parties have had much impact on their development. This contrasts with

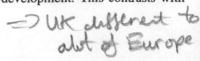
⇒ UK different to alot of Europe

most other European countries where, especially after the period of Fascism and the Second World War, Communist and Socialist political parties and the Catholic Church have fostered trade unions. For example, in France and Italy, union structure has been heavily influenced by the existence of Communist, Socialist and Catholic-sponsored unions.

In the UK, employees themselves have formed the major employee institutions and in order to understand the type of institution formed we need to focus on the factors which aid employee organisation. The formation of independent employee institutions is never simple. It requires the development of communication and resource networks, leadership and administrative roles, and ideological and material incentives to member loyalty. Nevertheless, there have been many attempts to create independent employee institutions and the first institutions to achieve any lasting success were organised around the possession of an occupational, market-based skill.

Market-based skill: occupational institutions

The earliest institutions to be formed by employees in Britain and most other western market economies were organised around clearly defined skills which could attract many buyers on an open market. The formation of institutions to protect and enhance a marketable skill pre-dates industrialisation. The feudal guilds were powerful economic, social and political institutions in the cities of Europe in the Middle Ages. The guilds were not employee organisations in a strict sense, for they were dominated by masters as well as covering journeymen, but their organisations were based around the possession of an occupational skill and their economic objective was to preserve and increase the value of that skill. To achieve this they attempted to monopolise the supply of their skill on the market. Using Weber's terminology we can say they adopted policies of *closure*.[1] They attempted to close social and economic opportunities to outsiders in order to maximise the advantages their skill could bring group members. They sought to close access to their advantageous market position by restricting numbers of apprentices taken on to learn their trade and by requiring long training and possibly the completion of a 'masterpiece' before potential recruits were allowed entry to the occupation. The guilds then attempted to stop any outsiders from breaking their monopoly over the supply of their skills on the market. They prevented the dilution of their market skills by laying down a network of rules, determined in guild meetings which regulated the apprentice system, methods of work, the pay of apprentices and journeymen, and the prices at which supplies should be bought and goods sold.

Many guilds were politically active and were able to gain charters from the crown or from national or city governments to protect and legitimise their market monopolies. At their height they were powerful self-regulating groups, able to maintain tight discipline and to dictate terms to their customers.[2] Guild controls decayed with the growth of industrial capitalism, but their closure policies have been copied by occupational groups, notably by professional associations and craft trade unions.

Professional associations

The ancient professions sought autonomy and self-regulation in their work and like the guilds used policies of occupational closure and monopoly.[3] The most powerful skill-based organisations in the UK today are still those for doctors, barristers and solicitors, and these bodies, such as the British Medical Association (BMA), the Bar and the Law Society, have wide-ranging, self-regulatory powers backed by royal charters. The associations attempt to control or influence recruitment to training; the length and content of training; qualification as a practitioner: standards of work and the disciplining of sub-standard work. They prevent competition by laying demarcations around jobs which only their members can do and by controlling advertising among their members; traditionally they sought to fix the price of labour by establishing scale fees and minimum rates. Political lobbying has resulted in state backing for some of these professional controls. Acts of Parliament may restrict certain key professional activities – such as signing death certificates in medicine or the traditional rights of representation in the courts – to practitioners whose names are included on the register kept by the professional association. As a result of these practices the ancient professions can exercise an extraordinary degree of occupational control over recruitment, work methods, discipline and the rewards received for work.[4]

The ancient professions' extensive control over the terms and conditions of work of their own members has been the envy of many other groups. Today there are over one hundred significant professional associations, ranging from the ancient Inns of Court and Royal College of Physicians, to institutions for accountants, various professional engineers and architects, and to societies for physiotherapists and hospital technicians. All are concerned to establish training systems and examinations to be used to register professionals as competent to undertake particular areas of work. Many of these qualifying associations also attempt to raise their group's status and increase their autonomy by the elaboration of codes of ethics and the disqualification of members who break these codes. Most take part in publicity and pressure group activity directed towards government, major employers and the public at large.[5] Professional controls are supported and professional association activities justified by ideologies which emphasise the importance of the group's skill for society as a whole and the need for the occupation itself to act as the best and only custodian of standards.

Attempts to form professional associations by new occupational groups continue. However, no new occupation is likely to achieve the very extensive self-regulation and unilateral control exercised by the ancient professions, for reasons we will discuss below. Before that discussion, however, we turn to the other form of occupational organisation stemming from market-based skill, but catering for manual workers, namely, craft trade unions.

Craft trade unions

Skilled craftsmen were the first manual workers to form organisations capable of operating beyond a single workshop. Evidence of trade societies of skilled men, organising on a district or town basis, can be traced back to the seventeenth century, and by the end of the eighteenth century we know that local trade societies had been established for many workers, including printers, shoemakers, weavers, spinners, hatters, coopers and various building tradesmen. The earliest craft societies attempted to achieve unilateral control of their wages and work methods. For example, members of the Shipwrights Society, which flourished in the Thames shipyards, drew up stringent rules for the employment of their members, for their pay and conditions of work, and insisted on a high standard of professional knowledge on the part of foremen.[6] Millwright societies circularised employers in their districts with their rates of pay and enforced craft methods and practices. Direct strike action was occasionally threatened and used against recalcitrant employers, but industrial action was generally less important than unilateral regulation – the policy of closure and the imposition of craft rules. Societies attempted to limit the numbers of apprentices taken on by employers and to insist on long (often seven-year) apprenticeships. They tried to ensure that their traditional areas of work were undertaken by their own time-served members and that traditional craft methods, work practices and standards were maintained. The solidarity of the craftsmen in maintaining these practices was supported by policies of mutual insurance. The societies organised insurance for sickness and death benefit among their members. Unemployment benefit and the system of 'tramp relief' (whereby skilled journeymen travelling in search of work would be helped by the appropriate trade society in each town) served not only as an insurance benefit to members but also acted to prevent the undercutting of the society's wage rates through competition from unemployed craftsmen.

The success of the craftsmen's policies depended not only on the coverage and discipline of the craftsmen's organisation but also on employers' demand for their skills. Craft bargaining power was rarely sufficient to dictate to employers all the terms on which craftsmen would work, but in times of economic prosperity, for example, when the engineering industry faced relatively soft markets or building faced a construction boom, craftsmen found many employers willing to accept, or at least bargain on, the trade societies' preferred terms of employment.[7] Thus local societies of artisans grew in the mid-nineteenth century to become the first national trade unions in the UK. In 1851 the Amalgamated Society of Engineers was established, followed in 1860 by the Amalgamated Society of Carpenters and Joiners, and in 1866 by an Amalgamated Society of Tailors. These amalgamated societies centralised their administration and the control of their funds and began to employ full-time staff. Their bureaucratic institutional structure earned them the label 'New Model Unions' from the Webbs.[8]

Thus craft unionism, which had its roots in the early period of industrialisation, has had a significant effect on the historical development of unionism in the UK. Craft unions were the first stable manual-worker unions. They operated horizontally, following their members across firms and industries. Thus the Boilermakers Society was to be found in shipyards, railway workshops, and engineering factories. Later the Electricians Union organised those with electrical skills on building sites and in maintenance departments. Their objectives were sectional, designed to exploit their craft skills in the labour market and to preserve the privileges of the 'aristocracy' of labour. At times their policies were explicitly justified by reference to the old professionals and, like the professions, their ideology was generally elitist. The craft unions were therefore based on very different principles from those of the unions of unskilled and semi-skilled workers which were later to develop alongside them and which we will discuss below.

The occupational control of the ancient professions and the self-regulation and autonomy of the old crafts have been envied by many other occupations. However, few have been able to match the old professions and most craftsmen have seen their old, unilateral controls whittled away. We need to explain why certain occupations have been able to achieve unilateral controls over their own working conditions.

Factors affecting the success of occupational institutions

There are variations in the success with which different occupations have been able to control their own working conditions through policies of closure and monopoly. An occupation's success will depend on the power resources available to the occupational group and the countervailing power of any rivals.[9] The power resources available to the occupation itself centre on their position in the labour market and factors which facilitate group organisation.

Power resources held by an occupational group

The *sine qua non* of occupational organisation is marketable skill. If the occupation is to achieve any monopoly control over the supply of its labour, then it needs to provide a form of labour which employers will find difficult to replace or substitute from the general labour market. As Braverman noted, deskilling work, so that unskilled labour can be substituted for skilled, has been an employer strategy in reducing the power and control of once-skilled groups.[10] It will be more difficult for employers to find easy substitutes for certain skills if those skills include diagnostic expertise only gained after long practice, or if the knowledge base of the skill is not understood or available to anyone outside the skilled group itself.

If a group possesses a non-substitutable skill, then the extent to which they can bargain to achieve good rewards and a high degree of self-determination in their work, will depend on the buyer's need for the skills they offer. If their skills are essential to their employer, having an immediate and pervasive impact on the latter's ability to achieve objectives, then the occupation has a potentially powerful resource.

In order to protect and take advantage of the labour market power provided by skill, an occupational group needs to build occupational institutions capable of enforcing the necessary closure policies. It is not easy to build long-lasting organisations, and organisation is facilitated if an occupation's members are able to communicate easily and are brought together by long periods of training when they can develop strong social ties and a sense of occupational identity. The earliest professional associations and craft unions – the Inns of Court barristers and the London printers – were favourably placed in these respects. Once a group forms to protect and enhance a marketable skill, its success in imposing its terms on the buyers of its skill will depend not only on the market demand for its labour but also on the group's success in its conflicts with rivals. Leadership, effective strategic planning, and the development of ideologies to give group claims legitimacy play a part in this. In battles for control the group's links with other power-holders may also be significant. If a group can guarantee recruits of high social status so that its members have powerful family and social contacts in, for example, the courts or government, then it is less likely to find its occupational claims successfully challenged.[11]

Power resources held by rivals to the occupation

There will always be other parties interested in challenging occupational controls. The most powerful rivals are employers and the government.

The countervailing power of an employer depends on the employer's position in the labour and product market and on the organisational and political resources which he commands. If an employer monopolises the demand for labour in his labour market or dominates his product market, then his bargaining position is obviously greater than if he does not. Clients buying the skilled labour of solicitors or barristers are usually scattered individuals, often in a personally vulnerable position which makes them highly dependent on the skills they seek. Such employers are much less powerful than the large company with monopsony control of its local labour market. Though doctors have considerable power, this is to some large extent countered by the fact that the government, through the National Health Service, is the major employer.

Occupational controls flourished in the nineteenth century in Britain, when employers were small and competitive. The growth of modern, large-scale organisation has threatened occupational control in two ways. First, the concentration of business activity makes it more likely that there will be employers who dominate labour and product markets. Second, as we have seen in previous chapters, the growth in the size of companies has been accompanied by the development of bureaucratic management structures and specialised hierarchies. These enable an employer to develop policies to make him less dependent on externally generated, market-based skills. As was described in Chapter 3, two types of policy may be used. Jobs may be redesigned in order to deskill the labour process and enable the employer to substitute new types of skill or unskilled labour for traditional skills. Or the employer may develop an internal labour market within his company such that any necessary skills are created within the organisation itself and are not easily sold on the open market.[12] Labour in this instance is not unskilled, but the skills are learnt by company training and experience and are likely to become more company-specific because they derive in part from an understanding of company policies and procedures. An employee with this background may find it difficult to find another market for his skill. Under either the deskilling or the internal, bureaucratic personnel policy, the conditions for the development of occupational, market-related employee groups are weaker.

Occupational controls are most likely to flourish under a passive government. If governments take an active interest in the regulation of employment affairs, then an occupation is less likely to find itself with a free hand. For example, the teaching profession, developing in conjunction with the modern state, has never achieved the self-determination of the legal or medical profession, which developed before it. Even when the National Health Service was introduced in 1948, doctors bargained to maintain many of their advantages. The BMA insisted that the relationship between government as employer and the occupation be kept at arm's length, and general practitioners, unlike teachers, are not direct employees of the state. In the 1980s, however, the Thatcher government sought to bring about major changes in both the legal and medical professions. In the case of lawyers it also tried to introduce more competition and break down barriers between solicitors and barristers. In the case of doctors it introduced competitive pressures and has imposed new constraints on those working in the National Health Service. However, in practice, changes in the NHS affected doctors, especially consultants, much less than other groups such as nurses. The old professions still remain powerful institutions.

Varying success of market-based occupational controls

With so many factors affecting the formation of occupational institutions and the power that they can exert, it is not surprising that there are marked differences in the occupational institutions of different societies. On the one hand, groups like medical doctors and lawyers, or craft printers and some building workers, have succeeded in forming occupational institutions with relatively high degrees of self-regulation in many societies. The success of less powerful groups is very varied. For example, midwives have survived as a coherent and separate occupational group within the medical profession in the UK, whereas a similar group lost the battle for survival in the US.[13] Occupational groups of both the professional and the craft type are more firmly entrenched in the UK than in societies where government or state agencies have always intervened in the regulation of economic affairs or where industrial management has traditionally been highly centralised and bureaucratic.

However, as we have already said, even well-entrenched occupations like doctors face challenges to their occupational controls. As NHS administration has grown, doctors are challenged by administrators and technical specialists within the hospital service. The knowledge base of the doctor's skill has become accessible to outsiders with the growth of the study of biochemistry and greater sophistication in diagnostic machinery. Centralised government reform of the NHS also presents a continuing challenge. Reflecting such changes, the BMA has increasingly had to adopt direct bargaining tactics in attempts to reinforce its traditional use of unilateral regulation and lobbying to protect its interests.

Challenges to occupational controls can be seen most clearly in the case of manual craftsmen. Unilateral craft controls which flourished in the second half of the nineteenth century were attacked as employers came to use new technology to deskill jobs. As was described in Chapter 3, the pioneering ASE suffered major defeats soon after it was formed, on the 'machine question' and the replacement of apprenticed engineers by unskilled or semi-skilled labour and machine tools. After losing major strikes and lockouts, the union was forced to loosen its original skill-based policies of closure and self-determination. The national union gradually lost its powers of craft protection, although craft controls survived in some local districts amongst powerful workgroups and among more skilled workers in toolrooms and maintenance shops.[14] A similar decline in craft controls can be traced in many industries. Shipwrights lost influence with prefabricated ships; vehicle builders were largely bypassed by the assembly-line technology of the motor car industry; in the case of printing, one of the last bastions of craft controls, the skill base of compositors has been virtually destroyed in the 1980s by new technology, especially computerised print-setting.

Monopoly control over jobs has become increasingly difficult to maintain in the face of managements' use of both technology and more sophisticated policies aimed at reducing its dependence on externally generated skills. Nevertheless, well-organised groups, who have tight membership discipline and who retain some vestiges of non-substitutable skill, have been able to cling to their monopoly of certain work and demand a high price for the buying-out of their traditional job-rights.

The problems facing new groups who wish to establish professional self-regulation can be illustrated by the fate of the United Kingdom Association of Professional Engineers. UKAPE was formed in 1969 and limited its membership to professionally qualified engineers. It devised codes of professionally approved behaviour, espoused a 'responsible' ideology, abjured strike action and sought recognition by engineering employers as the body with which they should agree the employment conditions of their professionally qualified staff. However, it provoked hostile reactions not only from the trade unions already in the area, but also from professional associations and from employers who argued that the category of 'professional staff' did not fit in their bureaucratically organised staff-grading structures. UKAPE could not muster the resources or political support necessary to overcome this opposition and to establish itself as a powerful professional body.[15]

In conclusion, occupational institutions protect and enhance the value of market-based skill. In the UK they grew to strength in the nineteenth century when governments did not actively intervene in the regulation of employment and when employers were small and non-bureaucratic. However, many employees do not have non-substitutable skills and many of the old skills have been undermined by developments in technology and in managerial controls over the labour process. What types of employee institutions are formed by those without a clear market-based skill? We turn first to look at the institutions that were formed in the late nineteenth and early twentieth centuries to cater for the unskilled or semi-skilled manual worker without a high level of non-substitutable skill.

Unskilled trade unionism

Most workers in the developing industries of the nineteenth and early twentieth century had no clearly defined skill which could be used to support policies of closure and monopoly control. Many attempts were made to mobilise workers in local areas to try to improve their working conditions, but these faced constant difficulties because such unskilled, low-paid and ill-educated workers could not control the supply of labour and had few resources with which to build effective organisations. Employers could use the generally anti-union laws particularly successfully against such groups and could all too easily replace protesting employees with new recruits.[16] In the face of these barriers to organisation, ideologies were gradually developed to help underpin the mobilisation of these hard-to-organise workers. Ideas spread that the difficulties facing employee organisation were worth surmounting, that risks were worth taking because radical improvements could be achieved. For employees with few power resources in the existing structure of society, the prospect of radically changed industrial and social arrangements became one of the anchorages of employee organisation.

General trade unionism

The ideology and practice of General Unionism developed to help counter the fact that unskilled workers had no significant labour-market power as long as employers could replace dissidents from the mass of the un-employed. It declared that all workers could and should unite to form a single, general union. In a single union the united class of workers, it was argued, would have the power to demand major industrial and political concessions.

The practice of General Unionism first had an appeal during the 1830s.[17] The most spectacular general union was the Grand National Consolidated Trades Union, created by Robert Owen in 1834. Formed initially to support workers in a local dispute, it quickly expanded its coverage, aims and membership. It proposed to rationalise the sectional, splintered craft unions into a united structure which would include agricultural and other labourers. It advocated production through cooperatives and aimed to provide assistance for any worker on strike. Even at its peak it never attracted a large membership and its organisation could not be maintained. Persecuted by employers and the government – the deportation of six Dorset labourers, the Tolpuddle Martyrs, being the most famous case – it was unable to provide the cohesion or level of assistance that strikers expected or to develop effective organisation.

Similar problems dogged the many more localised attempts to establish unions for unskilled labourers in the nineteenth century. Such organisations made progress in periods of rising prices and strong markets only to be broken when economic recession occurred. It was not until the 1880s that general unions achieved any permanent success. In 1888 a strike in London by women at Bryant and May's match factory attracted considerable public sympathy, and in conditions of unusually full employment general unionism sprang up in the nearby docks and in the gas industry. The high point of this development was the dockers' strike in 1889 when a five-week strike, with widespread support, achieved six pence an hour and eight pence for overtime. Some unskilled workers were beginning to make an impact through organisation, but the idea of a single, general union which would organise all of them faded. The organisation of the entire working class was too difficult, common interests seemed too insubstantial, and, given continuing competition in the labour market, general organisations were too weak. The general union organisers retreated to concentrate on areas that could be more effectively organised, like the new gas industry or the docks, where a highly united labour force could use strike tactics to exact concessions from the most profitable employers.

It is traditional in Britain to identify two main general unions which can trace their origins to the general unionism of the nineteenth century. The Transport and General Workers' Union (TGWU) developed from the organisation of the dockers and the General Municipal and Boilermakers' Union (GMBU) from that among the gas workers. The illogicality of having two general unions has often been noted, but with the decline of the general union ideal they remain distinct and separate institutions. Indeed, as we will see, one might argue that there are now more general unions since more and more unions have opened up and taken wider groupings into membership.

Industrial trade unionism

As the difficulty of general unionism was perceived, the idea of one union for each industry developed as a way of achieving working-class organisations, with sufficient common interest and control over their labour markets, to achieve industrial and political objectives. If all the workers within an industry could be organised, it was argued, then there would be little possibility of employers introducing substitute labour and an industrial union would be in a good position to fix favourable wages and conditions for the whole industry. The most radical advocates of industrial unionism were the Syndicalists, to which we referred in Chapter 2. Syndicalist ideas developed in France and the US and spread to Britain in the early twentieth century. Syndicalists argued for the merger of sectional union interests into industrial groups capable of radical action against employers and government. After the destruction of private ownership, industrial unions would govern industry. Syndicalist ideas were not widespread or long-lasting within the UK but Tom Mann, an engineer, started a monthly syndicalist journal in 1910 and an articulate expression of syndicalist thought was published in 1912 by the Unofficial Reform Committee of the South Wales Miners' Federation. *The Miners' Next Step* called for the end of private ownership and the administration of the economy by industrial unions.

Syndicalist ideas were anathema to many of the skill-based trade union officials who were attached to the more respectable notion that any political action should be conducted through Parliament. Such officials and many others were more receptive to the moderate, non-revolutionary philosophy of workers' power through industrial unions which was developed by some British intellectuals under the label 'Guild Socialism'. This sought to vest ownership in the hands of the state and put the government of each industry in the hands of industrial unions or 'guilds'. 'Collective contracts' between the state and 'worker guilds' would establish the output and price of an industry's goods.[18]

The advocates of industrial unions, like their general union predecessors, were therefore opting for various radical ideas to mobilise less skilled workers. Unlike the craftsmen their members were not the 'aristocracy of the working class', able to afford high subscriptions and with the skill base to use closure and monopoly tactics to achieve job control. Instead their organisations were fragile, they needed to support mass membership on very low funds, and their industrial muscle seemed slight. The problems facing the organisers of the 'New Unionism', as it was termed by the Webbs, and the way that they were gradually brought to adopt and accept collective bargaining as their dominant method, may be illustrated by the case of the miners.

The case of the miners

The earliest and classic example of industry-based trade unionism in a number of countries comes from coal mining.[19] Organisations of miners formed in the early period of industrialisation in the isolated mining villages, and local miners' societies gradually linked together to form regional and national bodies. The mining industry grew in size and importance throughout the nineteenth century, but despite this the early miners' unions proved extraordinarily difficult to maintain. Organisations claiming thousands of members arose in boom periods, only to disintegrate when the trade cycle brought falling prices, and the fragile unions were unable to resist employers' wage cuts. There were may difficulties. In any confrontation with employers, trade unionists could easily be replaced by the importation of 'blackleg' labour from the large numbers of unemployed agricultural or Irish labourers. Miners were highly dependent on their employers' goodwill, not only for wages but also for housing and food in what were often company-run villages. Local magistrates could be relied upon to favour the owners rather than their men in any dispute that reached the courts. Low pay entailed low subscriptions, inadequate funds and limited organisational resources. Differences in regional interests worked against the establishment of organisations able to maintain their unity or build up reserves to carry them over recessions. Before 1850 miners typically alternated between outbursts of militancy, often associated with riots, and a despairing apathy.[20] It was not until the second half of the nineteenth century, when the industry became a major exporter and rising prices and profits bought more prosperity, that any stable district or industry-wide association developed.

Even when miners' organisations became more established, the occupational strategy of reducing labour supply by closing jobs to outsiders was not really tenable. There was a ready army of unemployed always available to take their jobs. The first national miners' association, formed in 1842, therefore adopted a policy designed to increase the value of coal, and hence miners' labour, by restricting output. To support this policy a legal fund was created to defend miners prosecuted by employers for breach of contract. However, the Miners' Association of Great Britain did not survive a bitter strike in 1844, and with its defeat its policies were discredited. Thereafter, though workgroups working underground might have considerable control over the method of work, miners' leaders sought to achieve their broader objectives not by unilateral action, but by extracting concessions from government and employers. They formulated demands for higher wages or improved conditions and addressed them to whoever was thought to have the power to take decisions. Demands for wage increases were sent to local employers, backed by the threat of strikes. Other demands – for shorter hours, improved safety, the abolition of abuses related to truck (payment in kind) and the fair measurement of coal mined – were addressed to the government, backed by lobbying and the funding of Liberal miners' MPs.

Slowly the combination of industrial and political tactics achieved success which lasted beyond immediately favourable market conditions. Employers moved cautiously towards an accommodation with union officials as a means of controlling the miners' intermittent 'guerrilla war'. First, they accepted a system of 'sliding scales', which linked alterations in wages to changes in the price of coal, the scales being administered by independent committees of local dignitaries. Then, when the unions became strong enough to resist the wage reductions often derived from this system, employers accepted direct negotiations with union officials on wage issues through District Conciliation Boards. In this way collective bargaining was established.[21]

Achievements in the political sphere started with legislation on pit safety, checkweightmen (to measure the coal dug), and limits on working hours of boys underground. The miners retained their interest in direct political solutions, calling for the nationalisation of their industry by a Council on which their union would have controlled half the seats. It pressed for this through the interwar years, but did not achieve it until the nationalisation of the coal industry after the Second World War.

The National Union of Mineworkers (NUM) today is one of the closest to being a 'pure' industrial union, recruiting only within one industry and attempting to recruit all employees in that industry. Even in the mines, however, the vertical principle of organisation is not total for supervisory grades and colliery managers have separate unions. Also, since the miners' strike of 1984–5, a rival union, the Union of Democratic Mineworkers, has existed, with membership mainly in the Nottinghamshire coalfields. As the coal mining industry has declined, the NUM, as a union which restricts itself to one industry, has seen its membership fall to about 40,000, a fraction of its former size, and it is today a candidate for takeover by one of the large general unions.

In other industries there were attempts to create industrial unions by mergers or membership exchanges between existing unions, but the prior existence of craft and general unions hindered success. The major result of the syndicalist and guild socialist call for industrial unionism was the merger of three unions in 1913 to form the National Union of Railwaymen (NUR). This union has also declined in membership over the years with the contraction of the railways and has recently taken over another old industrial union, the National Union of Seamen, to form the National Union of Rail, Maritime, and Transport Workers (RMT).

Thus the new unionism of less skilled, non-craft workers developed on both general and industrial lines. The hopes of the early organisers were not met, for the new unions did not sweep all before them, uniting the working class into one big union or rationally structured industrial organisations.

The new unions did not herald the development of workers' control of production nor of revolutionary political change. Nevertheless they survived, despite many early failures, based on pockets of strength and areas of sectional interest. Since they could not unilaterally control pay and conditions, they became heavily reliant for their achievements on collective bargaining with their existing employers. In the case of the general unions they have grown by being open and expansionist. In the case of many of the industrial unions, the limits of the union have been fixed by the boundaries of the industry, and, as industries have contracted, so many of the former industrial unions have declined in membership.

Contrasts between market-based skilled and unskilled unions

The contrasting power resources of the market-skilled and less skilled or unskilled workers is reflected in the organisation and methods of the institutions they formed. Even when craftsmen could no longer retain unilateral control over their wages or work methods, they still sought to enhance their bargaining power by closure policies, trying to close access to their skill, to control the quantity of labour, and thereby to enhance its market value. The new unions, with few skills to protect, adopted different tactics, based more on the solidarity of large numbers, wider organisations and direct collective bargaining with employers about the price of labour.

Policies towards recruitment and union security provide an obvious contrast. Craft-based unions sought for longer to limit their membership to qualified, skilled workers and to close access to their traditional job territories to all but their own members by *pre-entry* closed shops. They insisted that their employers only employ people who were already members of their union for their traditional areas of work. In contrast, the new unions were more open in their recruitment of members and were always less likely to seek and obtain pre-entry closed shops. If they wished to consolidate a high union membership at a particular workplace, they tried to establish *post-entry* closed shops or 100 per cent union membership agreements. Under these the employer agreed to make it a condition of employment that a new employee had to join an appropriate trade union once he or she has started work. The basis of this policy was not the exploitation of skill, but resentment of 'free riders' who eroded employee strength in collective bargaining and benefitted from union members' negotiating activity.[22]

Skill-based and non-skilled unions also differ in their policies towards the organisation of work. Craft unions, with their continuing desire to maximise the relevance and value of scarce skills, have traditionally taken a close interest in the details of how their work is organised and still attempt unilateral regulation of working conditions. The leaders of other unions have often found it difficult to formulate bargaining objectives on the complex issue of the management of detailed work. The craftsmen's interest in work methods and their pressure to retain traditional working rules are commonly and derogatively labelled 'restrictive practices', and their concern to preserve a division of labour which maintains their skill base lies behind so-called demarcation disputes. Both restrictive practices and demarcation issues are less likely to arise with less skilled workers. Although the general and industrial unions originated with the most radical, anti-managerial ideologies, they have often been more passive towards the managerial use of labour because of the limits of their negotiating resources. They have focused instead on the collective bargaining of basic pay and terms of employment.

A related way of looking at trade unions and professional associations, associated with Turner, rests on the distinction between 'open' and 'closed' unions.[23] This hinges on how trade unions or other employee associations define their areas of recruitment and their job territory. Closed unions or associations limit recruitment to a specific type of worker or industry, such as the train drivers' union (the Associated Society of Locomotive Engineers and Firemen (ASLEF)) or the doctors' professional association (the BMA). Closed unions are concerned with preserving the jobs of their members, establishing tight boundaries around them, restricting labour supply and defending the status and wage differentials of their members. To these ends they often have devices such as apprenticeships or other qualifying arrangements, pre-entry closed shops or the equivalent, and unilateral regulation of terms and conditions. Open unions, by contrast, recruit much more broadly, they are expansionist, and are more concerned with the level of wages rather than relative wages. Because they cannot control the supply of labour or unilaterally lay down terms and conditions, they have relied much more on collective bargaining and financial and political muscle. Open unions try to grow and increase their power by being expansionist; closed unions, perhaps paradoxically, survive and seek to wield power by being small and restrictionist.

The distinction between skilled and less skilled, closed and open, unions is analytically useful because it highlights the importance of varied power bases. As we will see below in the discussion of trade union government, the type of membership organised by a union could also affect the methods of internal government adopted: with the craftsmen and closed unions exercising more control over their officials and adopting methods of government which decentralised power to local or occupational labour market levels; and with the industrial and general unions giving more power to regional and national full-time officials who were more likely to lead in collective bargaining and political lobbying. (However, this is not to deny that some groups of less skilled workers who are in a powerful position within their union, such as carworkers, dockers and busdrivers in the TGWU, have had considerable independence from, and control over, their officials.)

However, the distinctions between craft and unskilled, closed and open, unionism have never represented a rigid division. The new unions' often more socialist-inclined ideology influenced some craftsmen and helped integrate the different types of trade union into a common movement. Over time the methods of the different unions have also blurred together. Almost all craft unions have seen the value of their skill eroded and have adopted more open recruitment policies and direct collective bargaining with employers. For example, the Amalgamated Engineering Union (AEU) now often acts as an industrial or general union. (In 1992 it joined with the Electricians Union to form the Amalgamated Engineering and Electrical Union (AEEU).) On the other hand, some sections of the unskilled unions have been able to develop such a cohesive and united organisation that they have been able to gain a form of group monopoly over their jobs and substantial unilateral regulation. For example, this was for long the case with the TGWU in the docks before the deregulation of the industry in 1988 and it is still the case with drivers and guards on London Underground.

The slow, historical development of employee organisation based on craft, general and industrial unionism created a complex network of inter-meshing organisation across the manual workforce. The multi-union picture of employee organisation, a strong characteristic of British industrial relations, was to be made more complex by the separate development of trade unions for non-manual, white-collar employees. Before we turn to the growth of white-collar trade unionism in the UK, however, we need to consider the type of institution formed by workers who have skills which are needed by their employer, but which are gained through employment rather than by apprenticeship or professional training.

Organisation-based skills

Some workers possess a form of skill derived entirely from work experience rather than craft or professional training. The institutions developed to exploit and protect such skills have been called 'promotion-line unions' by Clegg, and he notes that in industries like iron, steel and cotton-spinning there were no apprenticeships but that the top manual workers were skilled by experience. They formed unions to systematise the rules governing the size of work teams and to regulate the promotion from labourer to the top man in the team.[24] The top men of these unions did not use them to exclude all unskilled workers, instead they sought to recruit those placed at lower rungs of their promotion ladder. Junior workers who could potentially act as substitutes for the skilled men were therefore joined into unions with them, although usually in a subordinate position, for the top men dominated the government of promotion-line unions.

With the growth of large-scale business organisations, some employers, pursuing strategies of internalisation, built promotion ladders into the structure of their organisations. Rather than deskilling the labour process by buying in skills from outside, these employers controlled the development and transmission of the skills they required. Necessary skills were learned through work experience and company-sponsored training, and employees were appointed to the more highly skilled and rewarded jobs by internal recruitment. Employees entered the organisation at the bottom of the career ladders and not in mid-career. Such policies were usually accompanied by an emphasis on the importance of company loyalty.[25] Historically, the Civil Service, the Post Office and many of the railway companies were the first to adopt such policies.

What type of institutions are formed by employees in these conditions? Generally it would seem that when careers are shaped within single organisations, then employee institutions follow the structures established by management and shape themselves around promotion ladders. If the employer endorses or encourages employee organisations, then something like enterprise trade unions or staff associations are likely to develop. If the employer resists employee organisations, then the institutions which form will start with a more confrontational ideology, but will still be patterned in part to follow the career interests of their members and their structure will tend to be closed. Civil Service and Post Office unions have from the start been structured around their members' organisational grades and career lines. The early railway companies were paternalistic but strongly anti-union. The railway industry eventually developed an industrial union for most railway workers, but this did not attract the footplatemen who established in ASLEF a promotion-line union assertively protecting the organisation-based skill of the train driver.

Employees with organisation-based skills are likely to be highly dependent on their employer for their career prospects. Job security is likely to be of crucial importance for such people, and they can be expected to be particularly concerned with the regulation of promotion criteria and promotion procedures. In achieving their ends they will not have the market-based power to use craft or professional policies of 'closure'. Their methods are therefore likely to involve some mix of confrontational collective bargaining and attempts to become part of, or at least to influence, normal managerial decision-making. In the twentieth century private employers in the UK have rarely provided career ladders for manual employees. However, such policies are common for white-collar workers and help explain the character of some of the white-collar trade unions.

White-collar trade unionism

The extension of British trade unionism in the period between the Second World War and the late 1970s largely occurred because white-collar workers – i.e. office and managerial employees, technicians and scientists – have increasingly joined trade unions. White-collar trade unions like the National and Local Government Officers' Association (NALGO) or the Association of Scientific, Technical and Managerial Staffs (ASTMS) (one of the predecessors of the present-day Manufacturing Science and Finance union (MSF)) showed phenomenal growth in the 1960s and 1970s. Some, such as the Banking, Insurance and Finance Union (BIFU) and the Royal College of Nurses (RCN), have continued that growth in the 1980s. In addition, and further complicating trade union structure in the UK, white-collar workers have also been recruited into the manual unions, often in special sections like the Managerial, Administrative, Technical and Supervisory Association (MATSA) of the GMBU or the Association of Clerical, Technical and Supervisory Staffs (ACTS) of the TGWU. Today, few unions can afford not to recruit white-collar workers, who have for some time been the main growth area in the labour force. Although it is difficult to distinguish white-collar from manual union membership, it is clear that much of the growth in trade union membership over the postwar period came from an expansion of unionism among white-collar workers. From the late 1960s to the late 1970s white-collar union density increased from 33 to 44 per cent and this accounted for just over two-thirds of union growth in this period. Over the same period white-collar union membership as a percentage of total union membership rose from 32 to 40 per cent.[26] The latest figures show that white collar union density in 1987 stood at 40.2 per cent, and that this constituted 48 per cent of total trade union membership in Britain.[27] White-collar workers are still less likely to join trade unions than their manual colleagues, but this expansion of white-collar trade unionism saved the British trade union movement from the membership consequences of heavy job loss in the traditionally well-unionised sectors of manufacturing, coal mining, railways and the docks.

Traditionally it was assumed that the generally more conservative orientation and more privileged work situations of the white-collar worker would prejudice him or her against trade unionism. In addition, employers tended to be more hostile to the unionisation of their white-collar staff. On the other hand, it had long been noted that the unionisation of white-collar workers was closely associated with bureaucratisation.[28] As business

Now nearly 50% of Union members are white collar.

organisations grew and became more bureaucratic, white-collar workers felt impelled to create their own separate and formal representation to influence events. However, white-collar workers might have chosen to express their interests through professional or staff associations. It has been estimated that if this type of institution is included, the density of organisation by white-collar and manual workers is roughly the same.[29] The tendency to join trade unions rather than other types of institution has been affected by the limited power resources of most white-collar workers and by managerial and government policies. Bain's studies pointed to several variables affecting white-collar union growth: these included growing employment concentration and the bureaucratisation of work; economic conditions causing inflation and narrowing white-collar pay differentials; union determination to recruit and diminishing employer resistance; and government policies which at the time favoured unionisation.[30]

The following conclusions might be drawn about white-collar unions. Some are structured around a distinct marketable skill, for example, the British Airline Pilots' Association (BALPA) regards itself as a professional association as well as a trade union. Other white-collar workers aspire to the occupational controls of the professions, but few have the market-based skill to make professionalism meaningful. Some white-collar unions, such as the National Union of Teachers, are rather like industrial unions in that they recruit only schoolteachers and aspire to be the only union for such teachers. However, in this case this is prevented by the existence of a number of other teachers unions and professional associations. Other white-collar unions have strong organisation-based skills such as the Inland Revenue Staff Federation in the Civil Service. Other white-collar unions have become more like general unions. For example, NALGO began as a union for higher level white-collar employees in town halls; it then opened up to recruit lower grades; it now recruits white-collar staff very generally in the public sector and it has some members in the private sector as a result of privatisation. The proposed merger of NALGO, the National Union of Public Employees and the Confederation of Health Service Employees will create a new conglomerate organisation within the public sector. (The new union, with the name UNISON, will have a membership of 1.4 million.) The MSF Union, an amalgamation of various scientific, technical and administrative staff unions, now acts very much like a general union for white-collar and professional staff and it also organises blue-collar workers.

TRADE UNION STRUCTURE AND MEMBERSHIP

The slow, organic growth of trade unionism in Britain, based on a number of organising principles, created a complex structure of multi-unionism.

Many unions compete for members in the same job territory and many employers are faced with the need to deal with several different unions. Multi-unionism exists in that within most unionised workplaces there are two or more unions organising adjacent groups of workers and in many there are two or more unions organising the same group of workers. This complex structure has long been criticised for being unwieldy, involving much duplication of effort, and causing industrial relations and economic problems. It stands in contrast to the single-company unionism which exists within each firm in Japan, to the exclusive representation which exists within each plant in the US, and to the single unionism which is derived from the industrial sector union structure of Germany. At one time the Trades Union Congress (TUC) strove to rationalise British union structure to create the industrial unionism the TUC recommended to the postwar Germany union movement. However, the many resolutions passed by TUC conferences on rationalisation have always foundered on the practical impossibility of equitable exchanges of membership for the old craft and general unions. More recently, the value of industrial unionism has been questioned as industrial unions have been shown to be relatively powerless in the face of their industry's decline, as industrial boundaries have shifted, and as conglomerate companies develop across the old industrial divisions.

There are various ways of dealing with the problems of multi-unionism. British trade unions have proved able to operate together in national-level collective bargaining by jointly working on negotiating committees or by forming federations – like the Confederation of Shipbuilding and Engineering Unions (CSEU) – to coordinate bargaining tactics with common employers. The TUC acts to regulate membership disputes arising from multi-unionism through the Bridlington Agreement of 1939. It also encourages mergers as a means of reducing the numbers of unions and enabling unions to benefit from economies of scale. Merger has indeed always been a policy pursued by unions. The TGWU, GMB and MSF are notable examples of unions which have absorbed large numbers of other unions. However, though mergers have sometimes sought to bring together unions with similar craft or industrial interests, such as the recent merger of the print unions to form the Graphical Paper and Media Union (GPMU), they have often been based as much on expediency, with the results determined by the chance that a particular union seeking expansion happened to be at hand when a weaker union was foundering or that the political orientations of union general secretaries coincided.

Processes of union expansion and amalgamation have acted to concentrate the bulk of union membership into a few large unions, many of whom represent a complex mix of different interests. Sixty per cent of trade unionists in the UK are now members of the ten largest trade unions[31] (see

Tables 6.1 and 6.2). There are many smaller unions with long histories of sectional representation, but the weight of numbers of trade unionists is concentrated in large unions which are now best regarded as conglomerates, spanning many different labour markets and types of skill.

Table 6.1 The twenty largest trade unions in Britain, 1990

Union	Membership (000s)
Transport & General Workers Union	1,229
General Municipal & Boilermakers Union	933
National Association of Local Government Officers	744
Amalgamated Engineering Union	702
Manufacturing Science & Finance Union	653
National Union of Public Employees	579
Union of Shop Distributive & Allied Workers	362
Electrical Electronic Telecommunications & Plumbing Union	367
Royal College of Nursing	293
Graphical Paper and Media Union	288
Union of Construction Allied Trades & Technicians	207
Confederation of Health Service Employees	203
Union of Communication Workers	201
Banking Insurance & Finance Union	171
National Union of Teachers	169
National Communication Union	155
Civil & Public Services Association	123
National Association of Schoolmasters / Union of Women Teachers	120
National Union of Rail, Maritime, and Transport Workers	118
National Union of Civil & Public Servants	113

Source: Trades Union Congress Annual Report (1990) and Annual Report of Certification Officer (1990).

The emergence of such conglomerates and the reduction in the number of smaller unions has still left British trade union representation complex and has not reduced problems of multiunionism. Such problems include: jurisdictional disputes which from time to time occur as to which union organises which group of workers; demarcation disputes as to which union members can do which job (a problem that persists especially on the divide between production and maintenance workers); and collective bargaining ineffi-

Table 6.2 The concentration of union membership

Number of members	Number of unions	Membership (000s)	Number of unions (%)	Membership of all unions (%)
Under 100	48	2	15.5	0.02
100–499	73	19	23.6	0.2
500–999	19	14	6.1	0.1
1,000–2,499	49	81	15.9	0.8
2,500–4,999	27	93	8.7	0.9
5,000–9,999	18	123	5.8	1.2
10,000–14,999	5	61	1.6	0.6
15,000–24,999	12	230	3.9	2.3
25,000–49,999	24	876	7.8	8.6
50,000–99,999	7	496	2.3	4.9
100,000–249,999	13	2,032	4.2	20
250,000 and more	10	6,131	3.2	60.4
*Membership unknown	4		1.3	
All	309	10,158	100	100

Source: Department of Employment Gazette, June 1991.

ciencies which arise from a number of unions pursuing different objectives and claims. Concentration has in fact led to a smaller number of general type unions competing aggressively with one another for membership.

To avoid some of the problems of multi-unionism, in recent years employers have pursued new polices. Those who have recognised unions for the first time or who have opened new plants on greenfield sites have gone for so-called single-union agreements. A few employers, already with a number of unions, have sought to reduce the number to one and so to gain the benefits of single-unionism.[32] Where this has not been possible, employers have increasingly insisted on so-called single-table bargaining, namely dealing with their unions through a joint committee and negotiating a single agreement which covers all of them. The TUC and the unions themselves have supported this latter way of dealing with multi-unionism and in practice this is likely to be the most significant.[33]

The membership of employee institutions

The total membership of all employee institutions is hard to gauge, for there are no national figures combining trade union and professional and staff association membership. As many as 2 million people may belong to the various staff associations and professional associations.[34] However, more detailed data is available on the membership of trade unions since they have to notify their membership to the government's Certification Officer.

Figure 6.1 charts the growth of trade union membership in UK from 1900 to more or less the present day. Fluctuations in union membership can be seen with peaks and troughs very much reflecting the business cycle. Thus membership grew in the 1910s, through the economic recovery from the mid-1930s onwards, and in the 1960s and 1970s; the major economic recessions of the 1920s and 1980s caused the substantial loss of members through high unemployment. The density of union membership, i.e. union coverage of potential membership (expressed in Figure 6.2), rose from 11.2 per cent in 1892 to 23 per cent just before the First World War. In 1920 it stood at 45.2 per cent, but fell to 22.6 per cent by 1933. Union density then increased steadily and in 1948 was up to 45.5 per cent of the employed population (excluding employers, the self-employed, members of the armed forces and the unemployed). It hovered at around 43 and 44 per cent for many years before rising from the late 1960s onwards to a peak of 56.1 per cent in 1978. From then onwards, it fell to 46.3 per cent of the employed population in 1987 and since then has fallen even further. (It should be noted that density figures are somewhat lower if one calculates density in terms of the working population, including the unemployed: such a calculation gives a peak of 53.4 per cent in 1979 and 41.0 per cent in 1987. Density is lower still if one uses sample survey methods such as the National Labour Force survey, which showed a density of 39 per cent in 1989.)[35]

Trade union density rose between the late 1960s and the late 1970s as a result of a combination of factors. Important among these were the still relatively low unemployment during most of those years, high price inflation and threats to real wage, rising differentials of union over non-union members, and a political and legal environment which was not overtly hostile to, or which positively encouraged, union membership. Other factors that may have boosted union membership were the growth of the public sector and, in the case of white-collar workers, as discussed above, fears that their wage and employment situation was deteriorating and that there might be remedies from union membership. In these circumstances, employers were prepared to recognise and deal with unions and to allow union membership to spread to new groups such as managerial staff.[36] Indeed, by being prepared to enter into closed-shop arrangements and to deduct union dues at source through 'check-off' arrangements, managements helped unions consolidate their position.[37]

The advent of mass unemployment in the 1980s and the reduction of the workforce in manufacturing industry which accompanied it, had obvious

Table 6.3 Union density in Great Britain, selected years 1948 onwards

Year	Male	Female	Total
1948	56.2	24.5	45.5
1950	54.7	24.0	44.3
1955	55.3	24.5	44.5
1960	53.9	25.3	44.0
1965	52.3	26.1	43.0
1966	51.8	25.6	42.4
1967	53.4	26.3	43.6
1968	53.7	27.2	43.9
1969	55.0	28.5	45.1
1970	59.0	31.2	48.5
1971	59.6	31.1	48.8
1972	60.4	32.4	49.6
1973	60.0	32.9	49.4
1974	61.2	34.1	50.4
1975	62.7	36.4	52.0
1976	64.7	38.3	54.0
1977	66.2	39.4	55.3
1978	68.0	39.1	56.1
1979	66.9	40.4	55.8
1980	65.0	39.9	54.5
1981	64.6	40.6	54.4
1982	63.3	39.9	53.3
1983	62.3	39.3	52.3
1984	59.1	38.0	49.8
1985	58.3	37.3	49.0
1986	56.5	36.2	47.4
1987	55.2	35.7	46.3

Source: J. Waddington, 'Trade Union Membership in Britain 1980–1987', *British Journal of Industrial Relations* (1992); Department of Employment Gazette, June 1991.
Note: The denominator for calculating density excludes the self-employed, members of the armed forces and the registered unemployed.

negative implications for trade union membership. Trade unions have seen and are seeing the decline of many of their traditionally organised industries, not just in manufacturing but also in the public sector, and the shift in economic activity to the less well-organised and more difficult to recruit service sectors. However, other factors in the 1980s have reduced trade

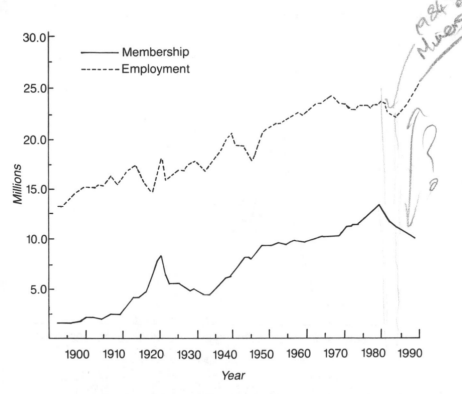

Figure 6.1 Trade union membership and employment in the UK, 1892–90
Source: Historical Abstract of Labour Statistics; Department of Employment Gazette, June 1971; A. Carruth and R. Disney, 'Where Have Two Million Trade Union Members Gone?', *Economica* (1988); J. Waddington, 'Trade Union Membership in Britain 1980–1987', *British Journal of Industrial Relations* (1992).

union membership and density. Some of these have also been economic, such as the fall in inflation in the 1980s and the decline in the wage differential which many union workers have enjoyed over non-union workers. Other factors have been more political. The Thatcher government removed many supports for trade unions and was seen to set an anti-union example. The labour legislation, which will be described in detail in Chapter 10, has led to the abolition of many closed-shop arrangements and has progressively weakened unions' bargaining power.[38] Also, the government's rejection of incomes policies meant that unions seemed less important to many potential recruits. In addition, new employer policies and strategies, which will be discussed in detail in Chapter 9, may have reduced the attractiveness of union membership.[39] Despite these forces, however, unions continue to cover a substantial proportion of the working population

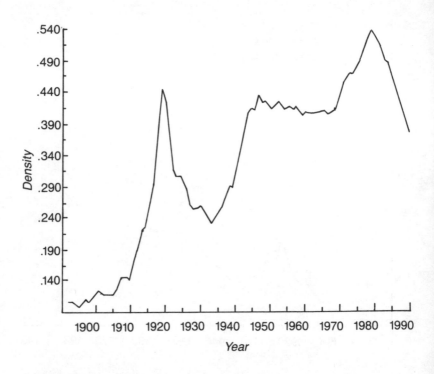

Figure 6.2 Union density in Great Britain, 1982–90
Source: Historical Abstract of Labour Statistics; Department of Employment Gazette, June 1971; A. Carruth and R. Disney, 'Where Have Two Million Trade Union Members Gone?', *Economica* (1988); J. Waddington, 'Trade Union Membership in Britain 1980–1987', *British Journal of Industrial Relations* (1992).

of the UK. Overall trade union density in the UK is not as high as it is in Sweden (where unions have a role in administering unemployment benefit and job programmes) some of the other Scandinavian countries or Australia, but it is higher than is found in Germany, France or the USA.

Average figures of union density disguise many variations. In 1987, 55 per cent of men were organised in trade unions as opposed to 36 per cent of women, though taking a long-term perspective over the last twenty years the ratio of female to male trade union density has risen. In 1987, 53.9 per cent of manual workers were organised in trade unions as opposed to 40.2 per cent of white-collar workers, though again the ratio of white-collar to blue-collar density has risen.

The lower organisation of women relates in part to the fact that much female employment is part-time and in part to the tendency for female

less women - pt time + smaller establishment where it is harder recr

Table 6.4 Comparative trade union density

Country	1970	1975	1980	1985	1988
United Kingdom	49.7	53.6	56.3	50.5	46.1
Australia	50.2	56.0	56.4	56.5	53.4
Canada	31.1	34.4	35.1	35.9	34.6
France	22.3	22.8	19.0	16.3	12.0
Germany (FR)	37.9	41.7	42.9	44.0	40.1
Italy	36.3	47.2	49.3	42.0	39.6
Japan	35.1	34.4	31.1	28.9	26.8
Sweden	64.2	82.1	89.5	94.2	96.1
United States	30.0	29.1	24.7	18.0	16.4

Source: OECD, *Employment Outlook* (Paris, 1991).
Note: It should be noted that different countries have different methods of recording membership and that slightly different denominators are used for different countries. For France and Italy, membership is expressed over those in employment, as it is for the US for 1985 and 1988.

employment to be concentrated in smaller establishments and in the less well-organised service industries. However, women such as schoolteachers and nurses are well organised. Industries with high levels of density are electricity, coal mining, the railways and other transport industries; those with low levels of density are distribution, entertainments and miscellaneous services. Industry differences in union organisation are illustrated in Table 6.5.

One major factor which helps place industries at the top or bottom of Table 6.5 is establishment size. On the whole, if employment is concentrated, then it is very much easier for employee institutions to become established and to maintain their organisation. The traditionally well-organised motor car plants, steel works and coal mines have heavily concentrated workforces, whereas in construction, agriculture, distribution and catering, employees are scattered and harder to organise.[40]

UNION GOVERNMENT AND ADMINISTRATION

How are employee institutions administered and governed? Many of the problems surrounding the maintenance of formal organisations mentioned in Chapters 3 and 4 apply, but with the added complication that the organisations' members are both the rulers and the main resource. In order to survive, independent employee institutions must gain their members' loyalty and subscriptions by acting on their behalf. However, to achieve

Table 6.5 Union density by industry, 1987

Industry	Union density (%)
Electricity	98.2
Coal mining	97.9
Railways	96.2
Gas	94.5
Water	94.2
Cotton and man-made fibres	93.4
Post and telecommunications	91.7
Sea transport	91.5
Printing and publishing	86.0
Air transport	83.1
Port and inland water transport	82.7
Local government and education	82.6
Road transport	76.6
National government	75.8
Health services	72.9
Metals and engineering	68.6
Glass	66.4
Footwear	65.8
Food, drink and tobacco	62.3
Bricks, building materials and pottery	55.9
Chemicals	54.6
Insurance, banking and finance	53.8
Other textiles	39.0
Leather, fur and clothing	38.6
Other manufacturing	34.4
Other mining and quarrying	33.2
Paper and board	30.7
Construction	29.8
Lumber and furniture	24.9
Distribution	13.0
Entertainment and miscellaneous services	7.7

Source: J. Waddington, 'Trade Union Membership in Britain, 1980–1987', *British Journal of Industrial Relations* (1992).

any success against rival interests, the institutions need to unite and co-ordinate their members' behaviour in a way that will require some member sacrifices and will curtail individual freedom. Some coercion lies behind the maintenance of any formal organisation. In self-governing institutions the question of who has the power to call for member sacrifices, and in pursuit of what policies, is a live issue.

Like most self-governing institutions, those for employees have constitutions designed to make the executive responsive to members' wishes. A broad model is that members are grouped into branches and elect their own branch committees. Through their branches members elect delegates who represent their branches on higher-level committees and who are sent to the annual conference chaired by the general secretary, or in some cases, a president. This determines policy by debating and voting on policy resolutions submitted through the branches. To implement policy and act for the institution between conferences there is an executive committee, which operates through a staff of full-time officers headed by the general secretary or president. Different employee institutions vary in their detailed interpretation of this broad model; for example, some conferences are biannual and large unions, such as the TGWU and the GMBU, are usually subdivided into specialised trade or regional groups with conferences and executives of their own, but all adopt some constitution of this form.

How trade unions should behave and whether or not they are democratic institutions has been a subject of considerable debate. Those on the left-wing of politics, who are sympathetic to trade unions, have traditionally called for the decentralisation of power within trade unions and the greater accountability of union executives to delegate conferences. This is seen as a way to prevent oligarchical tendencies, to reduce the influence of full-time officers who have to make accommodations with employers and government interests, and instead to increase the influence of lay activists who are less likely to be committed to established methods.[41] Those on the right wing of politics call for 'responsible' trade unionism, which they feel is in line with the moderate majority in trade unions. They call for postal ballots to be used both for the election of senior officials and for decision to strike. This is in the belief that secret ballots will show that militant leaders are often out of touch with members or will give conservative union leaders the backing of the less active, more conservative members, bypass-ing more radical lay activists.[42] Significant changes in the law in the 1980s, requiring more elections and balloting, will be discussed in Chapter 10.

Some variations in existing trade union constitutions relate to the vary-ing bases of organisation discussed earlier in this chapter. The governing structure of the craft unions reflects the craftsmen's old control of local labour markets and a self-confident control of their own officials. Craft unions have been more likely to decentralise many decision-making powers to local or district levels, and full-time officials are likely to be elected and subject to periodic re-election by the membership. For example, the Engineers' Union is often held up as the union with a very democratic constitution: it has an elaborate separation of powers between a powerful president, a general secretary, a national executive committee, district committees, an annual conference, a final appeals court and all-elected officials. Clegg notes that this parallels the structure of federal and state government in the US, with checks and balances between executive, legislative and judicial bodies.[43] However, despite these formal structures of government and representative democracy, in recent years direct participation in the branch life of the union has declined and this has tended to strengthen the power of national full-time officers.

In contrast, power in the general and industrial unions has tended to be more centralised. The members of the old general and industrial unions did not have the skill to regulate their local labour markets and such a strong incentive to be so directly involved. In addition, the high labour turnover of unskilled members and the mix of different job interests often made participation in branch life more difficult for them than for the craftsmen. Their unions developed centralised structures of government, relying heavily on a staff of paid officials who were sometimes appointed rather than elected and, if elected, were less likely to be subject to re-election. The staff-based general secretary was likely to be more powerful than the conference-based president. Nevertheless, to cope with the large and sprawling membership of such unions, trade-group subdivisions were usually added to branch and regional structures to give more channels through which members could influence policy-making. Thus the TGWU takes decisions about union rules and general union government at regional and national level, but decisions about collective bargaining are decentralised to trade groups such as motor cars, the docks and bus transport. Workers in these industries have had considerable independence from, and control over, their officials, reflecting their strong strategic position within their union.

Over the last quarter-century enterprise- and company-level structures have developed more prominence within union government. Trade unionists with organisation-based skills, such as the railwaymen and some civil servants, relate best to enterprise groupings. Most white-collar unions have workplace branches and unions such as the MSF, pursuing its policy of growth by merger, attracted many recruits by guaranteeing considerable autonomy to company sections or groups within the union. With the development of more formal workplace and enterprise bargaining for manual workers in the 1970s and 1980s (see Chapter 9), many manual unions also adjusted their structures to place greater emphasis on workplace branches and to give enterprise-based shop stewards a more prominent role in their union's activities. These developments have tended to make British unions more responsive to their workplace-based membership. On the other hand, legal changes and liabilities have tended to work in the opposite direction to centralise authority. Equally, higher unemployment in the early 1980s and 1990s and managerial counter-offensives have also tended to shift the power from local and domestic to national trade unionism.[44] In the future it seems that these conflicting tendencies will continue: legal requirements and pressures to maintain the union as an organisation will make for a concentration of power at the top; on the other hand, in terms of bargaining about pay and conditions, reflecting employer policies of internalisation, power will stay with the domestic union.

In the case of the professional associations, there is also great diversity as to how they run their affairs. Some of the larger ones, such as the RCN, have elaborate governmental and administrative structures and because of their size have similar problems of control and accountability. However, some of the smaller, more specialist associations are able to exist with less complex structures and yet maintain high levels of commitment and involvement. This would apply to organisations as diverse as the Hospital Consultants and Specialists Association at one end of the spectrum and more trade union-type associations such as the British Airline Pilots Association and Actors' Equity at the other end of the spectrum. In some ways these smaller associations can operate like some of the original, more primitive, direct democracies of the old craft unions.

To summarise, the structures of union government vary. The differences can often be linked to the original bases of organisation but union constitutions have also adjusted over time to reflect changing power-bases within the unions and changes in the level of collective bargaining. As constitutions not only reflect, but help to entrench the distribution of power in institutions, as trade unions usually contain a complex mix of pressures towards different policies, and as many within and without the trade union movement take an interest in the policies which are finally adopted, we can be sure that trade union constitutions will continue to attract attention. Much of the debate on union government is conducted in terms of the emotive word 'democracy'. However, democracy is a concept that can mean many things. For some, democracy requires the use of individual, postal ballots rather than votes taken at branch meetings, even if this voting technique serves to reduce the influence of active trade unionists and entrench the hegemony of union officials. For others, union democracy means pluralism and requires a two-party system or some degree of factionalism among the minority who take an active interest in the details of union affairs, so that full-time officials are subject to constant challenge and the membership has a clear choice between different policies at elections. This sort of factionalism, usually based on left v. right divisions, has been strong in unions such as the TGWU and the AEU. For others, democracy means direct participation in the trade union at the level where key decisions for the members are often taken, mainly at workplace level. This direct participation and democracy is seen as being the most meaningful for the members. For others the debates about democracy are a red herring. These argue that union officials at all levels are accountable to, and constrained by, their membership to some degree. They maintain that unions operate within constitutions that are as democratic as are found in most institutions in British society and that, because unions are only as strong as their members' support, union officials cannot in practice pursue wildly unpopular policies for very long.[45]

THE TUC AND INTERNATIONAL FEDERATIONS

The existence of union federations and joint working to coordinate trade unions in industry or local-level collective bargaining has already been mentioned. Employee institutions also form national federations to provide mutual services and to coordinate approaches to government. In the UK the main federation is the TUC, which has in membership the vast majority of organised workers. There is no significant formal federation for professional associations. The TUC in 1990 consisted of seventy-four trade unions with a total membership of 8.2 million workers, which constituted more than 80 per cent of all trade union members.[46]

The TUC was initially formed in 1868 by trade unions who wanted an annual meeting for the discussion of union affairs and the coordination of lobbies of Parliament to press for changes in law to protect trade unions. It has remained essentially a service organisation to its membership of autonomous trade unions ever since. As the trade union movement grew, the TUC slowly adjusted to include the newer unions. The new general and industrial unions affiliated as they developed and from the mid-twentieth century the TUC has recruited significant numbers of the white-collar unions. At the present time the main organisations outside the TUC are the Electrical Electronic Telecommunications & Plumbing Union (EETPU), which was expelled over a disagreement on policy about recruitment and no-strike agreements, and the RCN, which has never been a member. (The EETPU might rejoin in the guise of the new AEEU union created by merger with the Engineers.) The TUC gives British trade unions unity within one central national federation that does not exist in countries such as France or Italy. However, it is not as strong as the national federations in Germany and Sweden where, as we saw in Chapter 4, such federations have developed more extensive relations with national governments and employers' federations.

Member unions send delegates to the annual Congress each September. In between times, a General Council acts as the executive committee of the TUC. Its composition attempts to reflect the TUC's diverse membership, with the larger unions automatically allotted the majority of seats, but with representation also for smaller unions and women. The administration of TUC business is led by a General Secretary, elected by Congress 'for life', and an appointed staff at Congress House, organised into departments to service the various sub-committees of the General Council and to provide services such as educational courses and advice on health and safety.

Although there were attempts in the 1920s to give the TUC a stronger, coordinating role in trade union affairs, with the failure of the General Strike in 1926 and subsequent abortive talks with employers at national level, the TUC reverted to the servicing role it has held for most of its history. As we have suggested, it has never succeeded in acting for its members in direct bargaining with employers. In part this has been because of the opposition of constituent unions and in part because of employer refusal to enter into national bargaining. Instead the TUC administers the Bridlington principles, regulating inter-union membership disputes through a TUC disputes procedure, it services a network of inter-union committees, liaises with locally based inter-union Trades Councils, acts in consultation with or lobbies government, and represents British unions in international forums.

In the 1960s and 1970s the growth of government intervention in the economy and in employment affairs increased the significance of the TUC. In 1962 the government established the tripartite National Economic Development Council (NEDC). The TUC provided the employee side of this and all subsequent tripartite institutions. Through the 1970s the TUC produced an annual economic review, detailing and forecasting national economic trends and advocating economic policies of an expansionary, protective and interventionist nature. As governments moved to intervene in wage determination through incomes policies, the TUC at times supported and at times opposed incomes restraint, but the existence of such policies always gave it a certain importance. We will see later that this importance declined in the 1980s, and the NEDC was abolished in 1992.

International confederations

International federations and confederations were first formed at the end of the nineteenth century by unions seeking to exchange information and stop strike-breaking by employers who were importing workers or exporting jobs. The first international federation was formed by printers in 1889, followed by one for miners in 1890, and later international trade secretariats were established for other workers. These international federations suffered many reverses as national trade union movements became divided by the two world wars and the Cold War. Today the main confederation is the International Confederation of Free Trade Unions (ICFTU), which has in membership over 100 trade union bodies from nearly as many countries. In addition there are a number of international trade secretariats, catering for different industries, such as transportation, metalworking and chemicals. The power of these has always been limited because of differences between national union movements, the difficulty of generating international solidarity across international boundaries and the refusal of most employers to bargain or consult internationally. Some regional federations are quite strong. In 1973 a European Trades Union Congress (ETUC) was formed from two previous groupings and it now coordinates national federations from most European countries and has established industry committees for the European unions. The ETUC has achieved some success in campaigning for cuts in hours and better holiday entitlement and for the European Social Charter. It is consulted, along with its employers' counterpart, as one of the 'social partners', and in this way it is helping to shape European social policy and labour law.[47] However, even within the European Community and emerging single market, unions have rarely been able to use their international links for more direct assistance in bargaining with employers. Despite the growth of multinational enterprises and the increasing internationalisation of much business activity, unions so far have had great difficulty in establishing permanent negotiations with companies on an international basis.[48]

CONCLUSION

Employee institutions in the UK developed slowly and organically as different groups found ways of establishing permanent institutions to further their interests. The process started when occupational groups built institutions to protect scarce, marketable skills. Professional associations and craft unions adopted closure policies, restricting entry to those with the relevant training and closing access to jobs to untrained men in order to monopolise skilled labour supply. They aimed to use this monopoly control unilaterally to dictate employment terms to their employers. Later, mass general and industrial organisations developed to cater for the less skilled worker. With much less labour-market power to exploit, these were from the start more involved in collective bargaining with employers. This often led them to adopt a more open, confrontational stance and to espouse radical, socialist changes. With their more openly political objectives they were instrumental in the formation of the Labour Party.

Workers who are skilled but whose skills are based on work experience rather than apprentice or professional training tended to develop institutions that related to the structure of their employing organisations. In other ways also it might be said that trade union structure has been shaped by employer structure. Thus, historically small craft-based firms provided the basis for skill-based unionism in the nineteenth century; the resort to employers' organisations led to an increasing centralisation of union organisation and decision making in the early twentieth century; the persistence of loose forms of corporate organisation and the weakness of employers' organisations in Britain ensured the strength of fragmented and decentralised shopfloor unionism through the first three post-Second World War decades; more recently, the development of stronger corporate structures has encouraged a more enterprise-based and enterprise-orientated trade unionism.

To manual-worker unionism was added white-collar trade unionism, especially after the Second World War. The result of slow, organic growth has been that a complex multi-unionism has been created in the UK. This has been modified to some extent by waves of mergers, such that more than two-thirds of the UK's trade unionists now belong to the ten largest unions. Many of the large unions are now open conglomerates, spanning different occupational, industrial, and company interests. The differences in tactics and organisational structure which derived from different organisational bases have been blurred. Most trade unions of any size in the UK are now affiliated to the TUC. The TUC's role has traditionally been a limited, service role towards its affiliates, though in the 1970s it was very involved in the political sphere with government. In the 1980s and 1990s it has paid more attention to developing an international role.

Trade union government has attracted considerable attention. Trade unions have formally representative constitutions within which internal power battles occur. In most unions there are tensions about policy between lay activists and full-time officials. Many also need to accommodate sectional interests within the membership. Despite some gaps between theory and practice, most British unions are democratic in their government, though in all unions there is scope for greater membership participation.

The biggest question for unions in the future is membership. The number of union members and trade union density rose substantially from the late 1960s onwards and reached an all-time peak in the late 1970s. Since then, as a result of economic, structural and political changes, membership and density have fallen considerably. If unions are to grow in the future, they need to attain higher levels of membership in areas where there are already strong and, above all, to recruit in areas where they have traditionally been weak.

7 The role of the state – an historical perspective

In the nineteenth and well into the twentieth century industrial relations in the UK appeared to have little to do with politics. Employment relations were, for the most part, sorted out between employers and employees without obvious political activity and without much intervention by politicians or government agencies. With the exception of abnormal situations, such as the two world wars and major national disputes, the government did not intervene directly in industrial relations except to provide a very basic framework of law and some protection at work for women and children.

From the late 1960s, however, industrial relations became more intertwined with politics and politics with industrial relations. All recent governments have been concerned to introduce major changes in industrial relations law and practice. Both the TUC and the CBI have favoured legislative changes that have provoked opposition from the other side. Fundamental differences in policy towards industrial relations have never been far from the centre of political debate.

This change in the level of political activity in industrial relations has stimulated an academic debate on the role of the state in employment relations. The state can be described as the institutional system of political government with a monopoly over taxation and the legitimate use of force in a society.[1] The state is not synonymous with government. Obviously the government of the day is an important part of the state, as the grouping formally invested with state power and as the representative or spokesman of the state. We take the set of state institutions to comprise the legislature (Parliament); the executive (government ministers); the judiciary; central administration (the Civil Service); the police and army, which from time to time have played an important role in industrial relations, especially in industrial disputes; local government and specialist agencies such as, in the employment field, industrial tribunals, conciliation and arbitration services, equal opportunities commissions, and health and safety inspectorates. What role do these complex institutions play in employment relations? Are they a background, neutral force merely setting the scene within which employers and employees govern their own affairs, or do they play a more positive role? To what extent are the resources of state power used by employers or by employees in pursuit of their own objectives? Why has public policy on industrial relations been so controversial within the UK?

This chapter begins the analysis of the role of the state in industrial relations by reviewing the historical development of public policy, especially labour law, and by looking at the political activities of employers and employees and the impact they have on the behaviour of state institutions. At the end it then takes up more theoretical perspectives on the role of the state. This provides an essential background for further discussion in Chapter 10 of attempts by governments to reform British industrial relations.

EARLY STATE INTERVENTION AND THE DEVELOPMENT OF LABOUR LAW

A review of early state intervention and the development of British labour law shows the state varying its approach to the regulation of employment relationships. The approach adopted in the nineteenth century was encouraged by the development of a particularly 'voluntary' form of industrial relations in the UK. Voluntarism means a preference by employers, unions and the state for the voluntary regulation of employment relations and a preference for a non-legalistic form of collective bargaining. In the British case it has meant, in particular, a suspicion of judicial intervention in industrial relations.[2] It has helped to engrain a suspicion and distrust between unions and certain state institutions which still exists today and is more evident in the UK than in many societies abroad.

In pre-industrial Britain, occupational groups that combined the functions of capital and labour were often able to gain state support. As we saw in Chapter 6, the guilds and early professional associations sought and gained political protection for their organisations and for their economic functions of price, wage and apprenticeship regulation. When the medieval guilds declined, their control of employment and trade was increasingly taken over by the state. A series of enactments empowered local magistrates to fix wages and regulate labour markets by specifying numbers of apprentices and other aspects of employment. Indeed, the dominant industrial policy in the early modern period was the establishment of some regulatory authority to perform the services formerly rendered by the craft guilds.[3] The policy of state regulation of labour and product markets did not imply support for associations nor did it usually mean equivalent treatment to masters and men. A succession of acts prohibited the formation of organisations by employees and subjected workmen who failed to fulfil their duties to their masters to criminal penalties including imprisonment. Many thousands of workers were imprisoned under the various Master and Servant Acts for crimes such as leaving or neglecting their work, and the legislation was widely used in periods of social upheaval.

Paternalistic state intervention in employment and trade came under attack in Britain with the rise of the new entrepreneurial class of the Industrial Revolution. Petitions from workers for the enforcement or up-dating of the regulatory laws were met by arguments from the new masters that they needed freedom to use new methods and machines, freedom to recruit cheaper unapprenticed labour and freedom to conform with market rates if they, and the economy, were to prosper. The state, in the form of magistrates and Parliament, responded by dismantling the old regulatory laws. Thus, by the early nineteenth century, state regulation had been replaced by *laissez-faire* and the state refused direct intervention in the regulation of the labour or product markets. In place of the old paternalistic policies of state regulation was put the doctrine of freedom of movement, freedom of contract and the notion that free and equal individuals should regulate their own affairs by concluding voluntary contracts. In the employment field, even when no contract had been written down or verbally agreed, it was argued that the courts could interpret the terms of an individual's employment contract in the light of normal custom, and could therefore resolve, by litigation, any dispute between employer and employee. Herein lay the origins of what in Chapter 2 we called the liberal individualist approach to industrial relations.

The shift in public policy from state regulation to *laissez-faire* had a profound effect on the development of industrial relations. The Webbs argued that this shift in policy, stimulated by employer pressure, had the direct, though unintended consequence, of first stimulating trade union consciousness:

> So long as each section of workers believed in the intention of the governing class to protect their trade from the results of unrestricted competition, no community of interest arose. It was a change of indus-trial policy on the part of the government that brought all trades into line, and for the first time produced what can properly be called a trade union movement.[4]

Employees, faced with employer-dictated terms of employment, did not readily accept the doctrine of freedom of contract. The doctrine represented an advance from feudal ideas of servitude, but the assumption that the employment contract expressed a free bargain between equally powerful parties was a legal fiction. Inequality between employer and employee was embedded in contract law because the service sold by an employee was thereafter regarded as his employer's property, to be protected as such by the full weight of the law.[5] Employees, therefore, still sought protection against employer-dictated terms of employment, but were now deprived of their old channel of protest to the state. They turned, therefore, to develop more independent forms of trade union activity, but they found their attempts to mobilise group pressure attacked through the courts. Between 1858 and 1875, thousands of employees were prosecuted under the Master and Servant Acts and many trade unionists were imprisoned.[6] The old criminal sanctions against groups of employees had been strengthened by the Anti-Combination Acts (1799 and 1800) but even when these had been repealed in 1824 and 1825, unions were still liable in the courts for conspiracy and action in restraint of trade.

Despite the hostile legal climate, trade unions continued to develop. With their continued existence and pressure, the most repressive anti-union legislation was gradually removed during the course of the nineteenth century. However, the methods used to grant trade unions scope to operate within the law took a unique form in Britain compared with other countries.

As trade unions developed, the first stage, throughout Europe, was to make the formation of employee organisations lawful. Legislation in the UK in the early nineteenth century and in the late nineteenth century in Germany, France and Italy, granted some freedom of association. Unions henceforward were free to exist, although their activities were severely restricted. The next step was to legalise trade union activities and permit the industrial bargaining or political pressure needed if unions were to regulate employment conditions. In most countries this was to be achieved through laws which clearly specified trade union rights. Thus, in European countries, union rights were incorporated in constitutional provisions or in laws granting unions a clear legal status, and codes of positive labour law had their origins. In the UK, however, there was no legislation to codify union rights to organise, strike or participate in decisions affecting employment. In the absence of positive legislation specifying trade union rights and the trade union role, British unions operated lawfully because Parliament enacted *immunities* designed to protect them from the prevailing judge-made laws.[7] Well into the twentieth century, there was a pattern, in which periodic attempts were made by the judiciary to impose penalties on certain types of union activity through their interpretation of the law on breach of contract or restraint of trade. These judicial challenges were then followed by union pressure on Parliament to grant statutory immunities to protect unions from the new, judge-made liabilities. In this way trade unions were taken outside of, or given protection from, many aspects of the law, especially the common law. Thus, the system of immunities recognised that trade unions had a unique function and that some protection from the normal operation of the law was necessary if they were to represent their members. In Britain, then, voluntarism meant a freedom *from* the law and not a freedom *to* have certain things under the law; it meant negative immunities rather than positive rights.

The battle between unions and the judiciary over the scope of trade unions activities involved a number of famous cases. The judgment in *Hornby v. Close* in 1867 found that, although the repeal of the Combination Acts had made unions technically lawful, union objectives were still illegal under common law being deemed to be in 'restraint of trade'. This case occurred at a time when there were widespread calls from the press and Conservative politicians that 'something be done' about growing union influence, and the first Royal Commission to investigate trade unions was set up in the same year in 1867. Unions responded by mobilising a political defence. A group of union leaders from the craft unions presented liberal collectivist arguments to the Royal Commission, emphasising their respectability and the social value of trade unionism as a form of collective *laissez-faire*.[8] In 1868 the first Trades Union Congress was held to organise joint representation of the union case to Parliament. The unions' political lobby was aided by the extension of the right to vote to most urban male workers in 1867. The campaign achieved the Trade Union Act of 1871, which gave trade unions protection from the 'restraint of trade' doctrine. In 1875 two other major, reforming acts were passed. The Employers and Workmen Act removed the threat of imprisonment from employees in breach of contract of employment, and the Conspiracy and Protection of Property Act gave unions immunity from the crime of conspiracy when the combination was 'in contemplation or furtherance of a trade dispute'. This creation of immunities set a precedent for future labour law in Britain.

The growth of new unionism from the 1880s increased the concern of the business and propertied classes about union activities and provoked a new wave of judgments against trade unions based on civil, rather than criminal, liability. Judges found that strike action could be construed as a *civil* wrong, on the grounds that union objectives were unlawful, and the injured party could therefore claim damages. The most famous case was the *Taff Vale* judgment of 1901, which awarded a railway company damages and costs against the railwaymen's union. This award against a trade union, rather than against an individual union official, undermined the apparent legal status granted to unions over the previous forty years. The new legal threat served as a considerable stimulus to the formation of the Labour Representation Committee in 1900 and the election of twenty-nine Labour MPs in 1906. The incoming Liberal government was persuaded to pass the

1906 Trades Disputes Act which gave unions immunity against judge-made civil liability, especially over breaches of the contract of employment.

However, as unions succeeded, by political lobbying, in re-establishing their ability to act in industrial bargaining, the courts struck another blow against their political activities. In the *Osborne* judgment (1909) the Law Lords decided that trade unions could not use their funds to support the new Labour Party. Again it was another statutory intervention by Parliament which reversed this. The Trade Union Act (1913) legalised the creation of political funds by trade unions, but only after the approval of a ballot of union members and as long as individual members had the right to contract out of paying the political levy.

These conflicts between unions and the courts were followed by a long period of inaction in which both the courts and Parliament essentially left trade unions and industrial relations alone. In the wake of the General Strike, a restrictive Trade Disputes Act of 1927 introduced measures against sympathetic strikes and political action and introduced contracting in to the political levy. However, this act was not used,[9] because in a period of high unemployment it was not necessary, and from the late 1920s onwards public policy supported a system of industrial relations that was remarkably unencumbered by law. It was not really until the mid-1960s that intervention began, when the judges again intervened in a number of cases.[10] The liabilities which were discovered in these judgments were removed, as they had been in the past, by the state stepping in with the 1965 Trade Disputes Act.

Thus, Kahn-Freund was to argue: 'there is perhaps no major country in the world in which the law has played a less significant role in the shaping of relations than in Great Britain and in which the law has less to do with labour relations'.[11] As Flanders put it, the British industrial relations system was 'voluntary' not only in the sense that it relied on collective bargaining rather than law to establish the individual terms and conditions of employment, but also (unlike, for instance, the US and much of continental Europe) because collective agreements were not legally enforceable.[12]

This 'voluntary' approach also extended to individual employment matters where, with a few exceptions, it was also felt best to keep the law out (see Chapter 9). Before we turn to the reasons for this voluntarism and for its decline, we need to review the political activities of unions and employers.

THE POLITICAL ACTIVITIES OF EMPLOYERS AND UNIONS

Many commentators, unions and employers included, have drawn a distinction between (a) industrial activity such as collective bargaining, (b) pressure group activity such as lobbying, and (c) political activity such as direct involvement in the political process and the making of political choices. They have argued that union and employer involvement in the two former is legitimate, but not so in the latter. However, this is a difficult distinction to maintain both analytically and practically. Both employers and organised groups of employees are bound to be political, for they inevitably have an interest in political decisions that affect them. 'A completely non-political trade unionism hardly makes sense, and would today be about as unrealistic as a motor industry which claimed to have nothing to do with roads'.[13] The demand that certain large pressure groups keep out of politics may be good propaganda by opposing interests, but, if seriously meant, must rest on unrealistic liberal individualistic perspectives.

Social groups seek political influence in a number of ways. If group members have strong social contacts with people in political power, they will use the most direct method of personally influencing political decisions and will lobby the executive. Groups with less access to those in power will attempt to sway Parliament or public opinion by more indirect methods.

The first trade unions had no access to political decision-makers and initially relied on demonstrations and direct action to draw attention to their political demands. However these methods were soon supplemented by political pressure on Parliament. Unions joined the lobby for universal suffrage and began to encourage and support the election of labour-minded MPs. In the period from 1900 to 1906 trade unions formed a significant part of the alliance of socialist and working men's groups that eventually established the Labour Party. Today unions sponsor Labour MPs; they provide the majority of Labour Party funds; they control a large part of the vote at Labour Party conference; and they play a significant part in the election of the Labour Party national executive and leadership.[14]

Despite the close institutional ties between the unions and the Labour Party, a division separating the industrial and political wings of the Labour movement, has traditionally been maintained. Unions tended to use their political contacts for the narrow defence of their industrial activity, leaving most of the more general policy formation to the politicians. The sponsored MPs were usually used as spokesmen on any issue that directly affected a trade union's activities, but were not mandated on wider-ranging politics and unions traditionally concentrated their political lobbying on the executive and Whitehall. This policy changed with the development of proposals for trade union legislation from the late 1960s. Union-sponsored MPs threatened to vote against the Labour government's proposals for more restrictive legislation and this marked the start of a period in which trade unions sought to be far more actively involved in Labour Party policy-making.

The political activity of employers is usually less visible. Only recently have companies been legally bound to disclose their 'political funds' and there is not the same open, institutional link between business and the Conservative Party. Nevertheless, all employers' associations, most large companies and many medium-sized firms can make a case heard within Parliament by using MPs, usually from the Conservative Party, as consultants or associates and as spokesmen. The CBI, large employers' associations, and many large companies maintain close contacts with the executive and Whitehall.

Thus both unions and employers seek political influence. The political power they can muster in their own cause is difficult to assess with accuracy. Both sides can use constitutional pressure through Parliament, they can lobby the executive, or mount publicity campaigns. The publicity campaigns of unions tend to feature demonstrations, mass meetings, and marches. Employers' publicity campaigns favour the use of the communications media by mass advertising or by funding events to attract media attention, like opinion surveys. Both unions and employers have also adopted policies of non-cooperation against legislation they opposed.[15]

The relative political power of employers and trade unions is hard to assess. Objective studies of political power are difficult to conduct because power is difficult to measure and the exercise of power may be unseen. As a result, discussions of the political power of unions and employers readily degenerate to propaganda, with the 'other side' invariably being portrayed as 'too powerful'. In the case of the CBI, it may have influence on detailed technical matters, but its broader influence is more problematic.[16] Under the Thatcher government in the 1980s its relationship with the government was rather hesitant and cool and its influence declined as the government preferred not to work through such intermediate institutions. In the case of the TUC, its power rose in the 1960s and 1970s,[17] but declined precipitately in the 1980s when the government refused to consult with it. It is therefore difficult to gauge the relative political power of employers and trade unions, not least because studies of employer or union impact on particular policies cannot deal with the important question of 'invisible power'. The ability to 'mobilise bias', i.e. to prevent certain policies even reaching the agenda of debate and to suffuse other proposals with legitimacy, is a powerful if subtle tool.[18] Such ideological influence is extraordinarily difficult to assess, but in this context the link between business interests and the ownership of the press and media needs to be taken into account. Several studies of television and press news have suggested a bias against trade unions which should be of some significance in assessing the political influence of employers and employees.[19] Indeed, it could be argued that overt attempts to exercise power should often be seen as evidence of a lack of covert or invisible power. On the other hand, the relative lack of attempts to exercise overt power may indicate possession of real power.

Thus employers and trade unions have an interest in, and access to political decision making. Nevertheless, traditionally they deliberately sought to exclude the state from British industrial relations, and state intervention only began to increase in a substantial way from the 1970s onwards.

THE PERIOD OF VOLUNTARISM: COLLECTIVE BARGAINING AND THE WELFARE COMPROMISE

The period of voluntarism, which lasted for many years in Britain, meant that neither employers nor unions relied much on the state and its institutions to achieve their objectives. What were the reasons for this voluntarism?

Reasons for union commitment to voluntarism

In the nineteenth and early twentieth centuries the general and industrial unions did press for legislation on individual issues like the protection of women and children, health and factory safety, and the removal of the worst injustices of truck (i.e. payment in goods or credit, rather than cash). However, as the new unions developed their collective bargaining strength they increasingly adopted the preference of the craft trade unions for industrial bargaining rather than political campaigns for legislation as their method of achieving results. The TUC constitution adopted in 1922 did contain a commitment to seek minimum wage legislation, but this was never seriously pursued. Sporadic calls after the Second World War for legislation to enforce a shorter working week and for more weeks' paid holiday never developed into a concerted political campaign. British unions have relied on collective bargaining as their favoured method for improving employment conditions, and this contrasts sharply with the more politically orientated union movements in Europe. In France, for example, unions have over the years lobbied for and obtained statute laws on hours of work, holidays with pay, minimum wage levels and many other aspects of employment. In many countries on the continent the law is used to consolidate gains made by bargaining. British unions did not usually seek to legitimate or support their collective bargaining achievements by legislation. Instead the law has only been used where union organisation was weak or non-existent, for example, among juveniles, women and in selected low-paid industries (see Chapter 9). When laws on individual employee rights of the European type began to appear in the UK from the mid-1960s, the stimulus came from outside the British union movement.

Why have British unions not sought state support for minimum terms and conditions of employment when this is a common tactic for union movements elsewhere? Wedderburn and Phelps Brown suggest the reason lies in the historical development of the British union movement in the crucial formative period of the late nineteenth century.[20] In this period, when the relationship between the unions and the law was evolving, the UK had a relatively strong labour movement, but its strength was entirely industrial not political, and it did not have a well-developed political counterpart and the right to vote was only slowly extending to male workers. Unions gained industrial bargaining functions prior to the full extension of the franchise and before unions were able to exercise much political muscle. When they first began to act on the political front, their demands were pragmatic, not ideological, and were processed through a Liberal–Labour alliance, not a strong or cohesive working-class party. The Labour Party was not established with a political platform until 1906, and even then it was less socialist or ideological than the socialist parties on the continent. The Labour Party was an uneasy alliance of radical socialists and trade unions; many of the latter were notably 'moderate' – i.e. holding liberal collectivist values and not strongly committed to radical ideologies or to the desirability of major social change. These tensions on political policy were exacerbated by the defeats suffered by the left with the collapse in 1921 of the so-called Triple Alliance of miners, railwaymen and transport workers and the defeat inflicted on the TUC in 1926 when the government clearly outmanoeuvred the unions' General Strike. These were important factors in the unions' retreat from attempts to achieve major political changes.

Union suspicion of legal intervention was heightened by the difficult, if not hostile, relationship between trade unions and the British judiciary in the early development of British labour law.[21] The dominance of judge-made law in Britain, particularly in the employment area, gave the judiciary a particularly significant role, and union folklore quotes many cases where judicial interpretation clearly stretched or redefined the law against union interests, the *Taff Vale* and the *Osborne* judgments being the most famous historical cases. More recently unions have pointed to judicial decisions in the 1980s, such as those in the Wapping and P&O disputes, to support the contention that judicial interpretation still moulds the law against trade unionism (see Chapter 10).

The reasons for the unusually high degree of tension between unions and the judiciary in the UK are complex. In part they relate to the narrow social class from which British judges are recruited. This has been recognised as a problem by many. Winston Churchill once argued:

> It is not good for trade unions that they should be brought in contact with the courts, and it is not good for the courts. The courts hold justly a high and unequalled prominence in respect of the world in criminal cases, and

in civil cases . . . but where class issues are involved, and where party issues are involved, it is impossible to pretend that the courts command the same degree of general confidence. On the contrary, they do not, and a very large number of our population have been led to the opinion that they are, unconsciously, no doubt, biased.[22]

In a statement, a leading judge, Lord Justice Scrutton, said:

> The habits . . . the people with whom you mix, lead you to having a certain class of ideas of such a nature that . . . you do not give as sound and accurate judgments as you would wish. This is one of the great difficulties at present with labour. Labour says 'where are your impartial judges? They all move in the same circles as the employers, and they are all educated and nursed in the same ideas as the employers'. . . . It is very difficult sometimes to be sure that you have put yourself into a thoroughly impartial position between two disputants, one of your own class and one not of your class.[23]

Another reason for trade union distrust of the judicial process derives from the common law's emphasis on notions of individual property and contractual rights which give little recognition to collective pressure group action. The training and traditions of British lawyers are orientated towards nineteenth-century liberalism. Neither the collective pressures of unions nor intervention by state agencies accord well with this tradition. However, many trade unionists would add that historically, British judges have upheld the individualist, liberal traditions more consistently against trade unions than against employers' organisations and business cartels. The traditions of British law and the historical experience of relationships between unions and the British judiciary have therefore helped deter British unions from using the law as a method for achieving their objectives.

Employer acceptance of voluntarism until the 1960s

The historical preference for voluntarism and the opposition to legal intervention was shared with employers. For the most part, employers did not favour protective labour legislation, though they acquiesced in it for special cases such as women and children. Nor did British employers seek to use the law to contain the industrial strength of trade unions nor to structure the developing bargaining relationships. Collective laws have often developed in other countries as a result of employer pressure for state aid against trade unions. In Britain, the absence of employer pressure in the late nineteenth and early twentieth centuries was because unions only affected a minority of employers and those who were affected felt able to cope with trade unionism by multi-employer bargaining through employers' associations.[24] After the General Strike and during the depression of the interwar years employers did not feel any need to take unions to court and from the end of the Second World War up to the mid-1960s they were reluctant to take unions to court because of the changed economic and political situation. Employers were not therefore concerned to make use of the legal sanctions opened up for them by the *Taff Vale* judgment of 1901 and they did not campaign either to prevent the passage of the 1906 Act or to repeal it once passed. Equally they did not choose to use the 1927 Trade Disputes Act. With the increase in foreign competition after the Second World War, the employers' main preoccupation was with shopfloor productivity and the prospect of increasing control over the shopfloor by tighter management techniques.[25] In this situation legal immunities posed less of a threat to managerial prerogatives on the shopfloor than a positive legal right such as a 'right to strike' or more active political and judicial intervention. It was only from the mid-1960s onwards, as a result of increasing competition and the growing perception of a union 'problem', that pressure from employers for restrictive legislation on strikes, picketing, the closed shop, and the enforceability of agreements emerged. This is also to be seen in the context of the weakening of the Welfare Compromise.

The Welfare Compromise

The voluntary, non-legalistic system of industrial relations was supported in the quarter-century after the Second World War by social and economic politics which established conditions under which voluntary collective bargaining was seen as broadly acceptable by unions and employers. It was the breakdown of these policies from the late 1960s onwards which threw industrial relations back into the type of political controversy that had not been seen since the beginning of the twentieth century.

The period of 'Welfare Compromise' began with the postwar Labour victory in 1945.[26] Labour won this crucial postwar election with a commitment to full employment and a Welfare State. These objectives were to be achieved by the use of Keynesian economic policies in which government acted to regulate demand and smooth the business cycle by public expenditure. The policies involved increased employment, more state expenditure on such things as education, health and housing, and rising wages. Government intervened to regulate macroeconomic variables but left the details of employment relationships to be resolved by employers and employees. The policy was a clear move away from the *laissez-faire* philosophy, which argued for no state interference and the free play of market forces. Nevertheless, it did not seriously threaten either capital or labour interests, it maintained the key levels of voluntarism in industrial relations and received the support of both business and unions for many years.

Employers supported the Welfare Compromise policy because it offered to protect them from the sloughs of the trade cycle and from the social upheaval and class strife of the interwar years. When the Conservatives returned to government in 1951, they did not abandon the Keynesian economic policies; instead, they accepted the development of a mixed economy and union leaders still found their views were listened to in Whitehall. Indeed, the most important and long-lasting institutional expression of the involvement of unions in government was established by the Macmillan government in 1962. The National Economic Development Council (NEDC) was set up to enable unions, employers, and government jointly to discuss and study problems of economic policy and growth. In this respect there was a growing trend towards corporatism, but still within an overall voluntarist set of attitudes. (We will see below that the significance of the NEDC declined in the 1980s and it was abolished in 1992.)

Unions supported the policy because they believed it enabled them to maintain their autonomy in negotiations with employers while guaranteeing their members an improved and more secure life-style because of the support for employment and improvements in welfare. Trade union leaders could remain free of government pressure and responsive to their members on the key issue of wage demands, and yet become more closely associated with government policy. Senior union leaders had experienced an involvement in the administration of government policy during the First and Second World Wars. The coalition government of the Second World War had placed Ernest Bevin, the general secretary of the TGWU, in the Cabinet as Minister of Labour and he had used this position to trade the unions' assistance in the wartime mobilisation of labour for state support in the extension of collective bargaining. With the policies of the postwar Welfare Compromise union leaders maintained their contacts in Whitehall and could encourage and participate in the extension of the welfare state without threat to their traditional collective bargaining activities.

In summary, there was a period of around a quarter-century after 1945 when there was a consensus between politicians, trade unions and employers about the form of the postwar political settlement.[27] This consensus was based on a sustained period of economic growth and relatively full employment.

THE COLLAPSE OF THE VOLUNTARY CONSENSUS

The Welfare Compromise, while it lasted, kept industrial relations away from political controversy and hence in the British voluntarist tradition.

However, strains on the policy began to show, and by the mid 1960s pressures were growing for radical changes in public policy towards trade unions.[28] There was increasing concern that a combination of full employment and trade-union wage bargaining, along with restraints on productivity, lay behind the inflationary pressures of the time. As a result, there followed various attempts by governments to establish incomes policies. Such policies have difficulty coexisting with voluntarism, and, once state institutions are concerned to regulate wage increases, a voluntary system of free collective bargaining begins to be untenable.

As governments became increasingly concerned with the international competitiveness of the British economy, other aspects of the employment relationship came under government purview on the grounds that the voluntary system was failing to satisfy national economic needs. First there were laws such as the Industrial Training Act of 1964 and the Redundancy Payments Act of 1965 designed to improve labour efficiency and labour mobility. Next came laws influenced by the individual rights legislation of continental Europe and the US, designed to provide a statutory floor of employee rights on contracts of employment, unfair dismissal, equal pay and opportunity regardless of race or sex, guaranteed pay levels and provisions for paid maternity leave. Many of these incursions into the old voluntary system of regulation were broadly bipartisan, backed by Labour and Conservative governments, and had the support of employers and trade unions. However, there were more fundamental pressures on the Welfare Compromise and the voluntary system of industrial relations with a source outside government circles.

The main questioning of the Welfare Compromise came from employers concerned that the Keynesian social and economic policies were increasingly threatening the interests of business. Employers argued that rising state expenditure burdened companies with heavy corporate taxation. Nearly full employment and the new statutory floor of individual rights after the mid-1960s (discussed in Chapter 10) increased employee power within companies and contributed to a squeeze on corporate profits. Initially, leading employers responded by attempting to increase the productivity of their labour force by renewed rationalisation and by the change in collective bargaining arrangements discussed in Chapter 9. However, some employers began to see the solution in terms of the need for political and legal changes that would reshape industrial relations in Britain.[29]

Employer dissatisfaction with the old welfare consensus policies did not lead to employer agreement on alternatives. Different sections of business developed different conceptions of desirable solutions. Many large multinational enterprises did not see a need for legal changes. They were capital-intensive and were confident that they could cope with their own labour relations by buying-out trouble or by developing bureaucratic, internalised personnel policies. In sectors like engineering small-scale businesses tended to feel far more vulnerable to rising labour costs and disruptive labour tactics. However, small-scale businesses were often still attached to *laissez-faire* policies and did not want extensive state intervention. Small-scale businesses who were most vulnerable to competition therefore called for laws which would weaken union power, but not involve intervention in the employment relationship. They sought curbs on the closed shop and on employee power to strike and picket. In contrast, larger national firms with some monopoly control over their markets, together with UK subsidiaries of multinationals in the car industry, were more interested in changes in union government and negotiating structures and the reform of collective bargaining arrangements. Different types of policy were therefore being supported by different industrial groups.

State response to these pressures was evidenced first when judges began to interpret the law more restrictively in order to curb trade unions' power to strike. Judgments in 1964 and 1969 all narrowed the protection of the old immunities and made unions more liable to labour injunctions if they struck.[30] The Labour government of the time set up the Donovan Royal Commission to investigate trade unions and employers' associations with the aim of reforming industrial relations and made an abortive attempt to introduce restrictive legislation. The Heath Conservative government of 1970–4 attempted a more comprehensive and fundamental restructuring of British industrial relations in the 1971 Industrial Relations Act, which combined legislation to reduce trade union power with attempt to reshape trade unions to fit them into more bureaucratic administrative structures. From 1974 to 1979 the Labour government, while repealing its predecessor's laws, also went ahead with its own extension of labour law, both collective and individual, and operated an incomes policy. From 1979 the Thatcher government sharply reversed the direction of public policy by changing the law to narrow trade union immunities and reduce union power by tight monetarist economic policies. In their fourth term of office under Mr Major, the Conservatives seem set to continue in this direction, though perhaps in a less radical manner. These contrasting policies are discussed in detail in Chapter 10.

PERSPECTIVES ON THE ROLE OF THE STATE

What general conclusions can we draw about the role of the state in British industrial relations? How, indeed, should we view the state and state intervention? In attempting to answer these questions, we can revert to some of the concepts set out in Chapter 2.

According to the unitarist perspective, the state is the neutral guardian of the superordinate national interest. Society is or should be hierarchically organised with 'leaders' directing affairs and the populace accepting state leadership. The state can or must be trusted to act in the best long-term interests of the people. Historically, this reflected medieval and early modern notions of the organic state and government by rulers, enlightened or otherwise. In modern times, extreme unitarist states have existed in Fascist and Communist societies. Less extreme, there is obviously also some overlap here with hierarchically structured corporatist type systems. In modern times, in Britain, even during wartime, such an authoritarian state and unitarist industrial relations system have never existed.

According to the pluralist view, the state is a complex set of institutions with different centres of power, responsive to different pressures from outside. Power is therefore not concentrated but is diffused and dispersed and the role of government is to be the *primus inter pares* or first among a set of relatively equal institutions in society. The separate institutions within the state apparatus do not necessarily act in concert and may even conflict and favour differing policies. For example, within the Civil Service, the Department of Employment and its agencies traditionally tended to favour collective bargaining as a way of determining pay, whereas the Treasury, with less contact with industrial relations and with different priorities, was always less likely to favour collective bargaining and more likely to support legislation to curb union power. A more public conflict has at times been seen between Parliament and the Judiciary, with the latter on the whole espousing a more individual view of the employment relationship and the former, until the 1980s, being historically rather more favourably inclined to a collective approach to industrial relations.

According to the corporatist view, or at least corporatism of a pluralist variety, civil society is made up of a set of institutions, the most important of which, along with government, are the two main producer interest groups, organised business and labour. It is in the best interests of the populace that these institutions recognise their interdependence and work in a partnership. At national level these governing institutions should establish tripartite arrangements which can represent and also contain their respective local constituents, namely the electorate, individual firms and trade union members. Under more thoroughgoing forms of corporatism, representatives of business and labour are incorporated into the state apparatus, gaining certain privileges in return for enforcing state goals on their particular constituents.

Liberal collectivists, with their preference for a passive state, tend not to give the relationship between the state and other parties too close attention, merely assuming that, under systems of collective bargaining, the state can 'hold the ring' or establish some sort of 'Queensberry Rules'.[31] The state should act as a good employer and should intervene to help disadvantaged groups and to provide a supportive economic context. Liberal individualists believe in less state intervention and in leaving employment relations more to market forces and individual contracts of employment. However, there are some contradictions in their position: in industrial relations, they have been quite prepared to see the state intervene to enforce individual against collective rights; also, despite their belief in market forces, they have been prepared to see state intervention to remove impediments to market forces.

Marxists and other radicals view the state in a capitalist society primarily as the agent of the capitalist class. According to them, far from being neutral, state institutions are usually used to support the interests of capital against labour. Some argue that this occurs because people from business-class origins dominate positions of power and use state institutions as instruments to their own ends.[32] Others argue that this occurs regardless of the class origin of those in power, because those who govern are subject to so much pressure from business interests that they have no choice but to maintain the long-term interests of capitalism.[33] They accept that the state has some element of autonomy from capital and may not always act in capital's interest, but there are divisions on whether social democratic reforms apparently designed to serve the working class *do* assist them or merely prevent more fundamental change. Orthodox Marxists have argued that though the state may adopt policies that appear to override short-term business interests, this is only done to protect long-term capitalist interests and ensure the survival of capitalism. Because labour is an effectively organised interest group, strategies may be adopted which incorporate the leaders of labour organisations into the administrative apparatus of the state. Under such a system labour may appear to have considerable formal power and influence, but it is, in effect, neutralised. Labour leaders do not have the real power or resources to oppose capital in such circumstances. In return for their responsibilities, they accept more restrictive legislation and act to discipline disruption from their own membership. Other radicals, however, see more value in social democratic policies and argue that such policies may represent a genuine advance in working-class interests and help to weaken the hegemony of the capitalist classes.[34] The mainstream of British socialism has always advocated state intervention on labour's behalf and believed in a kind of bargained corporatism where labour is strongly organised and is a counterweight to the state and business interests.

There are therefore a number of different answers to the questions 'Who rules?' and 'Who should rule?'. Unitarists would say that the state should rule. Pluralists believe that no one group does or should rule. In this category, liberal individualists believe the state should rule, but a minimal state; liberal collectivists believe the state should rule, but leave most aspects of industrial relations to regulation by employers and trade unions; corporatists believe that society should be ruled by the tripartite institutions of government, business, and labour. Radicals believe that ultimately capital rules and the state is in practice subservient to business interests.

In conclusion, the British state initially played a rather limited, role in industrial relations and employment matters. However, this was important in that it laid down and maintained certain ground rules. After the Second World War, the nineteenth-century policy of *laissez-faire* was replaced by the Welfare Compromise, which involved greater state intervention in the economy, but retained the voluntary regulation of the employment relationship. The system of legal immunities kept most trade union activities outside the scope of the courts. There was a continued abstention of statutory law, with little legal support for minimum standards or conditions at work, and little legal support for trade unions or collective bargaining, except for the system of immunities. Direct state involvement was minimal, limited to conciliation, arbitration and inquiry services. Even the government's conciliation and arbitration services were 'voluntary', for they were and are still normally used only if employer and employee both wish to make use of them, and an arbitrator's award is not legally binding. Inquiries could be set up by government in the form of *ad hoc* committees or courts of inquiry and these reported to government, but their use was exceptional and limited. The only other traditional state intervention was the attempt to prevent the worst cases of low pay through wages councils and even this intervention, as we will see in Chapter 9, was imbued with voluntarism and designed to promote collective bargaining.

The argument for voluntarism, as traditionally put for example by members of the 'Oxford School', was that a reliance on voluntary collective bargaining rather than state regulation ensured that the rules that regulated the employment relationship were flexible, relevant to the particular conditions of each industry, and democratically determined by the parties who had to live with the results. In the defence of a non-interventionist state it was not explicitly argued that the state was thereby neutral between the parties, that employers and employees necessarily had a balance of power, or that any power imbalance had been equalised by the state such that justice reigned in the employment field. Instead, these issues were not discussed in any detail. Certainly the Oxford School's view of the state was too scantily developed to be used to analyse the pressures for state action that have arisen in the recent past.

As we will see in Chapter 10, the British state is no longer passive. There was in the 1970s, under both Conservative and Labour governments, a build-up in both collective and individual labour law and a growing

concern with the procedural conduct and the substantive outcome of industrial relations. In the 1980s the Thatcher government, with its commitment
to *laissez-faire* economics, narrowed the ambit of statutory immunities in
order to bring trade unions under the closer regulation of the judiciary. The
British state has thus moved from its extraordinarily passive policies of the
past, but, with disagreements about the direction of change both between
and within the major interest groups and political parties, it is far from clear
what the more active state policy will look like. Under the Thatcher government, for example, we will see that there developed a kind of 'bastard
voluntarism', with less state intervention in the area of individual and
protective labour law, but more in the area of collective labour law.[35]

It is highly unlikely that the UK will return to a passive state role in
industrial relations. In the modern world state inactivity is unusual in
industrial and economic relations. The *laissez-faire* policy of nineteenth-
century Britain arose in unusual economic and social conditions. In most
countries the state has always been far more actively involved in developing and regulating its economy. Voluntarism in industrial relations was
largely confined to the UK (and the USA) and survived only while it was
supported by the factors outlined in the sections above. Employers and
employees are invariably political in their activities. They use political
pressure to achieve their ends and this, together with government concern
to manage the economy and improve economic performance, will ensure a
more active role for the state than was traditional in the UK.

CONCLUSION

The state plays an important part in any national industrial relations system.
However, in Britain for many years the state was unusually passive and
there developed a 'voluntary' system of employment regulation. Employers
preferred this because it left them free to exercise their managerial rights.
Unions used their political power to keep the state, and particularly the
judges and the courts, out of industrial relations. Of course, some of the
basic ground rules of what was and what was not permissible were laid
down by the state. In the area of social law there were also legislative
interventions to protect women, children and some low-paid workers. This
tradition of voluntarism slowly began to break down, certainly from the
1960s onwards as governments of both political persuasions intervened
more in industrial relations. In the 1970s, there was a tendency towards
corporatism in industrial politics in Britain. Through the 1980s and into the
1990s, there have been contradictory tendencies: on the one hand, there has
been an increase in state intervention in the area of collective labour
relations and stronger state interference in industrial relations; on the other

hand, in the area of protective employment law, there was in the 1980s a reduction of state intervention. There was also a movement away from incomes policies and attempts to intervene in the labour market directly to control wage movements. Overall, however, state intervention in industrial relations continued to increase through the 1980s and is likely to increase further in the 1990s. In the future, one important factor here will be the growing importance of Europe and political and legal interventions from that source. These trends and developments we will review in Chapter 10.

8 Decision making and bargaining at work

This chapter brings together employers and their associations, employees and their organisations, and the state and governmental agencies and looks at the interaction between them in decision making. We hope that at this point a theoretical discussion will illuminate the nature of the various processes of interaction at work and the various ways that employment rules are made.

In the economic and social life of organisations many decisions have to be taken. Some of these may seem to be only indirectly connected with industrial relations and in this category may be put decisions concerning investment, product development and divestment. These are the decisions which mainly interest senior managers, and such decisions are often taken without much thought for industrial relations consequences and without being integrated into human resource strategies.[1] However, decisions in these areas are very important and often shape industrial relations and personnel decisions. For example, a decision whether to invest may ultimately lead to closure and redundancy. Other sets of decisions are more obviously concerned with industrial relations, and in Chapter 3 we discussed decision making in three interrelated areas: decisions about work organisation cover the way workers are organised around production processes; decisions about employment conditions include the way people are recruited and employed, job tenure and promotion, and wage and benefit arrangements; decisions about management–employee relations cover methods of representation, the rights and obligations of the industrial relations parties, and procedures for handling grievances and questions of discipline. Industrial relations is the study of the processes of control over all of these areas, both those which have a direct and an indirect impact on people at work.

TYPES OF DECISION MAKING

In this chapter we are concerned with how decisions are made in all these areas and, in particular, the extent to which employees have a say or voice in decision making and in the creation and administration of rules which affect their working lives. It is possible to identify a kind of spectrum of different types of decision making, which range roughly across a dimension of employee influence, from ones where employees have minimal say to those where the intention is that they should have a total say in decision making.

At one extreme of the spectrum there is unilateral employer regulation, in other words, situations where the decisions and rules are made by one side, namely management. Very significantly this may include decisions not to decide, that is, not to put certain items on the agenda or into play, and this is where the exercise of covert or invisible power is important. In many respects unilateral management regulation is the most important method of rule making. It is the predominant form in firms which do not have formal joint consultative or collective bargaining arrangements. Even where such arrangements exist, unilateral management regulation covers those important strategic decision areas such as investment, product development, and acquisitions, mergers and divestments; these are areas which management usually seeks to keep as managerial prerogatives. From management's point of view, unilateral regulation has the advantage that it not only preserves managerial prerogatives, but also provides flexibility and control. However, it also has the disadvantage that it may lead to an alienated workforce which in the end becomes difficult to manage and unproductive. In practice, we will argue later that unilateral control is never total and unilateral management decision making always involves some element of negotiation and bargaining. No managerial control system can establish comprehensive rules to cover every contingency at the place of work, and, if management tried to do so, it would probably not be very effective or efficient.

The second form of decision making we identify along our spectrum is individual bargaining. This refers to situations where the individual bargains with his or her employer about wages and conditions, working arrangements and other employment matters. Again, this is an all-pervasive process within organisations and we will elaborate on it below. Here we would note that many workers bargain individually about initial terms of employment on which they commence work – though often the job is presented by the employer on a 'take it or leave it' basis. There is also often bargaining at work about questions such as work allocation and work methods. However, except in the case of workers with scarce skills or in strategic positions within the organisation, such individual bargaining is always circumscribed and, as we argued in Chapter 5, there is invariably a power imbalance between the employer and the individual employee. Individual bargaining is therefore likely to be replaced by some form of group or collective bargaining wherever groups form with the unity and strength to bargain their cooperation for some concessions in their terms of employment. From the employer's point of view, individual bargaining offers certain advantages of control and flexibility in work organisation and employment matters. It is also likely to preserve managerial prerogatives. The main disadvantages for the employer are that such bargaining is time-consuming, can create anomalies between different individuals and may generate discontents among workers who may feel that they are being dicriminated against and unfairly treated.

Along the spectrum, the third form of decision making we refer to is joint consultation. Again consultation is a process which is all-pervasive at work in that there is always some flow of information between employer and employee and always some discussion. By joint consultation here we mean more the use of various forms of representation and formal mechanisms which are intended to give employees a voice in decision making. Within this, again there is a spectrum from the very informal and limited types of day-to-day meetings and briefing sessions, through to more formal consultative committees, and through to elaborate systems of workers councils which exist on a voluntary basis in some British firms and by law in many continental countries. In Britain, joint consultation has a long history and has been associated with some major British firms such as ICI and Cadburys.[2] Sometimes consultative arrangements are non-union-based and unions say anti-union-orientated, but often they coexist alongside unions and collective bargaining. More than one-third of British workplaces now have formal consultative arrangements of some kind or other.[3] From the employer's point of view, joint consultation has the advantage that management retains ultimate discretion and control, but simultaneously joint consultation can give employees a voice and perhaps thereby increase employee commitment. Unions, however, have always been suspicious of joint consultation, arguing that the consultation is often about minor matters or, where it is about more important matters, the consultation is *ex post* and not *ex ante*, in other words, it is about the effects of decisions already taken and not about the decisions themselves.

The fourth form of decision making brings us to collective bargaining. We have already referred to collective bargaining throughout this book and presented various definitions of this important process of job regulation. It is important because in Britain it covers about two-thirds of full-time workers and therefore has a wide impact on the economy.[4] Here we would define collective bargaining as a form of bilateral decision making: it is collective because employees associate together in a workgroup, trade union or professional associations (it does not require collective organisation through an employers' association on the employer's side); it is bargaining because each side has something the other side wants, because each side is able to apply pressure on the other, and because there is a process of 'give and take' which in the end usually results in the negotiation of a compromise agreement.

Again we will have more to say about collective bargaining below and in the next chapter. Here we would make the following brief points. First, it is often assumed that collective bargaining introduced group negotiations into the workplace, replacing individual arrangements between employer and employee. However, in historical perspective, it is best to see collective bargaining as developing out of earlier forms of job regulation, in particular out of either unilateral-employer regulation or unilateral-employee regulation. In the first case, workers challenged managerial regulation and forced employers into collective bargaining. In the latter case, usually in craft-type industries, employers challenged the unilateral control which skilled workers often possessed and forced them into collective bargaining.[5] Second, collective bargaining should not be seen as just being about the negotiation of agreements (which is often only the most visible and dramatic part of collective bargaining), but also about their day-to-day implementation and administration. In this sense, collective bargaining is not a one-off exchange, but a continuous political and administrative process at work. Third, collective bargaining is a highly flexible process which covers many aspects of employment: it covers substantive matters such as wages, hours and other conditions; it provides procedural rules which govern the relations and standing of the parties; and it deals with the conditions of production, namely the effort side of the wage–effort bargain. It is, however, much less likely to cover more strategic business matters, such as those decisions surrounding planning, investment and divestment to which we have already referred. Finally, it is important also to stress that the frontier of bargaining is continually shifting and what is bargained about can and does change over time, as economic, organisational, and political circumstances change. For example, in Britain, the scope of bargaining tended to grow in the 1960s and 1970s and to shrink in the 1980s.

As with all these processes, there are advantages and disadvantages to collective bargaining. For employers, the advantages of collective bargaining can be as follows. There may be *market* advantages in that, through collective bargaining, the employer discovers the going rate for a particular class of labour, negotiates a deal which provides some predictability during the course of the agreement and, where bargaining is on a multi-employer basis, it may help firms by taking wages out of contention between them and so reduce competition. Collective bargaining may offer other economic advantages, since there is some evidence that where it exists workers are more satisfied, turnover is less, and absenteeism is lower.[6] Collective bargaining may offer certain *managerial* advantages for employers in that there may, on the part of the workforce, be more acceptance of, and commitment to, jointly created rules and these can be enforced with the authority of the union. On the other hand, there are some disadvantages for employers of collective bargaining: it tends to push up wage levels and narrow differentials; it may involve strikes and other forms of industrial action; it restricts managerial discretion, flexibility and control over the processes of industrial relations; and the evidence for Britain is that in many instances it has probably reduced productivity and profitability[7]. Needless to say, from the union's point of view, there are overwhelming advantages to collective bargaining, since it gives the union a position within the organisation and enables it to be seen to win benefits for its members. Similarly, employees may obtain real benefits such as higher wages and greater control over their working lives. However, there may simultaneously be costs for union members, for example, if collective bargaining pushes up wage costs and holds back productivity and profitability, then this may jeopardise employment prospects. Also, the possibility must be borne in mind that some of the benefits of collective bargaining may possibly be secured, without concomitant costs, by other processes such as joint consultation.

From a wider social point of view, liberal collectivists see collective bargaining as a fair and flexible way of resolving conflicts and of providing a safety valve at work; liberal individualists see it more as being disruptive of the relationship between the individual and the employer and as being socially undesirable; corporatists see it as a prerequisite for the creation of orderly and efficient institutional arrangements in the wider society; while radicals are likely to have very mixed feelings about it, seeing it as simultaneously providing a check on management while at the same time in the long term enhancing managerial control.

The fifth form of decision making to which we will refer is unilateral employee regulation. This refers to situations where employees themselves create work rules, acting through workgroups, trade unions or professional associations, or some other institutional mechanism. Again, under this heading, there is a wide spread of different types of rule making, from the partial to the much more comprehensive.

Many so-called 'custom and practice' rules which favour workers fall into the category. By this we mean work rules and arrangements which tend to grow up over time and often exist within the twilight zone in organisations. These customs and practices are usually not officially introduced by management or written down in employee handbooks and are not formally created by collective bargaining. In many cases, they derive from precedents which are the result of concessions by management (often lower-level management) and which are then enforced by workgroups. Custom and practice rules may cover matters such as starting times, finishing times, tea breaks, transfers and work allocation. For example, a custom and practice covering some workers, such as electricity board meter readers, is that they can take their company van home in the evening, but that in return for this their start time is at their first job next morning. Another example, among council dustmen, is the so-called 'job and finish' convention according to which they can knock off work when they have completed their quota of jobs. Another custom and practice among many workers in the Post Office and on the London Underground has been the right to move to more favourable jobs on the basis of seniority – the so-called 'Buggins' turn' system. Such rules often provide flexibility and even enhance efficiency within organisations and they can give employees control over small, but in their eyes important, aspects of their working lives.[8] From a management point of view, however, they can often develop into irksome restrictive practices. The withdrawal of such customs and practices, the movement towards a tightening up of managerial controls, has often led to conflict and other industrial relations problems.[9]

Historically, craft regulation of labour supply, wage standards and levels of output was an important form of unilateral employee regulation, or 'autonomous regulation' as it was sometimes called. Even in non-craft industries, such as in coal mining and on the docks, workers have unilaterally controlled many aspects of their working lives. Today some of the more obvious examples of employee regulation are to be found among professional and similar workers: doctors are a prominent example of workers who play an important part in regulating entry into their profession, lay down demarcations and control work schedules; university academics, though much less powerful, also exert considerable unilateral control over work content and work methods; actors lay down a quota on newcomers into acting and impose other working rules on employers.

At the furthest extreme of unilateral employee regulation, we might include more formal and elaborate methods through which workers have sought to control their working lives. Under this heading might be included various worker cooperatives such as exist in Britain and throughout the world and systems of worker self-management which have been tried in various countries. There is a considerable literature on these latter forms of unilateral employee regulation.[10] These suggest that employees appreciate the influence which they have and value non-hierarchical forms of decision making. However, in practice, autonomy and choice have usually been circumscribed by market forces. In addition, actual involvement has not always been high, and there are always dangers that oligarchical tendencies may develop and small groups, with administrative and technical knowledge, may come to exercise power in a conventional manner. In terms of economic performance, many cooperatives and attempts at self-management have not been notable successes, though their proponents point to the major obstacles and constraints under which they have had to operate.

Another method of generating employment rules, which does not fit really along our spectrum, but which is nevertheless of extreme importance, is statutory regulation, or what the Webbs called 'legal enactment'. In other words, this refers to state regulation of wages, conditions and other aspects of employment relations. It therefore covers aspects of individual or protective labour law on questions such as health and safety and unfair dismissal; it covers the "dos and don'ts" of collective labour law on matters such as strikes and trade union affairs. Under this heading also we would include the regulation of pay and conditions of certain industries and categories of workers, such as workers in industries where wages councils set minimum rates and employees such as doctors and nurses, some civil servants and schoolteachers, whose pay is fixed by review bodies. Of course, during periods when statutory incomes policies have operated, many more workers have had their pay and conditions affected by legal regulation.

In the following sections of this chapter, we adopt a more conceptual approach and focus on bargaining and negotiation as broad social processes which underlie many of these methods of rule making. We also discuss the relationship between bargaining and bureaucracy and the power that can be exercised through different types of bargaining arrangements.

BARGAINING AS A SOCIO-POLITICAL PROCESS

Bargaining is an all-pervasive social process which involves the interaction between two or more individuals or groups which are attempting to define or redefine the terms of their relationship.[11] Bargaining may take place between individuals or groups, it may be covert or overt, it may result in informal or formal outcomes. Studies of industrial relations have traditionally focused on collective bargaining about wages and conditions, which is certainly the most visible form of negotiation to occur at work: it is often conducted through formal and specialised machinery, it may involve visible sanctions like strikes, and the bargainers themselves often use the news media to explain their negotiating positions. However, the high visibility of collective bargaining obscures the existence of the many other negotiation processes at work. Industrial relations needs to be analysed in the context of all the types of bargaining which occur within the different decision-making processes.

Within the social sciences there has long been a divide between those who focus on cooperation and coordination in social life (somewhat akin to the unitarists) and those who focus instead on competition and social conflict (more pluralist in orientation). The former deal with organisations in a manner which focuses almost exclusively on management and which assumes that management gets its own way. The latter argue that business organisations are not totally structured and rationally administered by top management, but contain numerous internal conflicts over budgets, plans, priorities and ways of working which may be the subject of many different bargains. In a sense, organisations can be seen as comprising many over-lapping sets of 'bargaining zones' and held together by a 'negotiated order'.[12] Thus, bargaining may occur between different factions on the company board, between management at different levels, between different departments, divisions or functions; it may also occur between different groups of workers and between union members and their representatives. These are largely examples of *intraorganisational* bargaining and are very important for an understanding of industrial relations. In addition, there is *interorganistional* bargaining, where an organisation negotiates in external zones with other organisations. This would include bargaining between a firm and other firms, between a firm and a trade union, between an employers' association and a union, and between employers, unions and government agencies.[13]

The degree to which negotiation is formalised

If people negotiate on similar issues time and again they invariably develop structured procedures to regulate their bargaining relationship. The development of norms in any regular social interaction is a basic socio-logical and psychological process. We can, therefore, distinguish different types of negotiation in terms of the degree and form of normative regula-tion, or institutionalisation, that emerges.

A very low degree of formalisation exists when bargaining occurs in situations where the dominant norms are that one party should have the authority to take decisions or that decisions should be taken according to some sort of prearranged criteria. Examples are the covert deals done between lower and higher management and between foremen and employees. In both cases, bargaining tends to be furtive because the domin-ant norms do not legitimise negotiation and these norms are supported by one of the parties or by external powers no one cares to challenge. If bargaining continues in this form, then one norm likely to develop to protect the bargaining relationship is that knowledge of deals and accom-modations should be kept secret.

At very low levels of formalisation, negotiation may be difficult to detect and there is the problem of deciding where to draw the boundary between the unilateral imposition of control by one party and bargaining between the parties. A supervisor may tell a skilled man to sweep the floor, be met by a stare of disbelief because this is not the custom and practice of the workplace, and then have to ask an unskilled worker. Such an exchange can be classed as bargaining, even though no special meetings, no specialist negotiators and no elaborate procedures are involved. It is enough that there was the attempt to define or redefine the terms of the relationship. In this example, the negotiation, though brief, is governed by norms known to both parties about appropriate work for skilled men and the scope of supervisory authority. More generally, it has been suggested that 'it is possible to visualise the process of supervision as a method of bargaining between workers and supervisors; details of the arrangements are left to be worked out through direct interaction between them'.[14]

A high level of formalisation exists when an elaborate set of norms regulates the bargaining process. Norms then specify the parties entitled to negotiate, negotiable issues, the timing and format of meetings, the nature of agreements and procedures for the implementation and administration of agreed terms. When norms governing negotiation are so specific and elaborate they are likely to give rise to very visible and concrete outcomes. Some of the norms will have a formal status as 'rules' written into handbooks, agreements or government laws. There are also likely to be specialised roles to cope with the work involved, hierarchical structures of meetings and mountains of paperwork.

Bargaining over employment relationships therefore takes institutional and non-institutional forms and can be more or less formalised both between and within organisations. The degree to which bargaining is institutionalised both reflects and affects the power of the negotiating parties, but in all industrialised societies some type of institutionalised negotiation has developed around the employment relationship.

Types of negotiating institution

As we have already said, there has been a tendency in the British and American industrial relations literature to equate the institutionalisation of negotiation on employment matters with interorganisational negotiation and formal collective bargaining. This is, perhaps, understandable in the Anglo-American context where collective bargaining has been a dominant form of institutionalised negotiation, but by ignoring other types of institutional bargaining this tendency reduces our ability to analyse negotiation in industrial relations. Here we will explore as examples two levels: first, the negotiating institutions that can surround managerial organisation; second, the negotiations that can relate to state administration.

Institutionalised bargaining and management's structures of control

Bargaining on employment relations may be integrated with, completely separate from or parallel to the structures of management.

Many early industrial firms were based on subcontracting, where the subcontractor hired labour for a particular job, and negotiations took place between the entrepreneur and the subcontractor and the subcontractor and the worker.[15] In these circumstances negotiation was very integrated into the structure of management. As we described in Chapter 4, the history of organisational development in the UK has seen the virtual elimination of this type of arrangement outside of a few sectors such as the construction industry. In most industries management has built more centralised, bureaucratic organisations around a directly employed workforce. Although, in this way, employers may have hoped to eliminate negotiation from the new, centralised organisational structures (aided, if they were aware of them, by the organisational models of Taylor and others in the structural school of organisation theory), their hierarchical control was not sufficient to exclude all bargaining, especially at lower levels between foremen and skilled workers.

In the UK, distinct collective bargaining institutions, largely separated from the institutions for managerial decision making, developed not only because employees felt they had different interests from their employers and wanted to control aspects of their working lives, but also because employers wished to defend their managerial prerogatives against unilateral employee regulation and to externalise trade union activities.

Where collective bargaining could be restricted to industry level and confined to basic matters of wages and conditions, it could often be kept separate from the internal processes of organisational control. This has been the case in Germany, where collective bargaining usually only takes place between a trade union and employers' association at national level about general matters covering all the firms in an industry.[16] In Britain, it has been more difficult to maintain the separation of collective bargaining from the structure of management when it is conducted at the company and workplace levels and when negotiations can cover a broad range of conditions and work arrangements. For example, shop stewards may be used by local managers to gain worker acceptance of difficult managerial decisions; and, in the reverse direction, stewards may help managers in order to increase their mutual control of local events.[17] Nevertheless it may be possible to keep collective bargaining at the place of work separate from organisational structures by specialist meetings and refusal to negotiate on matters of managerial prerogatives.

In Britain, employment issues have traditionally been negotiated through collective bargaining, but examples of more integrated institutional structures can be found. A few British companies, often influenced by their founders' strong religious or philosophical commitment to employee participation, are managed through structures which incorporate employee representatives onto company boards and managerial meetings. The John Lewis Partnership and Scott Bader are examples. Various forms of producer cooperatives, usually small in size, also exist. In these, employees, as owners, have a say in determining employment relations and other aspects of work. The negotiation which takes place in these situations is very much integrated into the structures of management.[18]

Between the separated institutions of collective bargaining and the institutional integration of producer cooperatives lie various institutions which aim to run negotiation in parallel with the structures of managerial decision making. German codetermination provides the best example of parallel institutions. Under German law, companies must establish works councils, which are distinct from the trade unions but which represent employee interests and have rights to information, joint consultation and codetermination. Codetermination covers social welfare; personnel policies including criteria for recruitment, job evaluation, training, work methods, transfer or dismissal; and general economic issues such as acquisitions, mergers and divestments. Managers must secure works council approval of their policies in these areas, and the works councils' power to 'codetermine' these issues is backed by the right to take the company to arbitration, but not the right to strike. Also in Germany is another form of codetermination, namely employee representation on company boards. Depending on the industry and the size of the company, German employees have the right to elect a certain proportion of the supervisory board of public companies. These worker directors have to act in the best interests of the company, but they have rights to information and co-decision making and through these representatives a kind of bargaining takes place between representatives of shareholders, managers, and employees. German unions have supported this system as an essential complement to industry-wide collective bargaining and generally regard it as an effective way of institutionalising workplace negotiations.

In the UK the most widespread institutions running parallel to management structures have been joint consultative committees or councils, to which we referred above. Recommended by Whitley in 1917 as a means of involving employees in domestic decision making and containing militant trade unionism, they have traditionally had only consultative rights and none of the state-backed powers of the German works councils or worker directors. Joint consultation did not become widespread in the UK until the Second World War, when consultation and production committees were used to secure greater employee involvement in the war effort. Although the institutions persisted after the war, they tended to become discredited as ineffective 'talk-shops' and fell into disuse as domestic collective bargaining grew. However, there has been a resurgence of the joint consultation arrangements of various kinds from the late 1970s onwards as employers made concessions to the demands for worker participation. In the 1980s, the weakening of trade unions and collective bargaining has allowed a growing number of firms to develop joint consultation of various kinds, but usually controlled by management.[19] Many consultative arrangements are restricted to matters such as welfare arrangements, the organisation of work tasks and the quality of production. Fewer are concerned with broader policy questions which management usually still wishes to maintain as subjects of managerial prerogatives.

Institutionalised bargaining and state structures of control

If governments openly intervene in the regulation of employment relations in collaboration with employers and trade unions, then they create new levels of institutionalised negotiation. There are, as we saw in the last chapter, many variants of state intervention, and employee and employer representation may be integrated into state administration or separate institutions may be created for limited purposes. In the UK, at various times in the past, tripartite institutions have provided for bargained corporatism on a limited range of special areas of public policy.

The most extensive attempts to involve the state in the regulation of employment relations have been incomes policies. Many past incomes policies of the 1960s and 1970s were presented as government-designed and administered, that is, as *not* negotiated. However, both the design and the administration of incomes policy were usually negotiated, although with varying degrees of success, but the bargainers have normally been shy of acknowledging it.[20] British governments have sought the support of employers and trade unions for their incomes policies, although it has seldom been openly agreed in formal, tripartite negotiations. Most government policies were subjected to the lobby of interested pressure groups, and civil servants consulted with the relevant pressure groups on draft legislation. The 1974–9 policy was negotiated in a formal *bi*partite institution, the TUC–Labour Party liaison committee. The Thatcher administration, by contrast, refused to bargain in the same way with either unions or management about economic policy.[21] However, in the case of some powerful groups, such as doctors, the police and prison officers, even during that period there was a sort of bargaining between government and employee institutions. The Labour Party in opposition in the 1980s discussed various alternative economic policies and possible forums with the TUC and would be more likely, as a government, to enter into a bargaining relationship with unions and employers.

Thus, the various British incomes policies and other government interventions in pay determination can be seen as attempts to construct centralised institutions for the negotiation of pay. Despite various experiments with different types of institution, all these incomes policies have been broken as groups of employees, sometimes with employer support, protested at wage restraint in the context of rising prices. The anti-corporatist forces opposed to incomes policy in the UK have been strong, and Britain has failed to create bargaining institutions to integrate government, employer and employee influence on economic matters. The nearest prominent examples to this are to be found in Germany and Japan, though in both these instances the employers and unions remain largely separate from government processes.[22]

In summary, negotiations over employment relations take many forms and vary in the degree to which they are institutionalised. Institutions for negotiation can be integrated with, separated from, or structured to parallel the institutions of management or government control.

Bargaining and bureaucracy

In Chapter 3 we stressed the importance of employer control strategies based on bureaucratisation. It is sometimes assumed that bureaucratic structures of control exclude negotiation, and there has been a conventional division of academic labour between organisation theorists, studying bureaucratic structures of control, and industrial relations specialists, studying bargaining and negotiation. This section stresses that bureaucracy is usually negotiated and notes the bureaucratic rules that are likely to be supported or contested by employees.

Many writings in the structural school of organisation theory assume that the bureaucratic structures of modern business are designed and exclusively controlled by management. Similarly, much of the writing in Human Resource Management also assumes that management creates sophisticated systems and practices which are accepted by employees without any real contention or negotiation. In practice, this is not the case. Employee pressure invariably plays a greater role in organisational design than this implies and the best-laid plans of managers are subject to counterpressures, bargaining and compromise. One of the important contingencies affecting management's choice of organisational strategies is employee power either directly or indirectly applied.[23]

In Chapter 3 we saw that Edwards and Woodward showed how bureaucracy was a highly developed form of managerial control.[24] Edwards made the point that bureaucratic and administrative systems were developed in part in order to control and motivate employees as much as to ensure the production and distribution of goods and services. However, in some firms, much of the bureaucracy that governed industrial relations was bilateral in nature, in other words created by management and unions negotiating together. In Chapter 4 we saw how complex bureaucratic corporate structures such as U- and M-form structures have developed. Marginson has argued that, in Britain, the multidivisional form of organisation in part resulted from shopfloor bargaining pressure.[25] Such pressures induced management to develop new forms of bureaucratic organisation so as better to structure collective bargaining in ways more favourable to management, in particular by locating it at company, divisional, or plant level, but not at departmental or workgroup level. In Chapters 3 and 4, we saw how Gospel, in his discussion of externalisation and internalisation, also related bureaucracy to bargaining. There it was argued that policies of externalisation were in part shaped by the weakness of bureaucratic structures in Britain. The development of stronger bureaucratic structures enabled employers to internalise more aspects of employment and industrial relations. As a result of this collective bargaining has been internalised within the firm and often supplemented by other forms of decision making such as joint consultation.[26]

In two classic studies of bureaucracy, Gouldner and Crozier dealt with the significance of employee negotiation in the shaping of bureaucratic rules.[27] Gouldner produced a detailed case study of the bureaucratisation of a mine and processing plant in the US.[28] He charted the reaction to management's attempts to tighten control over labour and production processes by the imposition of more bureaucratic rules and noted that employee reaction to bureaucratic rules varied according to the rules' source and purpose. Some rules, for example safety regulations, had the support of both managers and employees on site: their purpose was approved and they were jointly enforced; they could be seen as 'representative bureaucratic' rules, but aspects of their implementation were still negotiated. The no-smoking rules, prominently displayed throughout the works, were ignored by the men. Their source was external – the plant's insurers – and Gouldner classifies these unenforced regulations as 'mock bureaucratic' rules. There were also rules imposed by management on, for example, lateness, absenteeism or poor work standards, which were regarded as 'punishment-centred' and were resented and opposed by employees. Punishment-centred rules were designed and seen as instruments to control employees and were opposed and negotiations took place around them. All in all there was bargaining around the creation and administration of the bureaucratic rules of the firm.

Crozier emphasised the control function of bureaucratic rules, but also stressed that employees as well as managers can use and shape bureaucratic rules as instruments of control.[29] He studied a highly bureaucratised company, concentrating on three plants, and showed how, in one plant, workers restricted management's supervision by insisting on the letter of the rule-book. (More generally, it should be noted the union tactic of work-to-rule provides a good example of turning management-originated bureaucratic rules against management.) Crozier also described how employees, as well as managers, act to structure their environment through the elaboration of regulations to make their situation more predictable. According to him, 'There is an important distinction to be made between rules prescribing the way in which the task must be performed and rules prescribing the way people should be chosen, trained, and promoted. Subordinates fight rationalisation in the first area and want it in the second, and supervisory personnel do just the reverse.'[30]

Crozier noted two types of pressure from workers. There is a constant attempt to evade and manipulate bureaucratic rules as a means of increasing their own autonomy and power.[31] At the same time, employees attempt to establish rules to regulate and control managerial behaviour towards them. Linking the distinction drawn in the quote above to the division in Weber's bureaucratic characteristics, we can say that, in general, employers press for the bureaucratisation of controls over work organisation and task performance, while employees are more interested in regulating bureaucratic personnel policies. Employers seek specific written rules to govern the division of labour and performance standards but like to be free to recruit and reward as they wish. Employees prefer autonomy in work methods, but seek the clear, legal-rational regulation of recruitment, discipline, pay and promotion prospects.[32]

In writing about bargaining Crozier was concentrating on small group, individual and shopfloor bargaining. Some of the rules and regulations that enmeshed his plants were more formally negotiated, at higher levels of the management and union hierarchies and, therefore, at plant level could be seen primarily as external bureaucratic rules. For example, pay, hours and seniority rules had been established by centralised collective bargaining. Crozier suggested that informal negotiations may be reduced as organisations become rigidly structured and highly bureaucratised. However, higher-level negotiation of bureaucratic rules does not exclude lower-level bargaining.

Of course, only a small proportion of organisational arrangements are under negotiation at any one time. Nevertheless, significant bargains from the past leave their mark on organisational arrangements. As we noted in Chapter 3, employers may adopt different bureaucratic strategies in response to differences in employee power. Friedman suggested that bureaucratic personnel policies of 'responsible autonomy' have been adopted by large, oligopolistic modern firms in response to employee pressure during periods of economic prosperity; during periods of depression firms are more likely to resort to 'direct control', using tighter, more punishment-centred rules.[33]

In Britain, employees have pressed for standardised rules on pay rates and hours, using arguments based on precedent and comparability. However, British trade unions have been less bureaucratic in their orientations than those of Japan or Germany or the USA, where bureaucratic personnel policies and internal labour markets have become more firmly established within large corporations. Because British unions were themselves structured to relate to the British labour markets of the late nineteenth and early twentieth centuries, when British firms were still small, highly competitive and pursued strategies of externalisation, such unions saw less advantage in the organisation-related polices of unions formed in the twentieth century, with their greater concern for seniority and organisational careers.

BARGAINING AND POWER

Any further assessment of the nature of bargaining needs to consider the complex question of power. Who exercises power in the various bargaining arrangements and to what extent do different types of institution affect the distribution of power? Such questions lie at the centre of the theoretical perspectives on industrial relations discussed in Chapter 2 and we have already started to consider power when we examined employer and employee institutions. Opinions range from those on the political far left, who assert that no negotiation within capitalism can do other than confirm the dominant power of business; through the liberal collectivist's insistence that employees can genuinely improve their position through collective action; to liberal individualists' counter-claim that such action provides no benefit to employees but merely increase unemployment and inflation; and on to the corporatist belief that only the integration of employee representatives into management or governmental bodies can create a balanced distribution of power.

As we have already seen, power is a notoriously difficult question to study. One way to view power is as the probability that one actor within a relationship will be in a position to carry out his or her will despite resistance. However, as others have pointed out, if there is a considerable disparity of power between parties, then the dominant party may be in a position, not only to carry out their will, but also to suppress all signs of resistance.[34] This may be because the weaker party is aware that their power is so limited or that they have suffered a massive defeat in this area in the past and are not prepared to mount another challenge while they believe they will be defeated. Alternatively, the dominant party may be able to mobilise matters in a way that ensures that their claim to control certain areas goes unchallenged because the weaker party accepts their claim to have a moral, legitimate right to control. The subordinate may accept, as morally right, their disadvantaged position and not attempt to pursue their real interests. If power is exercised indirectly and invisibly in this way, then it becomes extraordinarily difficult to study, but no less important. In this section we look at the bases of power before discussing the power relationships within different types of bargaining institution.

The structural bases of power

Power derives from relationships of dependency. A can exercise power over B, if B is dependent on A for the achievement of important objectives. In employment relations dependency works many ways. Employees are likely to be dependent on their employer for objectives such as income, job satisfaction and desired social contacts, though, of these, economic dependence is undoubtedly the most important. Employers are dependent on their employees' effort and cooperation to achieve quantity and quality of output and profit. Both employers and employees are dependent on the state for the maintenance of the infrastructure and laws which supports economic activity. In turn the state is dependent on employers and employees for economic activity and cooperation in the implementation of government policy. However, different degrees of power and degrees of dependency need to be explored.

The state of the labour market, the nature of the product market and the organisation of work all help to structure power relationships between employers and employees. As we saw in previous chapters, the structural bases of power which derive from these factors are often discussed in terms of non-substitutability (i.e. A exercises power over B because B depends on A's contribution and would find it hard to find a substitute if A withdrew it) and strategic importance (i.e. that A's contribution has a particular and strategic importance for B in the achievement of objectives). Strategic and non-substitutable positions can be held by both employers and employees. The earlier chapters noted that a high degree of skill or a crucial position in the workflow increase employee power, provided that the employer is dependent on the goods or services that the employees produce. Conversely, an employer exercises power over employees to the extent that the former offers employment opportunities that are in scarce supply and that the income from employment is crucial for the achievement of personal objectives. The power of the state increases as its activities become more important for the achievement of employer and employee goals. Relationships of dependency are ingrained into all social organisation and help structure the distribution of power at work.

Employee power rests, in the last resort, on the threat or possibility of the withdrawal of labour and cooperation needed by the employer. How significant is this power? Strikes are a well-measured and studied aspect of employment relationships and the impact of the strike weapon has been extensively discussed.[35] The right to strike is seen by many as a fundamental safeguard against the authoritarian and totalitarian use of labour, and yet strikes are not necessarily powerful. A strike is only likely to exert pressure on an employer to make a change if the employer is dependent on the labour provided by the strikers, and if the employers' ability to wait until work is resumed is lower than the employees' ability to withstand their loss of income. In fact, a firm can actually benefit from not having to pay wages at a time of excess supply and may be quite prepared to sit out a long strike.[36] The longer a strike lasts, the weaker the employee position becomes because strikers bear considerable personal costs and their resources are quickly used.[37] Employees may attempt to increase the impact of a strike by timing it to cause maximum embarrassment for employers or by attempting to borrow the bargaining power of other workers by widening the action to bring in other workers. However, in Britain, the law now sets real limits both to sympathetic action and to picketing. Employers may react to counteract the power of strikes by dismissing the strikers, by substituting their labour power by bringing in other workers, or by buying in the product they produced. Employees face personal costs when they take strike action, and striker unity is therefore never guaranteed. Employers can seek to weaken employee unity and strike capacity by mounting a campaign to persuade the strikers that their action is irrational and immoral and mobilising public opinion against disruptive action. Employers therefore have powers to offset the strike sanction, although, for most employers, it will still be a sanction to be avoided.

In the early decades of the twentieth century, when most industrialised countries were experiencing major, often violent, confrontations between capital and labour, the potential power of the strike sanction seemed considerable. Syndicalists believed that a general strike would eventually spearhead a workers' revolution. However, in Britain, at least, the strike weapon has not evidenced this potential. Even during crisis situations, such as during the First World War and the General Strike of 1926, radicals were unable to mobilise workers for any such campaign. More recently the major reasons why the miners' strike of 1984–5 failed were because of the lack of unity on the part of the miners, absence of solidarity on the part of other workers and the ability of the Coal Board, other employers and the government to resist the strike. Striking is a costly and risky process and workers are rarely prepared to shoulder the risks except on clear-cut defensive issues or for real improvements that seem to be achievable.

Although relationships of dependency and power sometimes seem impervious to change they are, of course, formed by human action, and current social structures can be influenced by managers and worker representatives acting to affect the non-substitutability and strategic significance of the employees' contribution at work. Some of the managerial strategies described in Chapter 3 are designed to reduce the strategic importance and increase the substitutability of employee work. Government policies can also have an impact: for example economic and monetary policies designed to let unemployment reach 'natural levels' crucially affect employee power; and restrictions on the right to strike, the weakening of the closed shop, and the reduction of supplementary benefit to strikers' families introduced by the Thatcher government were designed to weaken employee ability to present a united 'non substitutable' front towards employers. As groups manoeuvre to increase the power resources that they hold and weaken those of rivals, the influence of ideas and of subjective beliefs also comes into play.

Power and authority: the mobilisation of ideas

Ideas can reinforce or undermine objective power bases, and all bargainers will use such arguments as a means of boosting morale on their own side, gaining the sympathy of external groups, and attempting to convince their bargaining opponent of the legitimacy of their case. This aspect of bargaining power can be better understood by introducing Weber's ideas on legitimated power or authority. Weber argued that power arising from the possession of objective resources is not the only source of control in social relations because the beliefs that people hold also influence behaviour. Beliefs affect people's willingness to be influenced by power. If power-holders can convince others that they have the moral, legitimate right to control certain decisions, then they exercise not only power, but authority. Authority provides invisible power in bargaining, for ideas and beliefs are not simply used instrumentally by negotiators but may become part of the individual sense of self-identity and value. Negotiators are themselves likely to be influenced by dominant ideologies and this sets limits on the issues they raise and pursue with confidence and conviction.[38] Authority, therefore, is legitimated power and, whereas power can expect to be challenged by other power-holders, authority proclaims the moral superiority of being above such battles. Authority claims to be non-negotiable and assumes the right to decide issues irrespective of the immediate distribution of power. In practice this means that any group challenging an established authority will find it more difficult to mobilise sympathetic support from other power-holders and will find it difficult to convince the waverers on its own side that they have a good case and are not making unjustified demands.

Because authority is a valuable additional resource enabling its holder to economise on the use of power, most groups attempt to give their claims to power ideological support. What arguments are used in the battle for minds within British industrial relations?

Employer ideologies

As we saw in Chapter 3, employers claim the authority to manage industry and argue that this authority derives from property rights, or from greater technical expertise, or from the long-term interest of everyone concerned.[39] The case that managerial authority is in everyone's long-term interest can be supported by unitarist arguments that organisations need to be hierarchically structured and rationally organised and that managers have the necessary status and expertise to enable them to run the organisation in a rational and efficient way; or it can be supported by the more pluralist argument that most employees willingly accept the position of managers who are there to coordinate the different interest groups in the long-term best interests of everyone. Such arguments have been used to claim unilateral control of employment relations or, once some control has been ceded, to maintain control of areas like investment or commercial decisions affecting closure.

Employee ideologies

As we saw in Chapter 5, employee ideologies are less coherent or confident than those of employers, and dominant, subordinate and occasionally more radical value systems all make conflicting claims for employee support. Most institutionalised employee bargaining is backed by arguments based on subordinate values. These give a broad acceptance to managerial authority, but attempt to limit and contain its scope by demanding that the authority be exercised in a proper, fair or 'legal-rational' way. For example, employees can exploit the argument that managerial authority rests on the need for rational administration, and bureaucratic rationality is used to back employee claims based on precedent, comparability and seniority.[40] Precedent has been widely used by British workgroups demanding that management act rationally in the light of its own past decisions.[41] Comparability arguments state that if a pay structure or personnel policy is to be seen as rational and just, applying to everyone equally, then certain groups of workers need to receive the same pay or conditions as similar groups treated more favourably elsewhere.[42] British workers have often fought for tenure, or promotion on the basis of seniority, or for redundancy to be organised on a 'last in, first out' basis. The claim to job 'property rights' has sometimes been interpreted as an expression of radical values; however, it is more a disinclination to accept management's right to deprive others of work for other than good disciplinary reasons. As the right to tenure was recognised by Weber as part of the rational, bureaucratic employment relationship, this pressure from employees is best seen as a demand that management operates within certain rational constraints, rather than as a rejection of management authority. In this way, employees may argue that a rational criterion for the distribution of pay or promotion is seniority on the grounds that assessment of merit is too subjective.[43]

Thus, although material resources like capital or control over communications do give considerable advantages to employers in the struggle to influence people's views, nevertheless the ideological arguments of less powerfully resourced groups can mobilise bias and bring pressure to bear. In the UK, employees' claim to have a voice in the determination of pay and condition is, on the whole, accepted as legitimate, at least if this is through some form of collective bargaining or joint consultation rather than anything more radical. When employee claims are couched in bureaucratic terms they may be more difficult for employers to ignore and in this way employees have played a part in shaping modern bureaucratic organisations.[44]

Power within different types of negotiating institution

To what extent is the exercise of power affected by the form of bargaining institution? Does collective bargaining, with its institutionalised right to strike, provide the best countervailing power within industry? Would the constitutional right to a works council or to be represented on company boards provide a more effective base for employee representation?

Liberal collectivists insist that employees exercise little power unless their bargaining is backed ultimately by the threat of collective action, though in practice in 99 per cent of collective bargaining situations there is no resort to industrial action.[45] Given the 'harmony bias' that is widespread in society, there have, however, been many advocates of more peaceful 'integrative' or 'problem-solving' approaches to bargaining.[46] Many joint employer–employee institutions are premised on the assumption that genuine negotiations can occur without a confrontational setting or strike sanction. This integrative and non-conflictual collective bargaining starts to shade into consultation or codetermination.

In some institutions based on joint consultation, institutional arrangements definitely work against the exercise of power by employee representatives. Institutions established by management as part of a policy for improved communication rarely enable employees to oppose management effectively on issues where interests conflict. Employees in briefing groups or Quality Circles may be able to make some impact on managerial behaviour by the force of their argument, but they will not be given information with which to challenge the rationality of management's decisions, and, if they do not have their own independent organisational links with their constituents, they will not be able to back their arguments with effective sanctions.

Many arrangements for putting worker directors on company boards are similarly curtailed in effectiveness. A small minority of employee directors are likely to find themselves powerless to penetrate the complexities of boardroom politics. They are likely to be at a loss to analyse what is happening, because of insufficient information or because they have been deluged with incomprehensible statistics and outmanoeuvred as managers and shareholder directors settle major decisions outside the boardroom. Employee directors have often found themselves patronised by other board members and resented by their electors as puppets whose privileged position provides no tangible benefits for employees.[47] In the German case, moreover, they are legally obliged to act in the best interests of the company as a whole and certainly cannot be involved in any coercive sanctions.

However, there is evidence to suggest that institutions based on consultation or codetermination are not necessarily powerless and that, even within collective bargaining, sanctions other than the strike do have an impact. Defenders of adversarial bargaining argue that it must be more effective than codetermination such as exists in Germany because it involves the strike sanction. However, the issues being dealt with in collective bargaining are very similar to works council and board-level business and there are issues where works councils and worker directors have achieved more success. Both works councils and worker directors in Germany can obtain considerable early information and can use various forms of pressure to achieve outcomes favourable to employees. They also deal with issues such as investment decisions which collective bargaining rarely covers.[48] In some ways, therefore, the differences between different types of system are nothing like as great as immediately appears and it is important not to assume that one particular institutional form ensures greater employee success – people are likely to put to use whatever bargaining institutions are available. Indeed collective bargainers can often operate more successfully in a cooperative rather than an adversarial mode, and the best bargainers often win more by less conflictual methods.

The impact of institutional arrangements on the underlying distribution of power is therefore difficult to assess. Some radicals believe there can be no effective redistribution of power within present political and economic structures and they question attempts to increase employee influence on management or government. They argue that no government, constrained by market forces, could implement policies to increase employee power. Such arguments are often premised on the assumption that radical improvements can only be made if the tempting lure of institutional reform was rejected by employees. However, British workers have, for the most part, not shown themselves interested in such radical change and have sought institutional negotiation within the existing society. Consistent employee pressure for institutional negotiations and strong employer resistance to schemes like the Bullock proposals for industrial democracy or the European Community Social Charter, all point to the fact that employers also believe that institutionalised negotiations can reallocate power.

CONCLUSIONS

It is possible to identify a spectrum of methods of decision making and ways of generating rules which control the employment relationship, the organisation of work, and relations between employers and their employees. All of these have their advantages and disadvantages for employers, for employees and their organisations, for the state, and for the wider society. All of the processes involve elements of negotiation between individuals and between groups; within groups there will also be bargaining and it is important to recognise this as an important aspect of industrial relations. Even where there appears to be unilateral management regulation, there will always be elements of bargaining, though this will not tend to be highly institutionalised.

It is possible to identify a spectrum of degrees of institutionalisation of negotiation, ranging from situations where bargaining is not supposed to take place or is irregular, to situations where it is highly formalised as in many instances where there are elaborate collective bargaining and joint consultative arrangements. Institutions for negotiation with employees and their representatives can be integrated with, separated from, or structured to parallel the institutions of management. This means that bargaining will not always take the form of overt bargaining between apparently adversarial groups. The degree to which bargaining is institutionalised and formalised both reflects and affects the power of the negotiating parties. The bases of bargaining power can be both objective and subjective, overt and covert. It is often the case that overt attempts to exercise power are evidence of a lack of covert power. On the other hand, the relative lack of attempts to exercise overt power may indicate possession of real power.

In the next chapter we look more empirically at the development of collective bargaining in Britain and at how employers have attempted to reform this over the last quarter-century.

9　The changing system of collective bargaining

Collective bargaining sets basic terms and conditions of employment for a significant number of British firms and most British employees. A recent survey showed that 53 per cent of all firms in 1990 had pay determined by collective agreements. Around two-thirds of full-time workers are covered in the survey by collective agreements; in other words they have their basic pay and conditions either directly or indirectly fixed by collective bargaining.[1] This is a larger figure than for firms covered in the survey because larger firms and public-sector organisations are more likely to have pay and conditions determined by collective bargaining. Thus the coverage of collective agreements is wider than union membership, since, in industries and workplaces, there are many non-union workers whose basic pay and conditions are fixed by collective agreements. As one would expect, the coverage of collective bargaining varies greatly: overall it is higher in the public sector than in the private sector, in manufacturing than in service industries, for manual rather than white-collar workers, and for men rather than for women.[2] Collective bargaining is therefore an institution of major importance which dominates the determination of pay and conditions of employment for British employees.

However, in recent years it has been the subject of much controversy. Attempts to reconstruct the collective bargaining system by governments are discussed in Chapter 10. In this chapter we chart the development of Britain's system of collective bargaining and attempts to reform it by employers. We trace the turbulence created in the traditional national-level system by the development of local bargaining in the years after the Second World War and by the growth of state involvement in collective bargaining. We chart the growth of more formalised company- and plant-level bargaining in the 1970s in private manufacturing industry. In the 1980s collective bargaining came under attack and in the public sector there have been strong pressures for the decentralisation of bargaining. In assessing collective bargaining today we note the alternatives to the dominant tradition of free collective bargaining that may prove significant in the future.

THE DEVELOPMENT OF BRITAIN'S COLLECTIVE BARGAINING SYSTEM

As we saw in Chapter 8 collective bargaining can be viewed as an institutionalised system of negotiation in which certain decisions affecting employment are decided within joint employer–trade union negotiating committees. When collective bargaining developed in the UK, the negotiating committees formed tended to be multi-employer and often multi-union. Formal negotiations came to be conducted industry by industry at what was called the 'national' level, with little government support or interference. Such national agreements developed first, in the late nineteenth century, in the private sector, in industries such as textiles, engineering and shipbuilding and later in the twentieth century in the public sector in the Post Office and the Civil Service. After the Second World War, national agreements were extended to the nationalised industries and developed in some areas of private-sector, white-collar employment.

It is sometimes assumed that collective bargaining introduced employee-group negotiations into the workplace, replacing individual arrangements between employer and employee. However, it is best to see collective bargaining as developing, in the late nineteenth and early twentieth centuries, out of earlier forms of job regulation, in particular out of either unilateral employer regulation or unilateral employee regulation. In the first case, workers challenged managerial regulation and forced employers into collective bargaining. In the latter case, usually in craft-type industries, employers challenged the unilateral control which skilled workers often possessed and forced them into collective bargaining.[3]

The initial development of collective bargaining in craft industries such as engineering and shipbuilding can be explained also as the compromise reached between employers and employees in the transition to more centralised forms of work organisation. As employers attempted to impose more direct control over labour costs and worker performance, they met resistance from employees who organised both to oppose tightening managerial controls and to standardise and improve their pay and conditions of work. The compromise of collective bargaining was in some ways second-best for employers who sought total unilateral control over work and for skilled workers who sought to maintain and extend unilateral employee regulation. The compromise emerged as some employers agreed to negotiate with union officials on basic rates of pay and hours of work. Employers acted together in these negotiations, signing agreements which initially covered local districts and eventually spanned entire industries. Through employers' associations they sought to externalise industrial relations and to exclude trade unions from the workplace. The contents of the collective agreements tended to be limited to basic pay and conditions of work and procedures for handling disputes. Detailed issues such as pay structures, methods of work, supervision and discipline were rarely touched by the collective agreements. Such areas were left, depending on workgroup power, to the unilateral determination of management, to unilateral workgroup control or to the realms of informal compromise on the shopfloor, which resulted in custom and practice rules.

By the end of the nineteenth century, craftsmen had local agreements on standard wage-rates and hours in industries such as printing, shipbuilding engineering, building and woodworking. In other industries, employees demanded a say in the piecework schedules and price lists, and collective agreements on such lists in the coal mining, iron and steel, textiles and footwear industries had developed by the end of the century. At the turn of the century the craft and piecework trades were still the main base of collective bargaining, but demands for collective agreements were being copied by other groups of manual workers in industries such as railways and shipping. These and other workers in semi-skilled and unskilled trades formed unions and, often in the face of fierce opposition, forced employers into collective bargaining.

THE GROWTH OF NATIONAL, INDUSTRY-LEVEL BARGAINING

The first collective bargaining was very informal and at workplace or district level, but, once it was established, there were many pressures to lift negotiations to the national, industry-wide level.

Employer association strategy

Employers, as we saw in Chapter 4, acted through employers' associations to demand national procedure agreements. Under such agreements no strike or lockout was constitutional until a central meeting of employer and union officials had attempted to resolve the dispute. Some employers saw national, multi-employer agreements on substantive issues like pay and hours as a logical development from such procedures, as a way of taking wages out of competition between firms in the labour market. The first national substantive agreements were signed, primarily on the employers' initiative, in cotton textiles in the 1890s and were followed over the next twenty years in most British industries as employers developed strategies of externalisation. Most trade union full-time officers also saw advantages in industry-wide negotiation because it ensured formal recognition, emphasised the need for full-time officers and enabled unions to demonstrate their effectiveness.

Government pressure

As early as 1891 a Royal Commission on Labour had recommended the development of national collective bargaining and, with the First World War, the government took the initiative to encourage national levels of negotiation. The government prohibited strikes and instituted compulsory arbitration on industrial disputes for industries vital to the war effort. Pay settlements by arbitration acted as a pressure towards the rationalisation of numerous local agreements into single industry-wide settlements. The government also took direct control of munitions factories, railways and coal mines, favouring industry-wide pay settlements in these industries. Wartime inflation and the associated need for constant adjustments in wage rates encouraged both employers and union officials to accept the seemingly more rational, less time-consuming system of industry-wide negotiation.

After the war, government policy was heavily influenced by the reports of the Whitley Committee (1917 and 1918). The Whitley Committee on the Relations between Employers and Employed was appointed, in the context of considerable government anxiety about the management of postwar industrial relations, because of the high levels of prewar industrial unrest and the existence of a radical shopfloor movement for workers' control (see below). Whitley advocated the extension of industry-wide collective bargaining and proposed the establishment of formal, interlocking employer–union institutions at industry, district and workplace levels. It was not clear from the reports how wide the decision-making powers of the joint bodies would be nor how equally power would be shared within them. The proposals therefore could either be seen as heralding a new world of democratic decision making at work or, more accurately as it turned out, as a simple recommendation for the spread of industry-wide pay bargaining across industry with some formal provision for management to consult with employees at the workplace.

When voluntary pay negotiations returned at the end of the war, the newly formed Ministry of Labour set about the promotion of the Whitley Committee proposals. It advocated national joint industrial councils (NJICs), under which equal numbers of trade union and employer representatives would meet at regular intervals to discuss both wages and conditions and wider areas of cooperation and industrial relations. Seventy-three NJICs were established between 1918 and 1921, covering both private- and public-sector industries, but few extended their scope beyond basic issues of pay and hours. The Whitley proposals made little difference to the major industries, such as engineering, textiles and coal mining, where collective bargaining had already been established. However, they were very significant for the public sector: in central and local government, Whitley Councils were established and this helped spread collective bargaining to both blue- and white-collar staff.

The growth of industry-wide collective bargaining that occurred in the immediate postwar years ended as unemployment rose and as trade unions suffered major defeats in industrial conflicts in the 1920s. In a number of industries, NJICs collapsed as employers withdrew their support. In coal mining, negotiation reverted to the district level as employers, confident of their increased strength, refused to bargain at national level. The depression of the interwar years, therefore, caused some reversal in the development of the national collective bargaining system. But on the whole it is remarkable how well it survived. However, the worsening market for labour had a more crushing effect on workplace bargaining which had also developed between 1910 and 1920.

Workplace bargaining and the early shop stewards' movement

Formalisation of collective bargaining at national levels implied, at least for many employers, that no significant negotiation *should* occur at the level of the company, plant or workshop. This was one of the aims of what we have described as strategies of externalisation. But the national agreements were mainly skeletal, establishing only very basic terms and conditions but still leaving innumerable details to be decided elsewhere. Although employers might claim the exercise of managerial prerogative over all issues not determined at the national bargaining table, as we suggested in Chapter 8, some other negotiation was always likely to emerge. Some form of domestic, workplace-based bargaining was inevitable because of weak managerial control systems, rudimentary management hierarchies and national agreements which could not comprehensively establish rules to cover every contingency at the place of work.

Shop steward activities first caught public attention in the First World War, but negotiating shop stewards have a longer history. At the end of the nineteenth century, payment-by-results systems spread in British industry as employers sought to increase control over worker effort and to reduce the autonomy of foremen and workgroups. An important, though unintended, consequence of the change in managerial control techniques was usually the encouragement of bargaining between workers and foremen or rate fixers over the price or time for each job. It became a regular practice for workers to consult with each other before any questionable price was accepted and for workers to negotiate on such prices as a group. In some works special committees sprang up for the purpose, among others, of considering all prices before a worker was allowed to accept them.[4] Some committees were granted *de facto* recognition by local management, making their committee-men the first shop stewards in the modern sense of having powers of negotiation, in addition to the conventional workplace representative's role of collecting union subscriptions, maintaining membership and acting as a link with union branches.[5]

The First World War speeded up the spread of shop steward bargaining throughout the munitions industries and to new groups of semi-skilled and unskilled workers. Military conscription and the associated manning problems at home, the wartime passivity of the trade union leadership who were supporting the war effort and power derived from wartime full employment, all stimulated the growth of shopfloor bargaining with the result that 'workshop and works committees, with duly appointed convenors, in close touch with similar bodies in other establishments became a regular feature of factory organisation'.[6]

Actively negotiating shop stewards fitted uneasily into a system of national-level bargaining and into trade union hierarchies. The early trade union branch structure was usually based on a worker's residence, rather than the workplace, and so workplace negotiators might represent members in several branches of any one union. In addition multi-unionism made it even more difficult for higher trade union officials to coordinate the exercise of authority over workplace activities. In the early twentieth century, the divorce between shopfloor representatives and official union institutions was sometimes exacerbated by differences in ideology and policy. In areas like Clydeside, Sheffield and Coventry, workgroup activity became associated with the so-called Shop Stewards' Movement. This movement opposed the official unions' wartime truce, advocated an end to sectional divisions within the union movement, and argued for industrial unionism capable of class-based political action in the pursuit of workers' control. Although most stewards were not direct members, the movement influenced stewards in many big cities and served as an industrial link with radical political agitations.[7]

The shop steward activity of the First World War stimulated several reactions. Some unions changed their rules to give stewards limited formal status and negotiating responsibilities, and the Engineering Employers' Federation (EEF) and engineering unions formally gave some recognition to shop stewards and to works committees. The government's reaction was to set up the Whitley Committee, and the Committee's proposals for works committees were intended to provide a constitutional outlet for demands for greater worker influence on the shopfloor. Within public mythology the Shop Stewards' Movement identified shop stewards with political revolutionaries, a stereotype which fitted only a small minority at the time but which was revived for the new generation of stewards which developed during and after the Second World War.

Shop steward activity and workplace bargaining declined in the interwar recession. With high levels of unemployment, employers took the opportunity to terminate the recognition of shop stewards, to tighten up unilateral management controls and to insist that collective bargaining be confined to national level.

The strengthening of national bargaining during and after the Second World War

Renewed economic growth from the mid-1930s onwards and government intervention during the Second World War revived the national system of collective bargaining. During the war government again intervened to control the economy, unemployment disappeared and unions bargained their cooperation for the extension of industry-wide collective bargaining. As part of the arrangements for the direction of labour, employers found that they could not avoid recognising trade unions when they asked for it. Fifty-six NJICs were created or re-established from 1939 to 1945 and the wages council system of state-backed, national negotiating machinery was extended in the belief that this would protect the industry-level bargaining system if there were a postwar recession similar to that following the First World War.

However, wartime conditions again stimulated the growth of shopfloor bargaining, but government, employers and unions took care to provide institutional channels for increased local activity. Joint production committees were established in war-related industries to enable managers and stewards to argue about differences at the place of work. The extent and scope of domestic, shop steward bargaining expanded, especially in industries such as engineering and shipbuilding, and some measure of the increase in this local activity can be seen in the large number of short, illegal strikes. However, in the Second World War domestic bargaining was *not* seen as a serious challenge to either official trade union policies or industry-wide collective bargaining and shop stewards (though sometimes associated with the Communist Party) were not for the most part seen as the bearers of a radical counter-ideology.

Britain's national, industry-wide system of collective bargaining was therefore well established by the end of the Second World War, with all major industries and the bulk of manual workers affected by industry agreements. By this time opinion in government, union and employer circles supported the system as a mature, flexible and democratic method of determining pay and conditions. During this period collective bargaining had also developed in the US, though more at company and plant level. So confident were the Western Allies in this method of conducting industrial relations that, at the end of the war, collective bargaining was pressed on the defeated wartime powers of Germany and Japan as a means of creating a liberal, pluralistic bulwark against the return of totalitarian regimes. West Germany developed a system of industry-wide bargaining, akin to the British, but which was to prove more stable; Japan, after initial turmoil, developed a system of company bargaining, more akin to the American pattern and again one which was to prove stable.

In Britain, under the postwar Labour government, the Nationalisation Acts put a statutory duty on the new management to set up negotiating machinery for their employees, a requirement which spread collective bargaining to white-collar workers in the nationalised industries. The growth of education, health and the social services also encouraged the development of collective bargaining for white-collar professional employees. White-collar trade union membership rose by a third from 1948 to 1964, and although this increase did not quite keep pace with the growth in the white-collar workforce, it was to represent a significant change in the base of trade unionism. Collective bargaining for white-collar employees spread relatively smoothly through the public sector and here also national-level negotiation became widespread. The national collective bargaining system therefore seemed, at least on the surface, well established and secure. By 1965 there were 500 separate institutions for reaching national-level agreements. The system was complex but seemed comprehensive and had the support of the state.

THE STATE AND TRADITIONAL COLLECTIVE BARGAINING

As we have already seen, British public policy during the development of the national collective bargaining system was relatively passive and based on a preference for voluntarism. Governments for the most part, outside of wartime, avoided direct intervention on terms and conditions of employment and did not use the law to encourage the growth of trade unions or the spread of collective bargaining. This differed from the way in which collective bargaining developed in other countries such as the US and on the continent of Europe. Nevertheless, as is evident from the history above, especially during wartime, public policy did encourage the development of national machinery for collective bargaining. The state also acted to help stabilise the collective bargaining system by measures which provided some support for the bargainers and measures, though limited, became a part of traditional British collective bargaining.

Conciliation, arbitration, and inquiry

Under legislation of 1896 the government gave itself three types of power to intervene in collective bargaining. It could *inquire* into disputes and offer advice without the consent of the parties; it could appoint a *conciliator* or board of conciliators to try to help resolve a dispute, if asked by one of the parties; and it could appoint an *arbitrator* to make a positive recommendation, but only if asked to do so by both parties. In no case was an inquiry's advice or arbitrator's award to be legally binding and all the provisions for government intervention were only to be used after voluntary collective bargaining procedures had failed. The provision of voluntary conciliation, inquiry and arbitration continues to the present day. The services were put on a permanent basis on the recommendations of Whitley, arbitration being entrusted to an industrial court (now the Central Arbitration Committee) and conciliation became part of the function of the new Ministry of Labour in 1916 and since 1975 has been conducted by the Advisory, Conciliation and Arbitration Service (ACAS).

Extending the terms of collective agreements

Compared with all other countries operating collective bargaining systems, British governments have given little support to either trade union recognition or to the extension of collective agreements once made. Only during the 1970s did the state assist unions seeking recognition from reluctant employers. Public-sector employers were, however, expected to recognise trade unions and determine their employment terms by collective bargaining, and companies working on contract to the public sector were subject to so-called 'fair wages' resolutions passed in 1891, 1909 and 1946, which required all government contracts to observe fair wages, hours and conditions of work for their employees. 'Fair' was defined as being those terms established by collective bargaining for the trade or industry in the district where the contractors operated.

After the Second World War, wartime provisions to protect wages were replaced by the Terms and Conditions of Employment Act (1959) which enabled individual workers to claim that the provisions of the relevant industry agreement should be applied to them, even if their employer was not party to the agreement. This clause existed for many years without being widely used, although it may have encouraged the widespread practice of unfederated employers following their industry's agreement. In

1975, Schedule 11 of the Employment Protection Act strengthened this extension of collective agreements. Schedule 11's repeal in 1980 removed one of the slender supports given by the British state to collectively agreed terms. This stands in contrast to the legal situation in many other West European countries.

Despite the tradition of voluntarism, there has also always been a minimum of employment protection rights in the UK. The earliest legislation concerned the payment of wages and the hours of work of women and children. Factory legislation in 1802 and 1833 set limits to the hours worked by women and children in industries like coal mining and textiles. A series of Truck Acts, passed from 1831, ensured that employers paid their employees in cash and not in kind and did not dictate how employees' wages should be spent. There has also been a consistent government interest in health and safety legislation.

Health and safety at work

From 1802 a succession of Factory Acts were passed, laying down minimum standards on such things as ventilation and sanitation; on the guarding and proper maintenance of machinery and equipment; on the provision of drinking water; on the use of poisonous and dangerous substances; and on the notification of accidents and industrial diseases. A government-employed inspectorate and fines were used to enforce these laws and by the early 1970s there were nearly thirty separate Acts in the area. These were rationalised in 1974 in the Health and Safety at Work Act.

Low pay, trade boards and wages councils

The early general unions and their supporters demanded a national minimum wage to protect the lowest paid, a demand that was vigorously opposed by advocates of a free labour market. In 1909 the Liberal government produced a compromise in the Trade Boards Act. Trade boards, composed of representatives of employers, employees and independents, were set up for certain low-paid industries with the function of deciding a 'reasonable' rate of pay. The Whitley Committee in 1918 suggested that trade boards should be set up in any area not covered by collective bargaining and should regulate a wide range of subjects in order to mirror and, most importantly, stimulate the development of collective bargaining. This extended role for the trade boards was bitterly criticised by employers, and in the interwar recession the boards reverted to their old, limited function of establishing minimum wages. In 1945, however, the system was re-vitalised and extended in the belief that the renamed wages councils would give some statutory protection to low-paid workers and to encourage collective bargaining.

Wages councils, in industries such as clothing, retailing and catering, had therefore two complex functions: support for the low-paid and the encouragement of collective bargaining where it was weak. The two roles were in some respects contradictory. The function of encouraging collective bargaining hindered effective support for the low paid because wages council rates could not be set too high. In turn, the low pay function probably hindered the spread of collective bargaining by removing some of the incentive to unionise or set up more genuine bargaining machinery. It is still a question of debate as to whether the wages councils, which today set pay rates for 2.5 million workers, should be retained or abolished or replaced by a national minimum wage. We examine this argument in Chapters 10 and 11, where we also look at later changes in government attitudes towards collective bargaining and legal intervention.

Thus, into the early post-Second World War years, the UK had a comprehensive system of industry-wide, multi-employer bargaining and, despite the overall principle of voluntarism, this had government support. This system was to come under pressure after the Second World War and to be transformed in the 1970s and 1980s.

THE RISE OF DOMESTIC BARGAINING

From the early postwar years onwards there was a slow growth of domestic, shop steward-led bargaining which came to challenge the traditional national collective bargaining system. Full employment and the Welfare Compromise in the quarter-century after the Second World War increased the ability of workgroups to act on their own. Even though shop stewards were not usually associated with radical politics or with the explicit rejection of national collective bargaining, the increase in shop steward activity from the 1950s to 1970s undermined the regulatory force of the national collective agreements.

A rising number of small-scale, shop steward-led *strikes* was the most public indicator of the growth of domestic bargaining. As we will see below, after the Second World War, there were many fewer large national strikes, but an increase in the number of small plant and workplace strikes, which reflected the shift of collective bargaining to this level. Concern also grew about *wage drift* – i.e. the drift of take-home earnings away from nationally negotiated wage-rates.[8] This was seized upon by economists who argued that domestic bargaining was a prime source of inflation, because unregulated local additions to wages were pushing up costs. It was noted that the gap between national wage-rates and take-home pay had increased between the 1930s and the mid-1960s because piecework earnings, over-time payments and domestic additions to national rates had all grown until they together contributed a high proportion of actual earnings. All three sources of wage drift were seen as a cause for concern.

Rising piecework earnings were seen as evidence that piecework schemes, originally introduced as a means of motivating workers and giving employers tighter control over effort, had degenerated and were being used by workgroups and shop stewards to increase earnings by pre-senting claims based on comparability and precedent at every job change. Constant domestic negotiations over piecework prices and times served, in the context of tight labour and soft product markets, to weaken managerial control over labour costs.

Overtime was seen as a problem on the grounds that systematic and high levels of overtime were worked by workgroups wishing to increase their earnings, rather than because there was any real need for extra hours to be worked. The length of the working week specified in national agreements dropped from 47.2 hours in 1938 to 40.3 hours in 1966, and yet the actual hours worked between 1946 and 1966 fell only by one hour. The control and distribution of overtime opportunities formed a significant part of the shop steward's bargaining role.

Factory additions to nationally agreed rates, in the form of supplements, productivity payments and conditions allowances, mushroomed and most employers' associations turned a blind eye to the growing problem. At the time, Flanders argued that the new domestic bargaining was 'largely informal, largely fragmented, and largely autonomous' resulting in 'chaotic' relationships outside the control of senior managers or full-time union officials.[9] This argument had a profound effect on the Donovan Commission and was echoed by all who were concerned to introduce more rational and formalised pay determination into the British economy.

By the 1960s shop steward activities were therefore again defined as a major national problem. There were various demands for government action, from calls for changes in collective labour law to outlaw un-constitutional strikes and so curb workgroup power, to calls for the restruc-turing of collective bargaining to integrate domestic negotiations into a new framework of internal institutions. Government response to these proposals are discussed in Chapter 10. Here we concentrate on the employers' reaction to the perceived problem.

However, we should bear in mind that, although domestic bargaining was widely presented at the time as posing problems for managers, govern-ment and trade unions alike, not all groups shared this perception.[10] Many shopfloor workers and their shop stewards were reasonably satisfied with a system that gave them considerable autonomy and control. Most domestic bargaining took place between local workgroups and local managers, with the connivance or explicit acceptance of officials higher in their respective hierarchies. Domestic bargaining was not widespread in areas where management had for many years adopted bureaucratic, central controls over personnel policy, for example, in the public sector or for the white-collar workers of many private companies. Spontaneous domestic bargaining was essentially a feature of the less bureaucratic industries with weak managerial hierarchies, such as engineering, shipbuilding and construction, and even in these industries it was often not seen as a problem by the unions or all managers directly involved.[11] The government agency later established to restructure domestic bargaining found many employers and senior managers who were not prepared to view their existing domestic arrangements as in need of change.[12] It was mainly those employers faced with increased international competition, tightening product markets and a concern to cut labour costs, who viewed their domestic arrangements with concern and, for the most part, it was these who took the initiative in instituting or reshaping their own domestic negotiations. It could be argued that, along with these employers, domestic negotiations were primarily seen as a problem by the advocates of incomes policy who sought a more rational method to control inflation.

EMPLOYER REFORM INITIATIVES

Productivity bargaining

From the early 1960s onwards some large, multi-plant companies were moving to create new institutions for domestic bargaining which would enable them to develop more detailed agreements with their workforce than were possible in national levels of bargaining. This strategy we have earlier described as one of internalisation. It also involved the increasing bureaucratisation of collective bargaining.

One of the most famous early attempts at reform took place at Esso's Oil Refinery at Fawley.[13] Local management conducted a long and complex series of negotiations to centralise domestic bargaining into a single, plant-level agreement. In the negotiations the employer gained a reduction in the size of the workforce and changes in working practices (the relaxation of job demarcation, the reduction of overtime, the abolition of craftsman's mates and greater freedom in management's use of supervisors). In return, employees received large pay increases, a reduction of the working week, the extension of fringe benefits and promises of greater job security. This 'productivity bargain' was seen by many as a rational approach to the problems arising from the gradual *ad hoc* accretion of shopfloor bargaining power. It was innovative because of the wide scope of bargaining issues, the negotiation process which intimately involved shop stewards, and the formalised plant-wide nature of the bargaining. (As an aside, it might be added, however, that it never produced the productivity pay-off which management expected.[14])

The Esso initiative created a wave of interest in petrochemicals and other industries, and an increasing number of large employers began to establish plant- or company-level joint negotiating committees and to adopt policies of strategic independence and internalisation. The Chemical Industries Association came to welcome and encourage domestic negotiations, but other employers' organisations, such as the EEF, were initially less willing to accept the reduced importance of national negotiations and, as we saw in Chapter 4, several large engineering employers left the Federation in order to take charge of their own relations with trade unions at domestic level.

The development of formal plant and company-wide bargaining

Though a few large companies took the initiative and led the reform strategy, government encouraged other employers to follow the move to more formalised domestic bargaining. The Donovan Commission and the Commission on Industrial Relations endorsed and encouraged the formalisation of domestic bargaining and the National Board for Prices and Incomes (1965–70) expounded the advantages of formal domestic bargaining as a way to boost productivity. Both the 1970–4 Conservative government and the 1974–9 Labour government played a role in this extension and formalisation of collective bargaining. These government policies will be considered in Chapter 10.

Through the 1970s there were radical changes at the workplace with formal joint negotiating committees for domestic bargaining spreading throughout manufacturing industry.[15] By the late 1970s, 68 per cent of manual employees, in 53 per cent of establishments, had their pay principally determined by single-employer bargaining conducted at levels such as the individual plant or the whole company. Shop steward organisation also developed, matching the greater institutionalisation of domestic bargaining, with regular shop steward meetings and the development of steward hierarchies with senior stewards and multi-union convenors. By the late 1970s, shop stewards existed in three-quarters of establishments for manual workers and one-third of establishments for white-collar workers. At that time an estimated 3,500 manual stewards and about 300 white-collar stewards were full-time, representing more stewards paid by their companies to spend time on union business than there were union officers paid by trade unions.[16] Management not only paid to support the shop steward hierarchies, but aided trade union organisation through agreements on the closed shop and check-off. At its peak in the late 1970s, the closed shop had spread to cover about 50 per cent of trade unionists.[17] At the same time, check-off arrangements (in which employers collect union subscriptions by deduction from wages) had spread to cover nearly 60 per cent of establishments and over 70 per cent of employees in manufacturing. (Unlike the closed shop, which has been eroded by legal changes in the 1980s, check-off has continued to increase in the 1980s.[18])

These changes were pushed for by some trade union officials, but they were more often initiated and sponsored by management. Employers, faced with inflationary pressures, increasing foreign competition, greater overseas ownership of industry, growing industrial concentration and a marked increase in government intervention in employment relations, reacted by seeking a firmer grip on labour costs and a more effective control over the labour process. They saw more formalised domestic bargaining, at plant or company level, as the means to achieve the workplace changes they desired. Check-off and closed shops were supported by managers in the interests of simplifying union administration and helping create domestic union structures with sufficient cohesion to implement agreements.

Employers also replaced the old piecework incentive schemes with new pay systems. These were intended to provide more rational internal wage structures with fixed rates of pay covering a whole plant or company. The intention was also to end the constant steward bargaining at each job change and to facilitate greater management control via more centralised negotiations. There was thus a movement towards measured daywork schemes – payment by time dependent on the achievement of work-studied output targets.[19] (This and the diffusion of work study techniques were also part of the continuing, though not always successful, effort to deal with restrictive work rules.[20]) In addition, through the 1970s, there was a significant increase in job evaluation for blue-collar workers. Both measured daywork and job evaluation favoured plant-wide bargaining and involved the creation of more orderly internal wage structures.[21]

Shop stewards themselves provided some of the pressures towards formalisation and for the most part they did not resist moves in this direction. Stewards sought more bureaucratic arrangements as a means to greater effectiveness.[22] The traditional fragmentation of workplace bargaining had disadvantages for employees and the move to more structured steward organisation was thought to be essential if stewards were to retain or increase their influence in the face of more sophisticated managerial policies or were to affect decisions made higher in company management. Thus, plant-wide and sometimes company-wide joint shop stewards committees were established to coordinate strategy and to engage in the new collective bargaining arrangements.

Even at the height of stewards' bargaining power in the 1970s, formal domestic bargaining usually took place at the level of the individual plant or establishment rather than for an entire multi-plant company. By the late 1970s, in only 11 per cent of the establishments covered by formal domestic agreements did the agreement cover more than one plant and these multi-plant agreements were normally found in industries *without* a tradition of strong shopfloor bargaining.[23] Formal multi-plant bargaining occurred where the employer had taken the initiative to move straight from the old multi-employer to new single-employer bargaining, or in foreign-owned companies with a preference for centralised, bureaucratic personnel policies. Where shop steward organisations were already strong, employers were likely to keep the determination of pay and conditions decentralised to the establishment level even when formalising domestic bargaining arrangements. Only a very small proportion of the largest British companies gave any official recognition to combine committees representing stewards from different plants.[24]

Without employer assistance shop stewards found considerable difficulty in building the necessary communication and organisational links between the workgroups of separate plants of a company. Of course, the difficulties in the face of trade union coordination of the workforces of multinational enterprises were even greater. In the 1970s, because of management opposition, unions found it extremely difficult to breach this gap in the structure of union and workplace representation and operate effectively at the new levels determined by large-scale, complex company structures of the multidivisional kind. Formal bargaining may for a time have strengthened trade unionism within the plant, but the development of formal domestic bargaining in the 1970s did not give unions access to corporate levels of decision making.

Thus, the aim of many large firms through the 1970s and 1980s was to relocate and formalise collective bargaining. This meant bargaining somewhere *below* the level of the industry but *above* the level of the shopfloor. The intention was to internalise industrial relations and reduce the number of bargaining points thereby tailoring agreements to the firm's needs and strengthening management's position.

There are important differences between firms in manufacturing industry as to the degree of centralisation and the level of collective bargaining. In some firms, for example, ICI, Ford, Kodak and the British Sugar Corporation, collective bargaining is highly centralised, covering all or most of the firm's activities. These tend to be firms with relatively standardised products, integrated production systems and centralised, functional forms of organisation. Other firms, such as British Leyland, moved in this direction in the late 1970s. On the other hand, some firms, such as Pilkingtons, Rolls Royce, Lucas, Philips and Cadburys, began to decentralise their bargaining arrangements. Privatisation has also led to some companies, such as National Power, starting to devolve their industrial relations. Some diversified companies, such as Unilever, Imperial Group and Reed International, usually with clear product market categories and multidivisional structures, have chosen to bargain at divisional level for many of their activities. Many firms, where production units were not particularly integrated and where there was more plant autonomy, chose to bargain primarily at plant level. This included firms such as GEC and GKN in engineering and Courtaulds and Coats Vyella in textiles.[25] These differences in bargaining levels in large part reflected differences in corporate structure and showed the growing ability of managements to make new strategic choices in industrial relations. Later in this chapter we examine changes in collective bargaining structure in the public sector.

THE EMPLOYER COUNTER-OFFENSIVE OF THE 1980s

The advent of the Thatcher government and the recession of the 1980s weakened the shop steward organisations that had grown to such prominence in the 1970s. As unemployment rose and product market competition intensified, a significant minority of employers chose to mount an offensive against shop steward power and to reshape or reduce domestic bargaining arrangements.

For example, in British Leyland the changed climate was symbolised when the chairman, Sir Michael Edwardes, successfully dismissed the company's senior convenor, in 1979 and went on to adopt an aggressive labour policy. In 1981 he threatened to dismiss all unconstitutional strikers and countered the stewards' call for a strike over the annual pay claim by directly communicating to all employees that he would dismiss all the workers of the most affected plants. Across the motor industry, once the centre of domestic bargaining, shop steward strength was reduced, as employers pushed back the frontier of control on such issues as the length of rest periods, the speed of the line and payment of lay-off pay for workers affected by others' disputes. The short, shop steward-led strikes which had caused such concern hitherto became less of a feature of the industry's labour relations in the 1980s.

Elsewhere, in the public-sector, the government and public-sector employers challenged the unions and showed a preparedness to take major strikes. In the case of steel, the British Steel Corporation fought and largely won the first major strike in that industry for many years. Following on this, management closed a number of plants and generally tightened up managerial controls. With its own direct employees, in the case of the GCHQ electronic monitoring facility, the government withdrew union recognition, arguing that unionism was not appropriate and posed a threat to national security.

The major public sector dispute occurred in the coal industry with the miners' strike of 1984–5. In response to threatened pit closures, the National Union of Mineworkers, under the militant leadership of Arthur Scargill, took strike action, at first locally, but then extending the dispute to a nation-wide strike, though without having had a national ballot. The National Coal Board, under Ian MacGregor, a new and equally radical chairman recently imported from the US, was encouraged in its firm stand by the Thatcher government which from the start saw this as a major dispute which it was determined to win. As the dispute continued a number of factors combined to undermine the union's position – legal action against its funds, the continued working of the Nottingham coalfield, the availability of coal stocks for the power stations, police counter-action against picketing and the reluctance of other unions to break the law and take sympathetic action. As the government and management saw the possibility of winning and as the determination of the union continued, the dispute dragged on reflecting the irreconcilable positions of the two sides. However, finally, after twelve months, the miners returned to work in what might be seen as the most significant defeat for the unions since the General Strike. The outcome of the dispute for industrial relations in the industry was a divided and weakened union, a more confident and assertive management, and the downgrading of collective bargaining. For industrial relations in Britain as a whole, the dispute showed how changes in the political and legal environment had shifted the balance of power in management's favour.

In the private sector there were also major confrontations which, though small in numbers, had a wider demonstration effect on British industrial relations. In January 1986 a strike began at News International, the publisher of *The Times*, the *Sun* and the *News of the World* newspapers. The owner, Rupert Murdoch, dismissed 5,500 printworkers and announced the derecognition of the print unions. The dispute arose from a failure to reach agreement on company demands for new work rules and manning levels, but it also had origins in long-standing labour relations difficulties and conflicts at the shopfloor level. When the strike started, production of the company's newspapers was moved immediately from Fleet Street to a new plant at Wapping in London docklands, where the papers were produced by a new workforce hired to replace the striking printworkers. Despite heavy picketing at the plant, a large police presence ensured the unions were unable to stop the production or distribution of the newspapers. After one

year, during which time the unions faced heavy court fines and sequestration for unlawful picketing, the strike was abandoned in February 1987.
News International continues to operate without the print unions and with
unilateral management determination of pay and conditions. The Wapping
dispute had a broader impact on the newspaper industry; without having to
resort to such dramatic tactics, other newspapers followed its lead in
reducing manpower and obtaining changes in working practices from the
unions, which now put up little resistance. In another area of the media,
television broadcasting, a somewhat similar dispute occurred at TV-am,
when in the winter of 1987–8, management sacked striking technicians,
introduced new technology and ran the station with replacement labour.

Another major dispute occurred at Britain's largest shipping line. In
1988, increased competition and uncertainties in their cross-Channel ferry
operations led P&O to demand a reduction in manning levels, a simpli-
fication of wage structures and changes in shift rosters. The National Union
of Seamen at Dover strongly resisted. However, the union attempt to extend
the dispute to other ports and shipping companies resulted in substantial
fines and sequestration by the High Court. After four months' dispute, P&O
announced the dismissal of the majority of its seafarers and the withdrawal
of recognition from the union. The company then resumed ferry services,
sailing its ships with new crews hired to replace the dismissed strikers,
alongside its non-striking officers and a core of its employees who had
agreed to return to work on the company's terms. In the wake of the dispute,
P&O began to construct a non-union-based system of human resources
management. In both national newspaper printing and the shipping industry, long-standing national agreements virtually ceased to exist.

The 1980s saw important changes, but also considerable continuity in
industrial relations. In the changed economic, political and legal climate,
trade union membership fell by 3 million, legislative changes (to be discussed in the next chapter) considerably restrained union activities, and the
number of strikes declined substantially. At workplace level the closed
shop has been curtailed and the influence of shop stewards has been
reduced. In these circumstances, management seized the opportunity to
push through changes in industrial relations practices which resulted in
major defeats for unions, as described above. Less dramatic, but more
important in a broader perspective, employers have enforced concessionary
agreements allowing changes in working practices and greater flexibility
and have sought to reduce collective bargaining as a constraint on their
activities. In parallel they have increased the scope of unilateral management action (negotiating with trade unions over a smaller range of issues)
and have extended non-union-based consultation and participation systems.
This has been accompanied by some introduction of new human resource

management practices, including new forms of team working, flexible systems of employment, individual contracts, performance-related pay systems, and new, often non-union, consultative arrangements. Much of this has been aimed at integrating workers more into the firm and obtaining greater commitment.[26]

However, there have also been significant continuities with the 1960s and 1970s. Macho-management (defined in terms of attacks on trade unions and the forceful imposition of change) was relatively rare and most employers did not feel the need openly to attack trade unions and shop stewards. Much of the talk about a new period of human resource management is somewhat exaggerated: evidence suggests that so-called new policies and practices have not been widely introduced and have usually been applied in a piecemeal fashion by employers.[27] Changes in working practices have often been modest, especially between maintenance and production workers and within maintenance areas and has not resulted in broad flexibility and multi-skilling of the labour force. Major changes in this respect have been confined to a minority of plants, and the gap between these and the majority is often still large.[28] There have been relatively few cases of the derecognition of unions and collective bargaining still remains the main form of joint rule-making in industrial relations. While overall union membership and density has fallen, this has been because of the closure of large, heavily unionised manufacturing plants and the opening of new, smaller plants and service operations. In areas where union membership was traditionally high, it has tended to remain so. Despite a growing formality of industrial relations, in line with long traditions of informality in Britain, shop stewards have retained a degree of influence as evidenced by the price in terms of wage increases which employers have had to pay for change.[29] Money wage increases averaged 6–9 per cent through the 1980s. The trend towards internal, single-employer bargaining has continued, often with a further decentralisation to plant rather than company or divisional level.[30] There has also been a trend towards the insulation of bargaining from outside forces, with pay and conditions more related to inside forces such as productivity and profitability rather than cost of living or external comparability. Consequently, many of the changes of the 1980s have been built on the developments of the two previous decades.

Thus, Britain's traditional collective bargaining system, based on multi-employer, industry-wide agreements, was undermined, especially in the 1960s, and was altered in the 1970s by the growth and formalisation of single-employer, domestic bargaining. In the 1980s, there was some reduction in the scope and coverage of collective bargaining. However, in terms of the level of bargaining, the trend has been further away from industry bargaining and towards a greater decentralisation of single-employer bargaining. For the most part, national agreements now have much less significance except to act as a safety net for the support of the lowest paid.[31] However, national bargaining continues to be important

(a)   on certain issues e.g. hours,
(b)   in certain industries, albeit often small ones such as parts of construc- tion, textiles, clothing, printing, road haulage, baking and electrical contracting, and
(c)   in the public sector.

PUBLIC-SECTOR COLLECTIVE BARGAINING

Public-sector collective bargaining has tended to be rather different from that in the private sector, and the story of its development has also been different. After the First World War the Whitley Report played an important part in stimulating collective bargaining and, despite setbacks, it developed slowly through the interwar years. It came to cover not only manual workers in electricity, gas, local authorities and transport, but also white-collar workers in central and local government. After the Second World War, the public sector was greatly enlarged by the nationalisation of industries such as coal and the railways. Here formal industry-wide bar- gaining, which had origins in the interwar years, was established, and similar arrangements were also created for manual workers in other indus- tries such as electricity, gas and local government.

In the public services, such as central and local government, national Whitley machinery had been established during the First World War and was extended and consolidated after the Second World War. Of course these sectors employed a high proportion of white-collar workers, and one of the striking things about the public sector has been the high level of unionisation and collective bargaining coverage of such workers. Health Service workers, schoolteachers, firemen and the police have traditionally also had their wages determined at national level.

Thus, in the public sector, there traditionally existed a series of national, industry-wide agreements, negotiated by a strong trade union and a single employer such as British Rail or a consortium of employers such as the local authorities negotiating through their employers' association, the Local Government Management Board.[32] These national agreements tended to be highly formalised and comprehensive and established detailed substantive and procedural systems. They were not, for the most part, subject to the fragmented bargaining, wage drift and unofficial action such as developed with private-sector domestic bargaining in the 1960s. This was because, since public-sector bargaining units were more bureaucratised and homogeneous, there was less scope for domestic bargaining and it was easier for managements to administer central wage and salary structures and other rules. There were only limited exceptions to this, such as local authority manual workers for whom there developed some local piecework bargaining. However, there were problems associated with this highly centralised system of bargaining. One was a problem of efficiency and manpower utilisation: under such a system, it was difficult to provide wage incentives, to bargain in detail about productivity, and to swop off wage increases at the national level for greater efficiency at local level. Another problem concerned wage levels and their repercussive effect elsewhere in the economy: when pay settlements were high, given the large numbers involved and their high visibility, these had considerable implications for government spending and for the inflationary process throughout the economy. A further problem occurred when, from time to time, governments operated incomes policies and tried to set an example with their own employees by holding back public-sector pay. Governments were able to do this because they were in many cases the ultimate employer and intervention in the wage-fixing process was relatively easy given the centralised nature of bargaining units. However, such interventions tended to upset differentials and led to periodic major disputes in the public sector, which as a result became relatively more strike-prone throughout the 1970s and 1980s. Together these factors combined to create what some have seen as a crisis in public-sector industrial relations in the 1970s and 1980s.[33]

In part to prevent some of these problems, the pay of groups such as doctors, dentists, nurses and senior civil servants was made subject to independent pay review bodies. The police and firemen also have their pay index-linked. Since 1987, after a series of strikes and the intervention of the Conservative government, teachers had their pay fixed by government and now have a pay review body. However, the government has not always been happy with the outcome of these arrangements and from time to time has staged increases and sought to reduce index-linking.

Since the 1980s, public-sector collective bargaining has started to move in the same direction as the private sector moved in the 1970s and local autonomy in bargaining has slowly increased. In part this has been because of external pressures, in particular government encouragement of competitive tendering, opting-out and devolved financial management; in part it is the result of internal pressures, with some local authorities, civil service departments, and other bodies wishing to fix wages and conditions to suit their local economic circumstances. Significant breaks with national negotiations are in train. A growing number of local and county authorities, mainly in the South East, have broken away from national negotiations. Areas of the Civil Service are also in the process of similar fragmentation as a result of the creation of quasi-independent agencies and a greater preparedness by the Treasury to see bargaining occur at departmental level. In addition, in local government and the NHS, there has been a growth in individually negotiated contracts for more senior staff, and in school-teaching management now has more discretion to pay allowances on top of national scales. Finally, there has been an increased use of performance-related, incentive pay, mainly for senior staff, though this is now starting to percolate down to lower-level employees and to question the future of national bargaining.

It is still unclear how far this public-sector decentralisation and move away from national bargaining will go and in large part future developments will depend on which political party is in government. A future Conservative government would undoubtedly encourage these tendencies towards the decentralisation of collective bargaining and indeed towards its diminution. Whichever party is in power, it seems inevitable, however, that there will be more diversity between and within different parts of the public sector. There will probably also be more local flexibility and pay additions, though often on top of existing national agreements on pay and grading. However, one major constraint on decentralisation will be fears that movement in this direction may lead to higher-level settlements and pay leapfrogging.

THE USE OF THE STRIKE WEAPON IN COLLECTIVE BARGAINING

Phases in the development of Britain's collective bargaining system are in large part reflected in the pattern of industrial disputes. Three measures of industrial action are conventionally used – the number of strikes or lockouts in a year, the number of workers involved in strikes, and the working days lost in strikes, i.e. the number of workers involved times the duration of the stoppage. We will use the number of strikes and the number of working days lost as the best measures of strike frequency and incidence. Britain's strike figures are quite good and comprehensive compared to some other countries. The Department of Employment records stoppages due to indus-trial disputes which involve 10 or more workers and which last for at least one day or which involve over 100 days lost.

As can be seen from Figures 9.1 and 9.2 there were high levels of industrial action in the late nineteenth century and just before and just after the First World War. This was when the system of national collective bargaining was established, tested, and consolidated. These years were characterised by bitter, industry-wide confrontation, involving massive numbers of working days lost and involving union demands for recog-nition, national claims for wage increases and hours reductions, and later employer counterclaims for wage cuts. These major disputes reflected the national structure of collective bargaining and came to an end as a result of union defeats in the recession of the 1920s. They did not return when the economy revived from the mid-1930s onwards nor during and after the war.

After the Second World War the figures for annual days lost showed a remarkably peaceful picture for a time compared with earlier industrial conflicts. Indeed, the operation and widespread extension of the national collective bargaining system was now credited by some with the successful institutionalisation of industrial conflict in Britain.[34] The apparent success of the national institutions was greatly assisted, if not primarily caused, by the economic growth of the postwar period and by the policies of the Welfare Compromise discussed in Chapter 7. National disputes were rare, lockouts were even rarer and strikes became very much shorter and smaller in scale, giving a dramatic reduction in the figures for working days lost, despite a larger labour force and higher union membership.

Yet from the early 1950s there was an upward trend in the number of stoppages, triggered initially by the collapse of the Labour government's incomes policy, the subsequent change in government, and price rises initiated by the Korean war. Between 1953 and 1959 stoppages outside coal mining (which has had a somewhat exceptional pattern owing to the unique circumstances of that industry and its changing bargaining arrangements) rose by nearly 80 per cent; 1960 saw a big increase in stoppages, when the non-mining total first exceeded 1,000; and throughout the 1960s there was a more or less continuous growth in the number of stoppages.[35] Between 1960 and 1968 non-mining strikes rose by 85 per cent, working days lost by 83 per cent, and the number of workers involved by 283 per cent, and by 1968 the total number of strikes had exceeded 2,000.[36]

Though there had been some large national stoppages in the late 1950s in engineering, printing and transport, most strikes during this period covered only a single plant or department and were of short duration, reflecting the rise of domestic and more fragmented bargaining referred to above. In addition an increasing proportion of the strikes in these years were unofficial (in that they took place without the prior authorisation of the national union) and unconstitutional (in that they took place before an agreed procedure had been exhausted). The average strike in the 1960s directly involved around 500 workers and led to the loss of about 1,000 working days; it was estimated at the time that unconstitutional and unofficial strikes made up 95 per cent of all stoppages and accounted for two thirds of the total number of days lost.[37]

Underlying the rising strike trend were economic factors such as full employment, rising prices, and real wages which were increasing less rapidly from the mid-1960s onwards. Alongside these, though more diffi-

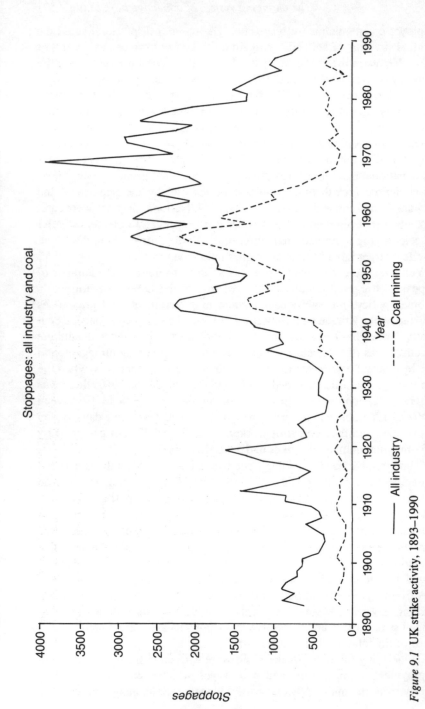

Stoppages: all industry and coal

All industry ——— Coal mining ----

Figure 9.1 UK strike activity, 1893–1990

Source: Historical Abstract of Labour Statistics; Department of Employment Gazette, July 1991; S. Milner and D. Metcalf, 'A Century of UK Strike Activity: An Alternative Perspective', Centre for Economic Performance, Discussion Paper Number 22 (1991).

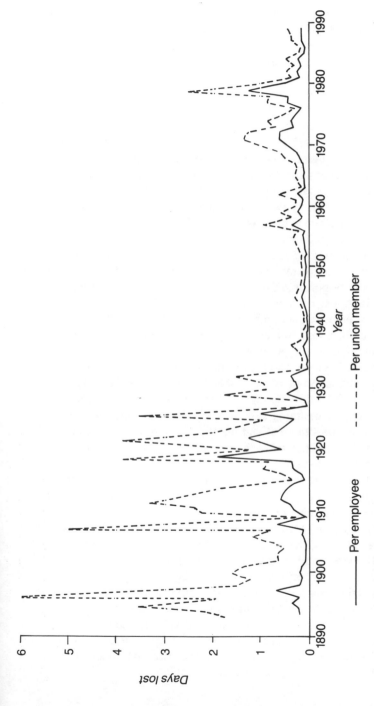

Figure 9.2 UK working days lost per employee and per union membership (excluding coal), 1893–1990

— Per employee   - - - - Per union member

Source: Historical Abstract of Labour Statistics; Department of Employment Gazette, July 1991; S. Milner and D. Metcalf, 'A Century of UK Strike Activity: An Alternative Perspective', Centre for Economic Performance, Discussion Paper Number 22 (1991).

cult to assess, were changing social factors such as rising expectations and a better educated and less deferential workforce. The trend also reflected the weakness and inability of traditional collective bargaining procedures to cope with the changed circumstances.[38] The fragmented nature of work-place bargaining, as we have described it, led to sectional stoppages over matters such as relative wages, the application of incentive schemes and working arrangements at shopfloor level. National disputes procedures were unable to contain the growing number of such disputes, and increas-ingly both management and unions found these procedures cumbersome and remote.[39] In engineering, for example, from its initiation on the shop-floor, through meetings at works level, to local conference and to central conference, with possible reference back, the hearing of a dispute could take several months. With a larger number of cases going through pro-cedure, the time taken to go through the various stages rose and the number of breaches of procedure grew.[40]

At the beginning of the century, strikes were limited to a very few industries where union membership was well established. Coal mining, for example, was responsible for a substantial proportion of the disputes and working days lost each year until the late 1950s. The increase in the incidence of industrial action from the 1960s onwards reflected the spread of trade unionism and collective bargaining to new groups of employees, such as white-collar and public-sector workers.

Britain's strike record was, from the mid-1960s, seen as demonstrating a growing national problem (see Table 9.1). The argument that Britain was 'strike-prone' fuelled mounting criticism of trade unions and of the tradi-tional collective bargaining system. There was growing concern, in parti-cular at the unconstitutional and unofficial nature of strikes, at 'wildcat' strikes which were felt to be particularly damaging, and the spread of strikes to more sectors.

In the 1970s there was some diminution of strike activity in the private sector, in part reflecting the beginnings of the reform and formalisation of plant and company bargaining referred to above. This was better able to contain industrial relations problems or it ensured that, when strikes took place, there were fewer of them, though they might be bigger in terms of the number covered. However, working days lost remained high throughout the 1970s and there were some years of very high levels of days lost, such as 1972, 1974 and 1979. In part this greater volatility in strike figures and high number of working days lost reflected the operation of incomes policies and the advent of major national confrontations surrounding wage claims in the public sector where, as we have seen, collective bargaining remained very centralised. At the same time there were some major private-sector disputes as in the motor car industry in the early 1970s and engineering in the late 1970s.

Table 9.1 UK strike statistics, 1960–91

Year	Stoppages	Workers involved ('000)	Working days lost ('000)
1960	2,849	819	3,024
1961	2,701	779	3,046
1962	2,465	4,423	5,798
1963	2,081	593	1,755
1964	2,535	883	2,277
1965	2,365	876	2,925
1966	1,951	544	2,398
1967	2,133	734	2,787
1968	2,390	2,258	4,690
1969	3,146	1,665	6,846
1970	3,943	1,801	10,980
1971	2,223	1,173	13,558
1972	2,497	1,734	23,909
1973	2,854	1,591	7,173
1974	2,992	1,626	14,750
1975	2,828	809	6,012
1976	2,016	668	3,284
1977	2,703	1,166	10,142
1978	2,471	1,041	9,405
1979	2,080	4,608	29,474
1980	1,330	834	11,964
1981	1,338	1,513	4,266
1982	1,528	2,103	5,313
1983	1,364	574	3,754
1984	1,221	1,464	27,135
1985	903	791	6,402
1986	1,074	720	1,920
1987	1,016	887	3,546
1988	781	790	3,702
1989	701	727	4,128
1990	630	298	1,903
1991	369	176	761

Source: Department of Employment Gazette, relevant years, December 1990 and July 1991.

Despite the above, a word of caution must be added concerning this picture of strike-proneness. It is possible to exaggerate the deleterious effects of strikes on British industry through these years. For example, it has been pointed out that in any one year most British employers were never confronted by a strike or the threat of a strike. Employers most likely to be affected were in motor vehicles, shipbuilding, mining and port transport, and within these industries strikes tended to be concentrated in a few large plants.[41] Differences in reporting the incidence of strikes make international comparisons hazardous, but they do broadly show that Britain was not too badly placed in terms of the proportion of working time lost through strikes. The USA tended to be higher; Japan was higher for a time in the late 1940s and early 1950s; and Canada and Italy also tended to be higher through most of these years. However, some of Britain's main European competitors, such as West Germany and France, were consistently lower. Moreover, from the 1960s onwards, Britain's relative position deteriorated. As Table 9.2 shows, the UK has tended to come about halfway down the international strike league table. On most recent averages the UK ranks lower than Italy, Canada or Spain in days lost per 1,000 employees, but still remains higher than major competitors such as France, Germany and Japan. The UK figures are not exceptional for a country which relies on collective bargaining as its main mechanism for handling conflicts in the employment relationship, which has problems associated with an ageing industrial base and contracting heavy industries, and where governments of all persuasions have tried to control inflationary pressures by seeking to influence highly centralised bargaining arrangements in the public sector.

In the 1980s the number of strikes, workers involved in strikes and working days lost all fell dramatically. In 1990 recorded strikes were down to 630 and working days lost to 1.9 million. This compared with an annual average number of 2,462 disputes in the 1960s, 2,631 in the 1970s and 1,129 in the 1980s; it compared with an annual average of 4.7 million working days lost in the 1960s, 12.9 million in the 1970s and 7.2 million in the 1980s. There are those who claim that this reflects better and more cooperative industrial relations, though evidence for such an improvement other than the strike figures themselves is not very conclusive.[42] The government and its supporters claim that in large part the fall reflects changes in labour legislation, making strikes more difficult. This argument about the changed legal situation and the tightening of managerial attitudes towards strikes is rather more compelling. However, legal changes do not explain why most of the reduction in strike activity has been in the private sector. Economic and institutional factors have probably been more important in the reduction in strikes.[43] The high levels of unemployment in the early 1980s and again in the early 1990s, the fall in price inflation in these

Table 9.2 Comparative strike-proneness (working days lost per thousand employees), 1980–9

Country	1980–4	1985–9	1980–9
United Kingdom	480	180	330
Australia	470	230	350
Canada	660	280	470
France	90	60	80
Germany (FR)	50	–	30
Italy	950	300	620
Japan	10	10	10
Spain	650	650	650
Sweden	240	120	180
United States	160	90	120

Source: Department of Employment Gazette, December 1991.
Note: France excludes public-sector disputes; from 1981 onwards the US has excluded strikes involving fewer than 1,000 workers; Canada made the same change in 1984.

same periods and the rise in real earnings of those in employment were probably more important factors. Significant also were the changes in collective bargaining which occurred in the 1970s and which private-sector management built on in the 1980s and used as the base on which to introduce more sophisticated pay systems and other personnel practices. By contrast, in the public sector, strike activity has remained relatively higher, reflecting attempts at macho-management in industries such as coal and the railways and reactions to wage restraint elsewhere in the public sector.

A number of caveats should be registered to the story of declining strike activity in the 1980s. First, there were still years in the 1980s when working days lost were high, largely the result of major public-sector disputes. It should be remembered that overall more working days were lost in the 1980s than in the 1940s to 1960s (suggesting that the 1970s may have been the exceptional decade rather than the 1980s). Second, when the reduction in union membership and the decline of traditional strike-prone sectors is taken into account, the fall in strike incidence does not appear quite so large. Third, there has been relatively more recourse to forms of industrial action other than strikes. Hence the incidence of overtime bans rose from under twice that of strikes in the early 1980s to up to two and a half times by the early 1990s. In recent years ACAS has had to deal with record numbers of individual disputes many of which have concerned working conditions.[44] Fourth, a similar reduction in strikes and working days lost occurred in most other major western economies, suggesting that more international factors such as high unemployment and lower inflation may have been more important in reducing strike activity than factors unique to British industrial relations.

It is difficult to predict what will happen in the 1990s. On the one hand, institutional and legal changes will largely remain in place and these will constrain strike activity; if unemployment remains high, if inflation is low, and real wages do not fall, then these economic factors will work to reduce strike levels. On the other hand, if inflationary pressures are strong and if real wages fall or if some groups (such as public sector workers) feel that they have fallen behind, then, when unemployment falls, there could be an upturn in strike activity. What is sure is that there will always be conflict in industry, and, so long as collective bargaining exists, this will from time to time take the form of strikes and will reflect collective bargaining arrangements.[45]

BEYOND FREE COLLECTIVE BARGAINING

Collective bargaining pervades employment relations within the UK, but since the 1980s it has been under considerable strain. It has come under pressure from a renewed advocacy of unilateral management, long heard in the US but previously seldom voiced in Britain. It has also come under attack, for the first time since the late nineteenth century, from a government committed to liberal individualist ideas. It has been constrained by legislation on collective labour relations and by the build-up of legislation on individual employment matters which we will discuss in the next chapter. In addition, there have been other pressures on collective bargaining.

One set of pressures has come from new developments within collective bargaining itself. On greenfield sites, where trade unions have been recognised for the first time, recognition has come about because of management's choice of a particular union to represent their employees in so-called 'beauty contests', where a union is selected by management to represent future workers. Traditionally this was not the way collective bargaining developed in Britain and it is yet to be seen how deep will be its roots in such situations. In addition there has been a growth in recent years of arrangements where union presence is restricted to individual representation but does not cover wider collective bargaining over terms and conditions. In some instances, especially on greenfield sites, where collective bargaining does exist, it is capped by no-strike agreements and pendulum arbitration which involves the use of an arbitrator being called in to resolve impasses by choosing one or the other side's final offer. Some argue that this removes the ultimate sanction from bargaining and changes its very nature. All these arrangements are still relatively rare, but they do represent a challenge to traditional collective bargaining and may in future have a broader effect on the conduct of industrial relations.[46]

We have already referred to some of the challenges posed by certain aspects of Human Resource Management. Here we would briefly note that at one extreme this has meant derecognition of trade unions and the removal of collective bargaining.[47] As yet such cases are relatively small in number. More often it has meant the move towards individual performance based pay, new non-union systems of joint consultation and employee involvement, and a by-passing or downplaying of collective bargaining. We will return to these developments in Chapter 11.

Another set of pressures on collective bargaining have come from government intervention in the form of incomes policies. Table 9.3 illustrates the complex history of government attempts to intervene in the regulation of incomes since the Second World War. Policies have been introduced by governments which favoured a system of economic planning – like the Wilson government in the late 1960s. They have also been introduced by governments which initially adopted market principles – like the Heath government between 1970 and 1974. They have been adopted by governments which, though initially non-interventionist, came to seek a corporatist solution to Britain's economic problems – the social contract Labour government of 1974 to 1979. Policies have sometimes been voluntary, sometimes compulsory; some specified simple pay norms or guidelines, some produced more complex formulae. All, however, restricted free collective bargaining by setting government objectives to override the possible outcome of negotiated settlements on pay.

Incomes policies had mixed success. Even those which succeeded in holding down pay increases for a time often degenerated in time into a backlash of claims based on upset differentials and major strikes such as the two major national coal disputes of 1972 and 1974 which challenged the Heath government's incomes policy. The following government's 'Social Contract' policies were initially based on firm trade union support, and industrial action fell to very low levels. However, further attempts to limit pay rises collapsed in a 'Winter of Discontent' in 1978–9. The Thatcher government therefore returned to free collective bargaining, at least in the private sector. But, in the public sector it imposed a system of cash limits and thereby indirectly retained tighter controls over pay bargaining than its predecessors. As we have seen, this caused industrial relations problems and instability in the public sector; arguably it would have created even more severe strains had not the private sector also been under great pressure at the time. The establishment of new pay review bodies for groups such as nurses and teachers have largely removed them from collective bargaining on wages and conditions. Thus, there have been numerous attempts to

Table 9.3 Policies on pay, mid-1960s–1990s

Year	Pay policy	Institutions
Labour		
1964	Voluntary policy	Tri-partite Declaration of
1955 (Apr)	3–3¹/₂% norm (Exceptions for productivity, low-pay man-power needs and anomalies)	Intent National Board for Prices and Incomes (1965–70)
1966 (July)	Six months freeze Six months severe restraint	TUC 'Early Warning System' (Nov 1965)
1968 (April)	3¹/₂% ceiling (Exceptions for productivity and anomalies)	
1969 (Dec)	2¹/₂–4¹/₂% norm	
Conservative 1970	No pay policy in private sector N–1% in public sector	
1972 (Nov)	Stage 1–six months' statutory freeze	
1973 (Apr)	Stage 2–£1+4% (Max £250 p.a.)	
1973 (Nov)	Stage 3–£2.25 a week or 7% (Max £350 p.a.; indexation)	Pay Board (1973–4) Price Commission (1973–4)
Labour 1974	No formal policy Wage increases in line with RPI Increases only every 12 months	Social Contract
1975 (July)	Phase I–£6 per week for those earning less than £8,500 p.a.	
1976 (Aug)	Phase II–5% (Min £2.50 per week and Max £4 per week)	
1977 (July)	10% maximum (Exception for productivity agreements)	
1978 (July)	5% maximum (Exceptions for productivity, low-pay, anomalies)	
		Standing Commission on Pay Comparability (for public sector) (1979–80)
Conservative 1979–	No pay policy in private sector Cash limits in public sector Exhortations to reduce expectations Monetarism and high interest rates	
		Entry into European Exchange Rate (Oct 1990): exit (Sept. 1992)

construct viable incomes policies in the UK; none, so far, has achieved lasting success. Nevertheless, state intervention in pay determination is never far from the surface and policies on pay may return to the agenda in the 1990s.[48]

In several periods there have been demands for industrial democracy which have also gone beyond traditional British collective bargaining. The first was in the early decades of the twentieth century, when demands for workers control were made by Syndicalists, Guild Socialists and advocates of industrial unionism who argued that trade unions should be involved, not in accommodative collective bargaining, but in the management and government of industry. The Labour victory in 1945 and nationalisation created high hopes for new arrangements for worker involvement going beyond traditional collective bargaining. However, nationalisation endorsed collective bargaining as the method of employee participation and left management to operate in the conventional way, through separate channels. For those who had hoped for more direct industrial democracy, nationalisation was a disappointment. Industrial democracy was again widely discussed in the general review of industrial relations in the 1960s and 1970s and proposals were made for the involvement of unions in management. The 1970s saw a spate of new workers' cooperatives, sit-ins or work-ins challenging managerial decisions to close plants, and some shop steward plans for alternative production.[49] Although the motive behind many of these was largely job protection and resistance to redundancy, they represented a different way of thinking about giving workers a say which diverged from traditional collective bargaining.[50]

Britain's membership of the EC brought European practices of worker participation by works councils and workers on company boards into discussions in the UK. Despite many union suspicions of such forms of industrial participation, the TUC was drawn into the debate on worker directors and in the mid-1970s proposed that half of company board seats should be taken by workers elected through trade union machinery[51] (see Chapter 10). At the time some unions were suspicious of this and opposed it as likely to undermine collective bargaining. At the same time, however, some management became more interested in consultation of various kinds. As a result, many introduced new consultative arrangements, often alongside collective bargaining. By the early 1980s more than one-third of manufacturing plants had some sort of consultative arrangements, most introduced during the course of the 1970s.[52] As we have suggested, the number of such arrangements has grown in the 1980s often reflecting new approaches to the management of human resources. At the present time, the creation of the European Single Market and the Social Charter has put joint consultation and European-style works councils (as discussed in Chapter 8) very much on the legislative agenda. Though the Conservative government and managements are hostile to many of its provisions, British unions, after their defeats in the 1980s and their realisation that collective bargaining can be reduced in coverage and scope, are now more interested in it as a way forward for giving workers a say in decision making.[53]

CONCLUSION

In the period immediately after the Second World War the traditional system of national, industry-wide collective bargaining, with the associated absence of government involvement in employment relations, was widely regarded as a firmly established, mature and democratic method for handling conflicts at work and giving employees a say in deciding terms and conditions of employment. From the 1960s onwards, the traditional system of collective bargaining became subject to strain arising from the growth of workplace, shop steward-led bargaining and of increased government intervention. In the 1970s and 1980s more formal plant- and company-level bargaining have replaced national and more fragmented bargaining as the main form of collective bargaining in British industry. The collective bargaining system in Britain is complex, with national bargaining still surviving in the public sector, though now itself under pressure; with some private-sector national agreements still continuing, though largely supplemented by domestic bargaining; and with company- and plant-bargaining of various kinds existing in the private sector. In the 1970s and 1980s, there was considerable questioning of collective bargaining from different perspectives. However, collective bargaining still dominates the determination of employment conditions for the majority of British employees.

10 Government attempts to reconstruct British industrial relations

In the last chapter we looked at management-initiated attempts to reform the British system of industrial relations. The last quarter-century has also seen a series of government-initiated attempts to reconstruct industrial relations. From the late 1960s onwards, the postwar consensus, which had supported collective bargaining and a voluntarist role for the state, gradually crumbled. All recent governments have produced major and radically different proposals for change.

An analysis of these differing government policies highlights the increasing significance of the role of the state, as discussed in Chapter 7 and illustrates the conflicting theoretical perspectives outlined at the start of this book. Government attempts to promote the reform of industrial relations have been premised on different presuppositions and perspectives. Liberal collectivist justifications for collective bargaining have been used to support state intervention both to increase and to contain trade union power. Macrocorporatist tendencies were evident in many of the institutions and laws of the 1970s, although corporatist arguments were often not openly used. In the 1980s, liberal individualism revived under the Thatcher government's attack on the institutions and practices of trade unionism and collective bargaining. In the 1990s, with a fourth term of Conservative government under Mr Major, there may be some signs of a less ideologically aggressive approach, though with a continued commitment to basic liberal individualist policies. The different interpretations and judgements of the policies have generated considerable academic debate on the success or otherwise of the reform proposals.

In this chapter we review the major prescriptions for changing industrial relations in the UK and analyse the theoretical perspectives underlying different government policies. Some policies were stillborn and have now been jettisoned; others have been eclipsed, but might in certain circumstances be reintroduced; others have brought about fundamental changes and now provide permanent institutions and practices in British industrial relations.

LIBERAL COLLECTIVIST REFORM STRATEGIES: THE EXTENSION AND RESTRUCTURING OF COLLECTIVE BARGAINING

Perhaps the best starting point from which to view modern attempts at reform is the Report of the Royal Commission on Trade Unions and Employers' Associations (1968). Known as the Donovan Report (after the Commission's chairman, Lord Donovan), it still in many ways represents a blueprint for liberal collectivist reform.[1] The Donovan Commission was set up by the then Labour government, in the context of mounting pressure from employers for legal changes to curb unofficial strikes, in the context of trade union concern at judge-made changes in collective labour law, and in the context of government concern to improve economic performance. The Commission's Report accepted that unofficial strikes were a cause for concern, but argued that they were only a symptom of underlying ills and not in themselves the most significant problem. Neither the strikes nor the underlying problems would be solved by changes in labour law; instead, British industrial relations were in need of procedural reform and a restructuring of collective bargaining.

It is worth spending some time analysing the Donovan Report because it was welcomed by many trade union and management specialists, it represented the view of the then prominent Oxford School of industrial relations, and it has arguably had an important impact on change in British industrial relations. Donovan advocated government action, but not the use of law, to encourage employers to shift the collective bargaining system to a more bureaucratic form that would match new levels of managerial decision making and would be consistent with a more orderly national system of industrial relations.

Procedural reform

Donovan advocated the reform of industrial relations procedures, rather than industrial relations laws. 'Procedure' meant both machinery for negotiating and dealing with problems and also more widely all non-substantive rules at work, including 'methods used in determining differential levels of reward, rights and privileges, or in recruiting employees and allocating them to jobs, or in promoting, supervising, disciplining and dismissing them.'[2] Procedural reform thus meant the restructuring of existing collective bargaining arrangements along more bureaucratic lines and the extension of collective bargaining to new groups of employees and new subject areas.

Procedural reform as the restructuring of collective bargaining institutions

This sort of reform (which we dealt with in Chapter 9) was presented as the solution to unofficial strikes and to the underlying problem of increased workgroup bargaining power in the tight labour market of the times. Restructuring was necessary because the old formal industry-wide negotiating institutions were ill-equipped to handle the pressures arising from informal shopfloor bargaining and because the UK had in reality developed two systems of collective bargaining: (1) the old national system with formal, industry-wide institutions playing an increasingly problematic role, and (2) informal, uncoordinated, 'chaotic' bargaining on the shopfloor. The shopfloor arrangements might satisfy those directly involved as they were loose and flexible, but they caused inefficiencies which acted against the long-term interests of management, unions and the broader society. Donovan therefore advocated the bureaucratisation of domestic collective bargaining. In place of constant, often covert, bargaining, it recommended formal and periodic negotiations conducted through more formal joint committees at company and plant level. Main board directors should be responsible for their managers' activities and the responsibilities of shop stewards should be more closely defined. The existing confusion of locally agreed terms – some written into agreements, some included in formal minutes, some based on custom and practice – should be replaced by single comprehensive agreements clearly specifying in written form the jointly determined rules applied to work.

Procedural reform as the extension of collective bargaining

The above proposals referred mainly to manufacturing industry, especially to sectors like engineering, shipbuilding and construction. More widely, Donovan argued that employment terms should be regulated by collective bargaining and supported this with the traditional liberal collectivist arguments that collective bargaining was democratic and flexible and provided the best channel for institutionalising conflict at work. Proposals for more direct industrial democracy were set aside by the Commission. Donovan supported collective bargaining, but the Report's proposals for the extension of collective bargaining were sketchy. It suggested that unions be given the right to a government-sponsored inquiry into recognition disputes where employers refused unions bargaining rights and that wages councils be reviewed to see if independent collective bargaining could replace them. It was hoped that the coverage and depth of collective bargaining would extend to cover matters such as shop steward facilities, matters of discipline, questions of redundancy and other employment matters.

The role of the state

In important respects the Donovan Report took a traditional voluntarist view of the role of the state. It opposed state intervention and the law as a principal agent of reform and it rejected mounting demands for legal changes. The law, it argued, was irrelevant to the structural problems underlying strikes and workplace inefficiencies and to use the law would only hamper the necessary restructuring, as it would be seen as unjust and irrelevant, merely bringing the law itself into disrepute. Only when domestic bargaining was reformed and formalised should the possibility of introducing the law be considered.

The Report therefore rejected the use of the law as a change agent, but it did call for government action to promote the procedural reforms it wished to see. Given its dislike for direct legal action, it suggested that a new state agency, combining investigatory and advisory functions, might be used to promote change. This Commission on Industrial Relations (CIR) would have powers to conduct inquiries and make recommendations, and, although these recommendations would not have the force of law, the CIR was envisaged as an interventionist body. Its brief was to promote the changes outlined in the Donovan blueprint and it was hoped that its advice would guide even reluctant parties along the specified path. Some legal pressures would be put on employers who refused to implement a recommendation to recognise a trade union, but even this would take the indirect form of compulsory arbitration on terms and conditions of employment.

The course of this reform strategy

How should we in retrospect view the Donovan proposals and their sequel? One view is to see the Report as strengthening the position of trade unions in British industrial relations and in particular the position of workplace trade unions. Donovan certainly did this and gave an impetus to the move towards formalised single-employer bargaining which we discussed in the last chapter. Another view is that Donovan sought to extend and restructure collective bargaining in order to create institutions consistent with increased state involvement in the regulation of employment. Although the Report did not deal with incomes policies or the details of individual labour law, it did implicitly favour these developments. For example, it argued that its proposals would make effective incomes policy easier to sustain and it saw its reforms as in line with the National Board for Prices and Incomes, which had already argued the need to rationalise domestic bargaining and increase labour productivity. It assumed that some sort of national, tripartite negotiations between government, employers and trade unions could, in a voluntary manner, provide a framework for incomes policy. More bureau-cratically structured negotiations would facilitate the administration and success of any incomes policy.[3]

The Donovan Report can therefore be interpreted as supporting collective bargaining, but wishing to reshape it so that it would fit in better with political objectives concerning national economic competitiveness and the control of inflation. This corporatist element of Donovan's prescription was not spelt out, but did, nevertheless, lie behind the main proposals.[4] However, these corporatist tendencies were certainly mild and not coercive. It was assumed that centralised regulation would derive from reformed bargaining, and the Report contained no proposals for tighter government control over trade unions. In this respect, the Report merely stated that union rule books should be clear and unambiguous, should contain safeguards for members in dispute with their union, and that there should be an independent trade union review body to hear union members' appeals against disciplinary action taken against them by their unions and to judge disputes between unions and the government registrar over the adequacy of union rules.

Though Donovan claimed to reflect the consensus of informed opinion at the time and though it relied on consensus for the implementation of its proposals, as things turned out, this consensus did not fully exist.

The Labour government in office at the time accepted some of the Report's elements, but not others. In a context of mounting economic and industrial relations problems, it did not fully accept the argument for gradual, non-legal reform and instead proposed legal sanctions in a White Paper entitled *In Place of Strife* (1969). This proposed legislation was to give the government power, in the case of disputes thought to harm the national interest, to impose a cooling-off period in unofficial disputes and to impose a compulsory ballot of union members before official strikes. The government announced that it was going to legislate on these so-called 'penal clauses', leaving the other matters until after an election. However, the proposals met with fierce opposition from the trade unions and some Labour backbench MPs, and the government was forced to climb down in return for an assurance of a 'solemn and binding' undertaking from the TUC to tackle the strike problem by itself intervening more in inter-union and unofficial disputes.[5]

Thus a Labour government started the first modern-day attempts to reform British industrial relations. This same government had already made history, in 1966, by introducing the first ever statutory incomes policy in peacetime, backed by criminal sanctions against those who disobeyed government orders to delay pay awards. In practice, however, the government did not use these legal sanctions. Though its policy started off as tight and tough, it was progressively weakened, as exceptions were allowed and as higher increases were allowed during a period which was seen as a run-up to a general election.

Reverting to the Donovan proposals, these the government also left to voluntary methods. It relied upon the CIR to promulgate and preach reform. In fact the subsequent activities and reports of the CIR provide an insight into the liberal collectivist reform strategy. It attempted to apply the Donovan blueprint wherever it found domestic bargaining, but some parts of the plan were more implementable than others. For example, it left more professional personnel departments and improved shop stewards' facilities in many of the companies it studied. By contrast, comprehensive agreements specifying all mutual obligations in a written form were not always accepted. The creation of new, formal bargaining committees at local level also frequently proved problematic. Although the need for such formal arrangements was often accepted, the level at which such committees should operate often created controversy as strong workgroups resisted negotiating with other workers and as managers often refused to negotiate at company level. Thus, there was not always consensus on the details of bureaucratisation.[6] Nevertheless, the CIR did help to extend and formalise company and plant bargaining in the 1970s.

On the expansion of collective bargaining, the CIR produced forty-five reports on recognition disputes. In general, advocacy of collective bargaining helped spread union recognition in areas, such as banking and insurance, where employer resistance was strong, and it acted as a block on the strategy of using internal, employer-sponsored staff associations. Eight reports were produced on wages councils, with the recommendation for rationalisation and the introduction of 'statutory' joint industrial councils which would bargain normally but have their agreements supported by the wages council inspectorate.[7] The extension of existing agreements to cover new topics proved highly problematic. The CIR met resistance from employers when it recommended that bargaining cover some areas previously determined by management and met resistance from workgroups when it called for bargaining over employee-determined work practices. Thus there proved to be less consensus on extending collective bargaining than many had imagined.

THE SECOND MAJOR ATTEMPT AT INDUSTRIAL RELATIONS REFORM: THE 1970–4 CONSERVATIVE GOVERNMENT

In 1970 Edward Heath's Conservative government came to power with the reform of Britain's industrial relations a major part of its manifesto. Rejecting Donovan's liberal collectivist prescriptions, industrial relations problems were seen as derived from excessive trade union power and it was confidently assumed that the creation of a new framework of collective labour laws would provide the solution. The 1971 Industrial Relations Act, which the government introduced, repealed much of the previous law on collective labour relations and, in place of the old immunities and legal abstention, introduced an interventionist system centred on a new labour court and a new list of civil wrongs, in order to reshape the trade unions' relationships with their members and to regulate workgroup power bargaining. Although the Act no longer survives on the statute book, its short and stormy history is worth studying because of what it tells us about industrial relations at the time and about contrasts with later Conservative government legislation.

The 1971 Industrial Relations Act

Before the Donovan Commission reported, the Conservative Party had produced a policy paper, *A Giant's Strength*, which identified the unions as the main cause of Britain's industrial relations problems and proposed the outlawing of the closed shop and the introduction of legally binding agreements and penalties on unofficial strikes. These more individualist and restrictive proposals were put into the 1971 Act; but, in addition, some of Donovan's arguments about the need to restructure collective bargaining and strengthen official trade unionism were also taken on board, together with institutions and laws transplanted from the US. This produced an Act of extraordinary length and complexity, the first major attempt in modern British history to use the law to reform industrial relations.

Briefly, the most important provisions included the following:

1 A new labour court was established, the National Industrial Relations Court (NIRC), with the powers of a High Court.
2 The Act created a Trade Union Registrar with powers to vet union rules, specifying requirements on such matters as who had the power to authorise official strikes. Unions which did not register were deprived of tax advantages, lost immunity against claims for breach of employment contracts, could be subject to unlimited damages in court actions, and could not benefit from the new provisions to assist union recognition.
3 Pre-entry closed shops were declared void and post-entry closed shops were nullified by giving all employees the right *not* to belong to a trade union. Only in certain special circumstances, where unions and workers might be particularly vulnerable, were the authors of the Act prepared to let collective rights override individual freedom.[8]
4 Written collective agreements were presumed to be legally binding unless otherwise specified. Shop stewards calling strikes in breach of

procedures could be sued if agreements were legally binding, and the CIR could draft procedure agreements to be imposed where none existed.

5 The Secretary of State for Employment could apply to the NIRC to prohibit, for sixty days, any industrial action thought to be gravely injurious to the economy and could order a compulsory ballot to gauge membership support for strike action.

6 In order to promote responsible trade unions and rational collective bargaining, registered unions could request CIR investigation of their recognition disputes.

New procedures were introduced for determining appropriate bargaining agents and bargaining units and the NIRC was given the power to enforce recommendations which benefited registered unions.

In contrast to the later Thatcher government legislation, the Act deferred to liberal collectivist traditions by emphasising the value of collective bargaining and voluntary conciliation before recourse to law. It acknowledged Donovan's influence by retaining the CIR's power to promote procedural reform and by instituting a 'Code of Practice' based on Donovan-type prescriptions.

However, the Act contained a number of fateful contradictions which, in the circumstances of the time, doomed its restrictive and interventionist approach to industrial relations.[9] As has already been suggested, some of the provisions, such as support for recognition, had some affinity with the reformist values of Donovan with its collectivist, mildly corporatist ideas for the strengthening and rationalisation of collective bargaining. However, other provisions revealed a unitarist and individualist dislike of unions and their activities. The outlawing of the closed shop, the right for individuals to join or not to join unions, provisions for small groups to challenge established bargaining arrangements were all desirable from a liberal individualist perspective. However, from a liberal collectivist or corporatist perspective, such individual rights were disruptive of effective collective regulation, they were likely to encourage the splintering of bargaining arrangements, and they weakened a union's ability to discipline members or maintain the unity necessary for effective bargaining. The 1971 Act sought to strengthen both the individual in dispute with his or her union and its regulatory arrangements *and* unions as agents of control over their members.

The contradictory provisions of the Act might be blamed on the contrasting influence of Conservative lawyers, with their strong individualist traditions, as opposed to Conservative businessmen, more predisposed at the time to a pluralist perspective or attracted to corporatist solutions.[10] However, businessmen were also increasingly open to ideas of restraints on the closed shop and curbs on union power. The unitarist, individualist perspective underlay much employer rhetoric and this encouraged the drafters of the law to assume that employers would not only support, but also use, the new provisions, an assumption which proved incorrect. In practice, not only was there widespread collusion between employers and workgroups to negate the legislation, but there was also considerable popular sympathy for the trade unionists who defied the new laws.[11]

The Act constituted one of the most ambitious attempts to reconstruct a major set of social institutions and it was the main plank of the government's domestic industrial and economic policy. However, as an attack on union bargaining power, it was attempted at a time when labour markets were still sufficiently tight to prevent employers risking outright confrontations with their workforces for the sake of an over-complex law of somewhat confused objectives. By 1974 the Act was discredited. Conservative politicians were admitting that major amendments were necessary and the director general of the CBI was saying that it had a detrimental effect on industrial relations.[12]

The actions and events which brought down the Act merit some further analysis.

The course of TUC opposition

The TUC strongly opposed the legislation and boycotted all the institutions of the Act. Many of the Act's controls depended on union registration, but only a few unions chose to register. The TUC's policy of non-registration was strengthened by a number of events which boosted union morale at precisely the time when the policy was being established. The first event was the NUM's successful 1972 strike which breached the incomes policy the government had introduced. This provoked a famous (Thatcherites within the Conservative Party would later say infamous) U-turn in government policy, and the earlier refusal to consult with the TUC was replaced by the establishment of tripartite talks on incomes policy. The Act had been premised on the removal of government from active intervention in the economy, relying instead on the new legal framework to help employers control their own affairs. Therefore, the U-turn towards more active government interference served to undermine the philosophical basis of the legislation and made the unions feel they could further exert pressure for the repeal of the Act.

Employer avoidance of the Act

From the start, the desire of employers to use the new legislation was limited and open disillusionment soon grew. Most employers were prepared to go to considerable lengths to give illicit support to their banned closed shops.[13] No large employers used their new rights to apply for court orders against so-called unfair industrial practices. Only individuals and small employers used the Act, and the employers who used it did so usually to sue other firm's workers, not their own. Even with the mass picketing and secondary boycotts of the miners' strike in 1972, the legislation was not used and there was a universal employer acceptance of union opposition to legally binding agreements. All major negotiations, even in the public sector, inserted clauses in their agreements that they were not legally binding.

Opposition from strong workgroups and unions

The law met with stubborn opposition from certain strong workgroups who were supported by their unions. Action by dockers to reserve to themselves work on containers brought them into conflict with owners and employees of inland container depots. Several of these disputes reached the NIRC and ultimately led to the imprisonment of five shop stewards, the so-called Pentonville Five. This in turn led to widespread sympathy action and the general council of the TUC voted for a one-day national strike in protest. The government was only saved from this crisis by humiliating interventions and an unusually speedy decision of the House of Lords, freeing the shop stewards from prison. The engineers' union was also involved in some fierce legal battles involving recognition procedures and the closed shop. These led to contempt of court proceedings and sequestration of union funds, followed by legal fiascos in the NIRC and further strike action outside. Together, these incidents ensured that the Court ended its life in a blaze of controversy and a widespread concern that the law was being brought into disrepute by legislation that did not have popular support and could not be enforced.

The experience of emergency ballots

The one and only experience of the emergency ballot provisions also proved a failure for the government. In 1972 it chose to use the cooling-off and emergency-ballot provisions against the railwaymen's union, which had started a work-to-rule after rejecting an arbitration award. The government was confident that a cooling-off period and ballot would prove the members to be unwilling to follow their 'militant' leaders into a strike. To the government's surprise, the resultant ballot showed the railwaymen to be six to one in favour of their leader's call for action. In these circumstances, British Rail conceded the claim in full. The government never used the emergency provisions again; when in 1974 they once more faced industrial action from the miners which they felt was gravely injurious to the nation, they tried a ballot of the electorate instead and called a general election.

The 1971 Act reflected the breakdown of the consensus on the postwar Welfare Compromise and demonstrated that at the time the unions were too powerful to be shackled by such a framework of legal controls. The dramatic failure of the Act influenced the contrasting policies of the governments which followed. The Labour government, which came into office in 1974, with the repeal of the legislation as a popular election pledge, responded to the greatly increased stature of the trade unions by involving them even more in high-level policy-making. When, in turn, the next Conservative government, under Mrs Thatcher, returned to office in 1979 and introduced its changes in labour law, it was careful to do so gradually and without conspicuous new institutions. For some union leaders, the experience of the 1971 Act convinced them that increased legislation was likely, but could be used to the unions' advantage. Thus, the TUC abandoned its abhorrence of legalism and began to think more and more in terms of positive, pro-union laws.

THE THIRD ATTEMPT AT REFORM: THE 1974–9 LABOUR GOVERNMENT AND THE SOCIAL CONTRACT

The TUC and the Labour Party were drawn together by their abhorrence of the 1971 Act and a desire not to repeat the confrontations of the previous period of Labour government. In opposition they agreed that the legislation and the statutory incomes policy would be repealed and that there would be a return to free collective bargaining. There would, however, then be new legislation to increase employment protection for individual employees, to strengthen collective bargaining and consultative rights, and to extend industrial democracy. After Labour's election victory in 1974, the TUC published *Collective Bargaining and the Social Contract*, which outlined what was, in effect, an agreement to exchange their support in voluntary wage restraint for legislation favourable to trade unions. This macro-corporatist approach was to be the essence of the third major attempt at government-sponsored industrial relations reform.

The pro-union legislation

The Trade Union and Labour Relations Acts of 1974 and 1976 repealed the 1971 Act and reinstated the statutory immunities to protect the right to strike. Only the 1971 Act's provisions on unfair dismissal were retained, and a Parliamentary battle developed centring on the position of employees in closed shops, which were again legal and spreading: was it possible for someone losing their job in these circumstances to claim unfair dismissal? In the end the government enacted the provision that dismissals arising from refusal to join a closed shop should be judged fair unless the individual had strong religious objections to trade unionism.

The Employment Protection Act of 1975 provided a range of new individual rights on guaranteed payment when laid off, paid leave in redundancies and the right to maternity leave (see below for more detail). On collective labour relations, along with reinstating statutory immunities, the legislation re-established several of the previous institutions, although with different names and powers. A Certification Officer replaced the Registrar, without the 1971 Act's power to vet union rules, but retaining the responsibility of judging a union's independence and suitability for collective bargaining. The Employment Appeals Tribunal replaced the NIRC in hearing appeals from industrial tribunals and the Certification Officer, but without wider jurisdiction; the Central Arbitration Committee replaced the old Industrial Arbitration Board and had the power to extend collective bargaining to give workers the 'recognised or general level' of pay and conditions in their area; and the Advisory Conciliation and Arbitration Service (ACAS) replaced the CIR as an independent, tripartite body.

The Employment Protection Act strengthened trade union rights within the workplace by giving shop stewards the right to paid time off work for training and union activities, by the reintroduction of a procedure to help unions gain recognition, and by a legal duty on employers to disclose information to unions for collective bargaining. The Act also created a period for compulsory consultation with recognised trade unions before major redundancies could be announced.

Thus there was no outright reversion to voluntarism and the Employment Protection Act marked a significant extension of state intervention, but in the direction of support for collective bargaining. The Labour government also enacted further consultation rights for trade unions in the Social Security Pensions Act of 1975, covering occupational pensions, and in the Health and Safety at Work Act of 1974, enabling recognised unions to appoint safety representatives with statutory rights to receive information and inspect work premises. Safety representatives were also given the right to call management to attend safety committee meetings, and in many smaller establishments this right stimulated union organisation and representation.[14]

The TUC also hoped for legislation on so-called planning agreements aimed to give unions and government a voice in the investment and employment plans of the largest manufacturing companies. Although the Industry Act of 1975 contained provisions on these lines, controls over private firms proved difficult to operationalise and the government was pushed back from these commitments and away from the initially close relationship with trade unions by mounting employer resistance and by growing economic difficulties. The proposed planning agreements were modified to exclude union involvement, but even then continued to be strenuously opposed by employers, and the ailing Chrysler Motors was the only company temporarily to sign a planning agreement, as a condition of a government loan to rescue its British plants.[15] Thus, there was the beginnings of a build-up of employer resistance to the extension of legal rights for employees and trade unions.

Proposals for industrial democracy

The TUC also sought legislation to introduce a new approach to industrial democracy into British industrial relations by giving trade unionists seats on company boards. Various proposals for worker directors (more or less along West German lines) had been under discussion in the UK since its accession to the European Community in 1974, and the TUC moved to support the idea of statutorily based worker directors, provided that (a) they represented trade unionists and did not introduce a new, second channel of employee representation and (b) they exercised real power, having parity with shareholders in the allocation of seats. In 1975 the government set up a Royal Commission on Industrial Democracy, chaired by Lord Bullock, with a brief to consider how best to put trade union representatives on company boards. Bullock proposed a statutory right for trade unions to claim seats on the boards of companies employing more than 2,000 employees. Any recognised trade union which represented 20 per cent or more of a company's employees would be able to request a secret ballot of company's employees to ascertain whether they supported the introduction of employee directors. If a majority, of at least one-third of those eligible to vote, agreed, then employee directors would be chosen through the trade unions, and the board would be reconstituted on a $2X + Y$ formula – employees and shareholders would have equal representation ($2X$) and there would be a small, uneven number of independents (Y) chosen with the support of the two sides. If employees chose to adopt worker directors, then all the unions in the company would establish a joint representation committee to decide how to allocate employee directorships and to coordinate the employee side.[16]

The Bullock proposals aroused a storm of protest from employers, and the CBI mounted a campaign of opposition threatening to match the TUC resistance to the 1971 Industrial Relations Act. In the end the Labour government could not resist the strength of this opposition. By 1977 the Social Contract between the government and the TUC was under strain as workers resisted further pay restraint in the face of rising prices and falling real wages. Government motivation to fight for the TUC-supported Bullock proposals was lessened as splits appeared within the union movement. Although the Bullock proposals were strongly supported by many unions, especially the TGWU, they were opposed by the Engineers and Electricians, who favoured free collective bargaining as the best way of giving workers a say at work. In these circumstances, the Labour government produced a highly tentative White Paper in 1978, suggesting the voluntary adoption of some form of minority employee representation, not necessarily selected through trade union channels and not on a company's main board, but on a more limited supervisory board. The White Paper did, however, support the creation of joint representation committees with statutory rights to discuss investment plans, mergers, acquisitions and contractions that would affect employees. These proposals for industrial democracy, when viewed along with the government's incomes policy, can be seen as a measure of the macrocorporatism of the 1974–9 Labour government.

The Social Contract incomes policy

The TUC support for voluntary wage restraint in return for pro-union legislation achieved some success for two or three years. The TUC initially produced guidelines on the time period which should elapse between wage claims and the types of claims to be submitted, and these were generally applied. However, the guidelines did little to ease the rapidly rising money wages which had been stimulated by the collapse of the Heath government's incomes policy and by worldwide inflation following the first oil shock in 1973–4. As early as 1975, the government found itself with inflation moving upwards towards 20 per cent, average earnings rising even faster, a massive balance of payments deficit and sterling under pressure. In these circumstances, official advisers started to propose a statutory incomes policy. Faced with governmental pressure for greater commitment to wage restraint, the unions proposed a simple flat-rate increase and a freeze on higher incomes, as long as the government tightened price controls and took measures to reduce unemployment. The government accepted these proposals, although with a rather lower flat-rate increase and without the tight price controls (see Figure 9.3).

The 1975 policy was succeeded by another agreed policy in 1976. Then, in 1977, income tax was reduced in exchange for a commitment to a 10 per cent limit on wage increases and the TUC acquiesced, although it was finding it harder to gain membership support for wage restraint in the context of a reduction in real wages, rising unemployment and public expenditure cuts dictated by the International Monetary Fund (IMF). Nevertheless the policy broadly held. From mid-1975 until mid-1978 the TUC therefore played an active part in developing and supporting a government incomes policy designed to reduce the level of real earnings in the hope of avoiding accelerating inflation, maintaining employment and keeping the Labour government in power.

However, pressure was on for an easing of the policy, and it was therefore rather surprising when the Prime Minister, James Callaghan, announced a 5 per cent pay guideline to operate from mid-1978, especially given clear warnings from union leaders that they could not support such guidelines and did not believe they would hold. The policy was subsequently challenged by several unions and was broken in the so-called 'Winter of Discontent' in 1978–9, which started with a successful strike at Ford and continued with a series of strikes in engineering, transport and the public services. Wage settlements accelerated and the government, which had arrived in office in the wake of a successful miners' strike against the Heath incomes policy, lost power in the context of another pay revolt of a wider magnitude.

Bargained corporatism from 1974 to 1979

The 1974–9 Labour government represented the high-water mark of macro-corporatism in Britain and the main attempt by a government to govern in open alliance with trade unions (though less so with employers). Between 1974 and 1979 in Britain, there had developed national-level negotiations between Labour ministers and the TUC. This macro-level of negotiation was dramatically illustrated by the government's offer to involve the unions in forming budget policy by exchanging tax cuts for wage restraint. At the level of individual companies, the Bullock proposals presaged a change in the nature of industrial relations in the direction of microcorporatism. By providing that shop stewards be given seats as employee directors on company boards, the proposals contained the potential for shifting domestic management–union negotiations from adversarial collective bargaining to supposedly more cooperative board level consultation and joint decision making. The traditional separation of collective bargaining from government and management structures of decision making was to some extent replaced by the closer integration of trade unions into the central decision-making bodies of government and industry. Criticism of this experiment in bargained corporatism were voiced from unitarist, liberal individualist, liberal collectivist and radical perspectives.

Those on the right of the political spectrum castigated the policies on two main grounds. The liberal individualist argument was put that such

arrangements undermined the sovereignty of Parliament by giving governmental status to groups who were not responsible to the electorate and by
putting collective interests above those of the individual. Unitarist arguments were also used against the extension of board-level employee representation, especially arguing that Bullock's interposition of employee
directors would make the efficient and profitable running of business
impossible to achieve.

From traditional liberal collectivists came fears that, once unions
became involved in the shaping and implementation of government and
management policies, they would inevitably lose their freedom to represent
their members. It was felt by some that the offer of tax concessions for wage
restraint marked the beginning of the end of collective bargaining.[17] Once
the trade unions became the agents of government policy, then they would
lose their independence and would no longer have the ability to represent
members and take up their grievances. Similar fears were echoed by many
of the trade unionists who opposed the Bullock proposals for industrial
democracy.

From a more radical perspective came arguments similar to those of the
liberal collectivists, but without the same faith in collective bargaining.
Some argued that trade union gains under corporatist bargaining were
inevitably limited by the dominant, class-based structures of power in
society which curtailed the advantages any government could offer its
workers.[18] In return for the illusion of some influence over government
policy, union leaders accepted greater restrictions over their use of industrial action and imposed tighter discipline over their own membership. So,
in the mid-1970s, the TUC allowed real wages to fall and issued restrictive
guidelines on the conduct of collective bargaining, but found its economic
policies rejected in the face of IMF pressure, planning agreements nullified
by employer opposition, and its demands for a return to free collective
bargaining rejected for rigid pay restraint.

Supporters of the bargained corporatism of 1974 to 1979 argued that
government intervention was inevitable, that intervention which enlisted
union support was better than the alternative, and that many of the Social
Contract policies brought real benefits for workers. The policies did bring
down price inflation from around 25 per cent to around 8 per cent and may
have prevented unemployment rising higher than it would otherwise have
done. Given the simultaneous extension of collective bargaining, these
policies may have increased union ability to represent members' interests
at the place of work. The Bullock proposals, had they been implemented,
would have enabled workers to extend their influence at work, statutory
representation might have provided the joint union coordination at company level which unions had found difficult to establish, and the

Reconstructing British industrial relations 249

arrangements would have kept British workers more in line with the European mainstream. On the other hand, there were costs. For a time during this period real wages actually fell, unemployment rose and growth was poor, and the collapse of the policy in the Winter of Discontent led to high levels of industrial militancy. For the supporters of the policy this was to lead to a discrediting of their approach in the eyes of the public and to defeat in the general election of 1979.

The situation quickly changed after 1979 as the succeeding Thatcher government adopted radically different policies, reverting to liberal individualist preferences and involving only the minimum recognition of, or consultation with, either organised business or trade unions. However, before we review the Thatcher period, we will examine the build-up of individual employment legislation which occurred under all governments in the 1960s and 1970s.

LEGISLATION ON INDIVIDUAL RIGHTS AND GOVERNMENT INTERVENTION

From the 1960s onwards British governments began, for the first time, to develop a substantial body of labour laws concerning individual rights. This marked an important shift away from the traditionally passive, voluntarist state role which had held that intervention should only be for limited classes of workers such as women, children and certain groups of the low paid. Through the 1960s and 1970s the following legislation was introduced.

1 The Contracts of Employment Act (1963) gave employees, for the first time in Britain, the legal right to written particulars of their terms and conditions of employment and it specified periods of notice that an employer must give before terminating employment.
2 The Industrial Training Act (1964) gave government support to the training of employees by requiring employers to pay a training levy which was used to fund government-approved training schemes approved or administered by the Industrial Training Boards. This was repealed by the Thatcher government.
3 The Redundancy Payments Act (1965) gave employees the right to claim compensation for the loss of their jobs, if dismissal was caused by technological or economic change. This acceptance by the state that workers had 'property rights' to their employment was a recognition of deep-seated feelings among employees, and was supported by managerial arguments that this would help overcome resistance to the restructuring of British industry.

4 Legislation against discrimination in employment on the grounds of race
or sex was passed in the Race Relations Act (1968), the Equal Pay Act
(1970) and the Sex Discrimination Act (1975). These attempted to
outlaw discrimination in access to jobs, treatment within jobs, and
payment. Discrimination has proved to be extraordinarily difficult to
prove in court and the practical effects of this legislation continue to
disappoint many of its advocates.

5 Legislation against unfair dismissal has had more impact. This was
recommended by the Donovan Commission and employees were first
given the right to claim compensation or reinstatement in the 1971
Industrial Relations Act. The provisions on unfair dismissal were
retained when that Act was repealed.

6 The Employment Protection Act (1975) added rights to a small guaranteed payment when laid off, to itemised pay statements, written reasons
for dismissal, paid time off to look for work or arrange training in the
event of redundancy, paid time off for shop steward training, the right
not to be dismissed for pregnancy and the right to reinstatement after a
period of maternity leave.

In 1978 many of these individual rights were drawn together in the Employment Protection (Consolidation) Act. In fifteen years a body of individual
labour law had been created, putting the UK in line with many other
European countries and in many respects ahead of countries such as the US
and Japan. However, as we will see below, when the Thatcher government
took office in 1979, it acted to restrict the scope and limit the application of
the employment protection given by its predecessors.

With the development of legislation on individual rights went a growth
of state agencies to implement and enforce such rights, many of them
structured on tripartite lines.

1 Industrial tribunals were established in 1964 and have since developed
to have jurisdiction over claims arising from the laws listed above. The
tribunals employ staff throughout the country and consider thousands of
cases a year. They are the nearest the UK has come to a well- established
system of specialised labour courts. However, the tribunals were
designed to make them as 'voluntary' as possible and to keep them out
of areas of collective labour relations. The tribunals themselves consist
of a chairperson, with legal experience, and two assessors, drawn from
two panels nominated by the CBI and TUC. Applicants and respondents
may present their own case without solicitors or barristers. Appeals on
points of law are heard by the Employment Appeal Tribunal (established
in 1975) and the House of Lords.

2 The Equal Opportunity Commission and the Commission for Racial Equality review and help promote the laws on sexual and racial discrimination. The Commissions are part of the state's administrative machine, responsible for administering public policy and law, and they were also set up on tripartite lines, with governing bodies composed of representatives of the CBI, TUC, and independents.

3 The Advisory, Conciliation and Arbitration Service (ACAS) continues the traditional conciliation and arbitration services once carried out by the Department of Employment. Its governing council consists of a full-time chairman, CBI, TUC and independent members. ACAS has staff in London and regional offices and handles thousands of requests for conciliation every year. By contrast there are considerably fewer cases of binding arbitration and, true to British tradition, these are still not legally binding. Some requests for arbitration and legal matters such as the disclosure of information for collective bargaining are passed to the Central Arbitration Committee (CAC), another tripartite panel.

4 The Manpower Services Commission was established in 1974 to take over traditional Department of Employment functions in manpower forecasting, the encouragement of training, and the administration of local employment offices and job centres, providing a placement service and employment advice. Some of this role is now handled by the Training Agency, though many of its functions were given over by the Thatcher government to local employer-dominated Training and Enterprise Councils.

5 The Health and Safety Commission was established to take over the administration of health and safety legislation, rationalised into a comprehensive Health and Safety at Work Act in 1974. The various inspectorates were grouped into a Health and Safety Executive which is responsible for the enforcement of the health and safety regulations, aided by union-appointed safety representatives at the place of work.

6 Wages councils, the tripartite institutions with the longest history, continue to exist in some sectors such as clothing, retailing, and hotel and catering, but have been reduced in number and coverage of topics and were under increasing threat during the 1980s from a Conservative government which has believed that they, along with other forms of employment protection, create inflexibilities in the labour market.

This build-up of individual employment law and of tripartite agencies in the 1960s and 1970s was supposed to complement free collective bargaining. As such it was supported by liberal collectivists. However, it is arguable that, largely unintentionally, it had started to impinge on and formalise, if not displace, voluntary collective bargaining. For example, law on redundancy payments and unfair dismissals led to a tightening up and formalisation of voluntary practices in these areas and to a tendency to look to the law rather than voluntary solutions.[19] On the other hand, to liberal individualists, this build-up of individual employment law represented a deviation from market principles and the growth of tripartite administration represented an undesirable movement towards corporatism. When the Thatcher government took office, it acted to restrict the scope and limit the application of employment protection. It began a programme of de-regulation of the labour market and the reduction of tripartite bodies.

THE THATCHER GOVERNMENT 1979-90: LIBERAL INDIVIDUALISM, MONETARY ECONOMICS AND RESTRICTIVE LEGISLATION

The economic and industrial relations policies of the incoming Thatcher government were far removed from most of what had gone before in British industrial relations.

The economic policy of the new government marked a radical change from the Welfare Compromise. Drawing on ideas from the nineteenth-century liberal tradition, from twentieth-century economists such as F. A. Hayek and M. Friedman, and the thinking of the so-called 'New Right', Britain was to be used as a major experiment in monetarism and in liberal individualist ideas. This meant that the government announced that it would not directly intervene in the economy via incomes policy-type measures aimed at controlling wages and prices. Instead the government was committed to using tight monetary controls and high interest rates to control the economy and to use deflation and unemployment to reduce wage claims and price inflation. Low inflation, rather than the prevention of high unemployment, became the ruling objective of policy. In line with a belief in limiting the role of the state and encouraging self-help, the public sector was reduced by widespread cuts in expenditure and by the growing privatisation of public-sector organisations. Direct taxes were cut and VAT increased to pay for income tax reductions. The government encouraged freer capital markets by lifting restrictions on the export of capital and made British markets more open to foreign competition. It announced that it would not bale out enterprises and organisations which could not withstand increased competitive pressures. These policies, combined with the worst international recession since the 1930s, led to a massive fall in national output and a dramatic rise in unemployment from just over one million when the government came into office to over three million, or 13 per cent of the labour force by 1983.

This recession was followed by a slow but long period of recovery up to 1989, during which years tight monetary controls were relaxed, Britain experienced favourable growth and unemployment fell from the mid-1980s onwards though not to the levels of the 1970s. In the late 1980s and early 1990s, Britain again suffered a severe recession as the government (from November 1990 onwards led by John Major) again used tighter monetary controls and high interest rates to tackle the inflationary problems which built up from the mid-1980s onwards. These two recessions were in part compounded by worldwide factors, but, in Britain, they were exacerbated by government monetary policies and they had to be absorbed by an economy which for many years had been growing relatively slowly and whose firms had for long been losing market share both at home and abroad.

The Thatcher government's industrial relations policy through the 1980s differed from those of previous governments and reflected radically different theories based on a faith in market forces and liberal individualism. As we have already said, the Thatcher government, from the outset, eschewed incomes policies, at least in the private sector, and turned its back on talks with the TUC and CBI on the management of the economy. In the private sector of the economy, employers and unions were left to free collective bargaining, but within the context of the government's overall restrictive economic stance: if, in their wage bargaining, the parties fixed wages and prices which were too high, then this would mean bankruptcy for firms and unemployment for workers. In the market-orientated public sector, such as telecommunications, gas and electricity, the government resorted to indirect pressures and incentives and later to privatisation to expose wage bargaining to market forces. In the non-market-orientated public sector, such as central and local government, teaching and the health services, the government introduced a tighter system of cash limits on spending and in this way tried to induce managements to stand firm against wage claims. At times this resulted in public-sector workers falling behind their private-sector counterparts and taking strike action in demand of higher wage increases. When this occurred the government was ready to take a firmer stand than its predecessors and put into place other measures to strengthen its hand.

The government believed that trade unions had a harmful effect on national competitiveness by imposing restrictive practices in the workplace, by exercising monopoly power in the labour market and by encouraging unrealistic expectations among workers. The solution was in part the adoption of the economic policy already referred to, but backed by legal changes designed to reduce union bargaining power and remove inefficiencies in the labour market. With the experience of the 1971 Act still in mind, the government made no attempt to repeat the massive changes of the early 1970s. Instead, along with reliance on its tough economic stance, gradual amendments were made in existing labour laws to restrict trade union power and to reduce the scope of employment protection legislation. The theory behind the legal changes was, however, straightforward: it was to introduce a restrictive framework of collective labour law and to de-regulate the labour market. There remained little of the liberal collectivism and none of the partial commitment to the corporatist integration of trade unions which had coexisted in the 1971 Act with a more restrictive approach to labour relations.

Changes in collective labour law

The Employment Act 1980

This Act repealed the procedures for aiding trade-union recognition and for extending collective agreements which we discussed in previous chapters. It gave employers legal remedies against secondary picketing and most other types of secondary, sympathetic action. In the first of a series of laws to reduce the effectiveness of the closed shop, it made it more difficult to introduce and maintain such arrangements. All new closed shops had to be approved by four-fifths of the workforce and a wider range of people, not just those with religious objections, could claim unfair dismissal if sacked for non-membership. For the first time, public funds were made available to encourage unions to hold postal ballots for the election of officers and for important policy decisions.

The Employment Act 1982

The 1982 Act further tightened the law on closed shops by requiring reviews in secret ballots and by outlawing union-labour-only contracts. Trade unions were made liable for damages if they instigated unlawful industrial action. Employers were also given legal remedies against politi-cal strikes. The general effect of these changes meant employers could sue unions directly for damages arising out of industrial action that was not protected by the statutory immunity applying to acts done in contemplation or furtherance of a trade dispute. These changes excluded from legality wide areas of industrial action which had been seen as lawful since the Taff Vale judgment at the beginning of the century and increased the scope for legal action over a wide range of industrial disputes.

The Trade Union Act 1984

Following on Mrs Thatcher's 1983 election victory, the main thrust of the Trade Union Act 1984 was against trade unions and the way they ran their internal affairs. Union executives had to submit themselves for re-election by secret ballot every five years and unions had to hold a secret ballot every ten years if they wished to keep a political fund. Pre-strike ballots were required for unions to retain their immunity from civil action for damages. However, this latter requirement only related to official strikes and not to unofficial action.

Employment Act 1988

After their third election victory in 1987, the Conservative government introduced the Employment Act 1988. This was again concerned with how trade unions were run internally and aimed to strengthen the rights of individual union members. Workers were allowed to apply for court orders instructing unions to repudiate industrial action organised without a secret ballot. Unions were banned from disciplining members refusing to support industrial action. All senior union officials had to be elected by secret ballot. A new Commissioner for the Rights of Trade Union members was created with, among other things, the duty in certain circumstances to support and fund union members' court action against their unions.

The Employment Act 1990

The 1990 Act removed all vestiges of legal protection for the closed shop by making refusal of employment on grounds relating to union membership unlawful. It also tidied up previous legislation by completing the process started by the 1980 Act by making nearly all forms of secondary action unlawful. It removed the immunity for organising industrial action if the action was not in contemplation or furtherance of a trade dispute or if the action was in support of an employee dismissed while taking unofficial industrial action. Alongside this it gave employers greater freedom to dismiss any employee taking unofficial industrial action and made unlawful industrial action taken to secure the reinstatement of selectively dismissed strikers. It made unions responsible at law if any other official (including shop stewards) called for industrial action and it further tightened up the law on ballots.

After the April 1992 election victory, the Major government has said that it will introduce what will be the final tranche of labour legislation. It will introduce a seven-day, pre-strike cooling-off period; a tightening of controls on the way postal strike ballots are conducted; and measures to render unions liable to be sued by customers for public-service disruptions even when the employer does not wish to take legal action. In terms of internal union matters, new controls over election procedures and union finances will be introduced; individuals will be allowed to join any unions of their choice, thus undermining the TUC's Bridlington procedures for dealing with poaching and interunion disputes; individual employees will also be required to give periodic written consent for the deduction of union dues through check-off arrangements, thus potentially undermining a major support for union membership and income. In the future, if there is to be any further legislation, a Conservative government might still feel tempted to introduce laws making collective agreements legally binding and outlawing strikes in essential services.[20]

Changes in protective and individual employment law

Substantial changes were made in the area of individual labour law in the 1980s. Here the government's stated aim has been to reduce what it saw as rigidities in the labour market and introduce new flexibilities into the employment relationship. Thereby it was believed that firms would be made more efficient and new jobs would be created. Opponents, on the other hand, have said that it has watered down legal rights for employees and made British workers some of the least protected in the European Community.

As we have already said, the Employment Act 1980 repealed procedures for extending collective agreements and ensuring that recognised pay levels were observed. It also limited employees' unfair dismissal and maternity rights by increasing the qualifying period of employment from six months to two years.

The Wages Act 1986 reduced the functions of wages councils in fixing rates of pay in industries where collective bargaining is weak by restricting them to fixing a single rate of pay and by removing young workers from their coverage. At the same time the government intimated that the funding of the wages council inspectorate was not a priority and that in future it planned to abolish wages councils altogether. Lack of employer enthusiasm for abolition and fears of the introduction of possibly more extensive measures from the EC are said to have stayed the government's hand.

The Employment Act 1989 continued the theme of deregulation. It repealed laws regulating young people's hours of work, exempted small firms from requirements to provide written statements of disciplinary procedures, and again increased the qualifying period for bringing complaints of unfair dismissal. (The law also took a sideswipe at collective matters by limiting the right to time off work for trade union duties.)

In line with this attitude to employment protection legislation, the government has also steadfastly opposed many of the proposals of the EC Social Charter on matters such as rights for part-time workers, maternity leave, and the restriction of overtime working. At the Maastricht summit in autumn 1991 the government chose to opt out of the so-called Social Chapter of the Treaty, which committed all the other EC countries to an extension of social legislation.

The industrial relations policy initiated by the Thatcher government was therefore to use the law gradually to reduce the threat of trade union industrial action and to weaken membership unity in such action. The objectives were not cluttered by any of the liberal collectivism of previous Conservative administrations such as the traditional obeisance to collective bargaining. It has sought to regulate collective relations at work and to introduce the threat of common law interventions into industrial relations. However, in the area of individual and protective labour law, it has de-regulated industrial relations and has changed Britain from being about average in Europe in terms of social and protective law to being towards the bottom of the EC league.

The legislation has had a major effect on industrial relations. It has changed Britain from being one of the least regulated western countries in terms of collective labour law to being one of the most regulated. It has made picketing much more difficult and has virtually stopped the use of secondary action in industrial disputes, with unions extremely wary to protect their funds. It has made the use of balloting in important union elections and before strikes the common practice in British industrial relations. It has gradually reduced the number and power of closed shops in British industry and ensured that no new ones are introduced. However, it has not stopped closed shops altogether which often continue to exist *de facto*, though without legal supports and much more vulnerable to those who decline to join or to employers who might seek to discourage membership.[21]

The reasons why this legislation seemed to have worked in contrast to the 1971 Act merit further analysis.

The approach of the law

The law was introduced piecemeal in a 'step-by-step' approach rather than as one major piece of legislation. This is not to say that there was, on the part of the government, a grand strategy from the start, other than to proceed in an incremental manner. However, the mistakes of the 1971 Act were not repeated. There were no major new institutions nor courts for the unions to mobilise against and it was left to union members and employers, rather than the government, to make use of the law.

The economic context

This was entirely different from the early 1970s, in particular with much higher levels of unemployment which discouraged many trade unionists taking action against the law. Moreover, the fact that the government was not trying to operate an incomes policy meant that it did not need to defer to the TUC and the unions. The restructuring of British industry, the decline of manufacturing industry, and the privatisation and deregulation of areas of the public sector were also important background factors serving to reduce trade union membership and undermine shopfloor organisation.

Employer attitudes

Management was rather more prepared to use the law than was the case in the early 1970s. Again, most major employers still did not have recourse to the law. But a few large firms, such as the Coal Board, News International and P&O showed what could be done. Other employers did not really need to follow suit, as most groups of workers sought to avoid such confrontations. Instead, the employers were able to take advantage of the changed economic and legal context and build on the reforms in bargaining structure and pay systems to which we referred in the last Chapter. However, it is significant that employers have not sought fuller juridification of British industrial relations via, for example, legally binding collective agreements.[22]

Changing attitudes within the Labour Movement

From the start, more trade unions were prepared to work with the law, especially in areas such as balloting where there had already been some growth in postal balloting. Other trade unions learned to live with the law and decided, in the face of judicial decision, that it was not worth jeopardising their assets. It is now clear that any future Labour government would not go back to the pre-1979 legal situation, in part for electoral reasons and in part because of European requirements. They would keep most of the present law on the closed shop and on balloting. Such a government would change some of the law on immunities and secondary action, allowing sympathy strikes and secondary picketing under certain circumstances. It would also probably introduce new laws: in the area of collective labour relations, it has promised to pass legislation on union recognition and bargaining rights; in the individual area, it would introduce law on minimum wage protection, rights to training, new legislation on sex equality and on many of the measures to be found in the European Social

Charter; in effect it would probably move Britain more towards a system of positive legal rights. Undoubtedly there would be no less labour law on the statute books under any future Labour government.

However, the legislation of the 1980s has not worked unambiguously, from its authors' point of view. For example, the legislative changes were posited on the presumption that trade unions were not democratic and were out of touch with their members. However, the legislation has not necessarily made unions more democratic or 'given unions back to their members'. Pre-strike ballots (most of which have gone in favour of the unions) have tended to strengthen the hand of unions in industrial disputes because, in situations where they have obtained a convincing majority, this has given them more credibility in bargaining. In the case of ballots on political funds, these all went in favour of unions having these funds and may even have encouraged some unions to institute such funds for the first time. In the case of ballots for union officers, these have tended to confirm incumbents in their posts and may indeed also have increased their legitimacy. They have not made union leaderships any more or less conservative.[23]

The law may have played a part in reducing strike incidence in the UK, by making it more costly to the unions if any breach of the law occurs. But it should be remembered that British unions still have essential immunities on core industrial relations matters; strikes have been falling since before the legislation was introduced; they have fallen also in other countries where there has been no such legislation; and other factors, such as high levels of unemployment, lower price inflation, and reduced union membership have probably been more important in reducing strike incidence. Also, there is little evidence that either reregulation (the advent of more restrictive collective labour law) or deregulation (the repeal of protective individual labour law) have had much effect on economic performance. Real gross domestic product grew over the 1980s by 2.2 per cent per annum compared with the same 2.2 per cent in the 1970s, 3.3 per cent in the 1960s and 2.5 per cent in the 1950s. It is true that in the 1980s Britain's growth performance was better relative to other countries, but this was because their growth rates decelerated more than Britain's. It is also true that in manufacturing industry productivity growth in the 1980s was better than in previous decades. Recent research has suggested that a weakening of trade union power may have played a part in this. However, plant closures, the fear of unemployment and a tightening of management control were probably more important than government legislative measures.[24]

We examine these and other effects and outcomes of the changes in labour law and of the Conservative government more generally in the next chapter. In conclusion here, we can say that the old voluntarist tradition in collective labour relations is now a thing of the past, except that British collective agreements are still not legally binding as they are in many other countries. On the other hand, in the area of individual labour law there has been something of a reversion to voluntarism with the repeal of much law in the protective and social area. However, given the build-up of collective labour law and the prospect of legal imposition from the EC, this can at best be seen as a bastardised form of voluntarism. In the future new European law will undoubtedly affect British industrial relations, despite the continued opposition of the Major government to the Social Charter and the opt-out from the Social Chapter of the Maastricht Treaty. This has already started to happen in areas such as equal pay and benefits for women for doing work of equal value to that of men and the protection of workers in business take-overs. Other areas of impact of European law may in the future include some reregulation of individual employment matters, with new rights and standards for groups such as part-timers, young workers, and immigrant workers; there may also be some impact on collective labour law, with rights to belong and not to belong to trade unions and with rights for trade unions to bargain with employers on certain specified topics. The impact of Europe may also bring new concepts and institutions into British industrial relations with notions such as 'social partnership' and employee participation in statutory works councils.

CONCLUSIONS: CONFLICTING PERSPECTIVES AND CONFLICTING PRESCRIPTIONS

The violent swings in government policy towards industrial relations over the last quarter-century highlight once again the existence of different theoretical perspectives on industrial relations and the decline of the postwar consensus.

In retrospect, the broad postwar consensus supporting the traditional collective bargaining system up to the mid-1960s can be seen as having been bolstered by the longest successful period of economic growth that the UK had enjoyed, even if that success was diminished by the faster growth of other industrial competitors. Most social institutions work more smoothly in periods of growing prosperity; in the period 1945 to 1965, the spread of collective bargaining, together with the growth of government-funded welfare, served to satisfy the expectations of most powerful groups of employees at a time when employers were not too severely squeezed by foreign competition.

However, from the 1960s onwards problems emerged. Employers, increasingly subject to fiercer competition, complained that collective bargaining led to too much conflict, generated unwarranted pressures on wages and costs, and restricted the efficient use of labour within the workplace. Employees felt that their incomes were not rising sufficiently fast or were being surpassed by others. Among the public there was some growing concern at the problem of strikes and other aspects of British industrial relations. Some workers, on the other hand, though probably always a minority, complained that collective bargaining was too narrowly based to meet their legitimate demands. Governments, for their part, became concerned with inflationary pressures, periodic outbursts of strikes and declining national competitiveness. In this climate of increasing criticism, there were a wide range of proposals for reform.

The liberal collectivist attempt at reform in the 1960s and 1970s brought about some important changes. In particular it encouraged the growth of single-employer bargaining and the reform of procedures, pay systems and wage structures. It also introduced a new set of individual rights for workers, but it fought shy of introducing a new framework of collective labour law. It is debatable to what extent it contributed to an improvement of Britain's economic problems of high inflation and declining competitiveness. The first major attempt at restrictive labour legislation and a more market-based approach to industrial relations under the Heath administration ended in a retreat from many of the initial policies of the government. In the 1980s, under Mrs Thatcher, the government more consistently pursued a more liberal individualist and *laissez-faire* set of policies: it eschewed incomes policies and favoured managing the economy by monetary controls and high interest rates; it introduced an extensive new framework of collective labour law; and, after repealing some earlier protective measures, it set itself against a further extension of statutory employment standards. It is also debatable to what extent it solved Britain's economic problems. The government of Mr Major, elected in 1992, seems set to continue with the basic framework of policies and laws which it inherited. However, under new pressures from Europe and continuing economic problems, there are suggestions that it may seek to pursue less radical and more consensual set of policies in the industrial relations area. We return to debates about outcomes of government policy and possible future changes in the final chapter.

11 Conclusions: issues, outcomes, trends

This book has been concerned with the processes of control over the employment relationship, the organisation of work, and relations between employers and employees in Britain. We have looked at employer strategies, structures and style in industrial relations. We have studied employee objectives and actions as individuals and in workgroups and have traced the development of trade unions as formal representative institutions. The politics of industrial relations have been considered, and we have examined the increasingly active role of the state and noted how very different policies have been advocated over the years by the main political parties. An important focus has been the development of the British system of collective bargaining and attempts to reform and change that system. This chapter concludes the book by restating the major themes and assessing the outcome of change over the last quarter-century. At the end we attempt a brief look into the future.

MAJOR THEMES AND ISSUES

One major theme throughout this book has been the existence of both cooperation and conflict at work. A degree of cooperation exists within all organisations and without it they would not be able to function. Similarly conflict also exists between individuals and groups, and it was argued at the beginning of the book that conflict is not always dysfunctional within organisations in that its successful handling and resolution can lead to more stable and fuller cooperation. From an analytical point of view, therefore, it is necessary to recognise the existence of both conflicts of interest and cooperation at work and to understand the different levels and forms which they can take. From a practical point of view, it is also necessary to recognise both cooperation and conflict in order to be prepared and equipped to deal with both of them.

Another major theme in the book has been the need to understand the sources and distribution of power within organisations and society. It is extraordinarily difficult to judge the distribution of power, not least because power can be both direct and indirect, overt and covert, based on objective and subjective sources. However, we have argued that while power is dispersed within organisations and in the broader society, this does not mean that there is some sort of parity of power between the groups studied. In the vast majority of instances individual employers have more power than individual employees, and this is one reason why employees turn to collective organisation. Even when this occurs, employee group power tends to be reactive and less initiatory than that of employers. In Britain, the state historically took a rather passive role in industrial relations, but when, at certain key junctures, it has intervened to support or change arrangements, its latent power has become manifest and has been seen to be considerable. On the whole we have stressed the power of employers in shaping the British system of industrial relations and of managers in determining day-to-day relations.

A further theme has been the existence of different ideological and theoretical perspectives on industrial relations. We identified a number of major perspectives. First of all, we made the broad distinction between unitarist and pluralist: the former stressing a single source of authority, common interests and willing cooperation between employers and employees, the latter allowing for conflicting interests and a power play within organisations. Within the pluralist perspective, we then identified a number of further approaches to industrial relations. Liberal individualists accept conflicts of interest within organisations, but believe that these should be settled between individual employers and employees through legal contracts and market forces. Liberal collectivists believe that conflicts are best resolved and cooperation best achieved by creating something like a balance of power in industry and by employees acting collectively. Corporatist perspectives have identified and favoured tendencies towards a higher-level institutionalisation of interest representation in society. Separate from unitarist and pluralist perspectives, radicals on the left have stressed the imbalance of power in society in favour of employers, have seen industrial relations as being shaped by fundamental conflicts of interest, and have advocated more thoroughgoing changes in order to make organisations and society more democratic. These different perspectives, and related academic theories, offer concepts and frameworks for an interpretation of industrial relations phenomena; an awareness of them also enables us to understand the assumptions and values of both academic writers and industrial relations practitioners.

A further theme has been that there are various forms of decision making within industry. These range from ones where unilateral employer regulation prevails to ones where unilateral employee regulation is predominant, and with various forms of joint regulation in between. However, we stressed that all of these involve elements of bargaining and negotiation. In British industrial relations, collective bargaining, of varying degrees of formality and informality, has been a central institution which dominates the determination of terms and conditions of employment for the majority of British workers, though this has come under increasing pressure over the last two decades from government intervention, new managerial initiatives, changing employee attitudes and doubts on the part of some trade unionists that collective bargaining is in itself a sufficient form of representation.

At certain key junctures employers, employees and their organisations, and governments have made major strategic choices which have had a profound effect on industrial relations. This is not to say that such choices have always been made consciously, and choices are inevitably constrained by economic, social and political circumstances and are subject to challenge from other interested parties.

We have suggested that employers are the prime movers and dominant influence shaping industrial relations. Employers can largely choose different approaches to the way work is organised, employment conditions are structured, and decisions at work are made. They can choose the structures through which labour is managed such as direct and indirect forms of employment, degrees of centralisation and decentralisation of management systems, reliance on line or staff managers, and the extent to which employers' associations are used. However, their choices are constrained by the contexts within which they operate. In Chapters 3 and 4 we placed considerable emphasis on the organisational context. Most modern organisations are bureaucratic, but the nature of bureaucracy within them varies greatly. Traditionally, in Britain, weak corporate structures and limited managerial hierarchies led to what we termed strategies of externalisation, with a reliance on employers' associations and a slow development of bureaucratic personnel practices. Managerial shortcomings in these respects lay at the heart of many of the traditional problems of British industrial relations. Strategies of internalisation and more sophisticated forms of bureaucratic control have developed only slowly and unevenly in Britain. Many of the changes in techniques and practices over the last twenty years (such as the development of better domestic procedures, new wage systems, and greater reliance on single-employer bargaining) can be understood as a part of this process of internalisation, at least for core workers. At the ideological level, while many British managers have (perforce) been pluralist in their orientation and while some have created sophisticated pluralist cultures within their organisations, there has often been a deep-seated unitarism and an underlying belief in managerial prerogatives. In recent years there has been a growth of a more sophisticated unitarism, reflecting the changed political climate, the decline in trade union power in some organisations, and the growth of new Human Resource Management perspectives.

Employees as individuals can influence industrial relations, but their main influence is when they act collectively in groups. Informal groupings are formed by employees themselves as a method of identification with work colleagues and a way of furthering their own interests, often in opposition to those of management. A recognition of such workgroup activity is very important for an understanding of industrial relations. In Britain, weak managerial structures and hierarchies traditionally allowed workgroups considerable latitude and power. This was the case during the long period of economic prosperity of the first three post-Second World War decades. In the 1970s, many employers sought to integrate such workgroups into more formal bargaining arrangements. From the 1980s onwards, they have tried in various ways, by reorganising work, to reconstitute workgroups and to place them more under management control. However, the success of such managerial techniques is always problematic and subject to challenge from employees.

Trade unions in Britain developed slowly and organically, especially from the latter half of the nineteenth century onwards. The process began when occupational groups built institutions to monopolise and protect scarce, marketable skills. Other workers, with more organisation-specific skills, developed institutions related to the structure of their employing organisations. General and industrial unions developed to cater for less skilled workers and to further their interests through collective bargaining with employers. To manual-worker unionism was added white-collar unionism, especially after the Second World War. The result of this growth pattern has been that a complex multiunionism emerged in the UK. This has been modified by union mergers, which have resulted in the emergence of a small number of large conglomerate unions which constitute the majority of union membership in Britain. It has also been modified in recent years by employer preference for single-unionism or more commonly single-table bargaining with all the unions within a company or workplace. Union membership has fluctuated considerably over time: it reached an all-time peak of 56 per cent in the late 1970s, since when it has declined to just over 40 per cent of the labour force. The present time is a major critical juncture for British trade unions: they have to decide on structures and forms of government suitable for the 1990s; on how to increase membership and recruit in new areas; and on the balance of methods which they will use, in particular between reliance on voluntary methods (such as collective bargaining) and other forms of representation and protection (such as legal rights and EC action).

The state is the third key player in industrial relations. In Britain, the state, though initially voluntarist in orientation, has had a major impact at certain key points in time. At the most fundamental level, from the nineteenth century onwards, the support for voluntarist employment principles and non-intervention in the employment relationship provided the basic framework within which employers, employees and unions operated. Similarly, from the nineteenth century onwards, the provision of legal immunities for unions and later the support for collective bargaining, especially during the period of the two world wars and in the first three decades after the Second World War, had an important effect on British industrial relations. In the 1960s and 1970s, government concern over macroeconomic management and international competitiveness was behind the tendency towards corporatist style arrangements. In the 1980s the Thatcher administration, with its neoliberal commitment to market principles and individualism and its introduction of legal restraints on unions, had a significant effect on the conduct of industrial relations, by reshaping the agenda and making possible what had previously seemed difficult for employers to attain. One of the major questions for the future, which we will discuss below, concerns the likely extent and nature of state intervention in the 1990s. This also means giving attention to the increasing role of the emerging European superstate which many believe the EC will become.

Over the last twenty years employers have sought to reform British industrial relations in various ways. In terms of work organisation, they have experimented with new ways of designing jobs which partially reverse Taylorist tendencies and seek to create more flexible, team working. There is also some evidence that in the 1980s there may have been an intensification of the labour process for some groups of workers as managements have tightened up their control over work organisation.[1] In terms of employment relations, employers have pursued different policies in different contexts and for different groups of workers. In the case of more skilled, core workers, employers have devoted greater attention to their recruitment and have developed more elaborate pay and benefit systems tailored to their own internal requirements; in the case of less skilled workers, employers have been more inclined to rely on the external market and to use part-time, temporary and subcontract working as a way of giving them more flexibility.[2] In their collective bargaining relationship with trade unions, employers have been the main force behind the important move from multi-level national and fragmented shopfloor bargaining to more formal single-employer bargaining. This reform has still left Britain with a complex collective bargaining system: national bargaining still survives in parts of the public sector, though there are growing tendencies towards decentralisation; some private-sector national agreements continue, though now largely supplemented by domestic bargaining; and company- and plant-bargaining predominates in the private sector.

There has been a growing questioning of collective bargaining *per se*. Employers, subject to fiercer competition, have complained that collective bargaining has led to too much conflict, generated unwarranted pressures on costs, and restricted the efficient use of labour within the workplace. Those employers who are non-union wish to remain so; from the 1980s onwards, a small but growing number have derecognised unions and got rid of collective bargaining; others have sought to reduce collective bargaining as a constraint on their activities and to supplement it with various kinds of non-union consultative arrangements. For their part, unions have become more aware that free collective bargaining cannot always deliver. They have also started to think about moving beyond collective bargaining and have looked more to the law, not only in areas of individual employment matters but also in collective areas. This latter inclination has been accentuated by the promise of EC legislation and social programmes.

Over the last quarter-century, all governments (concerned with inflationary pressures, periodic outbursts of strikes and national competitiveness) have produced major and radically different proposals for change in industrial relations. The liberal collectivist attempt at reform in the 1960s and 1970s brought about some important changes. In particular it encouraged the growth of single-employer bargaining and the development of personnel management and some reform of procedures and pay structures. In terms of legislation, it also led to a new set of individual rights for workers, but it fought shy of introducing a tight framework of collective labour law. The first major attempt at restrictive labour legislation and a more market-based approach to industrial relations under the Heath administration of 1970–4 ended in a retreat from many of the initial policies of the government. In the 1980s, under Mrs Thatcher, the government pursued, with greater consistency, a more liberal individualist and *laissez-faire* set of policies: it eschewed incomes policies and favoured managing the economy by monetary controls, high interest rates and tight fiscal policies; it introduced an extensive new framework of collective labour law; and, after repealing some earlier protective measures, it opposed any further extension of statutory employment standards. We will discuss the post-Thatcher era and the likely aftermath of the 1992 Conservative election victory in the section on future trends.

Before considering possible future trends, the next section will briefly survey the outcome of these reform and change strategies.

OUTCOMES OF CHANGE

There are a number of major areas where we may look at the outcomes of change over the last quarter-century. We will summarise some of the major outcomes, focusing on influence and decision making, the climate of industrial relations, economic performance, and the distribution of economic and non-economic rewards. Here we wish to bring out how the industrial relations institutions and the reform strategies we have described may have affected outcomes.

Turning first of all to influence in decision making and bearing in mind the difficulties we have cited in attempting to assess power, our analysis has suggested the following. Historically, the power of employers has always been considerable, especially during economic downturn when the relative input of employees in decision making has been weak. The countervailing influence of trade unions on political and managerial decision making rose during periods of economic upswing and abnormal periods such as the two world wars. During the Second World War and in the early years of the Welfare Compromise, union influence grew, and Clegg has suggested that it may even have peaked at that time.[3] During the 1960s and 1970s unions seemed to have considerable power in terms of pressure on employers and influence on government. Union membership rose and union involvement in decision making seemed to increase at shopfloor and national levels. Yet, much of this was the deployment of defensive power as unions reacted to changes initiated by management and government and to high inflation and threats to real wages. Nevertheless, during these years, both governments and employers had to involve unions more in decision making. In the 1980s, as a consequence of higher unemployment and a reduction of union membership, the balance of power shifted towards employers. The government also chose to realise its latent power, excluded trade unions from national influence, and played a critical role in reshaping industrial relations. During the last decade, employee influence in decision making through collective bargaining has been constrained and there has been an increase in more individual forms of employee involvement at work through mechanisms such as consultation and shareownership. Our analysis of power in earlier chapters would suggest that these voice mechanisms give employees less influence than either collective bargaining or legally based rights. This shift, we would suggest, is likely to continue through the 1990s as a consequence of political, economic and social changes.

If it is difficult to assess influence in decision making, it is equally problematic to judge the climate of industrial relations and the balance between conflict and cooperation. The term 'good industrial relations' has always been a difficult concept to operationalise. In terms of strikes, as we have seen, industrial relations could be said to have been better in the 1980s than in the 1970s – it will be remembered that in the 1970s the annual average number of disputes was 2,631 and of days lost 12.9 million, whereas this fell in the 1980s to 1,129 and 7.2 million respectively. Many managements have also reported better and more cooperative industrial relations. However, we should be wary of fully accepting these arguments. Strikes are a limited measure of the climate of industrial relations and the absence of strikes does not imply good and cooperative industrial relations. The propensity to strike is very much influenced by economic factors, such as the level of unemployment, and, moreover, strike levels in the 1980s were not noticeably lower than in the 1950s and 1960s. Other measures of the state of industrial relations, such as the filing of individual grievances and attitudinal surveys, suggest that conflicts of interest and feelings of distrust remain strong in British industrial relations. These are, however, held in check by a countervailing desire to cooperate and fears of the consequences of more adversarial attitudes.[4]

Turning to economic outcomes, it is again difficult to assess the effect of industrial relations changes because so many other factors affect economic performance. Indeed, industrial relations has probably been a less important determinant of economic outcomes than other factors such as levels of investment, quality of management, and government macroeconomic and industrial policy. However, industrial relations has undoubtedly had an important effect on economic outcomes.

In terms of economic growth and productivity, one of the most striking features of the British economy over the post-Second World War period has been that, though growth rates have been high by historical standards, they have been lower than in most other major industrial countries and Britain has fallen behind its major competitors in terms of levels of gross domestic product per capita.[5] Various industrial relations-type factors may have contributed to this. On the union side, one might cite the complex structure of unions in Britain and their historical strength at workplace level.[6] On the management side, taking a long-term perspective one might refer to weak structures and policies and a failure to develop strong internal arrangements for personnel management. In terms of the interaction between management and unions, one might cite excessive reliance on an adversarial type of collective bargaining. Those who would attribute responsibility to the state deploy rather contradictory arguments: either that historically the state was insufficiently involved (especially in terms of collective labour relations) or that, when it became involved, it interfered too much (especially in terms of individual employment relations); both, it has been contended, had a negative effect. On balance, after considering the evidence, Gospel has argued elsewhere that the management and mismanagement of labour has probably been the most important factor.[7] Unions have for the most part had insufficient power to have a major effect or to bring about positive changes for the better; state intervention in industrial relations has not had a significant effect on economic growth *per se*; but, over the long term, the actions and, often, inactions of employers have been very important. Significant employer action and inaction have included the following: a failure adequately to train employees or develop internal labour market-type arrangements to encourage commitment and productivity; weaknesses in terms of the management of production, especially in key manufacturing industries, such as motor vehicles and electrical products; and the slow development of internal systems of employee representation and collective bargaining.

How have different types of policies affected growth? The period of liberal collectivist, Donovan-type reform, from the late 1960s onwards, witnessed a slowing down of economic growth rates (real gross domestic product grew at 3.3 per cent per annum in the 1960s and 2.2 per cent in the 1970s). But, this slow-down was a world-wide phenomenon, and it might be argued that, had these reforms not taken place, then growth might have been even less in Britain.[8] Moreover, the reforms of that period, such as the development of personnel management and the move to single-employer bargaining in the private sector, provided a basis for further changes in the 1980s. The period of liberal individualist, Thatcher-type reform, in the 1980s, saw no overall acceleration in British long-term growth rates (real gross domestic product grew over that decade by 2.2 per cent per annum). However, since in the 1980s other countries performed less well than their historical record, Britain's performance improved relatively. Taking manufacturing industry alone, here productivity growth was higher in the 1980s than in the past and in relative terms compared better with other countries. Recent research has suggested that a weakening of trade union power and tighter management control from the early 1980s onwards were in part responsible for this. However, in the 1990s, other labour factors, such as a failure to invest in training or to develop a more positive climate of industrial relations, may constrain further gains in terms of performance and competitiveness.[9]

A further important economic outcome relates to the effect which industrial relations may have on inflation and unemployment. There are numerous theories of inflation and unemployment which give more or less prominence to industrial relations-type factors. However, it is inconceivable that the British system of industrial relations, based on entrenched and complex collective bargaining arrangements which we have described, has not contributed to wage cost inflationary pressures. The elaborate incomes policies of the 1960s and 1970s were certainly premised on this belief and were an attempt to deal with these pressures. In practice, they had only limited success and inflation, which averaged 3.8 per cent in the 1960s, rose to 13.2 per cent in the 1970s. Again the rise in inflation was a world-wide phenomenon, and the counter-argument is that inflation might have been even higher in the absence of such policies and that they at least allowed employment to remain at reasonably high levels. By contrast, in the 1980s, a more free-market-based approach to pay determination may have contributed to the lower level of price inflation at 7.5 per cent through that decade, but this has been at the cost of much higher unemployment (which averaged 1.5 per cent in the 1960s, 3.5 per cent in the 1970s and 9.5 per cent in the 1980s). For those in work in the 1980s, real wages rose more rapidly than during most of the two previous decades, though, as we will see below, they rose faster for some groups than for others. The British problem of how to control inflationary pressures and yet maintain full employment and obtain higher growth has still not been solved.

We turn next to outcomes in terms of the distribution of rewards, both wage and non-wage. Income differentials between different occupations tend to fluctuate over time, in part reflecting changes in the economy (they tend to narrow during periods of economic upswing) and major social upheavals (they narrowed during the two world wars). The long-term trend throughout most of the twentieth century has been towards a narrowing of differentials.[10] This was probably encouraged by industrial relations factors, such as the spread of collective bargaining and the operation of incomes policies in the 1960s and 1970s, both of which served to compress differentials. In the 1980s, income differentials between occupations and between those at the top and bottom of the income distribution have widened at a faster rate than ever before this century, certainly when post-tax income is considered. Differentials between broad regions such as the North and South and between the public and private sectors also increased in the 1980s.[11] This has been encouraged by the operation of more market-based economic policies, the eschewal of incomes policies (at least in the private sector), the move to more individualised pay systems and a weakening of collective bargaining.

Many non-wage benefits are positively correlated with wages so that those who earn the highest wages also have the most generous benefits. In the first thirty years after the Second World War, there was a spread of non-wage benefits, such as pensions and sick pay schemes, to non-manual workers. In recent years some firms have pursued a policy of so-called harmonisation, whereby they have sought to narrow differences between manual and staff employees. However, non-wage benefits are still very unequally distributed, with clerical and managerial staff enjoying more and better benefits than manual workers. Thus, fewer manual workers are covered by employer sickness schemes and these tend to be less generous, and fewer are members of pension schemes and, again, these are less generous.[12] Considerable differences also still exist with respect to time keeping rules, liability to lay-off and short-time, and redundancy arrangements.[13] For those who believe that people and rewards can never be equal and that inequality has economic advantages, the growing inequalities of the 1980s are to be applauded. For those who believe that greater equality is socially and economically beneficial, there is still a long way to go.

It is possible to draw attention to two other kinds of outcomes at work, relating to skill levels and employment prospects.

As we saw in Chapter 3, it has been argued that one tendency within capitalist society has been towards the deskilling of jobs. Some have seen this in terms of a general tendency towards the deskilling of all jobs; others have pointed to a polarisation of jobs in society, with some being deskilled, some retaining their skill content, and others being upskilled.[14] It is therefore inaccurate to talk about overall strategies of deskilling on the part of employers and it is more realistic to conclude that, while some employees and their children have experienced higher levels of education and training, many others in Britain are becoming relatively less well trained, certainly when compared to their counterparts overseas.[15] In this sense there may well have occurred a greater polarisation of skills within Britain. One major failure on the part of governments and employers over the last quarter-century has been the failure to raise the overall level of skill of the labour force, certainly when compared with other countries. One major objective of the 1990s must be to counteract this failure.

In terms of employment prospects, some have argued that over the last twenty years and especially in the 1980s, there has been a growth of a duality in the labour market. On the one hand, there are those who are well protected by internal labour markets and who have good job security and career prospects within a firm. Equally there are those with scarce skills who are able to take advantage of occupational labour markets. On the other hand, there are those, in secondary or peripheral jobs, who have less good job security and no real career prospects.[16] Sometimes these arguments are put in terms of the creation of a core of primary workers and a periphery of secondary, less secure and less well-advantaged workers. There has been some overstatement of the novelty of these developments, though it is probably true that over the last ten years there has been a growth in labour market structures on these lines.[17] This may have some economic advantages in terms of flexibility; it may also have some economic disadvantages in terms of the demotivation and under-utilisation of workers in the secondary sector; from a social point of view there are also disadvantages in terms of greater inequality in society.

WHAT OF FUTURE TRENDS?

In this final section we turn to underlying trends and possible future developments in industrial relations through the 1990s.[18] Here a systems-type framework is useful to structure these final thoughts; however, we stress that we are speculating about possible options and choices which will have to be made by the industrial relations parties. In this sense we are not saying that any future outcomes are structurally determined, but that there are choices subject to major constraints and environmental contexts.

The first context that must be taken into account is the technological. There is often much easy talk about rapid technological change, and all generations tend to think that they are living through such a period. At the present time, there is a good deal of truth in such assertions, and we are experiencing what might be called a Third Industrial Revolution. The First Industrial Revolution of the late eighteenth century was based on coal, iron and steam; the Second Industrial Revolution of the late nineteenth century was based on electricity and chemistry; the Third Industrial Revolution of the late twentieth century is based on microelectronics and information technology. This has already had profound effects on the structure of employment and types of jobs. In the future employment in manufacturing is likely to continue to decline and that in services is likely to continue to increase, though perhaps not at the same pace as in the 1980s. The new technology has enabled some firms to move, for some of their workers, from mass-production methods based on Fordist and Taylorist lines to more flexible and specialised systems of working.[19] There is a major set of choices to be made about the nature of jobs: in particular are we to see more deskilling, or a polarisation of skills, or a general upskilling? As we have already suggested, competitive forces are likely to put pressure on governments and firms in the 1990s for higher levels of training to equip the British labour force to use new technologies more effectively.

The second set of environmental factors relate to the market context. Over the postwar period, product markets have been growing in area and levels of competition have been intensifying. This is likely to continue for British industry through the 1990s, not least as the Single European Market is created and as Europe moves towards greater economic and monetary union. This new regime will put growing pressure on firms and on future governments to try to ensure economic competitiveness. In addition to these competitive pressures from Europe, there will also be greater pressures in global terms from American, Japanese and other competitors. In terms of the labour market, demographic projections are that the size of the labour force will continue to grow, but more slowly in the 1990s than in the 1980s, with much of the growth due to higher female participation; by the year 2000, women will make up more than 45 per cent of the workforce. The number of young entrants into the labour market will decline through the 1990s, but because of higher female participation rates, lower quitting rates on the part of older workers, and adjustments to fuller European economic integration, unemployment will probably remain high through the 1990s at over 2 million and it will obviously be higher during periods of cyclical downturn. In terms of the structure of employment, the labour force will be on average older and will contain more women; there will in addition be some further growth of part-time and temporary employment, though not as much as in the 1980s.[20]

The third context is the political environment, and here we must speculate about possible scenarios. One scenario is that the Conservatives, having won a fourth term of office under Mr Major in 1992, are in office throughout the whole of the 1990s. This would mean a government committed to market and liberal individualist policies, though probably less ideologically and aggressively so than during the Thatcherite 1980s. Another scenario is that the Labour Party, or some sort of coalition between Labour and the Liberal Democrats, come to power in the mid-1990s, in which case we will see a government more liberal collectivist and interventionist in orientation and this may lead to a revival of macrocorporatism under the new banner of Social Partnership. A third possible scenario is that, perhaps after a change in the electoral system, we see a period of greater political uncertainty over the decade of the 1990s, a development which would mean a state more open to pressure and bargaining with business and labour. One likely development is that through the 1990s we will see more intervention from Europe as the EC moves towards greater economic and political union. As the tide of Left Socialist and New Right policies ebbs, British politics are likely to move towards the centre and there will probably be less divergence on policy than in the 1980s.

In Britain and elsewhere in the advanced industrial world, the main debate at the political and public policy level will probably be between liberal individualist perspectives, with their belief in market mechanisms and unitarist arrangements within organisations (which were influential in the US and the UK in the 1980s); liberal collectivist perspectives, which are pluralist and more interventionist in nature (influential in the Social-Democratic and Christian-Democratic Parties of Europe); and various forms and levels of corporatism (also to be found in Europe and in Japan). With the demise of Marxism, what we have called radical perspectives will also be in eclipse, but they will not disappear, and major economic, social or political upsets could lead to the revival of new radical perspectives.

What likely impact will such changes in the context of industrial relations have on the main participants and the relations between them?

Turning first of all to employers. In the private sector of the economy it seems likely that, in key markets, large firms will remain dominant and may even grow further as a result of mergers, especially cross-frontier mergers within the EC. However, smaller firms will continue to grow in certain markets, and the average size of plants in terms of employment will probably continue to fall in part reflecting technological changes. Firms, facing an increasingly competitive market environment, will continue to look for flexibility and cost reductions via decentralisation and devolution. This in turn will put pressure on their industrial relations systems. In the British context employers are not likely to look to employers' organisations for industrial relations purposes but to the further development of in-house managerial capabilities among both line and specialist staff managers. Firms will pay more attention to human resource management policies in areas such as recruitment, training and remuneration systems.[21] There may be some further movement towards what we described as sophisticated unitarist policies, aimed at securing individual employee commitment, but the extent of this will depend very much on the economic environment and political pressures, not least from Europe, where notions of social partnership give more emphasis to collective relations. Probably the majority of large firms which already recognise trade unions for collective bargaining will remain largely pluralist in orientation, but with greater intra-organisational diversity and with reliance on both collective bargaining and sophisticated consultative arrangements. In this respect there may well develop a greater competition, both between and within firms, in terms of whether firms and plants are unionised and have collective bargaining or not.[22] Overall, the main strategy of large firms will be what we called bureaucratic, though with attempts simultaneously to achieve greater flexibility. It may also be in the direction of greater internalisation, though this will be supplemented by simultaneous policies of externalisation for some groups of workers and parts of firms. In the public sector, management will continue to be subject to more commercial and budgetary pressures and here the trend will be towards continued decentralisation and devolution, with greater emphasis on contracting out, individual relations with employees and forms of human resource management more like those in the private sector.

It is difficult to make predictions about the workforce other than the demographic projections which we have made above. There may be a continued trend towards more individualistic orientations and a diminution in the collectivist orientations we described in Chapter 5. This could be accompanied by a decline in ideologies based on opposition and resistance to management authority and a greater acceptance of, or acquiescence in, the dominant value system and conservative orientations. The traditional working class will continue to shrink in size, and a larger proportion of the workforce will come to see themselves more as middle-class, though less than in most industrial countries. It may also be the case that, with greater affluence and leisure, young people in particular will espouse post-materialist values, attaching more importance to non-work activities and at work stressing individual development. However, it was noted in Chapter 5 that the work ethic is still strong and may rise with higher levels of education. Similarly, post-materialist values also often contain a rejection of authority and a belief in commonly shared activities.[23] These will support collectivist orientations, and there will always be factors making workers act together at work.

Trade union membership will decline further, as the private services and higher-technology sectors of the economy grow and as female and part-time employment increases. The return of a fourth successive Conservative government in 1992 will not help union membership. Adverse cyclical factors will also have a negative effect on union membership. However, there will be counterpressures: having overcome some of the union prob-lems of the past, many managements may not wish to reduce union membership further and might aid membership by, for example, adhering to check-off arrangements. Unions may also be more successful in their recruitment strategies, especially if real wages are threatened, and pressures from Europe may contain employer anti-unionism and maintain member-ship. On balance, it seems likely that union membership will have stabilised at above one-third of the labour force by the end of the century.[24] There will be fewer unions, because of continuing mergers, but no less competition between such unions for membership, especially in the white-collar area, and the continued existence of some small closed unions will ensure a complex union structure in Britain. In terms of the distribution of power within unions there will be conflicting tendencies: legal requirements and the need for professional services will make for a concentration of power at the top; on the other hand, in terms of bargaining about pay and conditions, reflecting employer policies of internalisation, power will stay with the domestic union; and the role of the TUC will continue to decline in importance. The ideology of British trade unions will probably continue to adapt, as it has over the last decade, away from more radical orientations, towards more realistic accommodations with employers and government, based on the ideology and practice of Social Partnership. Links between the unions and the Labour Party will probably loosen, especially if the former feel that Labour cannot get elected to government and as the latter feels the need to distance itself from the unions in order to be elected.

As to the role of the state, in Chapters 7 and 10, we stressed the increase in state intervention over the last quarter-century, despite some deregulation of individual employment relations in the 1980s. Under Conservative governments, there will be more restrictive labour law, and, despite opposition to the social side of Europe, it would seem to be impossible to prevent a slow extension of individual labour law. Under a future Labour or coalition government, there would be some repeal of restrictive labour law, but new auxiliary labour law on such matters as union recognition and protective legislation would be introduced, including a full acceptance of the EC Social Charter. One of the big questions surrounds policies on incomes and the possible revival of some sort of macrocorporatism. Membership of the European Exchange Rate Mechanism, with its regime of fixed currencies and tight monetary policy, will put pressure on all the industrial relations participants to search for an alternative to high interest rates and unemployment as a way of controlling inflation and maintaining exchange rates. A future Labour or coalition government would probably move more in the corporatist direction and would engage more in discussions with employers and trade unions about economic prospects and the scope for pay rises. This might lead to some sort of national economic assessment with more coordinated bargaining on German lines. However, the degree of decentralisation in wage bargaining and the strength of liberal values in Britain will be major obstacles. It is unlikely that any Conservative government would attempt any such arrangements, though, paradoxically, such a government would be in a good position to enter into such a deal with unions desperate to obtain more say than they had in the 1980s and fearful of the effects of high interest rates and unemployment.

Collective bargaining will remain a central process in the economy and a way of handling conflicts of interest at work, with bargaining likely to remain at company and plant level and not revert to industry level. In the public sector there will be further decentralisation and it is likely that here there will be continued instability in bargaining, as governments try to control public-sector wages and restructure working conditions. The scope of bargaining will depend very much on the economic and political climate, though unions will want to extend bargaining to cover such areas as training, working time arrangements, equal opportunities provisions, and pensions. There will be some growth of single-union agreements and even more of single-table bargaining, though not much growth of no-strike agreements. Alongside collective bargaining there will be a further growth of direct communication and joint consultative arrangements of various kinds both in the non-union and the union sector.[25] Overall, it is probably true to say that the perimeter of collective bargaining will probably shrink and be replaced by more unilateral employer regulation and individual bargaining. One of the main imponderables must be the advent of other channels of representation which are not union-based but which formally integrate negotiation into the organisational structures of the firm. Here possible developments are legally based works councils or worker directors on companies boards such as exist in Germany. This will again depend entirely on the political environment and the impact of Europe. But it seems highly likely that there will be some developments in this area, given the fact that British multinationals with operations in other EC countries and multinationals based in other EC countries with British plants will be likely to establish European works councils.[26] Finally, there could also be, for some groups of workers (such as those in the international transport industries) and some companies (those which are very integrated in terms of production), a development of European-wide collective bargaining, though resistance to this from employers will be strong.

The processes of control over the employment relationship, the organisation of work and relations between employers and their employees have been the subject of considerable controversy within Britain for a quarter of a century. With no lasting solution having been found to many old problems, and with new pressures and challenges emerging, industrial relations will remain a topic of great social, economic and political importance and an intellectually stimulating field of study.

Notes

Except where otherwise stated the place of publication is London.

1 INTRODUCTION

1 Surveys for the 1977 Royal Commission on the Press and by the Glasgow University Media Group, *Bad News* (1976) and *More Bad News* (1980).
2 A. Flanders, *Industrial Relations: What is Wrong with the System?* (1965).
3 J. Dunlop, *Industrial Relations Systems* (1958).
4 A. Fox, *Industrial Sociology and Industrial Relations*, Research Paper No. 3, Royal Commission on Trade Unions and Employers' Associations (1966).
5 R. Dubin, 'A theory of conflict and power in union–management relations', *Industrial and Labor Relations Review* (1960).
6 M. Rose, *Industrial Behaviour* (1988), p. 335.
7 W. Ouchi, *Theory Z* (New York, 1981), p. 136.
8 R. E. Walton, 'From Control to Commitment', *Harvard Business Review* (1985).

2 PERSPECTIVES ON INDUSTRIAL RELATIONS

1 Commission on Industrial Relations, Report 29, *Alcan Smelter Site* (1972).
2 For a good summary see M. Rose, *Industrial Behaviour* (1985), Part 3.
3 See, for example, W. Ouchi, *Theory Z* (1981).
4 J. Storey (ed.), *New Perspectives on Human Resource Management* (1989).
5 S. and B. Webb, *Industrial Democracy* (1919) and *The History of Trade Unionism* (1920).
6 *Ibid.* For members of the Oxford School see the writings of A. Flanders, H. Clegg, O. Kahn-Freund, A. Fox, and W. McCarthy referred to elsewhere. H. Clegg, 'The Oxford School of Industrial Relations', Warwick Papers in Industrial Relations, No. 31 (1990).
7 R. Dubin in A. Kornhauser, R. Dubin and A. Ross (eds), *Industrial Conflict* (1954).
8 C. Kerr, J. Dunlop, F. Harbison and C. Myers, *Industrialism and Industrial Man* (1960).
9 J. Dunlop, *Industrial Relations Systems* (New York, 1958).
10 T. Parsons, *Economy and Society* (1956).

11 See N. Harris, *Competition and the Corporate Society: British Conservatives, the State, and Industry 1945–64* (1972).

12 P. Schmitter, 'Still the Century of Corporatism?', *Review of Politics* (1974) and L. Panitch, 'The Development of Corporatism in Liberal Democracies', *Comparative Political Studies* (1977).

13 Harris talks about pluralist and etatist corporatism: Schmitter refers to societal and state corporatism; Panitch uses the terms liberal and pure corporatism; and Crouch refers to bargained and pure corporatism. See above and C. Crouch, *Class Conflict and Industrial Relations* (1977).

14 G. Palmer, 'Donovan, the Commission on Industrial Relations, and Post Liberal Rationalisation', *British Journal of Industrial Relations* (1986); B. Jessop, 'Capitalism, Corporatism, Labour Exclusion or New Patterns of Cooperation', in O. Jacobi and K. Kastendieck (eds), *Labour Exclusion or New Patterns of Cooperation?* (Frankfurt, 1986).

15 G. Palmer, 'Corporatism and Australian Arbitration', in S. Macintyre and R. Mitchell, *Foundations of Arbitration* (Melbourne, 1989).

16 See the next chapter for some discussion of this.

17 E. Durkheim, *The Division of Labour in Society* (1933).

18 Milne-Bailey, a leading trade union spokesman, advocated a National Economic Council consisting of employer and employee representatives to advise Parliament and he envisaged a time when trade unionists would sit on the boards of nationalised industries giving a voice to ordinary people at work. W. Milne-Bailey, *Trade Unions and the State* (1934).

19 G. Palmer, 'Donovan, the Commission on Industrial Relations and Post Liberal Rationalisation', *British Journal of Industrial Relations* (1986).

20 F. A. Hayek, *The Road to Serfdom* (1944).

21 G. D. H. Cole, *Self-Government in Industry* (1917).

22 G. Sorel, *Réflections sur la Violence* (Paris, 1908).

23 For Marxist perspectives see R. Hyman, *Industrial Relations: A Marxist Introduction* (1975); T. Clarke and L. Clements (eds), *Trade Unions under Capitalism* (1977); R. Hyman, *The Political Economy of Industrial Relations* (1989); J. Kelly, *Trade Unions and Socialist Politics* (1988).

24 Over the last twenty years there has been an extensive debate among Marxists of various kinds on the nature of the labour process in capitalist society. For one survey see P. Thompson, *The Nature of Work* (1983).

25 P. Anderson, 'The limits and possibilities of trade union action', in R. M. Blackburn and A. Cockburn (eds), *The Incompatibles* (1967).

26 A. Gramsci, *Selections from Political Writings 1910–1920* (1977).

27 See J. Child, 'Organisational Structure, Environment, and Performance: The Role of Strategic Choice', *Sociology* (1972) and T. A. Kochan, H. Katz and R. B. McKersie, *The Transformation of American Industrial Relations* (New York, 1986).

3 EMPLOYERS AND THEIR STRATEGIES

1 D. McQuail, *Analysis of Newspaper Content*, Royal Commission on the Press, Research Paper 4 (1977); Glasgow University Media Group, *Bad News* (1976) and *More Bad News* (1980).

2 J. Gennard, *Financing Strikers* (1977).

3 See Chapters 7 and 10.

4 *Economic Trends* (December 1989).

5 G. Bannock and M. Daly, 'Size Distribution of UK Firms', *Department of Employment Gazette*, May 1990.

6 The average number of employees per plant in manufacturing industry fell from 60 in 1977 to 30 in 1988; the percentage of employees in plants employing more than 1,000 fell from 29 per cent to 18 per cent over the same period. *Annual Abstract of Statistics* (1981) Table 6.17 and (1991) Table 6.13.

7 Although in the 1960s and 1970s it may have been taken further in the UK than elsewhere. L. Hannah and J. Kay, *Concentration in Modern Industry* (1977).

8 A. Chandler, *Scale and Scope: The Dynamics of Industrial Capitalism* (Cambridge, MA, 1990).

9 K. Sisson, J. Waddington, C. Whitston, 'Company Size in the European Community', *Human Resource Management Journal* (1991).

10 H. Braverman, *Labour and Monopoly Capital* (New York, 1974).

11 J. Child, 'Quaker Employers and Industrial Relations', *Sociological Review* (1964).

12 See *ibid.* and the more recent study of Cadburys by C. Smith, J. Child and M. Rawlinson, *Reshaping Work: The Cadbury Experience* (Cambridge, 1991).

13 A. Berle and G. C. Means, *The Modern Corporation and Private Property* (Chicago, 1932); J. K. Galbraith, *The New Industrial State* (1967).

14 T. Nichols, *Ownership, Control, and Ideology* (1969); A. Francis, 'Company Objectives, Management Motivations, and the Behaviour of Large Firms', *Cambridge Journal of Economics* (1980); R. Edwards, *Contested Terrain* (1979); D. Gordon, R. Edwards and M. Reich, *Segmented Work, Divided Workers* (1982).

15 J. Child, *The Business Enterprise in Modern Society* (1969), pp. 36–51.

16 *ibid.*

17 For more details see Chapter 6.

18 E. Batstone, A. Ferner and M. Terry, *Consent and Efficiency: Labour Relations and Management Strategy in the State Enterprise* (Oxford, 1984); A. Ferner, *Governments, Managers, and Industrial Relations: Public Enterprises and their Political Environment* (Oxford, 1988).

19 *Ibid.*; A. Ferner and T. Collins, 'Privatisation, Regulation and Industrial Relations', *British Journal of Industrial Relations* (1991); T. Collins and A. Ferner, 'Holding the Line: Decentralisation and Line Management in Privatised Companies' (University of Warwick, 1991).

20 See H. Mintzberg, *The Nature of Managerial Work* (New York, 1973) and *The Structuring of Organisations* (Englewood Cliffs, NJ, 1979) p. 443.

21 H. F. Gospel, *Markets, Firms, and the Management of Labour in Modern Britain* (Cambridge, 1992).

22 A. Etzioni, *A Comparative Analysis of Complex Organisations* (New York, 1961).

23 J. Woodward, *Industrial Organisation: Theory and Practice* (1965).

24 R. Edwards, *Contested Terrain* (1979).

25 H. Braverman, *op. cit.*

26 See, for example, R. Crompton and G. Jones, *White Collar Proletariat* (1984); R. Scase and R. Goffee, *Reluctant Managers*, (1989).

27 C. Littler and G. Salaman, 'Bravermania and Beyond: Recent Theories of the Labour Process', *Sociology* (1982).

28 C. Littler, *The Development of the Labour Process in Capitalist Societies* (1982); D. Nelson, *Managers and Workers* (1975); J. Merkle, *Management and Ideology* (Berkeley, 1980).

29 M. J. Piore and C. F. Sabel, *The Second Industrial Divide* (New York, 1984).

30 See, for example, C. R. Littler, *op. cit.*

31 *Ibid.* and R. Edwards, *op.cit.*

32 M. Weber, *The Theory of Social and Economic Organisation* (New York, 1964 ed.).

33 C. Perrow, *Complex Organisations: A Critical Essay* (Glenview, IL, 1972).

34 R. Dore, *British Factory – Japanese Factory* (1973).

35 See two recent accounts of industrial relations in Japanese-owned plants in Britain: P. Wickens, *The Road to Nissan* (1987) and M. Trevor, *Toshiba's New British Company* (1988).

36 R. Dore, *op. cit.*

37 Advisory Conciliation and Arbitration Service, *Harmonisation*, (1989).

38 See, for example, Incomes Data Services, *Teamworking*, Report 419 (1988) and R. Collard and B. Dale, 'Quality Circles', in K. Sisson (ed.), *Personnel Management in Britain* (Oxford, 1989).

39 R. Fitzgerald, *British Labour Management and Industrial Welfare 1846–1939* (1988).

40 See, for example, H. Homburg, 'Scientific Management and Personnel Policy in the Modern German Enterprise', in H. F. Gospel and C. R. Littler, *op. cit.*

41 S. Meyer, *The Five Dollar Day* (Albany, NY, 1981).

42 For a good review, see S. Jacoby, *Employing Bureaucracy: Managers, Unions, and the Transformation of Work in American Industry* (New York, 1985); F. Foulkes, *Personnel Policies in Large Non-Union Companies* (Englewood Cliffs, NJ, 1980); T. Kochan, H. Katz and R. B. McKersie, *The Transformation of American Industrial Relations* (New York, 1986).

43 R. Coase, 'The Nature of the Firm', *Economica* (1937).

44 H. F. Gospel, *Markets, Firms, and the Management of Labour in Modern Britain* (Cambridge, 1992).

45 This is taken from G. S. Becker, *Human Capital: A Theoretical and Empirical Analysis with Special Reference to Education* (New York, 1964).

46 One of the earliest analyses of the internal labour market is to be found in C. Kerr, 'The Balkanisation of Labour Markets', in E. W. Bakke *Labour Mobility and Economic Opportunity* (Cambridge, MA, 1954) pp. 92–110. For a fuller analysis see P. B. Doeringer and M. J. Piore, *Internal Labor Markets and Manpower Analysis* (Lexington, MA, 1971).

47 This term is used in G. B. Richardson, 'The Organisation of Industry', *Economic Journal* (1972).

48 M. Wiener, *English Culture and the Decline of the Industrial Spirit, 1850–1980* (Cambridge, 1981); R. Locke, *The End of Practical Man: Entrepreneurship in Germany, France and Great Britain* (Greenwich, CT, 1984).

49 P. Wickens, *op. cit.* and M. Trevor, *op. cit.*

50 T. Burns and G. Stalker, *The Management of Innovation* (1961); A. Stinchcombe, 'Bureaucratic and Craft Administration of Production', *Administrative Science Quarterly* (1959); A. Stinchcombe, *Creating Efficient Industrial Administration* (New York, 1974); J. Pfeffer, *Power in Organisations* (Boston, 1981).

51 T. Burns and G. Stalker, *op. cit.*

52 A. Stinchcombe, *op. cit.* (1959).
53 M. Crozier, *The Bureaucratic Phenomenon*, (Chicago, 1964).
54 P. Doeringer and M. Piore, *op. cit.*; R. Edwards, *op. cit.*; H. F. Gospel, *Markets, Firms, and the Management of Labour*.
55 R. Edwards, *op. cit.* and W. Lazonick, *Value Creation on the Shopfloor* (Cambridge, MA, 1990).
56 A Friedman, *Industry and Labour* (1977).
57 H. F. Gospel, *Markets, Firms, and the Management of Labour*.
58 For a similar argument see H. Ramsay, 'Cycles of Control', *Sociology* (1977) and 'Reinventing the Wheel?: A Review of the Development and Performance of Employee Involvement', *Human Resource Management Journal* (1991).
59 K. Thurley and S. Wood, *Industrial Relations and Management Strategy* (1983); H. F. Gospel, *Markets, Firms, and the Management of Labour*.
60 H. Mintzberg, *op. cit.*
61 A. Fox, *Beyond Contract* (1974). R. Dore, *op. cit.*, pp. 73–94, gives a graphic description of the problems associated with individual piece work incentives in the British engineering industry.
62 C. R. Littler, *The Development of the Labour Process in Capitalist Societies*; H. F. Gospel, *Markets, Firms, and the Management of Labour*; C. Lane, *Management and Labour in Europe* (1989).
63 D. McGregor, *Leadership in Motivation* (New York, 1966); T. Burns and G. Stalker, *op. cit.*
64 A. Fox, *Industrial Sociology and Industrial Relations* (1966).
65 For a good statement of this philosophy see A. Roddick, *Body and Soul* (1991), which stresses the benevolent leadership and togetherness of the Body Shop group.
66 M. Poole and R. Mansfield, 'Changes in Managerial Attitudes to Industrial Relations 1980–1990', Paper presented at British Universities Industrial Relations Association Conference (1991).
67 J. Purcell and K. Sisson, 'Strategies and Practices in the Management of Industrial Relations', in G. S. Bain (ed.), *Industrial Relations in Great Britain* (Oxford, 1983).
68 J. Purcell, 'Mapping Management Styles in Employee Relations', *Journal of Management Studies* (1987).

4 EMPLOYERS AND THEIR ORGANISATION

1 A. D. Chandler, *Scale and Scope: The Dynamics of Industrial Capitalism* (Cambridge, MA, 1990) and O. Williamson, *Markets and Hierarchies* (New York, 1975), Chapter 8.
2 P. Marginson, P. Edwards, R. Martin, J. Purcell and K. Sisson, *Beyond the Workplace* (Oxford, 1988).
3 C. W. L. Hill and J. F. Pickering, 'Divisionalisation, Decentralisation, and Performance of Large UK Companies', *Journal of Manpower Studies* (1986); M. Goold and A. Campbell, *Strategies and Styles: The Role of the Centre in Managing Diversified Corporations* (Oxford, 1987).
4 A. D. Chandler, *op. cit.*, pp. 621–8.
5 P. Armstrong, 'Competition between the Organised Professions and the Evolution of Management Control Strategies', in K. Thompson (ed.), *Work, Employment and Unemployment* (Milton Keynes, 1984) and 'Engineers, Management, and Trust', *Work, Employment and Society* (1987).

6 I. Mangham and M. Silver, *Management Training: Context and Practice* (Bath, 1986); J. Constable and R. McCormick, *The Making of British Managers* (1987); C. Handy, *Making Managers* (1988).

7 See, for example, T. M. Mosson and D. G. Clark, 'Some Inter-Industry Comparisons of the Background and Careers of Managers', *British Journal of Industrial Relations* 6 (1968); A. I. Marsh and J. G. Gillies, 'The Involvement of Line Staff Managers in Industrial Relations', in K. Thurley and S. Wood, *Industrial Relations and Management Strategy* (Cambridge, 1983); S. G. Reading, *The Working Class Manager: Beliefs and Behaviour* (Farnborough 1979).

8 During the Second World War the Ministry of Labour introduced the American system of Training Within Industry. This continued to grow after the war. J. Child and B. Partridge, *Lost Managers: Supervisors in Industry and Society* (Cambridge, 1982).

9 J. Child and B. Partridge, *op. cit.*, p. 137. One indication of this is that from the mid 1960s British supervisory staffs increasingly joined trade unions. *Ibid.* pp. 11, 148–9, 169–88.

10 T. Lupton, *On the Shop Floor* (Oxford, 1963), pp. 180–90; S. Hill, 'Norms, Groups, and Power: The Sociology of Workplace Industrial Relations', *British Journal of Industrial Relations* (1974); W. Brown, *Piecework Bargaining* (1973), pp. 163–5. The traditional lack of information, if not interest, at senior levels, in the management of labour has been commented upon. See J. Winkler, 'The Ghost at the Bargaining Table: Directors and Industrial Relations', *British Journal of Industrial Relations* (1974).

11 National Economic Development Council, *What Makes a Supervisor World Class?* (1991).

12 D. F. Schloss, *Methods of Industrial Remuneration* (1892) p. 120, stated that subcontracting was 'practically ubiquitous'. For a recent analysis see C. R. Littler, *The Development of the Labour Process in Capitalist Societies* (1982).

13 M. M. Niven, *Personnel Management 1913–63* (1967), pp. 40–5.

14 In 1945 half of the 4,700 factories with over 250 workers employed a personnel manager. See Ministry of Labour and National Service, *Report of Conference on Joint Consultation, Training Within Industry, Works Information and Personnel Management*, Paper No. 4, 'Personnel Management', (1948) p. 42; A. Marsh, 'The Staffing of Industrial Relations Management in the Engineering Industry', *Industrial Relations Journal* (1976).

15 H. A. Clegg, *The Changing System of Industrial Relations in Great Britain* (Oxford, 1979), pp. 127–8.

16 W. Marks, *Politics and Personnel Management* (1978); W. W. Daniel and N. Millward, *Workplace Industrial Relations in Britain* (1983), Chapter 5; N. Millward and M. Stevens, *British Workplace Industrial Relations 1980–1984* (1986), Chapter 2; *Financial Times*, 10 February 1992.

17 See, for example, discussion in W. W. Daniel and N. Millward, *op. cit.* and N. Millward and M. Stevens, *op. cit.*, P. J. Buckley and P. Enderwick, *The Industrial Relations Practices of Foreign-Owned Firms in Britain* (1985).

18 See, for example, J. Storey, 'From Personnel Management to Human Resource Management' and D. Torrington, 'Human Resource Management and the Personnel Function', in J. Storey (ed.), *New Perspectives on Human Resource Management* (1989).

19 P. Geroski and K. G. Knight, 'Corporate Merger and Collective Bargaining in

the UK', *Industrial Relations Journal* (1984); P. Marginson, 'The Multi-divisional Firm and Control Over the Work Process', *International Journal of Industrial Organisation* (1985).

20 H. A. Turner, *Management Characteristics and Labour Conflict: A Study of Managerial Organisation, Attitudes and Industrial Relations* (Cambridge, 1977); E. Batstone, 'What Have Personnel Managers Done for Industrial Relations?' *Personnel Management* (June 1980).

21 P. Jackson and K. Sisson, 'Employers' Confederations in Sweden and the UK and the Significance of Industrial Infrastructure', *British Journal of Industrial Relations* (1976), speak in similar terms of defence, procedural/political, and market models of employers' association.

22 A. Smith, *The Wealth of Nations* (1970 edition), p. 169.

23 J. B. Jefferys, *The Story of the Engineers* (1945), pp. 10–11.

24 H. A. Clegg, *The System of Industrial Relations in Great Britain* (1972), p. 125; K. Burgess, *The Origins of British Industrial Relations* (1975), p. 180.

25 S. and B. Webb, *Industrial Democracy* (1898), p. 137.

26 H. F. Gospel, 'Managerial Structures and Strategies', in H. F. Gospel and C. R. Littler (eds), *Managerial Strategies and Industrial Relations* (1983).

27 H. A. Clegg, *Trade Unionism under Collective Bargaining* (Oxford, 1976).

28 K. Sisson, *The Management of Collective Bargaining* (Oxford, 1987).

29 See Chapter 6.

30 See Chapters 7 and 9. W. Grant and D. Marsh, *The Confederation of British Industry* (1977), p. 16.

31 *Manpower Policy and Practice* (Spring 1987).

32 R. Loveridge, 'Corporate Strategy and Industrial Relations Strategy', in K. Thurley and S. Wood (eds), *Managerial Strategy and Industrial Relations* (Cambridge, 1982).

33 H. F. Gospel, 'Employers' Organisations: Their Growth and Function in the British System of Industrial Relations' (London University PhD, 1974).

34 It only returned when the Chemical Industry's Association adopted a policy of accepting employers who did not have to conform to association-agreed rates.

35 For some statistical information on this see W. Brown (ed.), *The Changing Contours of British Industrial Relations: A Survey of Manufacturing Industry*, (Oxford, 1981), pp. 5–31. See also W. W. Daniels and N. Millward, *op. cit.*, Chapter 5, and N. Millward and M. Stevens, *op. cit.*, Chapter 2.

36 Royal Commission on Trade Unions and Employers' Associations, (Donovan Commission), Minutes of Evidence, 59, para 9384 (1966).

37 *Ibid.*, 20, para 2843, (1966).

38 Cadbury's *Board Minutes* 307, 18 December 1967, and Board File re Minute 61, 25 March 1968.

39 D. McIntyre, 'Inquest on the Engineering Dispute and the Future of Two-tier Bargaining', *Personnel Management* (December 1979).

40 E. Wigham, *Power to Manage* (1973), pp. 253–40; H. A. Clegg, *The Changing System of Industrial Relations in Great Britain* (Oxford, 1979), p. 88.

41 W. Brown and J. Walsh, 'Pay Determination in Britain in the 1980s: The Anatomy of Decentralisation', *Oxford Review of Economic Policy* (1991).

42 W. Brown, *The Changes Contours of British Industrial Relations* (Oxford, 1981), pp. 19–23; Commission on Industrial Relations, *Employers' Organisations in Industrial Relations* (1973).

43 W. Brown, *op. cit.*; W. Brown and M. Terry, 'The Nature of National Wage Agreements', *Scottish Journal of Political Economy* (1978); W. Brown and J. Walsh, *op. cit.*

44 G. Kelly, *A History of LACSAB* (1991).

45 Commission on Industrial Relations Study, *op. cit.*

46 See Chapter 3.

47 G. Ingham, *Strikes and Industrial Conflict* (1974).

48 K. von Beyme, *Challenges to Power: Trade Unions and Industrial Relations in Capitalist Countries* (1980); P. Jackson and K. Sisson, *op. cit.*; and K. Sisson, *op. cit.*

49 K. Sisson, *op. cit.*

5 EMPLOYEES AS INDIVIDUALS AND IN GROUPS

1 *Annual Abstract of Statistics* (1991) and *Department of Employment Gazette* (March 1991).

2 P. Brown and R. Scase (eds), *Poor Work* (1991); M. Jahoda, *Employment and Unemployment* (Cambridge, 1982).

3 M. Weber, *The Protestant Ethic and the Spirit of Capitalism* (1930).

4 P. Anthony, *The Ideology of Work* (1977).

5 R. F. Elliott, *Labour Economics* (1991), p.3.

6 J. Goldthorpe, D. Lockwood, F. Bechofer, and J. Platt, *The Affluent Workers* (Cambridge, 1968).

7 H. Beynon and R. M. Blackburn, *Perceptions of Work: Variations within a Factory* (Cambridge, 1972).

8 For a good review see K. Purcell, 'Gender and the Experience of Employment', in D. Gallie (ed.), *Employment in Britain* (Oxford, 1988). See also the results of the Department of Employment research programme: J. Martin and C. Roberts, *Women and Employment* (1984).

9 'Women in the Labour Force', *Department of Employment Gazette* (December 1990); S. Dex, 'Gender and the Labour Market', in D. Gallie (ed.), *op. cit.*

10 R. K. Brown, M. Curran and J. Cousins, 'Changing Attitudes to Employment', Research Paper Number 40, Department of Employment (1983); B. Ballard, *Department of Employment Gazette* (September 1984); J. Martin and C. Roberts, *op. cit.*

11 P. Elias, 'Family Formation, Occupational Mobility, and Part-time Work', in A. Hunt (ed.), *Women and Paid Work* (1988).

12 H. Beynon and R. M. Blackburn, *op. cit.*, p. 122; C. Cockburn, *Brothers: Male Domination and Technological Change* (1983); A. Pollert, *Girls, Wives, and Factory Lives* (1981).

13 Institute of Employment Research, *Review of the Economy and Employment* (Warwick University, 1987).

14 See, for example, R. Inglehart, *The Silent Revolution* (Princeton, 1977); D. Yankelovitch, *A World at Work* (New York, 1985).

15 M. Rose, *Reworking the Work Ethic* (1985); M. Rose, 'Attachment to Work and Social Values', in D. Gallie (ed.), *op. cit.*

16 P. Child, 'A Study of Industrial Relations in the Insurance Industry' (City University, PhD thesis 1981); D. Wedderburn and R. Crompton, *Workers Attitudes to Technology* (Cambridge, 1973); M. Rose, *op. cit.* (1985); M. Rose, *op. cit.*, in D. Gallie (ed.), *op. cit.*

17 R. M. Blackburn and M. Mann, *The Working Class in the Labour Market* (1979); B. Wootton, *The Social Foundations of Wage Policy* (1955); R. Hyman and I. Brough, *Social Values in Industrial Relations* (Oxford, 1975); F. Crosby, *Relative Deprivation and Working Women* (1982).
18 W. W. Daniels, 'Understanding Employee Behaviour in its Context', in J. Child (ed.), *Man and Organisation* (1973).
19 M. Jahoda, *op. cit.*
20 See, for example, H. Phelps Brown, 'The Counter Revolution of Our Time', *Industrial Relations* (1990).
21 J. Kelly and C. Kelly, '"Them and Us": Social Psychology and "the New Industrial Relations"', *British Journal of Industrial Relations* (1991); M. Rose, *Reworking the Work Ethic* (1985); R. Jowell, L. Brook, and B. Taylor, *British Social Attitudes* (1991).
22 W. W. Daniel, 'Industrial Behaviour and Orientation to Work', *Journal of Management Studies* (1969), p. 373; R. K. Brown *et al.*, *op cit.*
23 F. Parkin, *Class, Inequality, and Political Order* (1973).
23 See fuller discussion in Chapter 8. On issues such as the intensity of work, manning levels and work allocation, subordinate values can develop into more radical positions.
25 R. M. Blackburn and M. Mann, *op cit.*
26 B. Burkett and D. Bowers, *Trade Unions and the Economy* (1979).
27 For a good recent overview, see P. Edwards, 'Patterns of Conflict and Accommodation', in D. Gallie (ed.), *op. cit.*
28 R. M. Blackburn and M. Mann, *op. cit.*; C. Offe, *Industry and Inequality* (1976).
29 S. Hill, 'Norms, Groups, and Power', *British Journal of Industrial Relations* (1974); P. K. Edwards, *op. cit.*; M. Rose, *Industrial Behaviour* (1988), Part 3.
30 A. Sykes, 'Navvies: Their Work and Attitudes' *Sociology* (1969) and 'Navvies: Their Social Relations', *Sociology* (1969).
31 G. Mars, *Cheats at Work: An Anthropology of Workplace Crime* (1982).
32 W. J. Roethlisberger and W. J. Dickson, *Management and the Workers* (Cambridge, MA, 1939); M. Rose, *Industrial Behaviour*, Part 3.
33 See, for example, Incomes Data Services, *Teamworking*, Report 419 (1988) and R. Collard and B. Dale, 'Quality Circles', in K. Sisson (ed.), *Personnel Management in Britain* (Oxford, 1989).
34 J. Kelly and C. Kelly, '"Them and Us": Social Psychology and "the New Industrial Relations"', *British Journal of Industrial Relations* (1991).
35 M. Dalton, *Men who Manage* (New York, 1959).
36 C. R. Littler, *The Development of the Labour Process in Capitalist Societies* (1982).
37 Quoted in H. Beynon, *Working for Ford* (1973).
38 C. R. Littler, *op. cit.*; H. F. Gospel, *Markets, Firms, and the Management of Labour in Modern Britain* (Cambridge, 1992), Chapter 6.
39 S. Prais, *Productivity and Industrial Structure* (Cambridge, 1981); H. F. Gospel, *op. cit.*, Chapter 6.
40 S. Hill, *op. cit.*
41 Incomes Data Services, *op. cit.* and R. Collard and B. Dale, *op. cit.*
42 L. Sayles, *Behaviour of Industrial Work Groups* (New York, 1958).
43 See T. Lupton, *On the Shopfloor* (1963) for a good example.
44 E. Batstone, I. Boraston and S. Frenkel, *Shop Steward in Action* (Oxford, 1977) and *The Social Organisation of Strikes* (Oxford, 1978).

45 R. Brown, 'Divided We Fall: An Analysis of Relations Between Sections of a Factory Workforce', in I. Tajfel (ed.), *Differentiation between Social Groups* (1978); R. Brown and J. Williams, 'Group Identification: The Same Thing to All People?', *Human Relations* (1984); R. Brown, S. Condor, A. Mathews, G. Wade, and J. Williams, 'Explaining Intergroup Differentiation in Industrial Organisation', *Journal of Occupational Psychology* (1986).

46 E. Batstone *et al.*, *op. cit.* (1978), p. 28. See also M. Crozier, *The Bureaucratic Phenomenon* (Chicago, 1964) for a similar argument.

47 Named after the famous economists, Alfred Marshall and Sir John Hicks. For a full exposition see J. Peirson, 'The Importance of Being Unimportant: Marshall's Third Rule of Derived Demand', *Scottish Journal of Political Economy* (1988).

48 T. Nichols and P. Armstrong, *Workers Divided* (1976); T. Nichols and H. Beynon, *Living with Capitalism* (1977).

49 Incomes Data Services, *op. cit.* and R. Collard and B. Dale, *op. cit.*

50 J. Atkinson, 'Manpower Strategies for the Flexible Firm', *Personnel Management* (1984); National Economic Development Office, *Changing Patterns of Work* (1986); A. Pollert, 'The Flexible Firm: Fixation or Fact?' *Work, Employment and Society* (1988).

51 Incomes Data Services, *op. cit.* and R. Collard and B. Dale, *op. cit.* H. Ramsay, 'Reinventing the Wheel?: A Review of the Development and Performance of Employee Involvement', *Human Resource Management Journal* (1991).

52 See Chapter 9.

53 See, for example, J. Belanger, 'Job Control and Productivity', *British Journal of Industrial Relations* (1989) which makes the point that workgroup control is not necessarily detrimental to, and may even favour, productivity.

54 H. Dalton, *op. cit.*

55 Commission on Industrial Relations, *Industrial Relations at Establishment Level* (1973).

56 W. W. Daniels and N. Millward, *Workplace Industrial Relations in Britain* (1983), Chapter 2; N. Millward and M. Stevens, *British Workplace Industrial Relations 1980–1984* (1986), Chapter 5; M. Terry, 'How Do We Know If Shop Stewards Are Getting Weaker?', *British Journal of Industrial Relations* (1986).

57 C. Goodrich, *The Frontier of Control* (1920).

58 J. Purcell, 'The Rediscovery of the Management Prerogative: The Management of Labour Relations in the 1980s', *Oxford Review of Economic Policy* (1991).

59 E. Batstone and S. Gourlay, *Unions, Unemployment and Innovation* (Oxford, 1981).

60 W. Brown, *Piecework Bargaining* (1973); H. Beynon, *op. cit.*; E. Batstone *et al.*, *op. cit.* (1977) and (1978); P. Armstrong, J. Goodman, and J. Hyman, *Ideology and Shopfloor Industrial Relations* (1981); J. MacInnes, *Thatcherism at Work* (1987).

6 EMPLOYEE INSTITUTIONS – TRADE UNIONS

1 M. Weber, *The Theory of Social and Economic Organisation* (New York, 1947; reference to 1964 ed.), pp. 10–143.

2 *Ibid.*, E. Schneider, *Industrial Sociology* (New York, 1969).

3 T. Caplow, *The Sociology of Work* (1954) and T. Johnson, *Professions and Power* (1972).

4 T. Caplow, *op. cit.*, Chapter 5.
5 G. Millerson, *The Qualifying Associations* (1964).
6 H. Pelling, *A History of British Trade Unionism* (1987).
7 K. Burgess, *The Origins of British Industrial Relations* (1975); R. Price, *Masters, Unions and Men* (Cambridge, 1980); H. Phelps Brown, *The Origins of Trade Union Power* (Oxford, 1983).
8 S. and B. Webb, *Industrial Democracy* (1898), p. 16.
9 C. Turner and M. Hodge, 'Occupations and Professions', in J. Jackson (ed.), *Professions and Professionalisation* (Cambridge, 1970).
10 H. Braverman, *Labour and Monopoly Capitalism* (New York, 1974); R. Price, *Labour in British Society* (1988). See also Chapter 3 above.
11 C. Turner and M. Hodge, *op. cit.*
12 See the discussion of bureaucratic employment policies in Chapter 3.
13 J. Donnison, 'The Sex of Midwives', *New Society* (1 November 1973).
14 K. Burgess, *op. cit.*
15 L. Dickens, 'Staff Associations and the Industrial Relations Act', *Industrial Relations Journal* (1975).
16 See Chapter 7.
17 The Webbs, *op. cit.*, saw 1829–42 as the 'revolutionary period' of British trade unionism.
18 G. D. H. Cole, *Workshop Organisation* (1923).
19 S. D. Feldman and K. Tenfelde, *Workers, Owners, and Politics in Coalmining: An International Comparison of Industrial Relations* (Oxford, 1990).
20 Compare the behaviour of Sayles's erratic workgroups, discussed in Chapter 5.
21 K. Burgess, *op. cit.*; H. Phelps Brown, *op. cit.*
22 W. McCarthy, *The Closed Shop in Britain* (Oxford, 1964); S. Dunn and J. Gennard, *The Closed Shop in British Industry* (1984); W. W. Daniel and N. Millward, *Workplace Industrial Relations in Britain* (1983), Chapter 3; N. Millward and M. Stevens, *British Workplace Industrial Relations 1980–1984* (1986), Chapter 4.
23 H. A. Turner, *Trade Union Growth, Structure, and Policy* (1962). A further development of this is to be found in R. Undy, V. Ellis, W. McCarthy and A. Halmos, *Change in Trade Unions: The Development of UK Unions Since 1960* (1981).
24 H. A. Clegg, *The Changing System of Industrial Relations in Great Britain* (Oxford, 1979), p. 26. H. A. Turner, *op. cit.*
25 See Chapter 3.
26 G. S. Bain and F. Elsheik, *Union Growth and the Business Cycle* (Oxford, 1976); G. S. Bain and R. Price, 'Union Growth: Dimension, Determinants, and Destiny', in G. S. Bain (ed.), *Industrial Relations in Britain* (Oxford, 1983); J. Waddington, 'Trade Union Membership in Britain', *British Journal of Industrial Relations* (1992).
27 J. Waddington, *op. cit.*
28 D. Lockwood, *The Blackcoated Worker: A Study in Class Consciousness* (1966).
29 R. Lumley, *White Collar Unionism in Britain* (1973), p. 25.
30 G. S. Bain, *The Growth of White Collar Unionism* (Oxford, 1970). In the 1960s and 1970s, government policies encouraged unionisation through two channels. Recurrent incomes policies made it apparent that employees benefited from national-level representation backed by industrial sanctions, for such repre-

sentation was likely to give a place in the highly centralised negotiations on incomes policy. Second, from 1971 to 1980, governments endorsed collective bargaining and actively supported the recognition of trade unions. Unions could call for inquiries or ballots in companies where they sought recognition and, if the government agency – the Commission on Industrial Relations (CIR) or the Advisory, Conciliation and Arbitration Service (ACAS) – found support adequate, then recognition was endorsed. This had an impact on the spread of white-collar trade unionism to new areas and actively discouraged staff associations and the further development of professional associations. Staff associations were subject to the demand that they prove themselves independent of management. Faced with this, many staff associations merged with conventional unions and the formation of new associations was discouraged.

31 *Department of Employment Gazette* (May 1990).
32 P. Bassett, *Strike Free: The New Industrial Relations in Britain* (1986).
33 Industrial Relations Services, 'Single-Table Bargaining: A Survey', *Industrial Relations Services. Employment Trends*, Number 463 (1990).
34 R. Lumley, *op. cit.*, provides a figure of 2.25 million in the early 1970s.
35 J. Waddington, 'Unemployment and Restructuring: Trade Union Membership in Britain, 1980–1987', *British Journal of Industrial Relations* (1992); D. Bird, 'Membership of Trade Unions in 1990', *Employment Gazette* (April 1992).
36 H. F. Gospel, 'European Managerial Unionism', *Industrial Relations* (1978).
37 For the extent of the closed shop and check-off by the end of the 1970s, see W. W. Daniel and N. Millward, *op. cit.*, Chapter 3.
38 R. Freeman and J. Pelletier, 'The Impact of Industrial Relations Legislation on British Union Density', *British Journal of Industrial Relations* (1990).
39 For good reviews, see A. Carruth and R. Disney, 'Where Have Two Million Trade Union Members Gone?', *Economica* (1988); J. Waddington, *op. cit.*; D. Metcalf, 'British Trade Unions: Dissolution or Resurgence?', *Oxford Review of Economic Policy* (1991).
40 R. Price and G. S. Bain, 'Union Growth Revisited', *British Journal of Industrial Relations* (1976) estimated the impact of establishment size on all manufacturing industries in 1974. They calculated that the overall density of trade union membership was 62.2 per cent, but that if establishments employing less than 100 workers were excluded it rose to 76.9 per cent and excluding less than 200 workers, to 89.2 per cent. See also W. W. Daniel and N. Millward, *op. cit.*, Chapter 2, and N. Millward and M. Stevens, *op. cit.*, Chapter 3.
41 See R. Michels, *Political Parties* (New York, 1915) for the classic left-wing statement of the dangers of the so-called 'iron law of oligarchy'.
42 For useful summaries see R. Undy and R. Martin, *Ballots and Union Democracy* (Oxford, 1984); P. Elias and K. Ewing, *Trade Union Democracy, Members' Rights and the Law* (1987); P. Fosh and E. Heery, *Trade Unions and their Members* (1990).
43 H. A. Clegg, *The System of Industrial Relations in Great Britain* (1973).
44 W. Brown and S. Wadhwani, 'The Economic Effects of Industrial Relations Legislation Since 1979', *National Institute Economic Review* (1990).
45 R. Undy *et al.*, *op. cit.*, review these different perspectives. They contrasted the development of twelve major unions and assessed each union's government on the basis of effective adaptation to environmental change, rather than some formal model of democracy. It is interesting to note that, using this criterion, the

very formally democratic, faction-ridden AEU rated lower than the purportedly more centralised and full-time officer-led TGWU.
46 *Labour Research* (September 1991), p. 21.
47 Trades Union Congress, *Unions in Europe in the 1990s* (1991).
48 P. Marginson, 'European Integration and Transnational Management–Union Relations in the Enterprise', *British Journal of Industrial Relations* (1992).

7 THE ROLE OF THE STATE – AN HISTORICAL PERSPECTIVE

1 M. Weber, *The Theory of Social and Economic Organisation* (New York, 1947).
2 For a very good article, see A. Flanders, 'The Tradition of Voluntarism', *British Journal of Industrial Relations* (1974).
3 S. and B. Webb, *Industrial Democracy* (1898).
4 *Ibid.*, p. 41.
5 K. W. Wedderburn, 'Industrial Relations and the Courts', *Industrial Law Journal* (1980) and *The Worker and the Law* (1986).
6 D. Simon, 'Master and Servant', in J. Saville, *Democracy and the Labour Movement* (1954).
7 R. Lewis, 'The Historical Development of Labour Law', *British Journal of Industrial Relations* (1976) and R. Lewis, 'The Role of the Law in Employment Relations', *Labour Law in Britain* (Oxford, 1986).
8 R. Currie, *Industrial Policies* (Oxford, 1970).
9 The contracting-in provisions did have an effect on payment of the political levy.
10 See, for example, the *Rookes v. Barnard, Stratford v. Lindley, Torquay Hotel Company Limited v. Cousins* cases.
11 O. Kahn-Freund, 'The Legal Framework', in A. Flanders and H. Clegg (eds), *The System of Industrial Relations in Great Britain* (Oxford, 1954).
12 A. Flanders, *op. cit.*
13 E. Hobsbawm, 'Inside Every Worker there is a Syndicalist Trying to Get Out', *New Society* (5 April 1979).
14 K. Coates and T. Topham, *Trade Unions and Politics* (Oxford, 1986); A. J. Taylor, *The Trade Unions and the Labour Party* (1986); D. Fatchett, *Trade Unions and Politics in the 1980s* (1989).
15 As we will see in Chapter 10, the TUC successfully coordinated a policy of non-cooperation with the 1971 Industrial Relations Act. Employer non-cooperation was one factor which stymied the 1974–9 Labour government's proposals for extending industrial democracy.
16 W. Grant and D. Marsh, *The Confederation of British Industry* (1977).
17 A. Dorfman, *Government versus Trade Unions in British Politics since 1968* (1979); R. Martin, *The TUC: The Growth of a Pressure Group 1968–1978* (1980); J. Sheldrake, *Industrial Relations and Politics in Britain 1880–1989* (1991).
18 P. Bachrach and M. Baratz, *Power and Poverty, Theory and Practice* (New York, 1970); S. Lukes, *Power: A Radical View* (1974).
19 P. Hartman, 'Industrial Relations in the News Media', *Industrial Relations Journal* (1976); Glasgow University Media Group, *Bad News* (1976) and *More*

Bad News (1980); G. Palmer, 'Industrial Relations in the News', *British Journal of Industrial Relations* (1978).
20   K. W. Wedderburn, *op. cit.* (1980 and 1986); H. Phelps Brown, *The Origins of Trade Union Power* (Oxford, 1983).
21   A. Flanders, *op. cit.*
22   Quoted in *ibid.*
23   Quoted in P. O'Higgins, *Workers' Rights* (176).
24   J. England and B. Weeks, 'Trade Unions and the State', *Industrial Relations Journal* (1981).
25   H. F. Gospel, *Markets, Firms, and the Management of Labour in Modern Britain* (Cambridge, 1992).
26   C. Crouch, *Class Conflict and Industrial Relations* (1977) and *The Politics of Industrial Relations* (1979).
27   J. England and B. Weekes, *op. cit.*
28   C. Crouch charts the start of the breakdown from as early as mid-1950s, when the Conservative government produced a White Paper on the *Economic Implications of Full Employment* (1956) which questioned the commitment to full employment if price stability was to be maintained. It argued that full employment increased union bargaining power and was fuelling inflation. It urged employers to resist excessive wage claims and threatened 'wage restraint' in the public sector.
29   H. F. Gospel, *op. cit.*
30   See again *Rookes v. Barnard, Stratford v. Lindley, Torquay Hotel Company Limited v. Cousins.*
31   O. Kahn-Freund, *op. cit.* and *Labour and the Law* (1977).
32   R. Milliband, *The State in Capitalist Society* (1969).
33   N. Poulantzas, *Political Power and Social Classes* (1973).
34   A. Gramsci, *Selections from the Prison Notebooks* (1971).
35   R. Lewis, 'Reforming Industrial Relations: Law, Politics, and Power', *Oxford Review of Economic Policy* (1991).

8 DECISION-MAKING AND BARGAINING AT WORK

1   J. Winkler, 'The Ghost at the Bargaining Table: Directors and Industrial Relations', *British Journal of Industrial Relations* (1974); D. J. Hickson and G. R. Mallory, 'Scope for Choice in Strategic Decision Making and the Trade Union Role', in A. Thomson and M. Warner (eds), *The Behavioural Sciences and Industrial Relations* (Aldershot, 1981).
2   A. Pettigrew, *The Awakening Giant* (Oxford, 1985); C. Smith, J. Child and M. Rowlinson, *Reshaping Work: The Cadbury Experience* (Cambridge, 1990).
3   W. Brown (ed.) *The Changing Contours of British Industrial Relations* (Oxford, 1981), pp. 75–7; N. Millward and M. Stevens, *British Workplace Industrial Relations 1980–1984* (1986), pp. 138–48; Advisory Conciliation and Arbitration Service, *Consultation and Communication* (1990).
4   New Earnings Survey, relevant years, for details on proportions of employees covered by collective bargaining.
5   S. and B. Webb, *Industrial Democracy* (1898); A. Flanders, 'Collective Bargaining: A Theoretical Approach', *British Journal of Industrial Relations* (1968); A. Fox, 'Collective Bargaining, Flanders, and the Webbs', *British Journal of Industrial Relations* (1975).

6   R. Freeman and J. Medoff, *What Do Unions Do?* (New York, 1985).
7   D. Metcalf, 'Water Notes Dry Up', *British Journal of Industrial Relations* (1989); S. Nickell, S. Wadhwani and M. Wall, 'Productivity Growth in UK Companies 1975–86', Centre for Economic Performance Discussion Paper 26 (1991); P. Gregg, S. Machin and D. Metcalf, 'Signals and Cycles', Centre for Economic Performance Discussion Paper 49 (1991).
8   See, for example, J. Belanger, 'Job Control and Productivity', *British Journal of Industrial Relations* (1989), which makes the point that workgroup control is not necessarily detrimental to, and may even favour, productivity.
9   See the classic study by A. Gouldner, *Wildcat Strike* (New York, 1954).
10 For an overview see J. Vanek, *The General Theory of Labour-Managed Market Economies* (Ithaca, NY, 1970); F. Stephen (ed.), *The Performance of Labour-Managed Firms* (1982); S. Jansson and A. B. Hellmark (eds), *Labor-Owned Firms and Worker Cooperatives* (1986); M. Mellor, J. Hannah, and J. Stirling, *Worker Cooperatives in Theory and Practice* (1988).
11 R. Walton and R. McKersie, *A Behavioral Theory of Labor Negotiations* (New York, 1965).
12 P. Abell (ed.), *Organisations as Bargaining and Influence Systems*, Volumes 1 and 2 (1975 and 1978).
13 R. Walton and R. McKersie, *op. cit.*
14 W. Baldamus, *Efficiency and Effort* (1961).
15 C. R. Littler, *The Development of the Labour Process in Capitalist Societies* (1982). See Chapter 4 above.
16 K. Sisson, *The Management of Collective Bargaining* (Oxford, 1987).
17 See T. Nichols and H. Beynon, *Living with Capitalism* (1977) and E. Batstone, I. Boraston and S. Frenkel, *Shop Stewards in Action* (Oxford, 1977).
18 A. Flanders, R. Pomeranz and J. Woodward, *Experiments in Industrial Democracy: A Study of the John Lewis Partnership* (1968).
19 See note 1 above.
20 H. A. Clegg, *The Changing System of Industrial Relations* (Oxford, 1969).
21 J. Sheldrake, *Industrial Relations and Politics in Britain 1880–1989* (1991); J. MacInnes, *Thatcherism at Work* (1987).
22 R. Dore, T. Inagami and M. Sako, 'Japan's Annual Economic Assessment', Campaign for Work (1991); K. Koch, 'Wage Bargaining in Germany', Campaign for Work (1991).
23 J. Child (ed.), *Man and Organisation* (1973).
24 R. Edwards, *Contested Terrain* (1979); J. Woodward, *Industrial Organisation: Theory and Practice* (1965).
25 P. Marginson, 'The Multidivisional Firm and Control over the Work Process', *International Journal of Industrial Organisation* (1985).
26 H. F. Gospel, *Markets, Firms, and the Management of Labour in Modern Britain* (Cambridge, 1992).
27 A. Gouldner, *Patterns of Industrial Bureaucracy* (New York, 1954) and M. Crozier, *The Bureaucratic Phenomenon* (Chicago, 1964).
28 A. Gouldner, *op. cit.* (1954).
29 M. Crozier, *op. cit.*
30 *Ibid.*, p. 161, fn 33.
31 See also Terry's 'dynamic of informality', M. Terry, 'The Inevitable Growth of Informality', *British Journal of Industrial Relations* (1977).
32 To relate this more specifically to rules about seniority: employers are more

interested in generating bureaucratic rules which govern benefit seniority, for example, on pay, conditions and pensions; employees are more interested in creating bureaucratic rules which govern competitive status seniority, for example, on promotion, transfers, and lay-offs. R. Disney and H. F. Gospel, 'The Seniority Model of Trade Union Behaviour: A Partial Defence', *British Journal of Industrial Relations* (1989).

33 A. Friedman, *Industry and Labour* (1977), pp. 45–9.

34 P. Bachrach and M. Baratz, *Power and Poverty, Theory and Practice* (1970) and S. Lukes, *Power: A Radical View* (1974).

35 See Chapter 9.

36 This point is made in H. A. Turner, G. Clack and G. Roberts, *Labour Relations in the Motor Industry* (1967) and H. A. Turner, G. Roberts and D. Roberts, *Management Characteristics and Labour Conflict* (1977).

37 J. Gennard, *Financing Strikers* (1977).

38 P. Armstrong, J. Goodman and J. D. Hyman, *Ideology and Shopfloor Industrial Relations* (1981).

39 R. Hyman and I. Brough, *Social Values and Industrial Relations* (1975); R. Bendix, *Work and Authority in Industry* (Berkeley, CA, 1956).

40 Precedent, comparability and seniority can all be seen as both legal-rational and also traditional forms of rationality.

41 W. Brown, 'A Consideration of "Custom and Practice"', *British Journal of Industrial Relations* (1972).

42 W. Brown and K. Sisson, 'The Use of Comparisons in Workplace Wage Determination', *British Journal of Industrial Relations* (1975).

43 R. Disney and H. F. Gospel, *op. cit.*

44 For an argument on these lines in the American context see S. Jacoby, *Employing Bureaucracy* (New York, 1985).

45 This is the authors' (under)estimate based on the fact that over long periods of time, where collective bargaining exists, most workplaces do not experience a strike. See C. T. B. Smith, R. Clifton, P. Makeham, S. W. Creigh and R. V. Burns, *Strikes in Britain* (1978).

46 R. Walton and R. McKersie, *op. cit.*

47 P. Brannen, E. Batstone, D. Fatchett and P. White, *The Worker Directors* (1976); E. Batstone, A. Ferner and M. Terry, *Unions on the Board* (Oxford, 1983).

48 R. Herding, *Job Control and Union Structure* (Rotterdam, 1974); W. Streek, *Industrial Relations in West Germany* (1984).

9 THE CHANGING SYSTEM OF COLLECTIVE BARGAINING

1 P. Gregg and A. Yates, 'Changes in Wage Setting Arrangements and Trades Unions Presence in the 1980s', National Institute of Economic and Social Research (1991). See New Earnings Surveys, relevant years, for details on proportions of employees covered by collective bargaining.

2 See the relevant *New Earnings Survey*; *Department of Employment Gazette* (June 1989); W. W. Daniel and N. Millward, *Workplace Industrial Relations in Britain* (1983), Chapters 2 and 8; N. Millward and M. Stevens, *British Workplace Industrial Relations 1980–1984* (1986), Chapter 9.

3 S. and B. Webb, *Industrial Democracy* (1898); A. Flanders, 'Collective Bargaining: A Theoretical Approach', *British Journal of Industrial Relations*

(1968); A. Fox, 'Collective Bargaining, Flanders and the Webbs', *British Journal of Industrial Relations* (1975).

4 G. D. H. Cole, *Workshop Organisation* (1923); J. Hinton, *The First Shop Steward Movement* (1973).

5 See, for example, the Royal Arsenal shop stewards committee at Woolwich or the Piecework Committee at Crewe railway workshops.

6 G. D. H. Cole *op. cit.*; J. Hinton, *op. cit.*

7 J. Hinton, *op. cit.*; J. Goodman and T. Whittingham, *Shop Stewards in British Industry* (1969).

8 Donovan Commission, *op.cit.*

9 A. Flanders, *Industrial Relations: what is wrong with the system?* (1965).

10 Donovan Commission, *op. cit.*

11 E. Batstone, I. Boraston, and S. Frenkel, *Shop Stewards in Action* (Oxford, 1977). This study of domestic bargaining in the vehicle industry, conducted at the height of shopfloor power, found that stewards worked closely and co-operatively with their union full time officers.

12 See many of the reports of the Commission on Industrial Relations. H. F. Gospel, *Markets, Firms, and the Management of Labour in Modern Britain* (Cambridge, 1992), Chapter 7, makes the same point about many employers, especially in the 1950s and 1960s.

13 A. Flanders, *The Fawley Productivity Agreements* (1964).

14 B. Ahlstrand, *The Quest for Productivity: A Case Study of Fawley after Flanders* (Cambridge, 1991).

15 M. Terry and P. Edwards, *Shopfloor Politics and Job Controls* (Oxford, 1988); W. Brown (ed.) *op. cit.*, Chapter 2; W. W. Daniel and N. Millward, *op. cit.*, Chapters 2 and 8; N. Millward and M. Stevens, *op. cit.* Chapters 3 and 9; P. Marginson, P. Edwards, R. Martin, J. Purcell and K. Sissons, *Beyond the Workplace* (Oxford, 1988).

16 W. W. Daniel and N. Millward, *op. cit.*, Chapter 4.

17 W. Brown (ed.) *op. cit.*, Chapter 4; W. W. Daniel and N. Millward, *op. cit.*, Chapter 3.

18 W. W. Daniel and N. Millward, *op cit.*, chapter 3; N. Millward and M. Stevens, *op. cit.*, chapter 3; P. Gregg and A. Yates, *op. cit.*

19 Office of Manpower Economics, *Measured Daywork* (1973); A. Flanders, 'Measured Daywork and Collective Bargaining', *British Journal of Industrial Relations* (1973).

20 By 1978, 50 per cent of all manufacturing establishments were using work study techniques, W. Brown (ed.), *op. cit.*, pp. 113–14; W. W. Daniel and N. Millward, *op. cit.*, pp. 200–3.

21 A. Flanders ('Measured daywork', The National Board for Prices and Incomes, *Job Evaluation* (1968)) reported that 23 per cent of all employees in manufacturing were covered by job evaluation. W. Brown (ed.), *op. cit.*, reported that 55 per cent of manual and 56 per cent of non-manual are covered, p. 111. W. W. Daniel and N. Millward, *op. cit.*, put the figure lower at 23 per cent for all plants, but rising in size to 53 per cent in plants employing 500 or more, p. 204.

22 R. Hyman, 'The Politics of Workplace Trade Unionism', *Capital and Class* (1979).

23 W. Brown (ed.), *op. cit.*

24 W. W. Daniel and N. Millward, *op. cit.*, Chapter 2; N. Millward and M. Stevens, *op. cit.*, Chapter 5.

25 Along with W. Brown (ed.), *op. cit.*, and W. W. Daniel and N. Millward, *op. cit.*, see W. W. Daniel, *Wage Determination in Industry* (1976); A. Marsh, *Employee Relations Policy and Decision Making* (Aldershot, 1982), Chapter 6; N. J. Kinnie, 'Single-Employer Bargaining', *Industrial Relations Journal* (1983); P. B. Beaumont, 'Bargaining Structure', *Management Decision* (1980); P. Marginson *et al.*, *op. cit.*

26 National Economic Development Office, *Changing Patterns of Work: How Companies Introduce Flexibility to Meet New Needs* (1986); C. Curson (ed.) *Flexible Patterns of Work* (1986); J. Atkinson, *Flexibility, Uncertainty and Manpower Management* (Brighton, 1984); M. Cross, *Towards the Flexible Craftsman* (1985); W. W. Daniel, *op. cit.* (1987); Incomes Data Services, *Flexibility at Work* (Study 360, 1986); Advisory Conciliation and Arbitration Service, *Labour Flexibility in Britain* (1988); Incomes Data Services, *Teamworking*, Report 419 (1988) and R. Collard and B. Dale, 'Quality Circles', In K. Sisson (ed.), *Personnel Management in Britain* (Oxford, 1989); J. Storey, *New Perspectives on Human Resource Management* (1989).

27 D. Guest, 'Human Resource Management: Its Implications for Industrial Relations and Trade Unions', in J. Storey (ed.), *New Perspectives on Human Resource Management* (1989); J. Storey and K. Sisson, 'Limits to Transformation: Human Resource Management in the British Context', *Industrial Relations Journal* (1990); J. Kelly and C. Kelly, '"Them and Us": Social Psychology and "the New Industrial Relations"', *British Journal of Industrial Relations* (1991).

28 See, for example, National Economic Development Organisation, *op. cit.*; W. W. Daniel, *op. cit.*; M. Cross, 'Changes in Working Practices in UK Manufacturing 1981–1988', *Industrial Relations Review and Report*, Number 415 (1988); J. MacInnes, *Thatcherism at Work* (Milton Keynes, 1987); Incomes Data Services, *Flexibility at Work*, Study 454 (1990).

29 D. Marsden and M. Thompson, 'Flexibility Agreements and Their Significance in the Increase in Productivity in British Manufacturing Since 1980', *Work, Employment and Society* (1990) and P. Ingram, 'Changes in Manufacturing in British Manufacturing Industry in the 1980s', *British Journal of Industrial Relations* (1991).

30 For a good review see P. Edwards and K. Sissons, 'Industrial Relations in the UK: Change in the 1980s', ESRC Research Briefing (Warwick, 1979).

31 W. Brown and J. Walsh, 'Pay Determination in Britain in the 1980s: The Anatomy of Decentralisation', *Oxford Review of Economics Policy* (1991).

32 This body was previously called the Local Authorities Conditions of Service Advisory Board (LACSAB). G. Kelly, *A History of LACSAB* (1991).

33 For good accounts of public-sector collective bargaining, see D. Winchester, 'Industrial Relations in the Public Sector', in G. S. Bain, *Industrial Relations in Britain* (Oxford, 1983); P. Beaumont and J. Leopold, 'Public Sector Industrial Relations: Recent Development', *Employee Relations* (1985); R. Bailey and C. Trinder, *Under Attack: Public Service Pay Determination over Two Decades* (1989); R. Bailey, 'Pay and Industrial Relations in the UK Public Sector', *Labour* (1989).

34 A. M. Ross and P. T. Hartman, *Changing Patterns of Industrial Conflict* (New York, 1960).

35 Department of Employment, *British Labour Statistics: Historical Abstract*

1886–1968 (1971) p. 396; J. W. Durcan, W. McCarthy, A. Redman, *Strikes in Post-War Britain* (1983).

36 J. W. Durcan, *op. cit.*, Chapters 3 and 4. This increase was not concentrated in a few industries, but was spread throughout the economy.

37 Departments of Employment, *Labour Statistics*; figures for official and unofficial strikes only exist from 1960 onwards. See J. W. Durcan *et al.*, *op. cit.*, p. 130; Donovan Commission, *Report*, paras. 367–70.

38 E. H. Phelps Brown, *The Origins of Trade Union Power* (Oxford, 1983), Chapter 10; J. W. Durcan *et al.*, *op. cit.*, Chapter 12.

39 A. I. Marsh, *Disputes Procedures in British Industry*, Royal Commission Research Paper 2 (1) (1966); A. I. Marsh and W. McCarthy, *Disputes Procedures in Britain*, Royal Commission Research Paper 2 (2) (1968); N. Singleton, *Industrial Relations Procedures*, Department of Employment Manpower Paper 14 (1975), p. 64.

40 A. Marsh, *Disputes Procedures*; A. Marsh *Engineering*, Chapter 5; R. Hyman, *Disputes Procedures in Action* (1972) stresses procedure as an extension of bargaining.

41 C. T. B. Smith, R. Clifton, P. Makeham, S. W. Creigh and R. V. Burn, *Strikes in Britain: A Research Study of Industrial Stoppages in the United Kingdom*, Department of Employment, Manpower Paper 15 (1978), show that only 0.25 per cent of all manufacturing plants accounted for a quarter of all strikes and two-thirds of all days lost p. 55; J. W. Durcan *et al.*, *op. cit.*, pp. 425–8.

42 J. Kelly and C. Kelly, *op. cit.*

43 W. Brown and S. Wadhwani, 'The Economic Effects of Industrial Relations Legislation Since 1979', *National Institute Economic Review* (February 1991).

44 P. Edwards, 'Industrial Conflict: Will the Giant Wake?', *Personnel Management* (September 1991); Advisory Conciliation and Arbitration Service, *Annual Report* (1991).

45 The size and length of strikes also fluctuates with the state of the labour market and economic demand. On the whole, the tendency is that in periods of recession there are fewer strikes but they are longer, because major issues are at stake and there is little pressure on the employer for an early settlement. In periods of prosperity the tendency is for collective bargaining to generate more but shorter disputes.

46 P. Bassett, *Strike Free: New Industrial Relations in Britain* (1986); D. Metcalf and S. Milner, 'Final Offer Arbitration in Great Britain: Style and Impact', Centre for Economic Performance, Working Paper 174 (1991).

47 T. Claydon, 'Union Derecognition in Britain in the 1980s', *British Journal of Industrial Relations* (1989).

48 The Labour Party in opposition has talked about a National Economic Assessment and so-called synchronised or coordinated bargaining; since John Major became Prime Minister there has even been some talk of pay policies on these lines within the Conservative Party, *Financial Times* (13 November 1991); the Liberal Democrats have been interested in tax-based incomes policies of various kinds.

49 See, for example, G. Jenkins and M. Poole, *New Forms and Ownership* (1990); M. Mellor, J. Hannah, and J. Stirling, *Worker Cooperatives in Theory and Practice* (1988); see also the Lucas Aerospace Joint Shop Stewards' Committee Alternative Corporate Plan.

50 M. Mellor *et al.*, *op. cit.*
51 Bullock Commission, *op. cit.*
52 W. Brown (ed.), *op. cit.*, p. 76; N. Millward and M. Stevens, *op. cit.*, Chapter 6;
    M. Marchington and P. Parker, *Changing Patterns of Employee Relations*
    (1990), Chapter 2.
53 M. Hall, 'Behind the European Works Council Directive', *British Journal of
    Industrial Relations* (1993).

10 GOVERNMENT ATTEMPTS TO RECONSTRUCT BRITISH INDUSTRIAL RELATIONS

1 Royal Commission on Trade Unions and Employers' Associations (Donovan
   Commission), *Report* (1969).
2 A. Flanders, *Industrial Relations: What is Wrong with the System?* (1965).
3 Donovan Commission, *Report*.
4 More explicitly corporatist arguments were later developed in an article by A.
   Flanders and A. Fox, 'The Reform of Collective Bargaining: From Donovan to
   Durkheim', *British Journal of Industrial Relations* (1969). This argued that
   Donovan's reformed collective bargaining arrangements would cure the
   anomic loss of agreed regulation in British industry. This analysis may not have
   been endorsed by other members of the Oxford School, but it certainly
   highlights the corporatist elements in Donovan's thinking.
5 The 1969 Bill which emerged from this compromise excluded the penal clauses
   and concentrated on those aspects of the Donovan proposals which had TUC
   support. For a good, journalistic account of these events, see P. Jenkins, *Battle
   of Downing Street* (1970).
6 J. Goldthorpe, 'Industrial Relations in Great Britain: A. Critique of
   Reformism', *Politics and Society* (1974) and republished in T. Clarke and L.
   Clements, *Trade Unions Under Capitalism* (1977).
7 The CIR also sought to simplify the Wages Council system, but whether this helped
   the low paid or did much to extend collective bargaining is open to doubt.
8 Thus, provision was made for 'approved closed shops' for unions like Actors'
   Equity and the Seaman's Union and for 'agency shops' to provide a limited
   union security for other unions.
9 See B. Weekes, M. Mellish, L. Dickens and J. Lloyd, *Industrial Relations and
   the Limits of the Law* (1975).
10 See K. W. Wedderburn, 'Industrial Relations and the Courts', *Industrial Law
    Journal* (1980).
11 M. Moran, *The Politics of Industrial Relations* (1977).
12 B. Weekes *et al.*, *op. cit.*
13 B. Weekes *et al.*, *op. cit.*
14 S. Dawson, P. Willman, A. Clinton and M. Bamford, *Safety at Work* (Cam-
    bridge, 1988).
15 D. Coates, *Labour in Power: A Study of the Labour Government 1974–1979*
    (1980), pp. 100–6.
16 Royal Commission on Industrial Democracy (Bullock Commission), *Report*
    (1977). A new tripartite body, an Industrial Democracy Commission, would
    assist and guide the implementation of the necessary changes.
17 P. Anthony, *The Conduct of Industrial Relations* (1977), pp. 290–2.

18 L. Panitch, 'Trade Unions and the Capitalist State', *New Left Review* (1981).
19 R. Fryer, 'The Myths of the Redundancy Payments Act', *Industrial Law Journal* (1973); H. Collins, 'Dismissals on Transfer of a Business', *Industrial Law Journal* (1986).
20 Department of Employment, *Industrial Relations in the 1990s* (1991).
21 W. Brown and S. Wadhwani, *op. cit.*; P. A. Gregg and S. Machin, 'Unions, the Demise of the Closed Shop and Wage Growth in the 1980s', *Oxford Bulletin of Economics and Statistics* (1991).
22 See, for example, most employers coolness towards such proposals in the green paper, Department of Employment, *Industrial Relations in the 1990s* (1991).
23 R. Undy and R. Martin, *Ballots and Union Democracy* (Oxford, 1984); P. Elias and K. Ewing, *Trade Union Democracy, Members' Rights and the Law* (1987); P. Fosh and E. Heery, *Trade Unions and their Members* (1990); see various ACAS *Annual Reports* for information on balloting.
24 D. Metcalf, 'Water Notes Dry Up', *British Journal of Industrial Relations* (1989); P. Nolan and P. Marginson, 'Skating on Thin Ice', *British Journal of Industrial Relations* (1990); W. Brown and S. Wadhwani, *op. cit.*; D. Metcalf, 'Labour Legislation 1980–1990: Philosophy and Impact', Centre for Economic Performance Working Paper 12, London School of Economics (1990).

11 CONCLUSIONS: ISSUES, OUTCOMES, TRENDS

1 D. Metcalf, 'Water Notes Dry Up', *British Journal of Industrial Relations* (1989); P. Nolan and P. Marginson, 'Skating on Thin Ice', *British Journal of Industrial Relations* (1990); D. Metcalf, 'Union Presence and Labour Productivity in British Manufacturing Industry', *British Journal of Industrial Relations* (1990); S. Wadhwani, 'The Effects of Unions on Productivity Growth, Investment and Unemployment', *British Journal of Industrial Relations* (1990).
2 J. Atkinson, 'Manpower Policies for the Flexible Firm', *Personnel Management* (1984); National Economic Development Office, *Changing Patterns of Work: How Companies Introduce Flexibility To Meet New Needs* (1986).
3 H. A. Clegg, *A History of British Trade Unionism Since 1889. Volume III 1934–1952* (Oxford, 1992).
4 For a good survey see J. Kelly and C. Kelly, '"Them and Us"; Social Psychology and "the New Industrial Relations"', *British Journal of Industrial Relations* (1991). See also P. Edwards, 'Industrial Conflict: Will the Giant Wake?', *Personnel Management* (1991).
5 For good recent reviews see J. Muellbauer, 'The Assessment: Productivity and Competitiveness in British Manufacturing Industry', *Oxford Review of Economic Policy* (1986) and C. Johnson, *The Economy under Mrs Thatcher 1979–1990* (1991).
6 See D. Metcalf, *op. cit.*; P. Nolan and M. Marginson, *op. cit.*; S. Wadhwani, *op. cit.*; N. Oulton, 'Labour Productivity in UK Manufacturing in the 1970s and 1980s', *National Institute Economic Review* (1990).
7 H. F. Gospel, *Markets, Firms, and the Management of Labour in Modern Britain* (Cambridge, 1992), Chapters 6 and 9.
8 *Ibid.*
9 D. Metcalf, *op. cit.*; P. Nolan and M. Marginson, *op. cit.*; S. Wadhwani, *op. cit.* N. Oulton, *op. cit.*

300   *British industrial relations*

10 G. Routh, *Occupation and Pay in Great Britain 1906–79* (1980).
11 M. B. Gregory and A. Thomson, *An Analysis of the New Earnings Survey* (Oxford, 1990); S. P. Jenkins, 'Income Inequality and Living Standards: Changes in the 1970s and 1980s', *Fiscal Studies* (1991); *Social Trends* (1991); Low Pay Unit, *New Review*, Number 13 (1992).
12 F. Green, G. Hadjimatheou, R. Smail, *Unequal Figures* (1984) and Advisory Conciliation and Arbitration Service, *Developments in Harmonisation* (1982).
13 Incomes Data Services, *Harmonisation of Conditions*, No. 273 (September 1982); Advisory Conciliation and Arbitration Service, *op. cit.*; C. Roberts, *Harmonisation* (1985).
14 For a review, see D. Gallie, 'Introduction', in D. Gallie (ed.), *Employment in Britain* (Oxford, 1988); J. Child, 'Managerial Strategies, New Technology, and the Labour Process', in D. Knights, H. Willmott, and D. Collinson (eds), *Job Redesign: Critical Perspectives on the Labour Process* (Aldershot, 1985).
15 See, for example, D. Gallie, 'Patterns of Skill Change', *Work, Employment, and Society* (1991); S. J. Prais, 'Vocational Qualifications of the Labour Force in Britain and Germany', *National Institute Economic Review*, (1981); National Economic Development Council and Manpower Services Commission, *Competence and Competition – Training and Education in the Federal Republic of Germany, the United States, and Japan* (1984); Coopers and Lybrand for the Manpower Services Commission and National Economic Development Council, *A Challenge to Complacency: Changing Attitudes to Training* (1985).
16 P. Townsend, *Poverty in the United Kingdom* (1979) pp. 77–9; A. B. Atkinson, *The Economics of Inequality* (1975), Chapter 6.
17 J. Atkinson, *op. cit.*; National Economic Development Office, *op. cit.*; A. Pollert, 'The Flexible Firm: Fixation or Fact?', *Work, Employment and Society* (1988).
18 There have been numerous similar exercises to this. See, for example, M. Poole, W. Brown, J. Rubery, K. Sisson, R. Tarling, and F. Wilkinson, *Industrial Relations in the Future* (1984).
19 See, for example, M. J. Piore and C. F. Sabel, *The Second Industrial Divide* (New York, 1984).
20 J. McLoughlin, *The Demographic Revolution* (1991); Institute of Employment Research, *Review of the Economy and Employment* (1987); Confederation of British Industry, *Workforce 2000* (1989).
21 R. Chapman, 'Personnel Management in the 1990s', *Personnel Management* (January 1990).
22 This sort of competition has been charted in the US by T. Kochan, H. Katz and R. McKersie, *The Transformation of American Industrial Relations* (New York, 1986).
23 See, for example, R. Inglehart, *The Silent Revolution* (Princeton, 1977); D. Yankelovitch, *A World at Work* (New York, 1985); M. Rose, *Reworking the Work Ethic* (1985); M. Rose, 'Attachment to Work and Social Values', in D. Gallie (ed.), *op. cit.*; Social and community Planning Research, *British Social Attitudes: International Edition* (1989).
24 For a good survey article, see D. Metcalf, 'British Unions: Dissolution or Resurgence', *Oxford Review of Economic Policy* (1991).
25 H. Ramsay, 'Cycles of Control', *Sociology* (1977) and 'Reinventing the Wheel?: A Review of the Development and Performance of Employee Involvement', *Human Resource Management Journal* (1991).

26 P. Marginson, 'European Integration and Transnational Management–Union Relations in the Enterprise', *British Journal of Industrial Relations* (1992), and M. Hall, 'Behind the European Works Councils Directives', *British Journal of Industrial Relations* (1992); K. Sisson, J. Waddington, C. Whitston, 'Company Size in the European Community', *Human Resource Management Journal* (1991).

Index